Fifth Edition

Classroom Teaching Skills

Fall '03

Kenneth D. Moore

Eastern New Mexico University

Boston   Burr Ridge, IL   Dubuque, IA   Madison, WI
New York   San Francisco   St. Louis
Bangkok   Bogotá   Caracas   Lisbon   London   Madrid   Mexico City
Milan   New Delhi   Seoul   Singapore   Sydney   Taipei   Toronto

McGraw-Hill Higher Education

*A Division of The **McGraw-Hill** Companies*

CLASSROOM TEACHING SKILLS, FIFTH EDITION

Published by McGraw-Hill, an imprint of The McGraw-Hill Companies, Inc., 1221 Avenue of the Americas, New York, NY 10020. Copyright © 2001, 1998, 1995, 1992 by The McGraw-Hill Companies, Inc. All rights reserved. Previously published under the title of *Classroom Teaching Skills: A Primer.* Copyright © 1989 by The McGraw-Hill Companies, Inc. All rights reserved. No part of this publication may be reproduced or distributed in any form or by any means, or stored in a database or retrieval system, without the prior written consent of The McGraw-Hill Companies, Inc., including, but not limited to, in any network or other electronic storage or transmission, or broadcast for distance learning.

Some ancillaries, including electronic and print components, may not be available to customers outside the United States.

This book is printed on acid-free paper.

1 2 3 4 5 6 7 8 9 0 DOC/DOC 0 9 8 7 6 5 4 3 2 1 0

ISBN 0–07–232238–1

Vice president and editor-in-chief: *Thalia Dorwick*
Editorial director: *Jane E. Vaicunas*
Sponsoring editor: *Beth Kaufman*
Developmental editor: *Cara Harvey*
Marketing manager: *Daniel M. Loch*
Project manager: *Susan J. Brusch*
Senior media developer: *James Fehr*
Production supervisor: *Sandy Ludovissy*
Coordinator of freelance design: *Rick D. Noel*
Cover designer: *Annis Wei Leung*
Cover image: *©PhotoDisc Volume 41 image, number 41288*
Senior photo research coordinator: *Carrie K. Burger*
Photo research: *LouAnn K. Wilson*
Senior supplement coordinator: *Audrey A. Reiter*
Compositor: *ElectraGraphics, Inc.*
Typeface: *10/12 Palatino*
Printer: *R. R. Donnelley & Sons Company/Crawfordsville, IN*

Chapter Openers

1: © Paul Conklin/Photo Edit; 2, 5, 9, 12: © Elizabeth Crews; 3, 4: © Jean-Claude Lejeune; 6: © Susan Lapides; 7: © Elizabeth Crews/Stock Boston; 8: © Education 2/PhotoDisc; 10: © Michael Newman/Photo Edit; 11: © Grant Le Duc/Stock Boston; 13: © Frank Siteman/Photo Edit

Library of Congress Cataloging-in-Publication Data

Moore, Kenneth D.
    Classroom teaching skills / Kenneth D. Moore. — 5th ed.
      p.   cm.
    Includes bibliographical references and index.
    ISBN 0–07–232238–1
    1. Teaching—Handbooks, manuals, etc.   2. Classroom management—Handbooks, manuals, etc.   I. Title.

LB1025.3 .M66   2001
371.102—dc21
                                             00–038697
                                           CIP

www.mhhe.com

Brief Contents

Contents

Preface

Classroom Teaching Skills was written with the belief that both preservice and practicing teachers can benefit from a text that presents essential teaching skills in a concise, easy-to-read fashion. Organized around a comprehensive model of teaching that includes planning, implementation, and evaluation components, the skills addressed in this volume are common to instruction at all grade levels and in all subject areas. Taken together, these skills may be thought of as a minimum repertoire that all teachers should acquire.

Because this book is brief, affordable, and self-instructional, it can be used as a core text for skills-oriented general methods courses; as a supplementary text for elementary and secondary methods courses; or as a handy reference for in-service seminars and workshops with a practical skills focus. It also makes an ideal reference volume for individuals wanting a skills refresher prior to taking state or national competency exams.

✎ Pedagogy

The text has been carefully designed to maximize instructional flexibility and to model established principles of instruction. Each chapter begins with specific learning objectives that help focus the reader's attention. Student application activities and Internet web activities are included in most chapters to enhance concept understanding. The reader's understanding of key concepts is then checked by a series of self-tests that appear at the end of subsections within the chapters. End-of-chapter answer keys provide immediate feedback on how well the chapter objectives were met. The final chapter gives readers the opportunity to apply the skills covered in the text in the development of a unit of instruction.

✎ New to This Edition

There have been a number of refinements and additions to the fifth edition. All chapters have been updated with new information and with a more interactive format. Chapter summaries have been redesigned into a more student friendly format and theory and research references have been added to each chapter.

A number of modifications have been made to individual chapters:

- Chapter 1. "The Teaching Process," has been expanded to include sections on school organization, curriculum, and strategies for school improvement.
- Chapter 2, "Planning for Diversity," Chapter 3 "The Supportive Classroom Environment," and Chapter 13, "A Well-Designed Unit Plan," are timely new chapters.
- Chapter 4, "Writing Objectives," has been modified to include material on outcomes based education.
- Chapter 5, "Planning for content and Thinking Skills," has been modified and updated with germane new materials and research-based instructional methods.
- Chapter 9, "Classroom Management" has been reorganized to include the material on motivation.
- Chapter 10, "Evaluating Instruction," has been expanded to address authentic assessment and the latest on rubrics.
- Chapter 12. "Instructional Media and Technology," has been updated to include a section on the Internet and material on the use of technology in the classroom.

Acknowledgments

A textbook represents the cooperative efforts of many individuals who have helped to shape its form and content:

Sheila Buckley, *Beaver College*
Timothy R. Homberger, *The College of New Jersey*
William E. Klingele, *The University of Akron*
Dona Thornton, *Palm Beach Atlantic College*
H. Jeanette Willert, *Canisius College*

I would like to express my gratitude and appreciation to the many students who have used past editions; to teachers and colleagues who continue to share their ideas; and to many others who have contributed to past editions. I would especially like to thank Cara Harvey for her criticism, editing, and guidance in the development and revisions of the fifth edition of this book and to the publication team at McGraw-Hill for their valued assistance. My final words are thanks to my wife, Susan Joyce, who offered much assistance in the writing and editing of the text.

Kenneth D. Moore

About the Author

KENNETH D. MOORE is Dean of the College of Education and Technology at Eastern New Mexico University. He received his Ed.D. degree in Curriculum and Instruction from the University of Houston. Dr. Moore has been involved in teacher education for more than 25 years at both the public school and higher education levels. He has authored three books, numerous journal publications, an ERIC monograph, and has presented many papers at regional and national conventions. Dr. Moore has also served as Director of the Southwest Regional Association of Teachers of Science, President of the Oklahoma Association of Teacher Educators, and President of the Oklahoma Association of Colleges for Teacher Education. Dr. Moore is presently involved in educational reform and authentic assessment and serves on the NCATE Board of Examiners (BOE).

Planning Instruction

Teaching is a challenge that requires long hours of work and preparation. But above all, it requires skill in planning and skill in the classroom.

The purpose of this first section is to help you gain insight into the process of teaching and to put that process into a framework that will assist you in preparing to teach. Chapter 1 addresses what it means to teach. We discuss the different roles of a teacher and develop a working definition of teaching. Since planning forms the core of the teaching process, a comprehensive seven-step planning model is presented. Various preinstructional, instructional, and postinstructional teaching skills associated with this model are then identified and described. Also, since these factors will impact the planning process, school organizational patterns, the school curriculum, and strategies for school improvement are addressed.

A major purpose of this section is to assist you in becoming a better planner. To do so you must decide where you want to go and the best method of getting there. Chapter 2 will help you plan for students with different abilities and for students from diverse backgrounds. Chapter 3 will help you plan a supportive classroom environment and provide information about different management models. Chapter 4 will help you determine where you want to go in terms of developing your skill at writing well-stated objectives. It will also help you gain an understanding of outcome-based education (OBE). Chapter 5 shows how to plan presentations that achieve the stated objectives and focuses on teaching content and thinking skills.

The Teaching Process

Objectives

After completing your study of Chapter 1, you should be able to:

1. Identify and describe the three major roles performed by teachers.

2. Define and differentiate between teaching and reflective teaching.

3. Describe decision making and its importance to the teaching-learning process.

4. Differentiate between theoretical knowledge and active knowledge.

5. Identify the teaching skills necessary for effective teaching at the elementary and secondary level.

6. Explain the importance of effective planning and describe the seven sequential steps in the planning process.

7. Identify and describe various generic teaching skills.

8. Describe the different school organizational patterns.

9. Define curriculum and describe the different kinds of curricula.

10. Identify and describe the various educational proposals for improving the quality of education.

One of the proudest and most important moments in the life of a teacher is the teaching of that first class. If you are an experienced teacher, that first day has come and gone and is recalled with fond memories. Or is it? If you are a novice teacher, you are probably looking forward to that first day with great anticipation. The years of work and preparation will finally pay off!

Whether you are an experienced teacher or a novice, you probably have some misgivings and apprehension about the teaching profession. Most likely you have concerns about being a "successful" teacher, a "good" teacher, an "effective" teacher.

What makes an effective teacher? Are there certain identifiable skills that make one teacher more effective than another? Some say that effective teachers are born with the skill to teach. Others scoff at this notion and declare that it is possible to develop and train someone to be an effective teacher (Carr, 1998; Hunt, Touzel, & Wiseman, 1999). This text identifies with the latter group.

✄ Teaching

What does it mean to teach? We must answer this question before we can decide whether someone is an effective teacher. To prepare for developing a formal definition of teaching, let us look at what a teacher does. What are the major roles of a teacher?

Roles of a Teacher

Teachers play many roles, some of which interlock and overlap. However, most of your teaching activities can be divided into three broad categories that describe what you as a teacher do to bring about desired learning and changes in student behavior and to enhance student development.

Instructional Expert   The first and most notable role performed by a teacher is that of instructional expert: the person who plans, guides, and evaluates learning. This role, in a sense, serves as a kind of core role that the others tend to support.

Information constitutes the foundation for learning and thinking. This basic information must be organized so it becomes the scaffolding of advance organizer to which students can add more complex information. Thus, information must be made meaningful so it is remembered and students are able to transfer it to a variety of situations. This is one of the major tasks of the teacher as instructional expert.

As an instructional expert, you must make decisions related to what to teach, what teaching materials to use, the best method to teach the selected content, and how to evaluate the intended learning. These decisions will be based on a number of factors, including state-suggested curricular goals, your knowledge of the subject, your knowledge of learning theory and motivation, the abilities and needs of your students, your own personality and needs, and your overall teaching goals. Effective teaching must go beyond simply knowing about a subject or topic to being aware of how it fits in and what it has to offer.

This means being aware of the relationships between the subject or topic and the rest of the curriculum.

Students will expect you, as an instructional expert, to have all the answers, not only to questions about your subject but to a multitude of subjects.

Manager   The second important job of a teacher is to order and structure the learning environment. Included in this role are all the decisions and actions required to maintain order in the classroom, such as laying down rules and procedures for learning activities. Sometimes this role is viewed as nothing more than that of disciplinarian, the person who must see that the classroom group and its individual members stay within the limits set by the school, the limits set by you the teacher, and the limits set by the tasks at hand. However, in its best sense, management is much more complex.

Teachers must manage a classroom environment. Therefore, teachers are environmental engineers who organize the classroom space to fit their goals and to maximize learning. The way the physical space of the classroom is organized can either help or hinder learning. Seating must be arranged; posters hung; bulletin boards decorated; extra books arranged, learning carrels, and bookshelves installed. You may even want to build or adapt furniture for use in your classroom.

Classroom management also involves modeling a positive attitude toward the curriculum and toward school and learning in general. Teachers who reveal a caring attitude toward learning and the learning environment help to instill and reinforce similar attitudes in their students. The results, hopefully, will be more self-disciplined students and fewer management problems.

Finally, teachers are required to manage and process great amounts of clerical work. There are papers to be read and graded, tests to be scored, marks to be entered, attendance records and files to be maintained, notes and letters to be written, and so forth. Sometimes there seems to be little time for anything else.

Counselor   Nearly all teachers need the basic skills to assume the role of counselor in the classroom (Kottler & Kottler, 1993). Counseling skills are needed to develop high degrees of interpersonal sensitivity and to deal effectively with day-to-day problems. Although you will not be a trained counselor or psychologist, you should be a sensitive observer of human behavior. You must be prepared to respond constructively when behavior problems get in the way of student learning and development. In almost every class there are students who will look to you for guidance. Thus you must be prepared to assist students and parents with these problems and be prepared to work with colleagues in making the school experience as supportive as possible.

Remember that teachers work with people: students, parents, administrators, and colleagues. You must possess good human relations skills and be prepared to communicate and work with these different factions on a day-to-day basis, sometimes under unpleasant circumstances. These interactions, both pleasant and unpleasant, will benefit from a deep understanding of people and their behaviors. Finally, you will need a thorough understanding of yourself— your own motivations, hopes, prejudices, and desires—all of which will affect your ability to relate to others.

Do you feel overwhelmed by all these aspects of teaching? You may be surprised to learn that many experienced teachers are too. With these roles in mind, let us develop a formal definition of teaching.

A Definition of Teaching

Teaching can be defined as the action of a person imparting skill or knowledge or giving instruction; the job of a person who teaches. Clark and Starr (1986) suggest that teaching is an attempt to assist students in acquiring or changing some skill, knowledge, ideal, attitude, or appreciation. Bruner (1966) defines instruction as "an effort to assist or shape growth" (p. 1). These definitions and the roles that teachers perform imply that teachers need to be concerned with all aspects of student development—physical, social, emotional, and cognitive. Therefore, a broad definition of teaching might be: the actions of someone who is trying to assist others to reach their fullest potential in all aspects of development. This is a tall order. What skills might one need in order to accomplish this noble task?

Central to the process of learning to teach is the concept of effective teaching. Trying to define the competencies needed to be an effective teacher has long occupied the thoughts of professional educators. Some will argue that effective teachers are those who are effective decision makers. Other educators feel that effective teachers are those with a superior command of the subject and the skills necessary to communicate that content.

Reflective Teaching

Recently, new ideas about effective teaching have emerged (Brookfield, 1995). Traditional teacher-training programs have been directive in nature, espousing what practices prospective teachers ought to be engaging in to be effective. The dynamic and complex nature of teaching, however, warrants that teacher educators prepare prospective teachers to be self-monitoring individuals. Self-monitoring requires that candidates have skills that enable self-analysis of teaching episodes, reflection and focusing on events rather than on personalities, and systematic observation for patterns and trends of teaching and learning behavior. These new ideas suggest that to be effective, teachers must inquire into students' experiences and build an empirical understanding of learners and a capacity to analyze what occurs in classrooms and in the lives of their students. Adapting your teaching to focus on inquiry and problem solving requires that you change your orientation from a view of teaching as static, with simple formulas and cookbook rules, to teaching as dynamic and ever changing. This change will require that you become a **reflective teacher.**

Donald Cruickshank (1987), one of the primary architects of **reflective teaching,** suggests that reflective teachers want to learn all they can about teaching from both theory and practice. They teach and reflect on the teaching. In effect, Cruickshank suggests that reflective teachers think deeply about the theory and practice of teaching. They deliberate on their teaching and through the process become thoughtful and wiser teachers.

Schon (1987) points out that reflective teaching requires careful planning and continual "reflecting-in-practice" and "reflecting-on-practice" with regard to the many dimensions of classroom teaching and learning. Such teaching re-quires that you be sensitive to the diversity of students' needs and family back-ground. You must view students as active learners whose intellects, emotions, self-esteem, and self-worth deserve respect and enhancement.

Reflective teaching means you must ask basic, but often difficult, questions about the appropriateness and success of your teaching. If students are not successful, you should be asking how you can change your teaching or class-room behaviors to improve on their success. If students aren't attentive, what can be done to change this behavior? If students are receiving poor grades, what can be done to motivate them? In essence, you must ask self-evaluative ques-tions and then conclude whether you are satisfied or dissatisfied. Reflection, then, is the continued self-monitoring of satisfaction with effectiveness. Such self-monitoring should result in growth as a teacher and more effective planning and teaching.

Teaching often becomes routine with time, and techniques are repeated with very little or no forethought. Through reflective teaching, however, teach-ers adapt their lessons to learner needs and examine student satisfaction with a lesson. They engage students in their lessons and encourage students to as-sume more responsibility for their own learning. Reflective teachers learn to adapt subject matter to the individual differences of students and formulate their own rules, principles, and philosophies for better classroom practices. In other words, teachers who reflect on their effectiveness—who submit them to examination—become better decision makers and, consequently, more effective teachers.

✖ The Teacher as Decision Maker

Madeline Hunter (1982) says that teachers must be effective decision makers. Indeed, she suggests that teaching is decision making. That is, teachers must make sound decisions in their interactions with students that will result, when implemented, in increased probability that students will learn.

Researchers suggest that regardless of who or what is being taught, all teaching decisions fall into three categories: (1) what content to teach, (2) what the student will do to learn and to demonstrate learning has occurred, and (3) what the teacher will do to facilitate the acquisition of that learning. When these professional decisions are made on the basis of sound educational theory and if these decisions reflect the teacher's sensitivity to the student and to the situation, learning will usually take place. Should errors be made in any of these three decision areas, student learning will generally be impeded.

The number of decisions teachers have to make daily is astonishing. Mur-ray (1986) estimates the number at fifteen hundred. Skilled teachers not only make numerous decisions but also make them well. The effective teacher struc-tures the classroom so that it runs smoothly and efficiently. This enables more teacher time to be devoted to the most important decisions—decisions that will improve student learning. For example, "How much lecturing should I do?" "How many questions should be asked?" "How much reinforcement should be used?" "What is the best method to assess students' acquisition of the stated objectives?" "How can Cindi be motivated?" "Can John do better in class?" and "Are students interested in the lesson?" represent only a few questions you may ask on a normal day. Also, note that these decisions are made before, during, and after instruction time.

When teachers make sound decisions, student learning will result. These decisions will be both informal and formal, conscious or otherwise. Applied in this context and format **decision making** can be defined as making well-thought-out choices from among several alternatives. These choices are usually based on judgments consistent with one's values and on the relevant, sound information available. In making sound decisions, teachers must constantly monitor the classroom environment and their teaching. Essentially, to make effective decisions before, during, and after instruction, teachers must be effective planners, observers, and managers.

What theoretical knowledge does a teacher need to be an effective decision maker? More specifically, what theoretical knowledge does a teacher need to make sound decisions?

Theoretical Knowledge

Theoretical knowledge is generally gleaned from the coursework required in an approved teacher preparatory program. In most programs, this knowledge will be derived from such courses as foundations of education, growth and development, exceptional child, multicultural education, educational psychology, tests and measurement, educational media, and methods. However, the theories and knowledge developed in these courses cannot be totally applied to the learning situation. You must adapt the theories and principles to the reality of your actual classroom before they become useful.

Your classroom will be subject to variables that were not present when the theories and principles that you study in class were developed. These theories and principles were developed in controlled experimental situations. Factors such as the weather, the date (week before holiday, Christmas, etc.), location of school, time of day, your teaching style, and your personality were not present in the experimental environment. Thus, when you make decisions you must have a command of not only the theoretical knowledge but also factors within the learning environment and with regard to yourself.

Theoretical knowledge, then, is of limited value if it cannot be applied to the learning environment; that is, unless it can become active knowledge. Active knowledge is the application of theoretical knowledge. It is based on the correct application in decision making of the concepts, pure theory, and principles learned in university and college classrooms.

Active Knowledge

As a teacher, you can apply theoretical knowledge in two ways: to interpret situations and to solve problems. For example, you may observe a student acting like a clown all the time and interpret the actions as a need for attention. In so doing, you are using theoretical knowledge gained in your classroom management class. To solve the problem, you give the student attention when he or she isn't acting like a clown. A teacher lacking the appropriate theoretical knowledge might reprimand the clowning behavior and in so doing would give the student the desired attention, which would reinforce the clowning behavior.

Problem solving is central to the decision-making process. A situation must be diagnosed, information collected and analyzed, alternatives identified, decisions made, and the decisions applied and tested. To carry out this process effectively, a teacher must possess a high degree of theoretical knowledge and be able to apply it to the reality of the classroom. Thus, as some educators will argue, effective teaching is sound decision making.

Some teachers, however, will make decisions intuitively. That is, decisions will be made without a systematic analysis of information or without much background information. The rapid pace of classroom interactions often leave little time for the gathering and evaluation of pertinent information. In these cases, teachers must rely on quick thinking, hunches, and related experiences to make the most appropriate decisions. They must use their storehouse of experiences and hunches to guide their actions. This knowledge represents "what has worked" or "best practices" discovered through experiences.

Other educators view effective teachers as those who have a superior command of their particular academic subject and the teaching skills (specific and generic) to communicate that content to students. Let us now look at these viewpoints.

✴ Specific Teaching Skills

Joyce and Weil (1980) suggest there are many kinds of effective teachers. They further suggest that different teachers are effective under different circumstances. For example, a teacher might be quite effective at the elementary level but quite ineffective at the secondary level, or vice versa. Since elementary teachers are required to teach all areas of the curriculum, whereas secondary teachers usually teach in only one or two curriculum areas, subject matter instruction will usually be much deeper at the secondary level. Thus, when observing instruction at the elementary and secondary levels, you should note which specific skills are necessary for effective teaching at each level.

Skill in teaching reading represents another area in which elementary and secondary teachers differ. Because elementary teachers are responsible for teaching basic reading skills, they need extensive training in teaching those skills. Although reading instruction has historically been neglected at the secondary level, the importance of refining secondary students' reading skills is now becoming apparent (Clark & Starr, 1986). In fact, many secondary teachers are now required to develop some skill in teaching content reading. Unfortunately, in most states, skill in teaching reading is still required only of elementary teachers.

Major developmental differences between elementary and secondary level students also help differentiate the skills needed by teachers at different grade levels. At the secondary level, adolescents are going through puberty.

They experience a spurt in growth patterns and are maturing sexually. These physical changes can lead to an exaggerated concern about appearance and size. Socially, adolescents try to achieve independence from the family and often become greatly influenced by peer groups and overly involved in extracurricular activities. Emotionally, there is a search for identity that can result in moodiness, experimentation with drugs and alcohol, and even suicide in extreme cases. At this stage, thinking becomes more complex, a value system is further developed and refined, and competencies for life goals are mastered. With all these changes, no wonder adjustment is a problem. Thus, adolescent students need teachers who can model and help them acquire complex physical, social, emotional, and cognitive skills. What is needed is a combination subject matter expert, counselor, social psychologist, mental health worker, and youth group worker.

In contrast, students at the elementary level, particularly in the primary grades, are still quite dependent and need teachers who can display and provide affection and act as surrogate parents. As a result of these developmental differences, vastly different skills are needed to work effectively with elementary and secondary level students.

⋇ Generic Teaching Skills

There are also certain teacher skills that are essential for effective teaching in all grades and in all curriculum areas (Cooper, Cognitive & Technology Group at Vanderbilt, Leighton, Martorella, Morine-Dershimer, Sadker, Sadker, Shostak, TenBrink, & Weber, 1999; Guillaume, 1999; MacDonald, 1999). These generic skills can be classified as preinstructional, instructional, or postinstructional.

Preinstructional Skills

The key to effective teaching is planning (Jacobsen, Eggen, Kauchak, & Dulaney, 1985). You must plan well to teach well. But what skills does one need in order to plan well? To answer this question, let us take a closer look at the planning process. Essentially, planning can be thought of as a sequential decision-making process. You must decide sequentially on answers to the following:

1. What content should be taught?
2. What are the desired learner outcomes?
3. What teaching materials will be needed?
4. What is the best way to introduce the subject?
5. What is the best instructional strategy for the intended learning?
6. How should the lesson be closed?
7. How should the students be evaluated?

This sequential planning process is illustrated in Figure 1.1. Step 1 involves identifying the content; step 2, writing objectives; step 3, introducing the lesson; step 4, selecting an instructional strategy; step 5, closing the lesson; step 6, evaluating the lesson; and step 7, identifying new content to be taught. Notice that step 7 uses the evaluative information in step 6 to determine the next

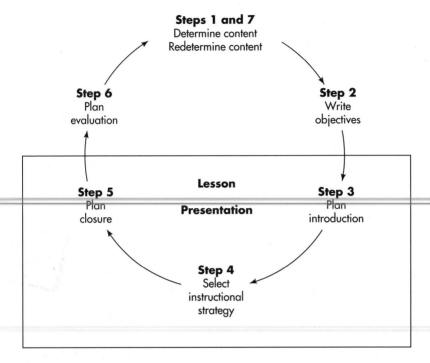

FIGURE 1.1   *Basic Seven-Step Planning Process*   The process is both sequential and cyclic in nature. Steps 3, 4, and 5 represent the component of the process that is implemented in the classroom.

lesson's content. Also, note that steps 3, 4, and 5 involve activities that form the class presentation component of the model. We will take a brief look at each of these steps before discussing them at length in subsequent chapters.

Step 1 involves selecting the content to be taught. The content can be determined by analyzing state-mandated learner outcomes and curriculum guides, by examining recommended textbooks, or by analyzing (diagnosing) student needs. Student needs are usually determined from past class evaluations (step 6) and from class observations during past lessons.

Once the content has been selected, step 2 is to decide exactly what students should know and exactly what attitudes and values should be developed with regard to that content. These specifics are stated in your lesson objectives and should be expressed in performance terms. In other words, objectives should specify exactly what students should be able to do upon completion of the lesson or the unit of study.

In step 3, the lesson introduction, your objective is to gain the undivided attention of the students. This introduction is commonly referred to as the **set induction** or the establishment of a **cognitive set.**

The selection of an instructional strategy is step 4 in the planning model and is of prime importance. Your task is to select the strategy that best fits your students' maturity levels, learning styles, and the classroom environment. This selection is determined from your knowledge of learning theory and from past observations of the class.

Step 5 involves ending the lesson. The closing must be planned so that the lesson content is made meaningful and is fully understood. This is referred to as your **lesson closure.**

Finally (in step 6), you must determine whether you have accomplished what you wanted. You must determine whether the students have mastered the specifics you have written into your objectives. However, your evaluation is not the end of the process; it is merely the starting point for the next planning cycle.

A thorough examination of the preinstructional and planning process reveals that it is a major undertaking requiring a number of skills. Specifically, you must be able to:

1. Make accurate observations.
2. Write objectives.
3. Select instructional materials.
4. Plan appropriate cognitive sets (set inductions).
5. Select appropriate teaching strategies.
6. Plan appropriate closures.
7. Determine and develop appropriate evaluations.

Whether you are a future teacher or an experienced one, you need to develop and refine these preinstructional skills. The results will be more effective planning and increased student learning.

Instructional Skills

Once you have planned a lesson, you must implement it. Implementing a lesson so that maximum learning takes place is a difficult task that requires special skills essential to all teachers.

Central to instruction is the ability to communicate. You cannot teach effectively if you are unable to communicate with your students. Moreover, you cannot communicate effectively without gaining student attention and arousing and maintaining their interest. This requires skill in the use of stimulus variation, questions, and reinforcement.

Management of the learning environment is also a skill that all effective teachers must master. You must be able to get students' cooperation, maintain their involvement in learning tasks, and conduct the business of the classroom smoothly and efficiently. Little teaching or learning can take place in an environment that is not well managed. Even well-planned lessons can fail if you lack the skill to manage a classroom. Specifically, you must be able to:

1. Establish cognitive sets (set inductions).
2. Communicate.
3. Use stimulus variation.
4. Use reinforcement effectively.
5. Use questioning techniques.
6. Manage a classroom.

7. Establish lesson closure.
8. Evaluate objectives.

Although the development and refinement of these instructional skills does not guarantee success, they should greatly increase your potential for success.

Postinstructional Skills

Teaching involves well-planned and organized evaluation. Evaluative information must be collected and analyzed with respect to your objectives, and judgments must be made regarding the level of student achievement. Consequently, data collection techniques, instrumentation, and data analysis techniques must be planned and developed prior to instruction.

There are two postinstructional skills essential to effective evaluation. Specifically, you must be able to analyze collected evaluative information and make judgments regarding evaluative information. Although these skills are used following instruction, they must be carefully planned prior to instruction.

As you can see, being an effective teacher is not an easy task. It takes hard work. You can now check your understanding of the teaching process by completing Web Search: The Teaching Process and Task 1.1.

The remainder of this book was written to assist you in developing and refining your understanding and use of preinstructional and instructional teaching skills. However, before we proceed, let us briefly look at school organizational patterns, the general structure of the school curriculum, and some of the various school reform issues.

⚹ School Organizational Patterns

Research has shown that there is nothing "magical" about rigid grade levels, fixed classroom space, rigid class size, or repetitive scheduling. Therefore, schools can be organized to allow for variety in schedules, class size, and teaching styles.

Web Search: The Teaching Process

Teachers often need ideas and resources to better motivate students and to make instruction more effective. The Internet can be a useful tool for this purpose. Access the following Internet URL sites: **http://www.iloveteaching .com/webmap/index.htm** and **http://www.teachers.net**. Analyze the ideas and resources available at these sites. Share your analysis with the instructor and class.

T A S K   1 . 1

The Teaching Process

Respond to the following items. Check your responses with those given at the end of the chapter.

1. Define teaching:_____

   _____

2. Teachers who think deeply about the theory and practice of teaching are_____

   _____ .

3. Madeline Hunter suggests teaching is _____ .

4. Differentiate between theoretical and active knowledge:_____

   _____

5. List the seven steps to the planning process in sequential order.

   Step 1:_____
   Step 2:_____
   Step 3:_____
   Step 4:_____
   Step 5:_____
   Step 6:_____
   Step 7:_____

6. The following items should be addressed in the planning process. Indicate which step of the seven-step planning process addresses each item.

   _____ a. An activity is planned to capture the undivided attention of the students.
   _____ b. The specifics that students should learn are identified.
   _____ c. The level of learning by the students is checked.
   _____ d. The activities to be used in teaching the content are developed or selected.
   _____ e. The content to be taught is determined.

7. Classify each skill or knowledge area listed below as being needed only by elementary teachers (E), needed only by secondary teachers (S), or a general teaching skill or knowledge area needed by all teachers (G).

   _____ a. Knowledge of the learning process.
   _____ b. Skill in handling discipline problems.
   _____ c. Skill in making observations.
   _____ d. Refined skill in teaching basic reading.
   _____ e. Sound decision-making skill.
   _____ f. Skill in listening.
   _____ g. Depth of knowledge in a single content area.
   _____ h. Skill in writing objectives.
   _____ i. Knowledge of adolescent behavior.
   _____ j. Skill in lesson closing techniques.
   _____ k. Skill in nonverbal communication.

Continued on next page

Analysis and Reflections

Teachers assume many different responsibilities in today's schools. Some say they are asked to do too much. Do you think teachers have too many responsibilities? If so, what can be done to improve the working conditions of teachers?

Continuous Progress Education

If schools are to be truly responsive to student needs, they would have to commit to a continuous progress education (nongraded pattern)—that is, grade-level barriers would be dropped. Schools would identify a continuum of learning objectives to be mastered in each academic area and students would work toward mastery at their own pace regardless of grade level. Advocates of continuous progress education suggest that age-grade school organizational patterns inhibit pupil learning, regardless of considerations of ability and interest.

The continuous progress movement has its roots in the nongraded movement which was relatively short-lived. The term "nongraded" has now given way to the term "continuous." The continuous progress education pattern has stalled to some extent. However, the movement shows promise as a viable school organizational pattern. Further research is needed on how the components of schooling are affected when continuous progress ideas are applied.

Self-Contained Classrooms

A self-contained classroom pattern holds one teacher responsible for all instruction in all subject areas to a group of students. Possible exceptions might be art, music, and physical education. Thus, the teacher would teach social studies, mathematics, science, language arts, and reading to the same group of students. This educational pattern gives great latitude to the teacher regarding what will be taught and how it will be taught. The quality of instruction depends to a high degree on the individual teacher. Most teachers lack the content knowledge in the required curriculum areas to make the self-contained classroom pattern viable at all school levels.

Although grouping students into self-contained classes based on ability and achievement is still widely practiced, the trend is changing. Many educators oppose the tracking of students. Indeed, educators have devised other methods for attending to student differences; that is, for providing challenging learning environments. Some of these methods include teaming, peer teaching, cooperative learning, continuous progress classes, individualized instruction, and magnet schools.

Departmentalization

The departmental organizational pattern holds one teacher responsible for each subject. Each department represents an academic discipline staffed with a group of teachers with preparation and certification in the specific subject. A departmentalized classroom organization compensates for teachers' academic weaknesses. In this plan, teachers instruct in their area or areas of specialization. Teachers teaching in the various departments have specialties such as science, language arts, or mathematics. The departmental pattern is usually the dominant pattern in junior and senior high schools.

Another organizational plan seen in some schools is the platoon system. The platoon system maximizes the availability of school resources and facilities to alternate groups and uses teachers' specializations to the utmost. Students are divided into two or more platoons. The platoons then take turns being instructed by their regular teacher or subject-area specialists. For example, designated subject-area classrooms can be established for mathematics, science, foreign language, and technology. Each platoon could then be scheduled into these designated subject-area classrooms.

When young adolescents enter middle school or junior high, they too often are confronted with departmentalization based on subject matter. The challenge for middle and junior high schools is to provide a smooth transition from the self-contained elementary school to the departmentalized high school. Thus, the departmental pattern needs to be modified to provide this transition. Interdisciplinary team organization that integrates the curriculum may provide the needed organizational pattern.

Teaming

Teaming, what is it? Basically, teaming (or team teaching) is a type of instructional pattern in which two or more teachers pool their expertise, interests, knowledge of students, and available resources and take joint responsibility for meeting a significant part of the instructional needs of the same group of students (see Figure 1.2). Teacher aides or assistants may also be included in the teaming arrangement. Teaming allows a school to make maximum use of teacher strengths and allows teachers to work flexibly with individuals and groups of students. This type of planning requires that a common group of students be assigned to a common group of teachers who share a common planning time, which results in a more efficient and productive classroom/school environment. Teaming gives teachers the opportunity to coordinate and reinforce subject matter.

One of the most important elements of teaming is cooperation. An effective team is formed as a combination of teachers that is able to accomplish cooperatively, better than individually, the tasks of meeting the needs of students. However, team teaching is not "turn teaching." Turn teaching differs in that two or more teachers bring their students together and conveniently take turns teaching. For example, a two-teacher team could join classes, with one teacher teaching language arts while the other teaches social studies. This form of

Period (20 minute modules)	Monday	Tuesday	Wednesday	Thursday	Friday
1	Homeroom	Homeroom	Homeroom	Homeroom	Homeroom
2	Language Arts and Social Studies	Language Arts and Social Studies	Language Arts and Social Studies	Language Arts and Social Studies	Language Arts and Social Studies
3					
4	Speech	Physical Education	Health	Speech	Health
5					
6	Recreation Period	Recreation Period	Recreation Period	Recreation Period	Recreation Period
7					
8	Lunch	Lunch	Lunch	Lunch	Lunch
9					
10	Math and Science	Math and Science	Math and Science	Math and Science	Math and Science
11					
12					
13	Exploratory	Music	Exploratory	Music	Exploratory
14					

FIGURE 1.2   *Block Scheduling with Team Teaching*

instruction is generally ineffective because of the lack of collaboration on lessons, strategies, student needs, and assessments.

Under the true **team teaching** concept, two or more teachers get together and join the instruction for their classes. Each teacher may be responsible for developing the plans for one particular subject, but they share the plans with each other and teaching responsibilities are shared. In some schools, an experienced teacher is appointed or selected by the team to assume overall responsibility for the team. This lead teacher organizes team meetings; facilitates meetings with students, parents, and school administrators; makes sure the team carries out its functions; and makes sure the team has the resources to put their plans into action.

Team teaching may also be used in nongraded and multigraded classrooms. This organizational plan allows students to be grouped by need rather than by grade. Students move from one group to another depending on the subject and the student's ability and interest.

One of the most difficult and yet effective instructional types of team teaching is **interdisciplinary team teaching.** The interdisciplinary approach calls for a team of teachers to integrate subject matter through focusing on meaningful themes. For example, a team could relate all instruction to a science theme such as the earth. This approach requires careful planning on the part of the participating teacher team. However, through careful planning, each instructional area can provide important concepts related to the thematic unit of study. This interdisciplinary team approach to instruction gives students the opportunity to see the interconnectedness of various subjects in the curriculum. Instruction can be balanced between such areas as a core curriculum, career exploration, and such associated areas as higher-order thinking and career education.

Interdisciplinary teams generally consist of two or more teachers with instruction in one of the following patterns: (1) at least two subjects are combined, mathematics/science or language arts/social studies; (2) four or more subjects are combined, such as mathematics/science/language arts/social studies; (3) the four core subject areas are combined with art, music, physical education, and so on. The most common subject matter combinations are math/science and language arts/social studies.

Flexible Block Scheduling

All school schedules are designed to repeat on some regular cycle. The most rigid basic cycle is the daily cycle, where every day basically repeats the schedule of the previous day. The schedule shows that all classes meet at the same time every day of the week, every day is the same for students and teachers, and all periods are equal in length.

Block scheduling is becoming the popular new instructional delivery pattern of choice for American schools. There is no standard form of block schedule. However, all have basically the same premise: School instruction need not be organized into the traditional seven- or eight-period day, but can allow for longer classes in most subjects. Many schools have used block scheduling for some time (Canady & Rettig, 1995). Rather than discuss all of the examples of block scheduling, two representative models will be presented.

Perhaps the most basic form of block scheduling consists of two classes "doubling-up" on alternate days. For example, we could double-up on language arts and social studies. On week one, language arts meets for two periods on Monday, Wednesday, and Friday; social studies meets the same periods on Tuesday and Thursday. On week two the schedule is reversed. The model could be modified to eliminate the confusing alternate weeks by having both classes meet for a "normal" 50-minute period on one day each week, Monday or Friday, perhaps.

Another common standard block schedule is the "Basic 4/4 Semester Plan," which is sometimes called an "intensive" or an "accelerated" model (Edwards, 1995). Under this schedule the school day is divided into four periods, and the school year is divided into two semesters. The traditional year-long

---

Expansion Activity: School Organization

The present school organizational structure is often criticized as being an industrial age factory model that has outlived its usefulness. Write a short reaction to this criticism and suggest possible changes needed in our educational system.

---

courses are scheduled for one semester of double-block periods. Teachers generally have three classes and use the fourth for preparation time.

Block scheduling offers several simple advantages. First, because there are fewer class changes, chaos in the hall is reduced. Second, teachers prepare for fewer classes and work with far fewer students each day. Third, students have the opportunity for in-depth study of subject matter. Finally, teachers tend to revise their teaching methods to more student-centered activities to accommodate the longer class periods.

This completes our discussion of school organizational patterns. Complete Expansion Activity: School Organization to further examine this critical issue.

⚔ The Curriculum

Content selection is of considerable importance in the teaching process. The content selection process cannot occur by chance: You must thoughtfully weigh the needs of students and the structure of the subject itself. That is, the learning situation and the subject itself must be accurately diagnosed as to the appropriateness of the curriculum to be taught. Once selected this curriculum is translated into instruction.

What is curriculum? Curricularists often have difficulty answering this question. Indeed, there are as many definitions of curriculum as curriculum textbooks. Broadly defined, curriculum is a systematic plan of instruction. However, curriculum must be viewed as different from instruction. In other words, *what* you teach is different from *how* you teach it. For the purpose of this text, we will define **curriculum** as all the planned and unplanned learning experiences that students undergo while in a school setting. Every school has a planned, formally acknowledged curriculum as well as an unplanned, informal, and hidden one. Basically, students experience four kinds of curricula in school settings: explicit curriculum, hidden curriculum, integrated curriculum, and extracurricular programs.

The Explicit Curriculum

The explicit curriculum is the formal acknowledged curriculum selected by a school or school district. The explicit curriculum focuses on goals, objectives, subject matter, and organization of instruction. Instruction has been carefully planned; resources—including personnel, materials, time, and space—have been allocated; the curriculum has been written into lessons and is taught in the classroom; and intended learning is formally evaluated. The formal curriculum encompasses the sequence of courses, goals, and objectives mandated by the state; the curriculum guide developed by the school district; and the textbooks used in the classrooms. Local curriculum development efforts are generally derived from the explicit state-mandated curriculum that is to be implemented by classroom teachers.

Some parts of the explicit curriculum are determined at the federal level. For instance, Public Law 94-142 dictates the degree and nature of the curriculum for children with special needs. Also, through grant programs Congress can often influence national curriculum decisions (Passe, 1995).

Local concerns—environmental issues, ethnic discord, and political problems—can have a tremendous impact on the school curriculum. For example, the Oklahoma City bombing led to the need for counselors in many schools in Oklahoma.

The Hidden Curriculum

The hidden curriculum is the "unintended" curriculum. It consists of those learning experiences, both negative and positive, that are not part of the explicit curriculum but that result in changes in the attitudes, beliefs, and values of students. Some students learn positive, worthwhile behaviors and attitudes, such as how to think independently, politeness, and the joy of mathematics. Still others may learn negative behaviors and attitudes, such as disdain for school, how to copy effectively, and how to hurt the feelings of others. As you can see, you must be constantly aware of the hidden curriculum that may be communicated or modeled in your classroom.

The Integrated Curriculum

Subject matter is usually organized as separate disciplines, each with their own time blocks. Or it may be integrated either on a schoolwide basis (as with the core curriculum) or at the classroom level (as with certain types of unit plans).

During the last few years educators have been rethinking the appropriateness of the separate-discipline approach. Indeed, many are calling for a restructuring of school subjects. Subject area leaders have long recognized that no subject can be taught in isolation; each is part of the whole. Curriculum developers should be working to create an *integrated curriculum,* in which disciplines are blended, fused, or unified.

Over the years two techniques have been used to create a more unified curriculum: correlation and integration. With *correlation,* subjects maintain their separateness but are related to each other. Students at a particular grade level are shown the relationships between subjects, as with speaking, reading, listening, and writing skills; mathematics and science; art and literature. This correlation can be horizontal, across one grade level, or vertical, across two or more. For example, mathematics may be correlated with science in the fifth grade (horizontal correlation), or Spanish, taught in the sophomore or junior year, may be correlated with literature, taught in the senior year (vertical correlation). Correlation becomes integration when the separate subjects lose their identities. Most curriculum planners focus on horizontal correlation and integration.

There are two basic approaches to *integration* of a district or school curriculum: adapting an existing curriculum and creating a new curriculum. The particular school situation dictates which approach should be used. Most teachers begin slowly by experimenting with integration. If successful, they expand its use.

The basic strategy for integrating existing curriculum is to look for common elements or connections. There are natural relationships between most subjects, and these can form the basis for integration. For instance, connections between social issues and measurements of time, distance, climate indicators, constructing and decoding graphs, and interpreting large numbers promotes social studies and mathematic correlation.

Creating a new curriculum is not an easy task. The first step in the process is to select an appropriate theme. This theme should be one that is exciting to students, educationally valid, of interest to the teacher, and manageable. Some common themes are pets, television, the human body, the West, and dinosaurs. Once the theme has been determined, the curriculum planners should identify subtopics related to the central theme and activities related to the subtopics.

Extracurricular Activities

Extracurricular activities are elective extensions of the explicit curriculum that do not carry credit toward graduation. Common examples are community work, band, clubs (French club, chess club, computer club, and so forth), and pep clubs. Some extracurricular activities, such as environmental cleanup projects or work on the school newspaper, can be direct spinoffs of the explicit curriculum.

Extracurricular activities are generally geared toward community needs, students interests and aspirations, and social issues. They serve to reinforce and add spice to the school's more formal curriculum.

Curriculum Selection

What should be taught in our schools? Since students and, ultimately, society will be the consumers of school curricula, the well-planned curriculum will take into account both the students' and society's needs. Moreover, the structure of the subject often dictates what and how a subject should be taught, that is, the content and the sequence of teaching.

Teachers and schools select subject content for a wide variety of reasons. Many teachers rely on textbooks and workbooks to determine the curriculum. Essentially, these teachers are turning the entire process of content selection over to the author and publisher of the adopted textbook. Other teachers use the adopted textbook as a base but integrate new material drawn from emerging social issues into the classroom content. These teachers do not blindly follow a textbook. They augment the textbook because they realize that textbooks are not all-inclusive. These teachers are not rigid. They are aware; they plan; and, finally, they enhance learning through involvement.

✄ Strategies for School Improvement

There have been numerous proposals for improving the quality of education. The discussion which follows considers only four of the major proposals.

School-Based Management

Many school districts are turning to **school-based management (SBM)** as a means of reform (David, 1995–96; Odden & Wohlstetter, 1995). Central to the concept of site-based management is the belief that school improvement is best achieved by giving the people closest to students the authority to make decisions. However, participatory management does not mean that everyone decides everything. Some decisions must be left with those who know the context in which the decisions will be carried out. As such, some decisions should be made by parents, some by school professionals, and others by the formal schoolwide body. The principal reason for initiating school-based management remains to increase student achievement.

The majority of schools that use school-based management (SBM) rely on a site council to make decisions about programs and resources. Most SBM councils are composed of parents, teachers, administrators, and classified employees, who are elected by their respective constituencies (Odden & Wohlstetter, 1995). In some schools, the council may share authority with the school administration or be merely advisory.

Parent and Community Involvement

Parent involvement and community involvement can be important factors in improving the academic learning of students. This process, wherein parents and educators are encouraged to cooperate in and support the education of students, can come in four different forms and levels: instruction at school, instruction at home, school governance, and community service.

Getting parents involved in the educational process can be a difficult task. Parents and teachers live in different worlds that are often separated by psychosocial barriers. Indeed, parents frequently have preconceived and sometimes biased views of school and teachers. Even with these constraints, however, parent and community involvement will generally positively impact the educational process.

Ultimately we must find ways to open and support culturally responsive communication between parents and schools. Too often minority and low-income families face sustained isolation from the school culture. Such isolation can result in an "us" versus "them" mentality. Teachers then often blame parents for student academic failures. However, because of changes in modern families (e.g., non-English-speaking, single parent families, urbanization, unwed mothers, decreasing family size, and poverty), it often takes a whole community to educate our young people.

Charter Schools

Charter schools offer a different approach to providing and managing schooling (Hassel, 1999; Nathan, 1999; Sarason, 1998). No one is forced to attend a charter school, a charter school represents a choice for students, parents, and teachers. In its purest form, a charter is a written agreement between a group of parents, teachers, or others from the public or private sector and a local school board, state education board, or some other public authority to carry out a specific instructional program (Bierlein & Mulholland, 1994). The charter school receives the full operating funds associated with its student enrollment. However, a charter school is an independent legal entity with complete authority over its finances and personnel. Once approved, a charter school is freed from many (or all) district and/or state regulations that are perceived as inhibiting innovation. Organizers tailor programs at the local level with few state restrictions.

Any group may propose a charter for a specific educational purpose. For example, a group of science and math teachers might wish to coordinate the teaching of these two subjects in an elementary, middle school, junior high, or high school. Or a group of parents might wish to replace a chaotic system of electives with a coordinated humanities program. Generally the charter school contract can be renewed if the identified student outcomes have been met. Thus, the charter school is accountable for its performance.

Year-Round Schooling

Some educators argue that the typical school calendar has outlived its usefulness (Ballinger, 1995). Originally designed to foster economic objectives it has little educational validity today.

To meet the demands of a growing student population without spending more money, some districts have implemented varying year-round schooling. The most popular schedule is the 45-15 plan where students attend school for forty-five days, followed by fifteen days of vacation. Thus, year-round students attend the same number of days as traditional schedule students (180), except the days are arranged differently. By running several simultaneous tracks of this schedule, schools can make better use of classroom space all year. There are numerous other types of year-round schedules, but the common factor is that students have several short vacations throughout the year, rather than one three-month summer break. Some schools have all students on the same instructional and vacation schedule (a single-track calendar). Others use a multi-track design which groups students onto tracks that have different instructional and vacation schedules. These tracks are varied so there is always at least one track on vacation.

Perhaps the most important reason for year-round school is to eliminate the significant learning loss that usually occurs during the summer. Thus, year-round schooling can reduce the amount of review time. Other advantages associated with year-round schooling are the opportunity it gives schools to offer advanced, remedial, and enrichment classes and the high student interest in learning resulting from the regular vacation.

There is also some opposition to year-round schooling. It is argued that there is no clear evidence that year-round schooling leads to higher achievement gains. Moreover, there are scheduling problems that must be overcome, conflicts with family lifestyles and extracurricular activities that present problems, and the increased operational costs associated with maintaining the school for the total year.

In order to review our discussion of the school organizational patterns, school curriculum, and strategies for school improvement, take a few minutes to complete Task 1.2, which will check your understanding of the concepts presented in these sections.

T A S K   1 . 2

Curriculum, Organization, and Reform

Respond to the following items. Check your responses with those given at the end of the chapter.

1. Define curriculum:_____

   _____

2. Describe the teaming concepts:_____

   _____

3. Describe flexible block scheduling:_____

   _____

4. Match the description on the left with the proper curriculum term on the right.
   - ____ a. A blend of different discipline areas
   - ____ b. Curriculum based on needs and interests of students
   - ____ c. The intended material to be taught
   - ____ d. The unintended teaching

   1. Explicit curriculum
   2. Hidden curriculum
   3. Integrated curriculum
   4. Extracurricular activities

5. Match the reform description on the left with the strategy on the right.
   - ____ a. Support provided for the education process
   - ____ b. Means for better use of school resources
   - ____ c. Gives people closest to students authority in making decisions
   - ____ d. Written agreement between groups to carry out a specific program

   1. School-based management
   2. Parent and community involvement
   3. Charter school
   4. Year-round schooling

Analysis and Reflections

Review the proposals for improving education. Write a short paper on the feasibility of each one. Submit papers to your instructor.

Summary

- It is possible to develop and train someone to be an effective teacher.

Teaching

- Teachers are expected to be instructional experts, classroom managers, and, to a limited degree, counselors.
- Some argue that effective teaching must be reflective teaching. Reflective teaching requires that teachers think deeply about the theory and practice of teaching and evaluate their own effectiveness.

The Teacher as Decision Maker

- Some educators argue that effective teaching is sound decision making. Teacher decisions fall into three categories: (1) what content to teach, (2) what the student will do to learn and to demonstrate learning has occurred, (3) what the teacher will do to facilitate the acquisition of that learning.
- Sound decision making requires a solid theoretical knowledge base and a storehouse of active knowledge (ability to apply theoretical knowledge).

Specific Teaching Skills

- There are many kinds of effective teachers. However, different teachers are effective under different circumstances.
- Required teaching skills often differ for elementary and secondary teachers.

Generic Teaching Skills

- Teaching skills fall into three distinct categories: preinstructional, instructional, and postinstructional. Preinstructional skills are those needed by teachers to be effective planners. Instructional skills consist of the skills needed by teachers to successfully implement planned lessons. Postinstructional skills are the skills needed by teachers to be effective evaluators.
- Attention to the development and refinement of preinstructional, instructional, and postinstructional teaching skills is important to all professional educators.

School Organizational Patterns

- To be truly responsive to student needs, schools should use a continuous progress pattern. The continuous progress movement has stalled to some extent.
- The self-contained classroom pattern holds one teacher responsible for all instruction. The quality of instruction depends on the individual teacher.
- The departmental organizational pattern holds one teacher responsible for each subject.
- Teaming is a type of instructional pattern in which two or more teachers pool their expertise, interests, knowledge of students, and available resources. Teaming gives teachers the opportunity to coordinate and reinforce subject matter.
- Interdisciplinary teaming is a difficult, but effective instructional pattern.

Interdisciplinary team teaching calls for a team of teachers to integrate subject matter.

- Block scheduling is becoming a popular new instructional pattern. Block scheduling organizes instruction so there are some traditional periods and some longer periods in a school day.

Curriculum

- A school curriculum is all the planned and unplanned learning experiences that students undergo while in a school setting. There are four basic kinds of curricula in schools: explicit curriculum, hidden curriculum, integrated curriculum; and extracurricular activities.
- The explicit curriculum is the formal school curriculum; the hidden curriculum is the "unintended" curriculum; integrated curriculum is blended, fused, or united subject matter; and extracurricular activities are the elective curriculum.
- The curriculum is selected on the basis of the needs of students and society. Teachers often select subject content for a wide variety of reasons.

Strategies for School Improvement

- School-based management is the belief that school improvement is best achieved by giving the people closest to students the authority to make decisions. Most school-based management patterns use site council to make decisions.
- Charter schools are a different approach to managing schooling. A charter is a written agreement between a group of parents, teachers, or others from the public or private sector and a local school board, state education board, or some other public authority to carry out a specific instructional program.
- Parent involvement and community involvement can improve the academic learning of students. This involvement can come in the form of involvement in instruction, instruction at home, involvement in school governance, and involvement in community service.
- There are numerous types of year-round schedules. Students usually attend school the same number of days as in traditional schedules. Year-round schooling is a pattern for using classroom space all year.

Activities

1. *Teacher roles*   Interview several teachers at different grade levels about their roles as educators. Do the teachers feel there is often too much to do? Do they often feel overwhelmed with the paperwork? Do they feel it is important to have good human relations skills?
2. *Classroom experiences*   Some knowledge is gained only through experiences and cannot be found in textbooks or college lectures. Do you agree with this statement? Give some examples of this kind of knowledge.
3. *Classroom observations*   Observe several teachers in an elementary and secondary learning environment. Make a list of the teaching skills observed in both the elementary and the secondary settings. Compare the

two lists. Do you note skills applicable only to the elementary setting? the secondary setting? Do you note any skills that apply to both settings?

4. *Self-analysis*   Make a list of personal traits you possess that will assist you in teaching at your grade level. If you are a future or experienced secondary teacher, compare your list with that of a future or experienced elementary teacher, and vice versa. Are there differences? In what areas do differences exist?

5. *Flexible block scheduling*   Visit with the principals of local secondary schools (middle school, junior high, or high school). Do they have a rigid basic daily schedule? flexible modular schedule? If modular scheduling is used, how long are the modules? How many periods in a school day? How do teachers feel about modular scheduling?

6. *The curriculum*   Obtain a state and district curriculum guide. How could the curriculum be improved at the level at which you plan to teach? Should teachers be free to determine their own curriculum? What forces commonly influence the school curriculum in your state? The explicit curriculum? the extracurriculum?

Answer Keys

Task 1.1 The Teaching Process
1. Teaching is the action of someone who is trying to assist others to reach their fullest potential in all aspects of development.
2. reflective teaching
3. decision making
4. Theoretical knowledge is the knowledge base needed to effectively carry out the teaching process. Active knowledge is the application of theoretical knowledge in making decisions.

5. Step 1: Determining content
   Step 2: Writing objectives
   Step 3: Planning introduction
   Step 4: Selecting instructional strategy
   Step 5: Planning closure
   Step 6: Planning evaluation
   Step 7: Redetermining content

6. a. Step 3   Planning the introduction
   b. Step 2   Writing the instructional objectives
   c. Step 6   Planning the evaluation
   d. Step 4   Selecting the instructional strategy
   e. Steps 1 and 7   Determining or redetermining content

7. a. G   All teachers must have a knowledge of the learning process.
   b. G   Handling discipline problems is an important aspect of classroom management.

c. *G* Making observations is important to all teachers.

d. *E* The major responsibility for teaching reading belongs to elementary teachers. However, current trends are for increased emphasis on secondary level reading.

e. *G* All teachers need to be sound decision makers.

f. *G* Listening is an important part of the communication process.

g. *S* Content knowledge depth is required only of secondary teachers. However, current trends are for greater emphasis on subject matter acquisition for elementary teachers.

h. *G* Writing instructional objectives is a skill needed by all teachers.

i. *S* Generally only secondary teachers work with adolescents. However, since some elementary teachers now teach in middle and junior high schools, these teachers too need training in working with adolescents.

j. *G* All teachers must be able to close a lesson.

k. *G* Nonverbal communication is a component of the communication process.

Task 1.2 Curriculum, Organization, and Reform

1. Curriculum is the planned and unplanned learning experiences that student undergo while in a school setting.

2. Teaming is the instructional pattern where two or more teachers pool their expertise, interests, knowledge of students, and available resources and take joint responsibility for the instructional needs of a group of students.

3. In flexible block scheduling school instruction is not organized into traditional periods, but instead, allows for longer classes in most subjects.

4. a. 3   b. 4   c. 1   d. 2

5. a. 2   b. 4   c. 1   d. 3

Theory and Research

Darling-Hammond, L. (1996). *What matters most: Teaching for America's future.* Washington, DC: National Commission on Teaching and America's Future.

Kellough, R. D. (1998). *Surviving your first year of teaching.* Paramus, NJ: Prentice-Hall.

Kronowitz, E. L. (1999). *Your first year of teaching & beyond.* White Plains, NY: Longman.

Means, B., & Olson, K. (1998). *Technology & education reform.* Upland, PA: DIANE Publishing.

Perelman, L. J. (1992). *School's out.* William Morrow and Company.

Perrone, V. (1999). *Lessons for new teachers.* New York, NY: McGraw-Hill.

References

Ballinger, C. (1995). Prisoners no more. *Educational Leadership, 53*(3), 28–31.

Bierlein, L. A., & Mulholland, L. A. (1994). The promise of charter schools. *Educational Leadership, 52*(1), 34–40.

Brookfield, S. D. (1995). *Becoming a critically reflective teacher.* San Francisco, CA: Jossey-Bass.

Bruner, J. S. (1966). *Toward a theory of instruction.* New York, NY: W. W. Norton.

Canady, R. L., & Rettig, M. D. (1995). *Block scheduling.* Larchmont, NY: Eye On Education.

Carr, T. (1998). *All eyes up here! A portrait of effective teaching.* Chattanooga, TN: Carr Enterprises.

Clark, L. H., & Starr, I. S. (1986). *Secondary and middle school teaching methods* (5th ed.). New York: Macmillan.

Cooper, J. M., *Cognition & Technology Group at Vanderbilt;* Leighton, M.S.; Martorella, P. H.; Morine-Dershimer, G. G.; Sadker, D.; Sadker, M.; Shostak, R.; TenBrink, T. D.; Weber, W. A. (1999). *Classroom teaching skills* (6th ed.). New York, NY: Houghton Mifflin.

Cruickshank, D. R. (1987). *Reflective teaching.* Reston, VA: Association of Teacher Educators.

David, J. L. (1995–96). The who, what, and why of site-based management. *Educational Leadership, 53*(4), 4–9.

Edwards, C. M., Jr. (1995). The 4×4 plan. *Educational Leadership, 53*(3), 16–19.

Guillaume, A. M. (1999). *Classroom teaching.* Paramus, NJ: Prentice-Hall.

Hassell, B. C. (1999). *Charter school challenge.* Washington, DC: Brookings Institution Press.

Hunt, G. H., Touzel, T. J., & Wiseman, D. (1999). *Effective teaching.* Springfield, IL: Charles C. Thomas.

Hunter, M. (1982). *Mastery teaching: Increasing instructional effectiveness in secondary schools, colleges and universities.* El Segundo, CA: TIP Publications.

Jacobsen, D., Eggen, P., Kauchak, D., & Dulaney, C. (1985). *Methods for teaching: A skills approach.* Columbus, OH: Charles E. Merrill.

Joyce, B., & Weil, M. (1980). *Models of teaching* (2nd ed.). Paramus, NJ: Prentice-Hall.

Kottler, J. A., & Kottler, E. (1993). *Developing the helping skills you need.* Corwin Press.

MacDonald, R. (1999). *Handbook of basic skills & strategies for beginner teachers facing the challenge.* Reading, MA: Addison Wesley Longman.

Murray, F. (1986, May). *Necessity: The developmental component in reasoning.* Paper presented at the Sixteenth Annual Meeting, Jean Piaget Society, Philadelphia.

Nathan, J. (1999). *Charter schools.* San Francisco, CA: Jossey-Bass.

Odden, E. R., & Wohlstetter, P. (1995). Making school-based management work. *Educational Leadership, 52*(5), 32–36.

Passe, J. (1995). *Elementary school curriculum.* Madison: Brown and Benchmark.

Sarason, S. B. (1998). *Charter schools.* New York: Teachers College Press.

Schon, D. (1987). *Educating the reflective practitioner.* San Francisco, CA: Jossey-Bass.

Planning for Diversity

Objectives

After completing your study of Chapter 2, you should be able to:

1. Explain why teachers need an understanding of diversity.

2. Define learning style and describe its various dimensions.

3. Explain the relationship between learning style and teaching style.

4. Describe techniques related to learning style that can be used to enhance student learning.

5. Explain the provisions of Public Law 94-142 and IDEA.

6. Outline procedures for modifying lessons to accommodate special needs students.

7. Explain how schools and teachers are addressing the various concepts of multicultural education.

Our schools face another historical reflection of a changing society. American schools in the twenty-first century will be populated by a new cultural mix (white, low-income, students of color, and non-English-speaking students). As such, a diversity of people, cultures, and values will be found in most classrooms (Latham, 1997). This means classroom teachers must be aware of and prepared to meet the special learning needs of a wide variety of students.

Today's students do not all learn and respond to learning situations in the same way. Indeed, learning is an individual experience. Along with the cognitive differences that influence learning, students will differ in learning styles, physical and learning disabilities, socioeconomic situations, and ethnic and cultural backgrounds. However, teachers are expected to teach the whole spectrum of students.

◈ Student Learning Style

Students learn through different learning styles. What is meant by learning style? Essentially, **learning style** can be viewed as the way an individual begins to process, internalize, and concentrate on new materials. Every person learns in a unique way, they have different learning channels. Some will be auditory learners, those who learn best by hearing; others will be visual learners, those who learn best by seeing or reading; and some will be physical learners, those who learn best through the manipulation of concrete materials (Shaughnessy, 1998). Some students will learn slowly; some rather quickly. Some will need substantial teacher assistance; others will be able to learn on their own. Most students will use each of these styles at one time or another. However, most will favor one style over others.

Researchers have produced valuable information about the relationship between learning and learner characteristics. Dunn and Dunn (1993) suggest learning styles are related to a person's preference in four main areas:

1. *Environmental:* The student's preference in terms of light, sound, temperature, and physical room when learning.
2. *Emotional:* The persistence and responsibility shown and the structure level, as well as the supervision needed when involved in learning.
3. *Sociological:* The adult assistance or group support (large group, small group, no support) needed when learning.
4. *Physical:* The need for movement, food intake, and time of day and sensory mode preference (e.g., visual, auditory, tactile, and kinesthetic) in learning.

These four factors can have a major impact on student learning. For example, some students will prefer bright lighting, while others will prefer dimly lit environments. Frequently, the noise level and room temperature will be the first learning style preferences communicated by students. These environmental effects are too often interpreted by novice teachers as simple complaining. Most experienced teachers, however, have come to realize that just as students are unique, they may learn in unique ways.

Processing Information

Students will all perceive reality differently. Some will immerse themselves in concrete reality; they connect experience and information to meaning. They learn best through empathy and their senses/feelings. They tend to be intuitive. On the other hand, some students think through experiences and react to the abstract dimensions of reality. They reason, analyze, and approach reality logically. Secondary schools generally do not value the sensing/feeling approach; therefore, it is often neglected and sometimes discouraged.

Students will differ in how they process experiences and information. Some will jump right in and try it (doers), while others will watch what's happening, reflect on it, and then do it (watchers). Doers tend to act on new information immediately. They try it out, and then reflect. Conversely, watchers need to internalize, reflect, and find personal meaning before acting. They associate information with their own experiences to create meaningful connections. As a teacher, you need to encourage watchers to develop the courage to experiment and try, while also refining their reflective skills. Doers need to be encouraged to develop the patience and ability to watch and be reflective, while also refining their experimenting gifts.

Kolb (1983) combined the two dimensions of perceiving information (concretely and abstractly) with the two dimensions of processing information (reflectively and actively) and formulated four different learning styles: divergers, assimilators, convergers, and accommodators. Divergers gather information concretely, and process it reflectively. The whole is processed before individual parts. Divergers like to work alone and slowly process and reflect upon new information. They like to develop a view of the whole picture before analyzing and grouping the parts for meaning. These learners will read all of the instructions before attempting to complete a task. The various components of divergers' learning style suggest that they should be given adequate time for private reflection and then given opportunities to work in groups to discuss and group their perceptions and plans. Assimilators gather information or perceive experience abstractly, and process that information reflectively. They are not interested in practical uses of theories. Assimilators are systematic planners and read and follow instructions carefully. They gather details first and formulate the whole by analysis. Assimilators are interested in the parts that make up the whole; they are inclined to complete a task as they read the instructions. Most classrooms are directed toward teaching this group. Convergers want to do it themselves. They like to process their experiences actively. Convergers prefer active experimentation to find out how something works. Convergers usually don't read instructions, but prefer to figure things out as they work with their hands. They just want the assignment and they will see if it works. Finally, accommodators gather information concretely and process it actively. They learn by trial and error and are often intuitive. They like to work from a whole to part perspective and are action oriented. They look for all the different possibilities that new information might offer. Accommodators may sometimes be impatient in their insisting that facts have many facets.

Cognitive Style

Differences in learning style are often due in part to differences in our **cognitive style,** that is, differences in how we respond to the environment and differences in the way information is processed and organized (Green, 1999; Riding & Rayner, 1998). An important aspect of cognitive style for teachers is the difference between field-dependence and field-independence. Field-dependent students usually see patterns as a whole and often have difficulty separating out the specific aspects of a situation or pattern, whereas field-independent students are usually better at seeing the parts that make up a large pattern. Field-dependent students will be people-oriented and prefer people-oriented subjects such as literature, history, and the social sciences and work well in groups. In contrast, field-independent students will be more likely to do well with problem-solving tasks and they often work well on their own. Finally,

Field Dependent		Field Independent	
Characteristics	Classroom Examples	Characteristics	Classroom Examples
Is global	Presents global aspects of concepts and materials. During instruction in general, student develops an overall feeling or general idea of material. Relates concepts to personal experiences.	Is analytical	Focuses on details of curriculum materials. Focuses on facts and principles. During instruction, develops a structure for categorizing the materials and clustering concepts.
Is extrinsically motivated	Seeks guidance and demonstrations from teacher. Seeks rewards that strengthen relationship with teacher. Relies on peers for direction and motivation. Prefers working in groups.	Is intrinsically motivated	Rarely seeks physical contact with teacher. Formal interactions with teacher are restricted to tasks at hand. Seeks nonsocial rewards. Develops a strong sense of personal directions and goals. Prefers to work alone.
Is socially oriented	Prefers to work with others and is sensitive to their feelings and opinions. Likes to cooperate. Prefers organization provided by teacher. Seeks to find social relevance of material presented in content areas.	Is content oriented	Prefers to work alone. Likes to compete. Can organize information by himself or herself. Focuses on nature of concept within and across content areas.

FIGURE 2.1 *Characteristics of Field-Dependent and Field-Independent Students*

field-dependent students often need more structure, need more reinforcement, react more to criticism, and require external cues to enhance learning, whereas field-independent students are usually internally reinforced, are less affected by criticism, are better at analyzing and reorganizing, and are better problem-solvers. Figure 2.1 gives the main characteristics that teachers should look for relative to students' cognitive style.

Another important aspect of cognitive style that teachers should be aware of is impulsivity versus reflectivity. Impulsive students will generally work and make decisions quickly and tend to concentrate on speed. They are usually the first to finish an assignment or task. In contrast, reflective students will more than likely take a long time considering all alternatives on an assignment or task and tend to concentrate on accuracy.

Impulsive students should be taught to be more reflective. They should be taught to pace their work by telling themselves to go slowly and carefully. Students can also be too reflective. In such cases, they should be assisted in pacing their work and helped in judging when enough analysis has taken place and it is time to make choices.

Identifying Learning Styles

Observations will often help sensitive teachers identify the learning preferences of students. A learning styles record form such as the four-category form shown in Figure 2.2 can be helpful for this purpose. Interviews are an excellent way to have students talk about their experiences as learners and will usually provide more accurate information regarding their learning styles. However, teachers often cannot identify students' learning styles accurately without some type of instrumentation. Some characteristics simply are not observable, even to the experienced educator. In addition, teachers can misinterpret students' behaviors and misunderstand their symptoms. A frequently used instrument for determining learning style with high reliability and validity is the Dunn, Dunn, and Price Learning Style Inventory (LSI), with subtests for students in grades 3 to 12. Teachers can have students take the LSI and receive a formal report on their styles. According to Dunn (Shaughnessy, 1998), the LSI does the following:

1. Permits students to identify how they prefer to learn.
2. Suggests a basis for redesigning the classroom environment to complement students' learning styles.
3. Outlines the group arrangements in which each student is likely to learn most effectively (e.g., alone, in a pair, with two or more classmates, with a teacher, or, depending on the task, with students with similar interests or talents; it also describes whether all or none of those combinations is acceptable for a particular student).
4. Tells which students should be given options and alternatives and which students need direction and high structure.
5. Sequences the perceptual strengths through which individuals should begin studying—and then reinforce—new and difficult information.
6. Tells how each student should study and do homework.

Learning Styles Record Form

Directions: For each student, record your observation regarding the following items related to the student's preferred style of learning.

Student's name: _____

Learning Style Attribute	**Findings (check when applicable)**	
	No	Yes
1. Style of working: Likes to work alone	_____	_____
Likes to work with others	_____	_____
2. Learning modality: Watching	_____	_____
Reading	_____	_____
Discussing	_____	_____
Writing	_____	_____
Moving	_____	_____
Touching	_____	_____
Listening	_____	_____
3. Need for structure: High	_____	_____
Low	_____	_____
4. Details versus generalities	_____	_____

FIGURE 2.2   *Sample Learning Styles Record Form*

7. Explains methods through which individuals are most likely to achieve (e.g., contracts, programmed learning, multisensory resources, tactual manipulatives, kinesthetic games, or any combination of these).
8. Tells which children are conforming and which are nonconforming and explains how to work with both types.
9. Provides information relative to the best time of day for each student to be scheduled for difficult subjects (thus, it shows how to group students for instruction based on their learning-style energy-highs).
10. Indicates those students for whom movement or snacks, while the students are learning, may accelerate learning.
11. Provides information regarding those students for whom analytic versus global approaches are likely to be important.

Some student differences related to learning styles can be accommodated; others are more problematic. As much as possible, you should see that students' learning needs are met. If sound is needed, you can allow students to use a CD player. When complementary resources fail, use personalized computer software packages. If discussion is important, block off a portion of the room for conversation. If complete silence is needed, provide noise filters. When bright lights are a problem, allow the student to wear sunglasses. For unmoti-

Web Search: Teaching/Learning Styles

Access search engine Yahoo, Northern Light, or Alta Vista on the Internet and conduct a "Lesson Plan" search or access URL **http://www.microsoft.com** and do a lesson plan search. Select a lesson plan that addresses at least two different teaching and/or learning styles. Share and discuss these styles with the class.

vated students, make sure you check on them, work with them, and give them encouragement. For motivated students, leave them alone, and monitor as needed. Finally, work with the administration and schedule students' toughest classes when they are in their prime. Some students will be morning learners, while others will be late afternoon. Teacher flexibility and a willingness to experiment with different techniques will provide opportunities to maximize learning. Complete Web Search: Teaching/Learning Styles for ideas on being flexible.

Learning Theories and Teaching Styles

Most teachers will develop a personal philosophy of teaching, so each will also have a unique personality and will develop a personal teaching style. This style is usually consistent with their learning style. Moreover, these teaching styles will generally be fairly consistent with the practical application of one of the theories of learning.

The learning theory preferences of teachers should be influenced by three factors: student characteristics, curriculum materials, and teaching style. These three factors should be considered when selecting a learning theory on which to base your instruction. The unique characteristics of younger students sometimes requires that teachers use an approach that differs from that used with older students. For this reason, it is often wise for the teachers of younger children to rely on the use and manipulation of concrete materials with a heavy reliance on behavioral learning theories. Indeed, some of your students will often be rather childlike while others will be quite mature. This diversity often requires the selection and use of innovative reinforcement techniques for motivation and classroom management.

Students need parental support. Indeed, conferencing with parents can be vital to meeting the learning needs of students (see Chapter 6). Parents should be given information about how and why their children learn and study the way they do. Too often parents think their children should study the way they did in school. After all, it worked for them, so parents often try to impose their style on their children. Parents need to learn to let their children learn and study in the manner that works best for them. If they need dim lights and the floor as a work area, these needs should be met. You, as a teacher, have a responsibility to communicate learning style needs to parents. Often students' good behavior at school and home will increase substantially when they are allowed to learn and study in the style that suits their needs. The better students understand themselves the more likely they are to accept themselves and the more apt they are to be responsible.

Sometimes teachers will have only limited influence over the choice of adopted instructional material for use in their classes. In some cases, the materials used will reflect a particular learning theory. In these cases, you will be compelled to use curriculum that rely extensively on a particular learning process. It is important that you understand this curriculum and that you support the viewpoint used to teach that curriculum.

To maximize effectiveness, you must understand your own teaching style because you will more than likely rely on the learning theory that complements your personal style. For example, if you feel teaching is the passing on of information, you tend to support a behavioral theory of learning. On the other hand, if you feel teaching is getting students to think, analyze, and organize information, you tend to prefer the cognitive learning theory or an information-processing approach. Factual information and the importance of observable behaviors is important to the former group whereas the latter group put a great deal of emphasis on thinking and problem solving.

No study of learning style would be complete without exploring the concept of multiple intelligences. The concept of multiple intelligences was developed by Howard Gardner (Armstrong, 1994) to broaden the scope of human potential beyond the confines of the IQ score. Let's take a brief look at Gardner's eight intelligences.

Multiple Intelligences

Intelligence is usually defined as the ability to answer items on intelligence tests. Gardner's theory of multiple intelligences questions this traditional concept of intelligence and expands it. It challenges the common idea that intelligence is a single general capacity and proposes that each person may have a number of different intelligences. Gardner (Armstrong, 1994; Checkley, 1997) has shown not only insight but also compassion with the development of the concept of multiple intelligences. Essentially, he suggests there are eight discrete different types of intelligence that students can display (Figure 2.3). These eight areas of intelligence relate to the individual's abilities linguistically, mathematically, spatially, kinesthetically, musically, interpersonally, intrapersonally, and naturally. Gardner's multiple intelligence theory provides the classroom teacher with two extremely valuable tools that will make learning more focused on individual abilities. First, it gives teachers help in assessing where students' abilities and strengths lie. Second, it is an effective guide for teachers in the design of classroom activities that will give students an opportunity to experience working in different areas of intelligence. Thus, discovering talents that may otherwise have gone unnoticed or untapped. The teachers of younger children function in a vulnerable position because their students are experiencing a bombardment of developmental changes. Thus, many times Gardner's multiple intelligences approach is especially important to these younger children who are attempting to discover who they are, where their

Intelligence	Core Components	Teaching Activities
Linguistic	Language utilization. Sensitivity to the sounds, structure, meanings, and functions of words and language.	Activities related to word games, discussions, choral reading, journal writing, etc.
Logical-Mathematical	Use of mathematics. Sensitivity to, and capacity to discern logical or numerical patterns; ability to handle long chains of reasoning.	Activities related to problem solving, mental calculations, number games, critical thinking, etc.
Spatial	Sensitivity to spatial world. Capacity to perceive the visual-spatial world accurately and to perform transformations on one's initial perceptions.	Visual activities related to art, mind-mapping, visualization, imagination games, etc.
Bodily-Kinesthetic	Body movement. Ability to control one's body movements and to handle objects skillfully.	Hands-on activities, drama, dance, sports that teach, tactile activities, etc.
Musical	Musical endeavors. Ability to produce and appreciate rhythm, pitch, and timbre; appreciation of the forms of musical expressiveness.	Songs that teach, rapping, superlearning, (enhance ability to learn) etc.
Interpersonal	Relate to people. Capacity to discern and respond appropriately to the moods, temperaments, motivations, and desires of other people.	Cooperative learning activities, community involvement, social activities, simulations, etc.
Intrapersonal	Self-understanding. Access to one's own feelings and the ability to discriminate among one's emotions; knowledge of one's own strengths and weaknesses.	Individual instruction, independent study, self-esteem activities, etc.
Naturalist	Nature understand. Ability to make distinctions in the natural world; capacity to recognize flora and fauna.	Activities related to the natural world and the biological sciences.

FIGURE 2.3   *Gardner's Eight Areas of Intelligence*

strengths lie, and what talents might be able to help them develop a greater concept of self.

You, as a teacher, need to develop a personal theory of learning that will complement your own personal philosophy of teaching. The adaptation of such a theory to your personal style will help you better understand your own strengths, weaknesses, and preferences. However, don't place all your emphasis on one type of learning. Remember that the teaching of factual information will be just as important as teaching the ability to think, reason, and analyze. Moreover, it will sometimes be necessary to adjust your teaching style to the learning styles and intelligences represented within a class.

This completes our discussion of teaching, learning styles, and multiple intelligences. Complete Task 2.1 before you proceed to the next section.

T A S K   2 . 1

Learning Styles

Respond to the following learning styles concepts. Check your responses with those given at the end of the chapter.

1. Define learning style:_____
   _____

2. Describe the four areas that appear to impact students' learning styles.
   a._____
   b._____
   c._____
   d._____

3. Describe the two dimensions for perceiving information and the two dimensions of processing information.
   _____
   _____
   _____

4. Individual differences in responding to the environment and the way information is processed and organized is called _____ .

5. Students who make decisions quickly and tend to concentrate on speed are referred to as _____ .

6. Describe the relationship between teaching style and learning style.
   _____
   _____
   _____

7. Gardner suggests there are eight areas of intelligence. Briefly explain this concept.
   _____
   _____
   _____

Analysis and Reflections

Do you see any problems relative to focusing on the different learning styles of students? How much should parents be involved? Write a paragraph or two about these concerns. Share your concerns with classmates.

⚔ Students with Disabilities

The most probable future of our public schools will be classrooms composed of a diversity of students with different needs. Thus, the more you know about your students the more effective you will be as a teacher. In short, to be effective you need to be aware of your students' strengths, weaknesses, aspirations, limitations, and deficiencies and have at your disposal a repertoire of instructional methodologies, as well as educational and assistive technologies. Some students may be deficient in mathematics or reading while others may be language or culturally different. Still others may be gifted. In addition, you must take into account students with disabilities, as well as differences in social and cultural background. An awareness of these differences and their impact on learning will help you devise ways to provide adequate instruction.

Exceptionality

Some of your students will be academically bright while others will be slow or disabled; some will be socially skillful while others are inept. **Disabled** can be defined as the inability to do something. On the other hand, **handicapped** refers to those individuals who are learning disabled, mentally retarded, emotionally disturbed, speech-impaired, deaf or hard-of-hearing, visually handicapped, emotionally disturbed, orthopedically impaired, autistic, traumatic brain injured, multihandicapped, or other health impairments, who need special educational services. Student differences and special needs will often require that you adapt the classroom's physical environment or your instruction in ways to accommodate the unique needs of students with disabilities or in inclusive environments. In effect, you must learn to modify your instruction to fit the unique needs of all students.

Legally the mandate for a free and appropriate public education (FAPE) came into existence in 1975 with the passage of Public Law 94-142, the Education for all Handicapped Children Act. PL 94-142 was amended in 1990 and is now referred to as IDEA (Individuals with Disabilities Act). IDEA requires that school districts provide a free, appropriate public education for every child between the ages of 3 and 21. One major provision of IDEA is that students should be educated in the least restrictive environment (Crockett & Kauffman, 1999). This means that whenever possible students should be integrated into the general education classroom. This practice is usually called **mainstreaming.** The term **inclusion** has largely replaced the use of the term mainstreaming. An inclusive classroom can be defined as a classroom that integrates students who have disabilities with their nondisabled peers in the general education classroom. Full inclusion refers to the placement of all students with disabilities in the general education classroom for the entire school day. Other inclusive models include "partial inclusion" where students with disabilities are in a general education classroom the greater part of the day or only for designated periods. Including students with disabilities in general education classrooms does not mean doing away with special education (Vaidya, 1997). Instead, it entails integrating the best that special education has to offer with general education for the benefit of all students.

Another major provision of IDEA is the establishment of a written individualized education plan (IEP) with nondiscriminatory evaluation procedures for each student with disabilities (Figure 2.4). It is important that parents work as partners with the school in this educational process. Indeed, parents should be seen as an agent for implementing some of the changes designed by professionals. The IEP program must give the present levels of functioning, long- and short-term goals, the services to be provided, and plans for initiating and

Child's name: _____ Birthdate: _____ Grade: _____
School: _____ Dominant Language: _____
Current Level of Performance (STRENGTHS AND WEAKNESSES):

Percentage of Time in the Regular Education Program: _____
Long-Term Goal:

Short-Term Objectives:

Special Education Services:

Related Services:

Describe modifications, supplementary aids and services, and additional support for personnel needed:

Describe the extent, if any, the child will not participate in the regular education classroom:

Evaluation Criteria:

Transition Services Required:
Beginning Date: _____ Frequency of Services: _____ Location: _____

IEP TEAM SIGNATURES: <u>Member Name</u>   <u>Signature</u>

                      _____   _____
                      Regular Education Teacher

                      _____   _____
                      Special Education Teacher

                      _____   _____
                      Public Agency Representative

                      _____   _____
                              Parents

                      _____   _____
                       Other   Title

Will the student participate in the statewide or districtwide assessment? ____ Yes ____ No
If yes, describe the modification needed for the child to participate: _____
_____
If no, describe why the student will not participate and what alternative assessment will be used:
_____
_____

Did the team consider the following:

        Behavior issues: ____ Yes   ____ No
        Language/communication needs: ____ Yes   ____ No
        Braille usage: ____ Yes   ____ No
        Assistive technology: ____ Yes   ____ No

FIGURE 2.4   *Sample Individualized Education Plan (IEP)*

SOURCE: Developed by Dr. Lisa Lawter, East Central University, Ada, Oklahoma. Used with permission.

evaluating the goals. Carrying out IEP goals and objectives may require lesson modifications or obtaining and using special equipment (Cornwall, 1998; Council for Exceptional Children Staff, 1999).

A prelesson planning task for all lessons is to identify your students' entry levels. This task requires that you find out what students already know about your proposed lesson and their mastery of necessary prerequisite skills.

How do you diagnose the needs of students, especially since you usually won't meet them until the start of the school year? Diagnosis is a two-phase process (see Chapter 10); an initial phase and a continuous phase. The initial phase takes place prior to the arrival of students whereas the continuous phase follows their arrival.

Based on diagnosis, you must learn to modify your instruction to fit the individual needs and interests of your students. Examples of appropriate modifications include developing special worksheets to help teach difficult concepts, modifying assigned work, developing special study guides, changing grouping patterns to fit special needs, and obtaining and using special equipment for gifted students or for students with physical disabilities. Instruction that is hands-on, involves activities, is participatory, and uses cooperative learning is usually more effective for all students.

The use of differentiated assignments is a must when working with students with disabilities. This can be accomplished by varying the difficulty of assignments, the length, or by individualizing the curriculum as much as possible (Bigge, 1999; Lewis & Doorlag, 1998). For example, you might provide an oral exam/activity for a student with motor difficulties or in a mathematics class, you might assign five problems to your students having academic difficulty, ten problems to the average students, and ten more difficult problems to the higher functioning students. Similarly, you might require only half as much writing from children who experience motor difficulties. Teachers can also use software to develop lessons tailored to their students' individual capabilities. For example, programs like HyperStudio will let you create multimedia programs. Such interactive programs encourage student participation and can help improve communication between themselves, other students, and you.

The Web can be a valuable resource for lesson ideas. Many of the lessons found at various sites can be modified to address your learning intent. Complete Web Search: Special Education for some useful ideas.

Another approach to assignment modification is to vary the type of work students do. Some students should be allowed to complete and submit their written assignments on a word processor. Creative student may occasionally be allowed to create something instead of writing a report. Students might sometimes be allowed to assist each other.

Some general planning guidelines for working with students who have disabilities include:

1. Learning about the nature of the disability and how that disability might affect the learning process.
2. Determining what assistance is available from a special-education or resource expert.

Web Search: Special Education

Special education resources can be found on the Internet at URL **http:// www.nhgs.tec.va.us/SpecialEd/sped_resources.html, http://www.rit.edu/~easi,** and **http://www.sau.edu/bestinfo/Disabled/disindex.htm.** Access these sites and generate ideas that would be useful for instruction in either a special education or regular classroom. Make a list of these ideas and share it with your instructor and with classmates.

3.   Determining the equipment needs for the student that will allow him or her to function at an optimum level.
4.   Considering how to adapt the curriculum and your teaching strategies to better serve the needs of the student with disabilities.
5.   Considering how to individualize the curriculum as much as possible.
6.   Providing for the removal of barriers, both physical and psychological, that inhibit the student with disabilities from fully functioning in your classroom.

Some districts develop classroom modification plans to assist teachers with their instructional modifications. Figure 2.5 shows a sample plan with three categories. The teacher checks those items that will apply to a specific student. Review Figure 2.5 and use ideas generated from the review to complete Expansion Activity: Students with Disabilities.

This completes our brief look at students with disabilities. Review Figure 2.5 and the list generated in Expansion Activity: Students with Disabilities and complete Task 2.2.

✖ Multicultural Education

As the population of the United States grows, multicultural education continues to be a critical issue for teachers. Central to the topic of multicultural education is a concern about equity and fair treatment for groups that have experienced discrimination in the past. Originally applied only to minority racial groups, multicultural education now applies to differences in gender, religion, language, class, and exceptionality as well as racial and ethnic differences.

Expansion Activity: Students with Disabilities

Form groups of about four members per group. Generate a group list of ideas teachers could use to ease learning for students with disabilities. Share the list with classmates and discuss the pros and cons of each suggestion.

Student: _____   Teacher: _____

School: _____   Grade/Course: _____

A. Exam Modification

___ 1. Reduce the number of exams to _____
___ 2. Open book exams
___ 3. Allow more time for regular exam
___ 4. Reduce the length of the regular exam
___ 5. Use more objective items (fewer essay items)
___ 6. Give same exam orally
___ 7. Write down test items for students
___ 8. Read test items to the student
___ 9. Substitute assignment for test
___ 10. Other (specify) _____

B. Modifications in Assignments

___ 1. Repeat instructions/provide more detailed directions
___ 2. Use individual learning packages with clearly stated objectives
___ 3. Give instructions through several channels (written, oral, etc.)
___ 4. Provide materials that are programmed/self-checking
___ 5. Brief the student on key points before starting an assignment
___ 6. Allow more time for regular assignments
___ 7. Reduce the length of the regular assignments
___ 8. Break the assignment into a series of smaller assignments
___ 9. Reduce the reading level of the regular assignment (reword, edit)
___ 10. Change the format of the instructional materials
___ 11. Use different format materials to teach the same content
___ 12. Provide study aids (hints, cue cards, spelling list, guides, calculators, computers)
___ 13. Performance/hands-on activities/physical assignments
___ 14. Oral presentations/reports/projects/role play, etc.
___ 15. Other (specify) _____

C. Alternatives in Presenting Content

___ 1. Make cassette recording of the lecture for individual playback
___ 2. Allow teacher aide/volunteer to take notes for student
___ 3. Allow classroom peer to make carbon copies for the student
___ 4. Use of visual (maps, charts, pictures, etc.) audio materials (tapes, CDs, records)
___ 5. Use of individualized learning centers, contracts, or computer learning packages
___ 6. Provide laboratory/hands-on/learning by discovery experience
___ 7. Use of programmed learning/self-checking materials
___ 8. Other (specify) _____
_____

FIGURE 2.5 *Classroom Modification Plan*

T A S K   2 . 2

Students with Disabilities

Respond to the following items. Check your responses with those given at the end of the chapter.

1. Differentiate between disabled and handicapped._____

_____

2. Outline the provision of IDEA._____

_____

_____

3. Outline possible lesson modifications that can be made for students with disabilities.

_____

_____

_____

_____

Analysis and Reflections

Write a paragraph regarding your interpretation of "least restrictive environment." Relate your interpretation to the idea of inclusion.

Your teaching credential allows you to teach at specific levels in any school in your state. As a result, you could be required to teach in a school that is culturally, ethnically, linguistically, or socioeconomically diverse. After all, the United States consists of a wide variety of different ethnic people—African American, Mexican American, Native American, Chinese American, Vietnamese American, Cuban American, Cambodian American, Jewish American, Iranian American, Laotian American, and Italian American, to name but a few. This mix has resulted in a highly diverse student body in many schools. The student bodies of some schools will represent forty or more languages. As such, it is extremely important that you determine the nationality and language groups of the students in your classroom.

Multicultural education is being implemented widely in our schools (Congressional Digest, 1999). Indeed, more classroom teachers have studied the concepts of multicultural education than in past years. Textbook publishers are now integrating ethnic and cultural content into their books. However, despite the growing successes, multicultural education faces serious challenges as we begin the new century. Factor into this equation legislation of the 1970s that mandated equal opportunities for children with handicapping conditions (again to take place in an integrated setting), and you can begin to appreciate the competing expectations and demands with which schools and teachers must contend. Most recently, state legislatures across the country have begun to mandate some kind of accommodation for Attention Deficit Disorder (ADD) or Attention Deficit Hyperactivity Disorder (ADHD) and some form of AIDS education—a direct reaction to the spread of AIDS in the United States.

Limited English Proficiency (LEP)

A major problem in some areas of the country is learning a second language, English. In many communities today, it is not uncommon for more than half the students to come from homes where the first language is not English. In the Los Angeles Unified School District, for example, more than eighty-one languages are represented. Big city school districts in New York City, Miami, and Houston, as well as many smaller districts now have populations of ethnic minorities that equal or exceed non-Hispanic students. Nationwide, the number of students whose first language is not English is expected to increase during the next quarter of a century. Yet standard English is necessary for success in school and society. Learning to communicate reasonably well in English will be a major task for many students. They will need your help. Some schools use a pullout system, in which part of the student's day is spent in special bilingual classes and part in the regular classroom. Other schools place students in sheltered classes consisting of specific cultural groups where the teacher is specially trained to work with LEP students. Whatever system is used, the teaching of students who have limited proficiency in English (LEP) should include the use of hands-on learning and cooperative learning (see Chapter 5).

A Multicultural Classroom

How does a teacher develop a multicultural classroom? There are many options available to creative teachers that will improve the multiculturalism of the classroom. These strategies can be organized into four categories: professional development, teacher expectations, curriculum, and instruction.

The first step toward developing a multicultural classroom is to improve your own knowledge of and attitudes toward different cultures. You should take the initiative to learn as much as possible about the subcultures in your area. To familiarize yourself with local subcultures, be an active participant in local community events. This active involvement, along with analysis and reflection, will give you valuable insight into understanding the behaviors and interactions of cultural subgroups in your classroom. Special attention should be given to subgroup attitudes toward work and the importance of social interaction, the needs of the group versus the individual, and learning styles. Differences in these areas consistently cause problems for beginning teachers.

Teacher expectations for individual students, and classes as well, does indeed affect classroom interactions and, in some instances, what students learn. Maximizing expectations and minimizing differential interactions are important ingredients in creating a classroom that is free of bias, that is, a multicultural classroom.

Evaluate your learning materials for bias—stereotyping, linguistic bias, and unreality. Issues related to bias can be discussed with students and examples given to illustrate various misconceptions. Multicultural topics and heroes of various cultures can be studied and lessons can be designed to recognize the holidays, art, music, literature, and language of different cultures.

Finally, there are numerous instructional strategies that you can use to enhance multiculturalism in the classroom. For instance, community problem solving is an effective way to aid understanding of subcultures and their concerns. Other effective techniques include having students work together in groups, designing activities so they mesh with a variety of learning styles, and planning lessons so students' existing abilities are used. When grouping students, avoid ability grouping and tracking. Too often, students from the same culture or ability level are assigned to the same group. Make sure your groups are heterogeneous with representation from different cultures and different ability levels.

Good multicultural education goes beyond special activities, ethnic heroes, and special days. It requires consistent day-to-day practices that focus on the diversity of our society. Nagel (1998) has synthesized a comprehensive list of useful strategies. Some of these strategies include:

1. Believe in students.
2. Appreciate the cultural background of all.
3. Promote family participation.
4. Help develop social skills.
5. Use interactive strategies.
6. Teach justice and caring.
7. Know your students.
8. Hold zero tolerance for put-downs.
9. Reflect your own culture.
10. Read multicultural literature.
11. Question for high-level, critical thinking.
12. Provide equal opportunity for access.
13. Reduce prejudice, understand privilege.
14. Have students negotiate meaning.
15. Align texts to needs.

These strategies are not intended to be all inclusive. However, they represent food for thought for you to develop your own strategies for inclusion in your classrooms. The Internet can also be a valuable source of ideas for multicultural learning opportunities (Gregory, Stauffer, & Keene, 1999). Using some of the ideas generated from these sources complete Web Search: Multicultural Education.

Web Search: Multicultural Education

Obtain at least five sample lesson plans. Sample lesson plans can be obtained at URL **http://www.askeric.org/virtual/Lessons/.** Form groups of about four members per group. How could the sample lesson plans be modified to make the classroom more multicultural? Share the ideas with classmates and discuss the pros and cons of each idea.

Restructuring schools for equity for all is not new to American education. Americans have traditionally looked to the schools both to change society and to respond to changes in society. Today schools continue to perform this historic role. Multicultural education will continue to be an important issue to beginning and experienced teachers. Complete Task 2.3 to check your understanding of multicultural education in the classroom.

T A S K   2 . 3

Multicultural Education

Respond to the following multicultural education questions. Check your responses with those given at the end of the chapter.

1. How have the basic application concerns of multicultural education changed from the original intent?

   _____

   _____

2. Most of today's schools will be diverse to some degree. (True/False)

3. A major problem facing many schools in some areas is _____ .

4. Outline some techniques for developing a multicultural classroom.

   _____

   _____

   _____

   _____

Analysis and Reflections

How will you make your first classroom more multicultural? Write a paragraph about how you will go about this task. Submit your paragraph to the class instructor.

Summary

- A mixture of people, cultures, and values will be found in most school classrooms.

Student Learning Style

- Students have different learning styles. Learning style can be viewed as the way an individual begins to process, internalize, and concentrate on new materials.
- Students learn through different learning channels. Some will be auditory learners, others will be visual learners, and some will be physical learners.
- Research suggests that learning styles are related to a person's environmental, emotional, sociological, and physical preferences. These four areas can have major impact on learning.

- Students differ in how they process experiences and information. Some will be doers, while others will be watchers. Doers jump right in and do it. Watchers watch what happens, reflect, and then do it.
- The concrete and abstract dimensions of perceiving information and the reflective and active dimensions of processing information have been combined to formulate four different learning styles: divergers, assimilators, convergers, and accommodators.
- Learning style can be due to differences in cognitive style. One important aspect of cognitive style is the difference between field-dependence and field-independence. A second important difference in cognitive style is impulsivity and reflectivity.
- Most teachers will have a personal teaching style that is consistent with their learning style. However, it will sometimes be necessary for a teacher to adjust his or her teaching style to students.

Students with Disabilities
- Students will be different. Some may be disabled and others may be handicapped. Students' differences will sometimes require that the classroom's physical environment and/or instruction be adapted to the unique needs of mainstreamed or special students.
- Public Law 94-142 or IDEA (Individuals with Disabilities Act) mandates a free, appropriate public education for every child. Whenever possible, special students should be integrated into the regular classroom. This is referred to as mainstreaming or the inclusion of special students. An individualized education program (IEP) must be written for each special student.
- Teachers must sometimes modify lessons for special students. Modifications can be made in materials, assignments, assistance, or assessment.

Multicultural Education
- Multicultural education has become an important issue for schools. Multicultural education applies to differences in gender, language, class, exceptionality, and race and ethnic background. Schools and teachers are now integrating multicultural content into the lessons being studied.
- Limited English Proficiency (LEP) is a major problem in some parts of the country. In some schools, more than half the students have a first language other than English. Some schools use pullout programs to address this problem. Others use a sheltered program.
- Teachers need to develop a multicultural classroom. To accomplish this task, teachers must focus on four areas: professional development, teacher expectations, curriculum, and instruction.

Activities

1. *Classroom observation* Complete an observation in an area school. Visit with administrators and teachers. Answer the following:
   a. Are different teaching and learning styles observed?
   b. Do teachers conference with parents regarding learning styles?
   c. Are the classes diverse?

    d. Are there language differences?

    e. What is the school and/or teachers doing to address multicultural education?

2. *Student learning* Remember that a teacher's job is to teach all students and assume an attitude that all students can learn. Suggest techniques and strategies that can be used to accomplish this task. Sources of information should include library research, Internet searches, current journals, and recent books.

3. *Self analysis* Think back to your own childhood. How would you describe your ethnic group? Where did your parents/grandparents come from? What traditions were important in your family? What holidays were celebrated and how? What practices and beliefs have you adopted from your family? What practices and beliefs have you rejected and/or modified?

Answer Keys

Task 2.1 Learning Styles

1. Learning style can be defined as an individual's best learning channel. It can be viewed as the way a person begins to process, internalize, and concentrate on new material.

2. a. Environment: A student's preferences relative to the environment.

    b. Emotional: Student persistence and responsibility as well as supervision needed when learning.

    c. Sociological: Needed adult assistance and/or group support.

    d. Physical: The needed movement, food intake (snacks), and time of day and sensory mode.

3. The two dimensions for perceiving information are concretely and abstractly and the two dimensions of processing information are reflectively and actively.

4. cognitive style

5. impulsive

6. A teacher's teaching style is usually consistent with his/her learning style. The teaching style will generally be consistent with a particular theory of learning.

7. Gardner suggests that individuals have eight different kinds of intelligence. These eight intelligences include: (1) linguistic, (2) logical-mathematical, (3) spatial, (4) bodily-kinesthetic, (5) musical, (6) interpersonal, (7) intrapersonal, and (8) naturalist. Students will learn best if there is a match between intelligence area and learning.

Task 2.2 Students with Disabilities

1. Disabled is the inability to do something whereas handicapped refers to individuals who need special educational services.

2. IDEA mandates a full, free appropriate education for every child between the ages of 3 and 21. This education is to take place in the least restrictive

environment and an individualized education plan (IEP) with an evaluation procedure must be written for each student.

3. Possible modifications include varying assignments, modifying evaluations, changes in pacing, modifications in materials, providing special equipment, or providing special assistance.

Task 2.3 Multicultural Education

1. The concept of multicultural education originally applied only to minority racial groups. It now applies to a wide array of different groups.

2. True. Most United States schools will consist of a wide variety of different ethnic individuals.

3. language

4. Techniques related to a better understanding of different cultures or integrating cultural strategies into the curriculum and your instruction represent a few techniques. Also, expect the best from all students to get their best.

Theory and Research

Caldwell, G. P., & Ginthier, D. W. (1996) Differences in learning styles of low socioeconomic status for low and high achievers. *Education, 117*(1), 141–148.

Dunn, R., Griggs, S. A., Olson, J., Gorman, B., & Beasley, M. (1995). A meta-analytic validation of the Dunn and Dunn learning styles model. *Journal of Educational Research, 88*(6), 353–361.

Gallavan, N. P. (1998). Why aren't teachers using effective multicultural education practices? *Equity & Excellence in Education, 31*(2), 20–28.

Knight, K. H., Elfenbein, M. H., & Martin, M. B. (1997). Relationship of connected and separate knowing to the learning styles of Kolb, formal reasoning, and intelligence. *Sex Roles: A Journal of Research, 37*(5–6), 401–415.

Miller, M. D., Brownell, M. T., & Smith, S. W. (1999). Factors that predict teachers staying in, leaving, or transferring from the special education classroom. *Exceptional Children, 65*(2), 201–218.

Park, C. C. (1997). Learning style preferences of Korean, Mexican, Armenian American, and Anglo students in secondary schools. *NASSP Bulletin, 81*(585), 103–112.

Pattnaik, J., & Vold, E. B. (1998). Preservice teachers' multicultural literacy: Are we missing the forest for the trees? *Equity & Excellence in Education, 31*(3), 73–74.

Silver, H., Strong, R., & Perini, M. (1997). Integrating learning styles and multiple intelligences. *Educational Leadership, 55*(1), 22–28.

References

Armstrong, T. (1994). *Multiple intelligences in the classroom.* Alexandria, VA: Association for Supervision and Curriculum Development.

Bigge, J. L. (1999). *Adapting curriculum and instruction for special needs students.* Belmont, CA: Brooks/Cole Publishing.

Checkley, K. (1997). The first seven . . . and the eighth: A conversation with Howard Gardner. *Educational Leadership, 55*(1), 8–13.

Congressional Digest. (1999). *The U.S. education system: Overview of the current environment.* Washington, DC: Author.

Cornwall, J. (1998). *Individual education plans (IEPs)*. London: David Fulton Publishers.

Council for Exceptional Children Staff. (1999). *IEP team guide*. Reston, VA: Author.

Crockett, J. B., & Kauffman, J. M. (1999). *The least restrictive environment: Its origins and interpretations in special education*. Mahwah, NJ: Lawrence Erlbaum Associates.

Dunn, R., & Dunn, K. (1993). *Teaching secondary students through their individual learning styles: Practical approach for grades 7–12*. Boston: Allyn & Bacon.

Green, F. L. (1999). Brain and learning research: Implications for meeting the needs of diverse learners. *Education, 119*(4), 682.

Gregory, V. L., Stauffer, M. H., & Keene, T. W., Jr. (1999). *Multicultural resources on the Internet*. Englewood, CO: Teacher Ideas Press.

Kolb, D. A. (1983). *Experiential learning: Experience as the source of learning and development*. Englewood Cliffs, NJ: Prentice-Hall.

Latham, A. S. (1997). Responding to cultural learning styles. *Educational Leadership, 54*(7), 88–89.

Lewis, R. B., & Doorlag, D. H. (1998). *Teaching special students in general education classrooms*. Englewood Cliffs, NJ: Prentice Hall.

Nagel, G. K. (1998). Looking for multicultural education: What could be done and why it isn't. *Education, 119*(2), 253–254.

Riding, R. J., & Rayner, S. G. (1998). *Cognitive styles and learning strategies: Understanding style differences in learning behaviour*. London: David Fulton Publishers.

Shaughnessy, M. F. (1998). An interview with Rita Dunn about learning styles. *The Clearing House, 71*(3), 141–146.

Vaidya, S. R. (1997). Meeting the challenges of an inclusive classroom of improving learning for all students. *Education, 117*(4), 622–627.

Establishing a Supportive Environment

Objectives

After completing your study of Chapter 3, you should be able to:

1. Identify and discuss factors that influence the general climate of a classroom.

2. Describe techniques for providing a supportive environment for learning.

3. Differentiate between the authoritarian, democratic, and laissez-faire approaches to leadership and between task-oriented and socioemotional leaders.

4. Differentiate between the five types of social power.

5. Compare and contrast the four different categories of time found in schools and classrooms.

6. Identify and describe characteristics of the different management models.

7. Identify and discuss organizational techniques that lead to effective classroom management.

No matter how well prepared you are for a class, limited learning will take place in a nonsupportive and poorly managed environment (Freiberg, 1996). Thus, it is extremely important to arrange and organize your classroom so that it is supportive of student learning. An ideal classroom climate should promote deep understanding, excitement about learning, and social and intellectual growth. All students should be able to achieve academically, socially, and emotionally (Jubala, Bishop, & Falvey, 1995).

Effective teachers believe they can teach and believe *all* students can learn. They expect *all* students to *want* to learn. They expect the best from students and establish a climate to get it. They establish a management system so that class time is most efficiently used with minimum of lost time. To this end, effective teachers thoroughly plan how the classroom will be arranged and procedures for managing the classroom before they meet students for the first time.

The learning of students will often be related to their perceptions of the outcomes. In effect, students must believe they are capable of learning and must see some value in the material. They must feel they can do, and before they will do, they must see an importance for doing. To this end, students must feel that you and the classroom environment will be supportive of their efforts and that they will be welcomed in that environment. Thus, classroom climate, classroom leadership, and management style will often determine whether the classroom is supportive and whether students will learn or not.

⚔ Classroom Climate

Teachers whose classrooms are pleasant, positive, supportive, and challenging will often find student achievement and behavior to be at a higher level than that of students in the classrooms of teachers who are harsh, negative, nonsupportive, and unchallenging. Teachers should create a climate at the beginning of the year where the exchange of ideas is encouraged, respect for all students and their work is fostered, and a sense of community is established. Other factors such as the physical environment, room arrangement, the use of time, and classroom communications will influence classroom climate. We will look at each of these factors later in this section.

Leadership Styles

What type of person are you? Are you commanding, dominating, sharp, critical, and harsh? Are you stimulating, warm, caring, fair, funny, and interesting? Or are you lackadaisical and permissive? Personal characteristics such as these influence your leadership style. Your leadership style will also be heavily influenced by such factors as the subject and grade you teach, the policies of the school, and the abilities of your students. Some students lack the maturity and ability to be involved in classroom decision making, and some school districts actively discourage such student involvement. Also, always keep in mind that you may, and should, change leadership styles as the situation warrants.

Although extensive research has identified several types of leaders, three basic approaches are often cited: authoritarian, democratic, and laissez-faire. As a teacher, you should be aware of these theories of leadership and the major characteristics of these leadership types.

Power, domination, pressure, and criticism typify the authoritarian leadership approach. The teacher uses pressure and punishment to demand cooperation. The teacher assumes the sole responsibility for making all decisions for the class. His or her role is to control student behavior and to force compliance with a sharp voice and the use of fear. The authoritarian approach seeks to achieve compliance through the use of forceful external controls.

The authoritarian teacher uses criticism and put-downs when students make mistakes. This style of leadership often results in an atmosphere of hostility and creates in students a feeling of powerlessness, competitiveness, high dependency, and alienation from the subject matter. Students in an authoritarian atmosphere often fear taking chances and often develop low self-esteem and a defeatist attitude. They tend to give up when faced with a new or difficult task.

The sharing of responsibility is the democratic approach to leadership. The democratic leader seeks compliance through encouragement rather than demands. The teacher is kind, caring, and warm, but also firm. Order is maintained by letting students participate as much as possible in decision making. Responsibility is taught on a firsthand basis by giving *students* responsibility. The democratic leader seeks to motivate through both internal and external means.

The democratic leader avoids criticism and put-downs. Instead, self-esteem is developed by sharing responsibility. If students are encouraged when they make mistakes, they develop a sense of belief in themselves. As a result, the classroom atmosphere is one of openness, friendly communications, and independence. Research has shown that productivity and performance are high in well-run, democratic classrooms (Wraga, 1998).

In a laissez-faire approach, the teacher is completely permissive. Anything goes! Everyone does his or her own thing. This style of leadership most often leads to chaos. It produces disorganization, causes student frustration, and results in little if any work getting done. In addition, students often experience stress and a feeling of being totally overwhelmed and lost.

Many classroom problems can be overcome if we turn from the obsolete authoritarian approach of demanding obedience and turn to a more democratic approach based on freedom, choice, and responsibility. However, freedom does not mean that "anything goes" or that you abdicate your role as a leader. It means freedom with limits. Students need limits and guidance to become responsible individuals. The amount of freedom and the limits you impose will ultimately depend upon factors mentioned earlier: subject and grade, student abilities, and school policies. Generally younger children need more guidance and limits than older students. Table 3.1 compares the characteristics of the authoritarian, democratic, and laissez-faire leadership styles.

There are several ways to explain leadership and to theorize about the role of the leader. Indeed, some research suggests that there is no single type of good leader for all situations. An effective leader in one situation may be ineffective in another. Instead, good leadership depends on a person's traits, on the

TABLE 3.1

Characteristics of the Different Leadership Styles

Authoritarian	Democratic	Laissez-faire
Punishing	Friendly	Permissive
Faultfinding	Firm	Allows total freedom
Demanding	Encouraging	Leads to anarchy and disorder
Commanding	Stimulating	
Critical	Helping	
Pressuring	Guiding	
Sharp-voiced	Winning	
Imposing	Warm	
Dominating	Caring	
Harsh	Fair	
Fearful	Influencing	

situation, and on the person's style of handling it. Some theorists will argue that there are two basic kinds of leaders, those who are task-oriented and those who are relationship-oriented or socioemotional. The task-oriented leader is concerned more with getting the job done than with the feelings of and relationships between group members. Their style may not endear them to group members. The socioemotional leader is primarily concerned with feelings of and relationships between group members. They are usually well liked by the group, even when they must reprimand someone.

No discussion of leadership would be complete without mentioning power, for power is the capacity to influence other people. Teachers must be viewed as having social power if they are to form and lead a cohesive classroom. There are five types of social power, or leadership, that a teacher can strive for: expert, referent, legitimate, reward, and coercive power.

1. *Expert power.* Expert power represents the legitimation of leadership because students perceive the teacher as an expert in a certain area. Successful teachers have expert power. Students see them as competent to explain things and knowledgeable about particular topics.
2. *Referent power.* Leadership earned because of a perception of a teacher's trustworthiness, fairness, and concern for students. Students will often accept as leaders teachers whom they like and respect. Students want to be like those teachers they admire.
3. *Legitimate power.* Leadership based on the specific role as a teacher. Legitimate power cannot be earned, it comes with the title. All teachers will have a certain degree of legitimate power.
4. *Reward power.* Leadership based on rewards or benefits that teachers can give to students. These rewards can take the form of grades, privileges,

Expansion Activity: Leadership and Power

Write a paragraph describing the type of leadership and power you think beginning teachers should most quickly achieve. How would you achieve each?

approval, or more tangible compensations, such as exemption from a test. To the extent that students desire the rewards conferred by teachers, teachers have a degree of leadership and authority.

5. *Coercive power.* Leadership based on punishment or coercion. Coercive power relies on threats and punishment in order to "influence." Because it is easy to use this type of power and it achieves quick results, coercive power is used frequently by teachers. Teachers, especially new teachers, should work to establish expert and referent power as the best way to guide a classroom. This will take time. It can often be accomplished by giving students a sense of belonging and acceptance. Complete Expansion Activity: Leadership and Power to express some of your own ideas about leadership.

Classroom Choice

Student misbehavior is one of the biggest concerns of many teachers. They fear open student defiance. In effect, many teachers are worried about classroom survival.

Some experts suggest that the best way to avoid many classroom problems and the associated concerns is through shared management. That is, students are given a voice and choices in what takes place in the classroom. Students can be given the opportunity to provide input and/or choices in establishing rules and in the curriculum to be studied (Kohn, 1996). Shared decision making and choices give students a stake in the educational process and a sense of ownership. The process, in effect, gives students some ownership of the classroom environment.

Physical Environment

An attractive room is conducive to learning. As a teacher you will in most cases have full responsibility for the appearance and comfort of your room. Will your room be attractive and colorful, or will it be bleak and drab?

Although most schools have custodians, during school hours it is your responsibility to keep a clean and neat room. Share this responsibility with students and make sure that places and procedures are designated for storing supplies, handing in papers, and disposing of trash. This kind of planning greatly enhances classroom functioning and helps to maintain a pleasant, productive working atmosphere.

Ventilation, temperature, and lighting of the classroom also affect student comfort and ability to concentrate. A room that is stuffy or too hot or cold, or a room that has dim or bright lighting, is often distracting, causing students to focus on their discomfort rather than on their work. It is your responsibility to adjust these factors properly, or to see to it that they are adjusted by the proper person.

Bulletin boards and displays can add much to the attractiveness and atmosphere of a classroom. They should be designed to be both informative and colorful, and when student work is prominently displayed, they can be quite motivating. Having students design and construct classroom bulletin boards and displays gives added meaning to the classroom environment. It becomes their room, a place to be proud of and to be cared for.

Room Arrangement

Think about the way your room will be organized. It is important to determine what areas need to be provided and what items and types of furniture are required before you arrange the room. The classroom environment should be arranged so that it is easy for you and the students to work and so that it does not encourage misbehavior. It should be arranged to aid teaching and learning and help maintain discipline. For example, it is usually unwise to place the pencil sharpener in a place where students must pass close to other students when going to use it. Some students can't leave each other alone as they pass nearby. In addition, it is generally unwise to place the wastebasket at the front of the room; it is an inviting target for basketball practice.

Your seating arrangements should be a prime consideration because seating can either facilitate or hinder what will go on in the classroom. The seating arrangement should focus on the chalkboard since most class instruction occurs there. Remember that you may be able to manipulate seating to foster a number of effects—from closeness to conflict. There are any number of ways to arrange seating (see Figure 3.1). You should experiment and solicit suggestions from students.

What, then, constitutes an effective seating arrangement? One possibility is to seat students in shallow semicircles, no more than three rows deep. If adequate space is interspersed within the three rows, the teacher and students can walk around within the arc of the semicircle with minimum disruption to students who are working at their desks. Moreover, this arrangement allows the teacher to move quickly to the side of a student who is disruptive or who needs individual assistance. Cluster seating can be used effectively when group work is a frequently used strategy. Indeed, cluster seating is ideal for cooperative learning. Discussions and demonstrations require that all students have a clear view of each other or the demonstration material. Square, circular, or horseshoe arrangements meet this criteria. These arrangements facilitate the give-and-take of conversation inasmuch as students can see one another when they talk. Students are also much more likely to get to know one another in a face-to-face seating arrangement and are more apt to stay attentive throughout the activity. Finally, theater-type seating is commonly used in secondary classrooms in which the lecture method is predominant.

Seating arrangements can be used to control student behavior. Appropriate behavior may be rewarded by allowing students individually or as a group

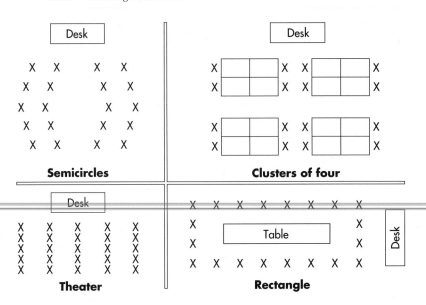

FIGURE 3.1   *Possible Seating Arrangements*

to select their own seating. Occasionally the class may even be given the opportunity to rearrange the seating as a reward for good behavior. In addition, disruptive behavior may often be controlled by simply moving the disruptive student away from certain individuals or away from the total group. Placement of a disruptive student's desk beside the teacher's desk often enables the teacher to give more attention, personal contact, and encouragement to the student.

Constructive use of wall space often evokes a more positive climate. For example, you can display motivational statements (teacher- or student-made or commercial), materials to spark interest in a topic, or classroom procedures. Moreover, before school begins, put up an interesting attention-getting bulletin board and be prepared to change it periodically. Make your bulletin boards interesting, attractive, and colorful so they help promote a positive attitude toward school and your room and subject. You might even want to devote one bulletin board to announcements, such as the bell schedule, the weekly lunch menu, news items of interest to the class, and classroom rules and consequences. Remember you must also provide easy access to pencil sharpeners, reference books, learning centers, trash containers, and so on. Place these accessories, if at all possible, behind or to the side of the students' focal points, since travel to and from them can be distracting.

Good environments are flexible. Most classrooms have moveable chairs. Therefore, don't get in the habit of seating students only in straight rows. You should feel free to have students move their chairs several times during a class. You might, for example, have them move into a circle for discussion, into a small group for in-depth exploration of a topic, and back to rows for a lecture. You should experiment with different room arrangements to find those that work best for you and students. Complete Expansion Activity: Positive Classroom

Expansion Activity: Positive Classroom Climate

Draw three diagrams of the features of a classroom, each illustrating how to promote a positive classroom climate and a different leadership style.

Climate which will give you the opportunity to illustrate some of your own ideas on how to arrange a classroom.

Time in Schools and Classrooms

Schooltime is obviously limited. In fact, schooltime can be divided into five different categories: mandated time, allocated time, instructional time, engaged time, and academic learning time. Figure 3.2 illustrates how the five different times relate to each other.

The total time available for school activities is essentially established by the state. A typical school is in session approximately six hours a day for 180 days. This set amount of time is referred to as **mandated time** and must be used for both academic and nonacademic activities.

During the mandated time, a variety of subjects must be taught, plus time must be used for lunch, recess, transitions between classes, announcements,

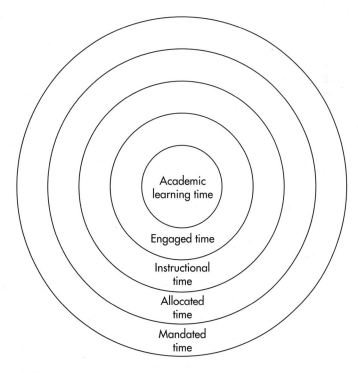

FIGURE 3.2   *Relationship between School Times*

and so on. The time appropriated for each of these activities is often called **allocated time.** For example, one hour a day may be allocated for reading instruction and one hour for housekeeping activities. Secondary schools tend to be subject-oriented and tend to allocate more time for academic content than do elementary schools. Elementary school children usually need more time to develop social and personal skills. However, some states will make recommendations for allocating time in curriculum content areas at the elementary level. Since students can learn only the material that is presented to them, an important goal of classroom management often is to expand the amount of time allocated for learning.

Teachers attempt to translate allocated time into learning through **instructional time.** That is, they attempt to translate the available, tangible blocks of class time into productive learning activities. Despite a teacher's best efforts, however, not all students pay attention or stay on-task all the time. For example, some students may be daydreaming during seatwork, some may be simply goofing off, and others may rush and finish early. As a result, we have another area within instructional time called *engaged time.*

Engaged time, or **time on-task,** differs from mandated, allocated, and instructional times in that it is the actual time individual students spend on assigned work. Students are actively (physically or mentally) participating in the learning process during engaged time. This active participation may include writing, reading, solving problems, or simply listening to a teacher's presentation. If students are not actually engaged in the learning process, they will, of course, not learn. A second goal of classroom management is, therefore, to improve the quality of time by keeping students on-task. Engaged time will depend on routine classroom practices, student motivation, and the quality of instruction. Typically, engaged-time rates range from lows of 50 percent in some classrooms to as high as 90 percent in others (Berliner, 1987).

Time on-task isn't always productive. Indeed, students often engage in an activity at a superficial level, with the result that little understanding or retention takes place. For example, they could be reading a social studies passage at a superficial level with little concentration on what is being read. If this is happening, the teacher must motivate the students to make time on-task more productive. In short, they must maximize **academic learning time.** For some educators (Block, Efthim, and Burns, 1989), maximizing academic learning time means that student performance must be at a high success rate (80 percent or more).

Too much instructional time is lost in today's classrooms. In fact, some educators contend that as much as 50 to 60 days may be wasted each year. Some commonly noted time wasters are as follows:

1. *Changing and beginning classes.* Teachers often use five to ten minutes per class to take attendance and make announcements. Thus, teachers need to devise systems for speeding up housekeeping chores. The use of assigned seats, printed lists, or diagrams, for instance, often speeds up these housekeeping chores.

2. *Excessive viewing of films.* Many teachers use films simply as time fillers, especially on Fridays. The use of instructional tools such as films and computer activities should be justified in terms of student learning and results.

3. *Not handling routine procedures smoothly and quickly.* Many teachers spend too much time on simple classroom routines. Procedures should be set up for routine activities. Procedures for lining up for lunch, going to the restroom, collecting papers, and sharpening pencils, for example, should be well planned and streamlined at the beginning of the year.

4. *Testing.* About three days a year are lost due to districtwide testing. Districtwide and standardized testing should be incorporated into regular class time. That is, normal instruction should be carried out during the portion of the day that is not used for testing.

5. *Spending too much time on discipline.* Disciplinary statements and actions often interrupt instruction. The use of nonverbal actions to curb misbehavior often allows a lesson to proceed without interruption. Nonverbal methods are discussed at length later in this chapter.

6. *Early finishes.* A surprising amount of time is lost through early finishing of lessons. You should avoid this tendency by planning more instruction than you think you'll need.

7. *Extracurricular activities.* Many times students are dismissed early for athletic events, music and band activities, school tournaments, and other such activities. Special events should be scheduled on activity days, or after school hours.

How can you tell when students are engaged, or on-task? Conversely, how can you tell when they are off-task? This job, needless to say, is not easy. You must sharpen your observation skills. Watch their eye contact: Are they watching you during your presentations? During seatwork, do their eye movements suggest that they are engaged in the directed work? Finally, do they raise their hands to ask or answer questions? You should be sensitive to these indicators, and you should also develop your own list of indicators that suggest students are engaged and on-task. Complete Web Search: Organizing a Classroom which may give you some tips on organizing your classroom for better on-task behaviors.

Web Search: Organizing a Classroom

Access Internet URL sites: **http://www.innovativeclassroom.com** and **http://www.pacificnet.net/~mandel/ClassroomManagement.html.** Analyze the ideas presented on organizing a classroom. Write a couple of paragraphs on the ideas gleamed for organizing your own classroom.

Communication

The topic of communication covers a broad range of complicated human relationships that are central to a smoothly functioning and positive classroom environment. Indeed, good communication between teacher and students is essential to learning. This means that more than the "teacher talks—students listen" pattern must be taking place. Real communication is an open, two-way street, in which you talk but you also listen. As a teacher, you must learn to listen, and you must allow students to talk and to give their input toward finding solutions to classroom problems. You must constantly strive to improve your ability to communicate and to listen with an open mind to the feelings, ideas, and opinions of your students. We will address the principal ideas related to communication in more detail in Chapter 6.

This completes our discussion of classroom climate. Take a few moments to complete Task 3.1, which will check your understanding of this section.

✖ Management Models

Classroom management is the process of organizing and conducting the business of the classroom so that intended learning takes place. Classroom management is too often perceived as related to the preservation of order and the maintenance of control. However, this view is too simplistic because classroom management is much more. Indeed, it involves the establishment and maintenance of the classroom environment so that educational goals can be accomplished.

Central to effective management is the ability to provide a positive social and physical environment conducive to learning and the well-being of students. As a teacher you must be aware of the principles and consequences of the various management models that will be available for your use. We will briefly discuss eight models that are widely used in schools today.

Assertive Discipline Model

We will first look at **assertive discipline.** Canter and Canter (1976), the model developers, advocate the need for teachers to be assertive. An assertive teacher is one who clearly and firmly communicates needs and requirements to students, follows up with appropriate actions, responds to students in ways that maximize compliance, but in no way violates the best interests of the students (Canter & Canter, 1976, p. 9). The intent of the assertive discipline model is to help teachers take charge in the classroom and to teach them to be calm yet forceful with students.

From the beginning of the year, assertive teachers refuse to tolerate improper behavior. Excuses such as emotional problems, poor home environments, hereditary weaknesses, and personal grievances are not accepted. The assertive teacher establishes rules for behavior along with consequences for proper and improper behavior. Students who follow the rules receive positive consequences such as some kind of material reward, free time, or special privileges, while students who break the rules receive negative consequences such

T A S K   3 . 1

Classroom Climate

Respond to the following items. Check your responses with those given at the end of the chapter.

1. It is usually unwise to involve students in the establishment of a positive classroom climate. (True/False)

2. Label each of the following items as characteristic of the authoritarian leadership approach (A), the democratic leadership approach (D), or the laissez-faire leadership approach (L).

   _____ a. Responsibilities are shared in the classroom.
   _____ b. The teacher decides, and students obey without question.
   _____ c. The teacher demands cooperation.
   _____ d. The teacher acknowledges and encourages achievement.
   _____ e. The teacher is firm and sets limits, but is warm and fair.
   _____ f. There is freedom, with few, if any, constraints.

3. Differentiate between task-oriented and socioemotional leaders.

   _____

   _____

   _____

4. Explain how the selection and changing of student seating can be used effectively to curb disruptive behavior in the classroom.

   _____

   _____

   _____

5. Match the time category on the left with its label on the right.
   ___ a. Time teacher uses for learning activities.   1. Allocated time
   ___ b. Time student is engaged in learning   2. Engaged time
          process with resultant high success rate.   3. Instructional time
   ___ c. Time set by state for school activities.   4. Academic learning time
   ___ d. Time during which students participate in   5. Mandated time
          learning process.
   ___ e. Time appropriated to individual school activities.

6. Explain how instructional time is lost in today's schools.

   _____

   _____

   _____

Analysis and Reflections

Reflect on what you consider to be your own emerging teaching style. What classroom arrangements will best suit it?

as losing recess time, staying after school, or going to the principal's office. These rules and consequences are clearly communicated to students and parents at the beginning of the year.

Assertive teachers insist on decent, responsible behavior from their students. It is assumed that all students can behave if they want. Proper behavior is a matter of choice. Assertive teachers make promises, not threats. That is, they do not threaten to enforce the rules and apply the consequences; they promise to do so. Assertive teachers are consistent and follow through with action.

Noncoercive Discipline Model

William Glasser (1965), the creator of the noncoercive discipline model, recommends reality therapy as a means to good discipline. **Reality therapy** is the act of guiding an individual toward reality—that is, assisting an individual in becoming responsible and able to satisfy his or her needs in the real world. Glasser believes that students are rational beings and can control their behavior if they wish. However, they often must be assisted in making good rather than bad choices; that is, they must be guided to become responsible individuals able to satisfy their real-world needs. It is the teacher's job to provide guidance so that students make good choices. According to Glasser, this guidance is a ten-step process (Glasser, 1977).

Rules are essential to Glasser, and they must be enforced. Reasonable consequences should always follow student behavior, and no excuse should be accepted for poor behavior. Factors such as unstable background and lax upbringing do not make poor behavior acceptable. Student responsibility must be stressed continually, and students must be forced to acknowledge their behavior and to make value judgments regarding it.

Glasser stresses the use of classroom meetings in addressing problems. Students sit in a small, close circle; discuss the problems; and seek solutions. The teacher's role is to stay in the background and to give opinions only sparingly. Class rules and reasonable consequences should be developed at these meetings, and all students should be expected to observe them. The rules should remain flexible and open to changes at future meetings in order to accommodate changing situations.

The Behavior Modification Model

Behavior modification is based on the behavioral philosophy of B. F. Skinner, who assumes that most behaviors are learned, that learning is largely controlled by the environment, and that behaviors that are rewarded or reinforced in some manner will occur again.

The basic premise of **behavior modification** is that behavior is changed by altering the consequences, outcomes, or rewards which follow the behavior (Presbie & Brown, 1976; Walker & Shea, 1980). In this model, reinforcement is used systematically to change some aspect of student behavior. Students who are good, who follow the rules, or who perform well are given reinforcers or rewards. The reinforcers may be praise, awards, grades, or even such tangible items as food or candy. Students who misbehave or who perform poorly are ignored, are removed from a reward, or are punished.

A system of reinforcement can be quite complex. One such program is the **token reinforcement system.** In this system, students earn tokens for both academic work and positive classroom behavior. The tokens may be points, chips, checks, play money, or anything else available. Periodically the students are given the opportunity to exchange their accumulated tokens for some desired activity or reward.

The Teacher Effectiveness Training Model

Teacher effectiveness training (TET), conceived by Dr. Thomas Gordon (1974), strives to instruct teachers in how to establish positive relationships with students. Gordon believes that teachers can reduce negative behaviors by using clearer, less provocative communications.

The TET model for dealing with classroom problems begins with the question, "Who owns the problem?" If the problem belongs to the student, Gordon recommends active listening (or empathetic listening) on the part of the teacher; that is, the teacher becomes a counselor and supporter. The teacher helps the student to find his or her own solution to the problem. On the other hand, if the teacher owns the problem, the teacher and student together must find a solution through mutual problem solving.

The key to the use of TET is determining who owns the problem in a troublesome situation. According to Gordon, if you are blocked from reaching your goals by the student's action, then you own the problem. For example, if a student continuously makes noises as you try to teach, you own the problem because you are being kept from reaching your goal of teaching. However, if you feel annoyed by a student's behavior, if you wish a student would act differently, or if you feel embarrassed for a student, then the problem likely belongs to the student. The student who tells you that he or she hates school or hates his or her parents has the problem.

Gordon further suggests that teachers too often attack students through the use of **you-messages** when, in fact, the teacher owns the problem. Rather than saying "You are slow," "You are no good," or "You are lazy," Gordon suggests that you send an **I-message** to tell a student how you feel about a problem situation and implicitly ask for corrective behavior. Examples of I-messages are "I am angry at what you are doing," "I am disappointed in your behavior," or "I can't hear myself think for the noise."

If an I-message does not correct the problem situation, the teacher and student are in a conflict situation. When this happens Gordon recommends that a **no-lose tactic** for problem resolution be employed. The six-step, no-lose tactic constitutes a form of negotiation to which teacher and student contribute relatively equally. The process begins with a determination of the exact problem. Possible solutions are then generated, with the teacher and student presenting the same number of ideas. The ideas are evaluated in step 3, and the unacceptable ideas are rejected. Step 4 is the selection of the best solution of those that remain. This is followed by a determination of how to implement the selected solution. The last step entails an assessment of how well the solution works. Generally, punishment is not recognized as a viable solution in the no-lose tactic, since it would place the student in a losing situation.

Positive Classroom Discipline Model

Frederick Jones (1987), the founder of positive classroom discipline, analyzed thousands of hours of classroom observations and found that most management problems result from *massive time wasting* by students. Jones found very little hostile defiance on the part of students. Instead, Jones found students commonly talked when they shouldn't, goofed off, and moved about the room without permission. In other words, most classroom problems result from students being off-task. In dealing with these off-task behaviors, teachers often lose as much as 50 percent of their instructional time. Jones contends that this wasted instructional time can be reclaimed when teachers correctly address four skill clusters that relate to: classroom structure, limit setting through the use of body language, incentive systems, and efficient help.

Jones emphasized that prevention is the best way to deal with behavior problems. In turn, the best way to prevent problems is by providing a classroom structure that focuses on room arrangement. In effect, one key to prevent students' goofing off is to minimize the physical distance between teacher and students, so the teacher can move to problem areas quickly. Through movement and proximity, along with a pause and look, most problems can be cured. Jones suggests that seating be arranged so the teacher can move freely among students. Second, specific and general classroom rules should be established. These rules should be few in number and define the teacher's broad guidelines, standards, and expectations for work and behavior. Third, Jones suggests that classroom chores be assigned to students. This will help students develop a sense of responsibility and give them a sense of "buy in" for the class. Finally, Jones contends that each classroom should have a "bell activity" that students get started on and complete when they enter the room. This activity can be related to the day's lesson, journal writing, or a brain teaser.

Jones suggests that 90 percent of discipline and keeping students on-task, problem behaviors, can be accomplished through the skillful use of body language. Effective body language use would include the use of various physical mannerisms to establish appropriate behaviors and to enforce them. Body language, Jones says, can be used to show that the teacher is calmly in control. The body language that tends to get students back to work includes physical proximity to students, direct eye contact, body position (body orientation toward student), facial expressions, gestures, and tone of voice.

Jones contends that incentive systems can be established to keep students on-task and to get them to complete their work. An effective classroom incentive can be anything outside the student that prompts the student to act. Jones suggests that preferred activities, such as time on the computer, free time, use of educational games, a popcorn party, and free reading, can serve as an incentive or reward for desired behaviors. Furthermore, Jones adds, the use of peer pressure represents an effective motivator. For example, time can be deducted from the class-allotted preferred activity time when a student misbehaves. The amount of time to deduct can be recorded with a large stopwatch placed at the front of the room, so the whole class can see. If a large stopwatch is unavailable, a standard amount of time (e.g., one minute) can be deducted for each misbehavior.

Finally, Jones suggests that providing efficient help is related to time on-task. His research revealed that teachers, on the average, spend approximately four minutes helping each student who is having difficulty with seatwork. Jones recommends that this time be cut to twenty seconds or less per student, with an optimal goal of about ten seconds. Doing so allows more students to be helped in a shorter period of time and reduces the tendency for students to work only when the teacher is helping them.

Proper classroom structure, using body language, implementing an incentive system, and providing efficient help will not eliminate all behavior problems. When problems do develop, Jones suggests that a backup system such as in-class isolation or removal from the room be used. This backup system should be discussed with students and used when students cause serious problems in the room.

Cooperative Discipline Model

Cooperative discipline is based on the ideas of Linda Albert (1996) who suggests that teachers need a management strategy that enables them to work cooperatively with students and parents. She adds that once a true cooperative understanding has been reached, the classroom can be transformed into a safe, orderly, inviting place for teaching and learning and students will have a good chance of learning to behave responsibly while achieving more academically.

Influenced by Adlerian psychology and the work of Rudolf Dreikurs, Albert is convinced that students' actions are based on their attempts to meet certain needs. Like Rudolf Dreikurs, Albert contends that most misbehavior occurs when students attempt unsuccessfully to meet a psychological need—the need to belong. But when students are unable, for whatever reason, to achieve the desired belonging, they direct their behavior toward mistaken goals: attention-seeking, power-seeking, revenge-seeking, and avoidance-of-failure. Students have a mistaken idea that through inappropriate behavior directed toward these goals they will somehow fulfill their need to belong.

Most students will get enough attention in the classroom. Some, however, require more and seek it actively—showing off, calling out, pencil tapping, and asking personal questions—or passively—not finishing work, being slow to follow directions, and lagging behind. When they don't receive the attention they desire, some students resort to power-seeking behavior. Through various verbal and physical actions they try to show that they will not be controlled by the teacher, they will do as they please. They may actively talk back, mutter responses, be defiant and throw temper tantrums, or passively be noncompliant with directions, forgetful, and inattentive. When the student suffers real or imagined hurt in the classroom, he or she may retaliate against teachers and classmates. Revenge-seeking can take the form of verbal attacks, destruction of materials in the classroom, or direct physical attacks on the teacher or other students. Finally, many student have a fear of failure. Indeed, a few will withdraw and quit when assignments or activities are too difficult.

Albert puts emphasis on strategies to prevent misbehavior, but also contends that teachers must be prepared to act the moment a student misbehaves. Albert suggests that the three Cs—capability, connection, and contribution—are essential to helping students feel a sense of belonging.

Albert suggests that students' sense of capability is one of the most important factors in school success. She calls this students' I-can level. The I-can level can be improved by communicating that making mistakes is okay, improving students' confidence, focusing on past successes, making learning more tangible through the use of portfolios and checklists, and recognizing students' achievements.

Albert considers it extremely important that all students initiate and maintain positive relationships with teachers and peers. That is, they need to make connections and become more accepting of others and their differences, more attentive to the needs of others, appreciative of the accomplishments of others, affiliative of the desirable traits of others, and kinder and more caring about people.

Albert contends that students also need to be helped in making contributions to the class. To this end, students should be encouraged to make contributions to the class, school, and community and encouraged to protect the environment and to help other students.

Albert strongly advises teachers to establish a classroom code of conduct for their classroom. Moreover, teachers should involve students and parents as partners in the formation of a management plan. This plan should include consequences that are related, reasonable, respectful, and reliably enforced. Students should be helped to learn to make better behavior choices.

Positive Discipline in the Classroom Model

The positive discipline in the classroom model aims at making students at all levels more successful, not only in the classroom, but in all walks of life. Nelsen, Lott, and Glenn (1997), the originators of the model, regard classroom management as developing classrooms where students are treated respectfully and are taught the skills needed for working with others. The vehicle for accomplishing this task is the class meeting.

Class meetings are used to teach students social skills such as taking turns, communicating, helping one another, listening, hearing different points of view, and taking responsibility for their own behaviors. Nelsen et al. believe that management problems diminish and academic skills are strengthened in the process.

Nelsen et al. contend that students benefit in seven ways from the use of class meetings that are an integral part of positive discipline in the classroom. These benefits include three perceptions that lead to success in the classroom and the development of four essential skills that contribute significantly in life. The three perceptions formed include:

1. A sense of personal capabilities. (*I can perception.*)
2. A feeling of significance in primary relationships. (*A belonging perception.*)
3. A sense of personal power to influence one's life. (*A feeling of control over the things that happen to me.*)

The four essential skills developed include:

1. Intrapersonal skill. (*I understand my feelings and am capable of controlling them.*)
2. Interpersonal skill. (*I can communicate and get along and work with others.*)
3. Strategic skill. (*I am adaptable, flexible, and responsible.*)
4. Judgmental skill. (*I am wise and can evaluate situations.*)

The approach advocated by Nelsen et al. suggests that teachers should focus on caring about students' welfare and should show students they care. However, certain teacher behavior barriers must often be overcome before the caring relationships can be developed, while other corresponding builder behaviors will help build such relationships. These barriers and corresponding builders are:

1. *Assuming vs checking.* Teachers should not assume how students think and feel. Instead, they should check with students.
2. *Rescuing/explaining vs exploring.* Teachers tend to rescue or explain difficult situations to students. However, students grow in knowledge and understanding when they are allowed to perceive and explore for themselves.
3. *Directing vs inviting/encouraging.* Directing students should be limited as much as possible. Instead of commanding, students should be invited and encouraged to become self-directed.
4. *Expecting vs celebrating.* Teachers should hold high expectations of students and believe in their potential. Moreover, teachers should call attention to success and celebrate accomplishments.
5. *"Adult-isms" vs respecting.* Nelsen et al. label the statements "adult-isms" when they tell the students what they ought to do. Such statements should be replaced with respect statements.

Classroom meetings are the primary avenue for providing a caring, supportive, and cooperative classroom climate. Nelsen et al. maintain that students should be trained during class meetings in the kind of classroom climate desired. Among other suggestions is the recommendation that teachers go beyond logical consequences. They urge teachers to think and plan in terms of solutions rather than consequences; democratic methods should replace authoritarian ones.

Discipline with Dignity Model

Discipline with Dignity, by Richard Curwin and Allen Mendler (1988), presents strategies for improving classroom behavior through maximizing student dignity and hope. Curwin and Mendler label students whose behavior prevents their learning and puts them in serious danger of failing in school, behaviorally at-risk. These are the students that are referred to as angry, hostile, lazy, irresponsible, turned off, or withdrawn. They often do not want to learn and make no effort to learn. They do not follow directions and teacher requests. They tend to provoke trouble in the classroom. They are not successful in school.

Curwin and Mendler contend that an effective management system must focus on helping behaviorally at-risk students regain a sense of hope and restore their sense of dignity. These students usually have a history of academic failure which has resulted in a loss of hope and a sense of being a loser. To help students overcome behavior problems, Curwin and Mendler maintain that an effective plan should focus on three dimension of discipline: (1) a prevention dimension, (2) an action dimension, and (3) a resolution dimension. The prevention dimension addresses what can be done to prevent discipline problems. The action dimension focuses on what teachers should do when discipline problems occur. The resolution dimension helps problem students learn to make and abide by decisions that serve their needs.

The prevention aspect of the discipline system focuses on motivating students and formulating class rules and consequences. The rules should specify behaviors that are acceptable, or unacceptable, whereas consequences specify the steps the teacher will take when rules are violated. According to Curwin and Mendler, these rules and consequences should be selected through group discussions and should be what is best for the class. The consequences should be logical consequences, students make right what they have done wrong; or conventional consequences, commonly used consequences such as time out or removal from class; or generic consequences, students given reminders or warnings; or instructional consequences, instruction on how to behave properly. These rules and consequences should then be posted and become the social contract for the class. Curwin and Mendler further suggest that a classroom Social Contract Test be given to prevent students from using the excuse that they didn't understand the rules. We will address the formulation of rules and consequences further in Chapter 9.

The action dimension refers to what teachers do when rules are broken. Curwin and Mendler advise teachers to select and apply the appropriate consequence for the situation. This application process should be viewed as an opportunity to interact productively with the student.

The resolution dimension is used to formulate a future plan of action for behaviorally at-risk students. The teacher should attempt to find out what is needed to prevent reoccurrence of the problem. A mutually agreed upon plan of action along with an implementation and monitoring plan should be formulated.

All teachers will experience undesirable behavior in their classroom at some time. The discipline with dignity model offers realistic help for teachers working with chronically misbehaving students.

The eight models of classroom management that have been discussed in this section can be characterized by certain similarities and differences. Table 3.2 shows the focus of the eight models we have addressed. Complete Expansion Activity: Determining Your Management Style which will address these characteristics.

TABLE 3.2

Overview of Classroom Management Models

I. Assertive Discipline Model (AD)
1. Students can control their behaviors
2. Firm, assertive approach
3. Insistence on appropriate behavior
4. Clear limits and consequences
5. Take action promptly
6. Follow through and reinforcement of rules

II. Noncoercive Discipline Model (ND)
1. Students rational beings
2. Poor background no excuse
3. Classroom meetings address problems
4. Reasonable rules with reasonable consequences
5. Student responsibility and self-direction
6. Good choices result in good behavior
7. Teacher support, fairness, and warmth

III. Behavior Modification Model (BM)
1. Behaviors learned
2. Reinforcement through rewards
3. Constant reinforcement produces desired behavior quickly and strongly
4. Tokens can be given for desired behavior; later traded for rewards
5. Rewards can be verbal comments, observations, practice, prizes, etc.

IV. Teacher Effectiveness Training Model (TET)
1. Clear communication
2. Determine "Who owns problem"

3. Send I-message when teacher owns problem
4. No-lose tactic used for conflict resolution
5. Punishment not usually viable solution

V. Positive Classroom Discipline Model (PCD)
1. Most problems due to massive time wasting
2. Prevention best way to avoid problems
3. Nonverbal behaviors key to prevention
4. Classroom rules established
5. Classroom chores assigned to students
6. Need "bell activity"
7. Establish incentive system
8. Provide help efficiently; less than twenty seconds

VI. Cooperative Discipline Model (CD)
1. Cooperative strategy
2. Actions attempt to meet needs
3. Misbehavior attempt to belong
4. Inappropriate behaviors directed to mistaken goals: attention-seeking, power-seeking, revenge-seeking, and avoidance of failure
5. Help develop capability, connections, and contributions
6. Establish code of conduct

VII. Positive Discipline in the Classroom Model (PDC)
1. Make students successful
2. Treat with respect and teach social skills

Continued on next page

TABLE 3.2 Continued

3. Use classroom meetings to teach skills
4. Focus on caring
5. Emphasize democratic methods

VIII. Discipline with Dignity Model (DWD)
  1. Maximize dignity and hope

2. Danger of failing students are behaviorally at-risk
3. Effective plans focuses on prevention, action, and resolution
4. Rules and consequences formulated through group discussion
5. Social Contract Test given over rules and consequences

Expansion Activity: Determining Your Management Style

Did you notice a pattern to the management models? Write a paragraph or two about how you might apply these management principles while teaching in your own subject area or grade level.

This concludes our study of classroom management models. Study Table 3.2, the results of Expansion Activity: Determining Your Management Style, and complete Task 3.2 which checks your understanding of the eight models.

T A S K   3 . 2

Management Models

We have briefly discussed eight models of management. Each of the following statements represents a position from one of the models. Identify each position as representative of the Assertive Discipline Model (AD), the Noncoercive Discipline Model (ND), the Behavior Modification Model (BM), the Teacher Effectiveness Training Model (TET), the Positive Classroom Discipline Model (PCD), the Cooperative Discipline Model (CD), the Positive Discipline in the Classroom Model (PDC), or the Discipline with Dignity Model (DWD). Check your responses with those given at the end of the chapter.

_____ 1. Teacher uses strategies that will develop a positive working relationship with students and parents.
_____ 2. The teacher rewards acceptable student behavior and ignores unacceptable student behavior.
_____ 3. The teacher takes charge in the classroom and is assertive and firm.

Continued on next page

_____ 4. The teacher reduces the occurrences of inappropriate behavior by establishing a positive, helping relationship with students.

_____ 5. Teacher uses class meetings to help students develop social skills and to formulate class rules and consequences.

_____ 6. The teacher establishes rules and continuously stresses student responsibility.

_____ 7. The teacher uses classroom meetings to discuss and handle problem situations.

_____ 8. The teacher attempts to minimize time wasting through use of prevention strategies.

_____ 9. Teacher uses strategies that will help misdirected students develop a sense of belonging.

_____ 10. The teacher views a token reinforcement system as an effective means of promoting proper student behavior.

_____ 11. The teacher uses I-messages rather than you-messages when problem situations occur.

_____ 12. Teacher attempts to improve behavior by maximizing student dignity and hope.

_____ 13. The teacher assists students in making good choices rather than bad choices.

_____ 14. The teacher uses the no-lose tactic when confronted with a conflict situation.

_____ 15. The teacher communicates needs and requirements to students and follows up words with actions.

_____ 16. The teacher assigns chores to students to develop a sense of class ownership.

_____ 17. The teacher uses a classroom Social Contract Test to make sure students understand the rules and consequences.

Analysis and Reflections

Write a couple of paragraphs about how you might incorporate the knowledge you've obtained about management into your own management philosophy.

Summary

- Classrooms must be arranged and organized to support student learning. Effective teachers believe they can teach and believe all students can learn.
- Learning is related to students' perceptions of their abilities and the importance of the material.

Classroom Climate

- Classrooms should be pleasant, positive, and supportive. Beginning teachers should create a classroom in which the exchange of ideas is encouraged, respect is fostered, and a sense of community is established.

- Classroom leadership can be authoritarian, democratic, or laissez-faire. Productivity and performance are usually higher in well-run, democratic classrooms.
- Many classroom problems can be overcome when teachers turn to a more democratic approach based on freedom, choice, and responsibility. Classroom freedom means freedom with limits.
- There are five types of social power: expert, referent, legitimate, reward, and coercive. New teachers should establish expert and referent power.
- Students should be given a voice and choices in what goes on in the classroom.
- An attractive, clean, and neat room is conducive to learning. It should be arranged to aid teaching and learning and to help maintain discipline.
- The total time available for school activities is referred to as mandated time. Teachers attempt to translate all classroom allocated time into instructional time. Instructional time is turned into engaged time and academic learning time.

Management Models
- The assertive discipline model advocates the need for teachers to be assertive. An assertive teacher is one who clearly and firmly communicates needs and requirements to students, follows up with appropriate actions, responds to students in ways that maximize compliance, but in no way violates the best interests of the students.
- The noncoercive discipline model recommends assisting students in becoming responsible and able to satisfy their needs in the real world. The teacher must guide the individual toward reality, that is, assisting an individual in becoming responsible and able to satisfy his or her needs in the real world.
- The behavior modification model is based on the premise that behavior is changed by altering the consequences, outcomes, or rewards that follow behavior. Students who are good, who follow the rules, or who perform well are given reinforcers or rewards.
- The teacher effectiveness training model strives to instruct teachers in how to establish positive relationships with students. Negative behaviors can often be minimized by using clearer, less provocative communications.
- The positive classroom discipline model suggests that most problems in the classroom come from massive time wasting and the key to preventing most problems is to keep students on-task. This can be accomplished through classroom structuring, limit setting through the use of body language, incentive systems, and efficient help.
- The cooperative discipline model emphasizes that teachers need a management strategy that enables them to work cooperatively; with students and parents. The teacher's goal is to assist students in their desire to belong.
- The positive discipline in the classroom model aims to make students more successful in the classroom and in all walks of life. This can be accomplished by treating students with respect and by teaching them social skills.

- The discipline with dignity model provides teachers with strategies for improving classroom behavior through maximizing student dignity and hope. An effective management plan should consist of a prevention dimension, an action dimension, and a resolution dimension.

Activities

1. *Classroom observation* Visit several different classrooms at different grade levels. Collect data relative to classroom climate and leadership.

    a. Compare the climate of the different classrooms.
    b. Compare the leadership of the different classrooms.
    c. Are the seating arrangements of the classrooms similar? Are they effective for the prevention of management problems?
    d. Is time used effectively in the classrooms? How could time management be improved?

2. *Behavior observation* Complete several observations in various classrooms at different grade levels. How do the observed teachers control behavior? Do the teachers use signals, warnings, nonverbal messages, or other subtle measures to prevent discipline problems from arising? Which techniques seem most successful? Do all students respond in the same way? Does there appear to be a difference in effectiveness at the various grade levels?

3. *Model analyses* Analyze the eight management models. Which model, if any, do you prefer? Why?

4. *Classroom diversity* If you were teaching in a culturally diverse classroom, what would you do to bridge the different cultures to form a more positive classroom climate? What leadership approach would you take with a culturally diverse class?

Answer Keys

Task 3.1 Classroom Climate

1. False. Students can and should be involved in establishing a positive classroom environment. It then becomes their room.
2. a. D   b. A   c. A   d. D   e. D   f. L
3. Task-oriented leaders are concerned with getting the job done while socioemotional leaders are mainly concerned with feelings and relationships between group members.
4. Desks that are too close to each other or that stand in the way of traffic often represent distractions to students. Sometimes changing seating to cut down on the tendency of friends to visit can curb behavior problems.
5. a. 3   b. 4   c. 5   d. 2   e. 1
6. Time is lost at the beginning of class in taking roll, lack of organization when changing activities during class, spending too much time on simple routines and behavior problems, too much testing, not using the total period for instruction, and losses due to extracurricular activities during instructional time.

Task 3.2 Management Models

The following responses would be appropriate. However, some of your responses may be different. Some of the statements represent more than one model. Therefore, if you disagree with this key, analyze your response carefully. If you feel comfortable with your response, stand by it.

1. CD	5. PDC	9. CD	13. ND	17. DWD
2. BM	6. ND	10. BM	14. TET	
3. AD	7. ND	11. TET	15. AD	
4. TET	8. PCD	12. DWD	16. PCD	

Theory and Research

Chemers, M. M., & Ayman, R. (Eds.). (1993). *Leadership theory and research: Perspectives and directions.* New York: New York Academic Press.

Eagly, A. H., Karau, S. J., & Makhijani, M. G. (1995). Gender and the effectiveness of leaders: A meta-analysis. *Psychological Bulletin, 117*, 125–145.

Kohn, A. (1996). *Beyond discipline: From compliance to community.* Alexandria, VA: Association for Supervision and Curriculum Development.

Kraut, H. (1996). *Teaching and the art of successful classroom management.* Staten Island, NY: Aysa Publishing Inc.

References

Albert, L. (1996). *Cooperative discipline.* Circle Pines, MN: American Guidance Service.

Berliner, D. (1987). Simple views of effective teaching and simple theory of classroom instruction. In D. Berliner & B. Rosenshire (Eds.). *Talks to teachers.* New York: Random House.

Block, J. H., Efthim, H. E., & Burns, R. B. (1989). *Building effective mastery learning schools.* New York: Longman.

Canter, L., & Canter, M. (1976). *Assertive discipline: A take-charge approach for today's educator.* Los Angeles: Canter and Associates.

Curwin, R., & Mendler, A. (1988). *Discipline with dignity.* Alexandria, VA: Association for Supervision and Curriculum Development.

Freiberg, H. J. (1996). From tourists to citizens in the classroom. *Educational Leadership, 54*(1), 32–37.

Glasser, W. (1965). *Reality therapy: A new approach to psychiatry.* New York: Harper and Row.

Glasser, W. (1977). 10 steps to good discipline. *Today's Education, 66*, 61–63.

Gordon, T. (1974). *Teacher effectiveness training.* New York: David McKay.

Jones, F. (1987). *Positive classroom discipline.* New York: McGraw-Hill.

Jubala, K. A., Bishop, K. D., & Falvey, M. A. (1995). Creating a supportive classroom environment. *Inclusive and Heterogeneous Schooling: Assessment, Curriculum, and Instruction.* (San Diego Unified School District, San Diego, CA), Baltimore, MD: Paul H. Brookes.

Kohn, A. (1996). What to look for in a classroom. *Educational Leadership, 54*(1), 54–55.

Nelsen, J., Lott, L., & Glenn, H. (1997). *Positive discipline in the classroom.* Rocklin, CA: Prima.

Presbie, R. J., & Brown, P. L. (1976). *Behavior modification.* Washington, DC: National Education Association.

Walker, J. E., & Shea, T. M. (1980). *Behavior modification* (2nd ed.). St. Louis: C. V. Mosby.

Wraga, W. G. (1998). *Democratic leadership in the classroom: Theory into practice.* Paper presented at the Czech National Civic Education Conference, Olomouc, Czech Republic. (ERIC Document Reproduction Service No. ED427998).

Writing Objectives

Objectives

After completing your study of Chapter 4, you should be able to:

1. Define learning.

2. Provide valid reasons for stating instructional objectives.

3. Define and contrast educational goals, informational objectives, and instructional objectives.

4. Compare and contrast overt and covert behavioral changes.

5. Name and define the four components that make up a properly written instructional objective.

6. Write objectives that include the four components of a well-stated objective.

7. Name and describe the three domains of learning.

8. Classify given objectives as being cognitive, affective, or psychomotor, and rate them as higher- or lower-level in each domain.

9. Prepare (write) educational goals, informational objectives, and instructional objectives at different levels of cognitive, affective, and psychomotor sophistication.

10. Describe outcome-based education and list major objections to the model.

11. Explain the importance of establishing educational standards.

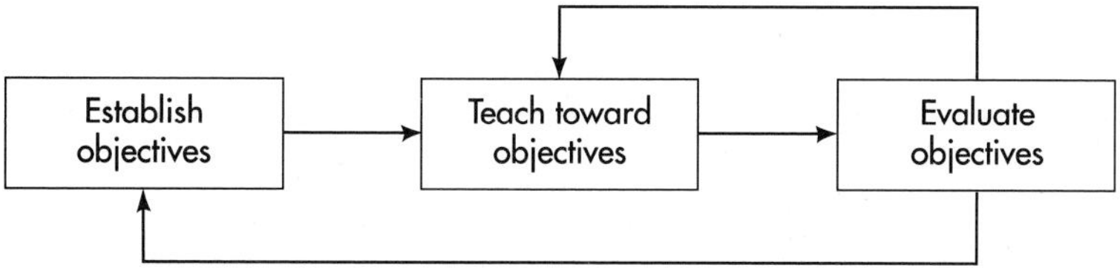

FIGURE 4.1 *Teaching Model*

Learning can be defined as change in a student's capacity for performance as a result of experience. Effective teaching should, therefore, be directed toward targeted changes in performance. Thus, in planning instruction you must first decide what changes you want to take place as a result of your instruction, or what will result from your teaching. The intended changes should be specified in your instructional objectives. Viewed in this context, an **objective** can be defined as a clear and unambiguous description of your instructional intent. An objective is not a statement of what you plan to put into the lesson (content) but instead a statement of what your students should get out of the lesson. Thus, your teaching model can be viewed as shown in Figure 4.1.

The model shows that the first task is to establish your objectives. Second, you teach toward the acquisition of the stated objectives using the selected teaching approach. Finally, you evaluate students' attainment of the stated objectives. If students do not achieve the intended objectives, you may either select a different approach or you may alter the original objectives. If students achieve the targeted outcomes, you are ready to go on to the next set of objectives.

Value of Objectives

Why should you take the time to write objectives? In the first place, as indicated in the preceding teaching model, your teaching approach will be dictated to a large extent by your objectives. These objectives demand certain learning environments and activity sequences. For example, if a lesson objective is the acquisition of a specific motor skill, your activities must include practice and refinement of that skill. If, on the other hand, the objective is related to the knowledge of specific muscles one uses in performing certain motor skills, a textbook and related diagrams would probably suffice (Beane, Toepfer, & Alessi, 1986).

Another important reason for stating objectives is related to the evaluation process. You will not know whether your students have acquired the targeted learning unless you know what you intended to teach and have evaluated that intent. Thus, your objectives set the framework for your evaluation. Of equal importance to the instructional process is the fact that objectives assist you in communicating with your students. When your objectives are shared with the students—and they should always be shared either verbally or in writing—students know what is expected of them. They do not have to guess what is important. They do not have to guess what will be on the test!

In our discussion thus far we have been concerned with stating objectives in terms of specific instructional intent that can be observed and evaluated. However, there are several levels to instructional intent. At the very general, abstract level are statements of the goals that a school might set for its graduates. At the other extreme are very specific statements of what students will be able to do following instruction. Let us now look at the different levels of instructional intent in greater detail.

⋈ Goal and Objective Specificity

Too often the terms *goals* and *objectives* are incorrectly interchanged. However, there is a difference in the level of specificity at which they should be written. **Goals** are extremely broad statements that are used to describe the purposes of schooling, a course, or a unit of instruction. Objectives, on the other hand, are narrower statements of the intended learning of a unit or specific lesson (Gronlund, 1970). Moreover, objectives also vary in the level of specificity depending on the type of objective written.

A nomenclature that differentiates between goals and objectives, as well as between the specificity levels of objectives, has been developed. Unfortunately there is little agreement about how this terminology should be used. The terms *educational goals, educational aims,* and *general objectives* are often used to denote broad general purposes, whereas the terms *specific objectives, informational objectives, behavioral objectives, performance objectives,* and *instructional objectives* are often used to denote the more specific learning targets.

Generally goals and objectives are written at three different levels (Kryspin & Feldhusen, 1974). In this text we label the three levels, in descending order of specificity, educational goals, informational objectives, and instructional objectives, as depicted in Figure 4.2. In theory and in their proper use, the more specific objectives are subordinate to and are contained in the more general goals. Thus, goals and objectives can be thought of as forming a continuum from general to specific, as suggested in Figure 4.2. Educational goals are usually written for a school, course, or unit, followed by (in descending order) informational and instructional objectives written for specific lessons and exercises. This sequence may vary somewhat depending on the writer. Some writers prefer using a combination of informational and instructional objectives for a unit of study or for specific lessons.

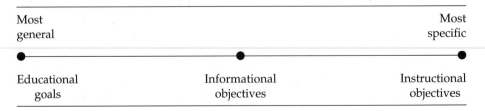

FIGURE 4.2 *General to Specific Continuum for Goals and Objectives*

TABLE 4.1	

Examples of Goal and Objective Specificity

Type	Example
Educational goal	The student will become a knowledgeable citizen.
Informational objective	The student will match major industries to their respective region in the United States.
Instructional objective	Given a list of industries and United States regions, the student will match each industry to its respective region with 90 percent accuracy.

Examples of the three different levels of specificity for goals and objectives from a social studies course are shown in Table 4.1. Note that the specificity increases as you move down through the examples. Thus, informational objectives are subordinate to educational goals, and instructional objectives are subordinate to informational objectives.

✷ Educational Goals

Educational goals are extremely broad and may take weeks, months, or even years to achieve. Note the broad terms of the goal in Table 4.1. It is the entire intent of the course or unit, that is, what the teacher wishes to accomplish in the broadest possible sense. The informational and instructional objectives then support the educational goal. That is, they tell what the students will do to show that they have become knowledgeable citizens. Other examples of educational goals are:

1. The student will learn to read.
2. The student will live a healthful life.
3. The student will appreciate art and music.
4. The student will know how to solve algebraic equations.
5. The student will think clearly and rationally.

Note the use of the verbs *learn, live, appreciate, know,* and *think* in the preceding examples. These verbs make the statements vague; they are not stated in observable, measurable terms. In fact, they appear to be so vague that they give no help at all in planning instruction. Yet, on closer examination they do set the general direction of instruction and, consequently, are the first step in deciding what to teach. The next step is to decide on the specifics related to these goals. That is, the teacher must now decide in a precise manner exactly what students should know and do to show that they have accomplished the goals. These decisions are then written up as more specific objectives: informational and instructional.

The point of all this is that in planning you must first develop your course goals, then develop informational and instructional objectives. The goals give the general direction to take and also give an overview of what the students will know or be able to do after your instruction. You then state specifically, in observable and measurable terms, exactly what the students will do to show you that you have accomplished your goals. These latter statements make up your informational and instructional objectives.

✵ Covert Versus Overt Behavior

The basic purpose of schooling and teaching is to cause students to learn something. Thus, as a result of the instruction, students should act or be inclined to act differently from before. There is a change in the individual. This change can be covert (not easily observed) or overt (observable). Writers of educational goals are concerned with covert, internal changes, which are less clearly measurable than are the behaviors associated with the more specific objectives. Verbs associated with educational goals include *know, understand*, and *appreciate*. Writers of informational and instructional objectives, on the other hand, are concerned with overt, observable behaviors which can be tested and measured. Thus, they tend to use measurable verbs, such as *list, explain*, and *match*.

Educational goals cannot be easily measured or directly observed. They lack the specification of exactly what, in observable terms, the student is to do to show that the intended learning has taken place. Thus, the verbs used in writing educational goals are often rather vague, ambiguous, and open to interpretation.

Table 4.2 lists verbs that are appropriate for writing educational goals (covert) and verbs that are appropriate for writing informational and instructional objectives (overt). Note the difference in clarity of language between the

TASK 4.1

Identifying Verbs

Given below is a list of verbs appropriate for writing goals and objectives. Label each verb as covert (nonobservable) (C) or overt (observable) (O). Check your responses with those given at the end of the chapter.

___ 1. tell   ___ 4. comprehend   ___ 7. pantomime
___ 2. place   ___ 5. sing   ___ 8. grasp
___ 3. design   ___ 6. know   ___ 9. appreciate

Analysis and Reflection

Educational goals give a broad direction for educational intent. Research the goals of the grade level or subject area you plan to teach. What are some of the broad goals for instruction at the grade level and in the subject area you intend to teach? Write a short paper on your findings and share them with your instructor and your class.

TABLE 4.2

Illustrative Verbs for Writing Goals and Objectives

Covert (Nonobservable) Verbs	Overt (Observable) Verbs	
apply	add	label
appreciate	analyze	list
believe	arrange	locate
comprehend	build	measure
cope	calculate	name
demonstrate	choose	operate
enjoy	circle	order
familiarize	classify	pick
grasp	compare	point
imagine	construct	pronounce
know	contrast	read
like	define	recite
realize	distinguish	select
recognize	draw	sing
think	explain	sort
understand	graph	underline
value	identify	write

two groups. After carefully studying Table 4.2, complete Task 4.1, which will test your skill at identifying covert (nonobservable) and overt (observable) verbs.

If you had trouble with Task 4.1, spend some time studying Table 4.2. We are now ready to look at writing informational and instructional objectives in detail. However, before we do, we shall look at what constitutes a well-stated objective.

Well-Stated Objectives

Mager (1984) and Kibler, Barker, & Miles (1970) have developed very influential systems for stating objectives. According to these writers, a well-stated objective should include four components: the performance, a product, the conditions, and the criterion.

The Performance

A well-stated objective must be written in terms of what students are expected to do, not what the teacher is to do. Suppose the following statement had been written for an objective: The teacher will pronounce the new vocabulary words.

It is evident what the teacher is to do, but there is no indication of what the students are to do. Since student learning is the purpose of instruction, well-stated objectives should always be written in terms of observable student performance. Thus, the preceding objective might be restated in this way: The student will pronounce the new vocabulary words.

Special care must also be taken to select the proper verb when writing objectives. Above all the language must be clear. There must be no ambiguity. Each verb in your objective must mean the same to you, an interested colleague, or the principal. Subjective terms, such as *learn, realize,* and *understand,* should not be used as performance verbs in writing objectives. These terms are open to interpretation and might have different meanings to different individuals. Instead use terms that denote observable actions (overt) or behaviors (see Table 4.2). For example, your intent might be for students to be able:

> To identify (in writing) . . .
> To explain (orally) . . .
> To list . . .
> To construct . . .

Certain verbs represent special cases in terms of our ability to directly view the performance. Verbs such as *identify, distinguish, compare,* and *add* represent internal (covert) processes in that the actions cannot be directly observed. You cannot directly see someone identify, distinguish, compare, or add, but you can see some action that shows that the process has taken place. The action could include such behaviors as circling, pointing, or checking to show identifying; checking, sorting, or writing the descriptions to show distinguishing; listing or writing the characteristics to show comparing; and writing or orally stating the sum to show adding. Mager (1984) calls these observable verbs "indicator verbs" and suggests that you add an indicator verb to the objective to specify the action when confronted with special covert verbs that cannot be observed directly. Applying this procedure to the verbs cited earlier, the objective could be rewritten as:

> The student will identify (circle) . . .
> The student will distinguish (check) . . .
> The student will compare (in writing) . . .
> The student will add (write the sum) . . .

The performance component in a well-stated objective specifies exactly what student actions should be observed as a result of instruction. If the objective verb represents an internal, covert process that might lead to vagueness, you would be wise to add an overt indicator verb for clarity. If, however, you feel the internal, covert process verb is clear and not open to interpretation, there is no need for an indicator verb.

The Product

The product is what students will produce by their action. It is that product which will be evaluated to determine whether the objective has been mastered. The product can be a written sentence, a written sum, listed names, a demonstrated skill, or a constructed object. We list here some statements that contain the first two components of a well-stated objective, the performance and the product. The portion of the statement that has been underlined is the product of the action.

> The student will write <u>the numerals to ten</u>.
> The student will identify (underline) <u>the nouns in a sentence</u>.
> The student will list <u>the main ideas in a short story</u>.
> The student will classify <u>leaves into groups based on texture</u>.
> The student will solve (write answer) <u>two-digit multiplication algorithms</u>.

The product then is the planned outcome resulting from the instructional process. It is what you want students to produce or be able to do.

The Conditions

Under what conditions will students perform the intended action? Will they be allowed to use an open book? What materials will be used? Where will they perform? These questions are answered in the conditions component of your objective. This component of a well-stated objective includes the information, tools or equipment, and materials that will or will not be available to students; any special limitations or restrictions as to time and space; and any other requirements that may be applicable. Examples of conditions that might be included in a well-stated objective include:

> Given a list of 20 authors . . .
> After reading chapter 2 . . .
> Using the class textbook . . .
> Given a ruler and protractor . . .
> Without the use of references . . .
> . . . on a multiple-choice test . . .
> . . . before the class . . .
> . . . during a 10-minute interval . . .
> . . . from a list of equations . . .

In writing the conditions component of a well-stated objective, you should attempt to visualize under what conditions the students will show mastery and try to duplicate these conditions as nearly as possible in your objective. Some teachers also believe that objectives should always begin with a phrase such as "Upon completion of the lesson (or unit, or course), the student will . . ." because the intended action is to take place only after instruction has been concluded. However, if you keep in mind that the intended action always represents terminal behavior, there is no real need to add the phrase. Whether or not you add the phrase is entirely up to you.

The Criterion

The fourth and last component of a well-stated objective is the level of acceptable student performance. Here you state the level of behavior you will accept as satisfactory or the minimum level for showing mastery. The criterion level may be stated as follows:

As the minimum number acceptable:
... at least three reasons ...
... all five steps ...

As the percent or proportion acceptable:
... with 80 percent accuracy ...
... 90 percent of the 20 problems ...
... nine of the ten cases ...

As an acceptable tolerance:
... within ± 10 percent ...
... to the nearest hundredth ...
... correct to the nearest percent ...

As acceptable limits of time:
... within 10 minutes ...
... in less than five minutes ...

As a combination of acceptable standards:
... at least two problems within a 5-minute period ...
... within 20 minutes with 90 percent accuracy ...

Or it may be stated as any other standard of acceptance. Usually your standard is selected on the basis of past experiences and class expectations.

This completes our discussion of the four components of a well-stated objective. Table 4.3 gives a review of these four components. Study the table and take a few minutes to complete Task 4.2.

Did you have any trouble with Task 4.2? If not, good work! Number 4 was a little tricky, and you may have included the phrase "a given Spanish dialogue" as part of the conditions. Technically you are correct; however, the dialogue also represents the product which will be evaluated. Therefore, you could have included it in both the conditions and the product. Now try Web Search: Behavioral Examples which will let you apply objective concepts.

Now that you know the basic components of a well-written objective, you are ready to differentiate between informational and instructional objectives.

TABLE 4.3

Components of a Well-Stated Objective

Part	Question to Ask	Example
Student performance	Do what?	Write
Product of performance	What is result?	Three sentences
Conditions of performance	Under what conditions?	Given three nouns and three verbs
Performance criterion	How well?	With no more than one error

T A S K 4 . 2

Identifying the Components of Well-Stated Objectives

For each objective given below, circle the performance, bracket the product, underline the conditions once, and underline the criterion twice. Check your responses with those given at the end of the chapter.

1. Given a set of pictures, the student will be able to place the pictures in proper sequence with no more than one error.

2. Given the necessary materials and the dimensions, the student will construct a polygon with all dimensions being within 5 percent.

3. The student will be able to identify (select letter) on a multiple-choice test the subplots of the poems read in class with 100 percent accuracy.

4. After completing a series of Spanish language tapes, the student will orally recite a given Spanish dialogue with no errors in pronunciation.

5. The student will write a 300-word essay on a given social studies topic with no sentence fragments and no more than two errors in grammar.

Analysis and Reflections

This section has focused on writing well-stated objectives. How important do you think it is to write well-stated objectives? Is it really necessary to write objectives for every lesson? How do they make instruction more effective? Write a paragraph or two on your conclusions and submit them to your instructor.

Web Search: Behavioral Examples

Access the example behavioral verbs and student activities on Internet URL site **http://www.adprima.com/examples.htm** and the submitted sample lesson plans at **http://www.adprima.com/usermenu.htm**. Analyze the example activities and lesson plans. Do you feel the objectives would be clear to students? Could you improve the lesson plans?

✖ Informational and Instructional Objectives

Informational objectives are abbreviations of instructional objectives. **Instructional objectives** contain all four components of a well-stated objective, but informational objectives specify only the student performance and the product. Consider the following example of an instructional and an informational objective written for the same instructional intent:

Instructional objective: Given a list of alternatives on a multiple-choice test, the student will select the definitions for the terms *triangle, rectangle,*

T A S K   4 . 3

Objective Concepts

Respond to the following items. Check your responses with those given at the end of the chapter.

1. List the three benefits derived from the writing of objectives.

   a. _____

   _____

   b. _____

   c. _____

   _____

2. It is sometimes unwise to share your objectives with students.(True/False)

3. List the nomenclature of learning intent in terms of specificity from least to greatest.

   a. _____

   b. _____

   c. _____

4. List and describe the four components of a well-stated objective.

   a. _____

   _____

   b. _____

   _____

   c. _____

   _____

   d. _____

   _____

5. Informational objectives usually contain all four components of a well-stated objective.(True/False)

Analysis and Reflections

Figure 4.1 depicts a simple model of the instructional process. From your experience as a student and from your school observations, do teachers follow this model? If yes, why do they do so? If not, why do you think they fail to follow this model? Discuss your conclusions with your classmates.

---

   square, trapezoid, circle, rhombus, and *parallelogram* with 100 percent accuracy.

Informational objective: The student will select the definitions for the terms *triangle, rectangle, square, trapezoid, circle, rhombus,* and *parallelogram.*

The informational objective is an abbreviation of the instructional objective in that it omits the conditions (given a list of alternatives on a multiple-choice test) and the criterion for judging minimum mastery (100 percent accuracy). The informational objective contains only the performance (to select) and the products to be selected (definitions for the terms *triangle, rectangle, square, trapezoid, circle, rhombus,* and *parallelogram*). Conditions apply only at the time of assessment and may not always be needed in your objective statement. That is, they will often be standard and understood by students. Likewise, the criterion may not always be needed and may be very artificial in that the mastery level will be determined when the evaluative information is processed.

Most teachers use informational objectives to share their instructional intent with students. In most cases this suffices. However, if more information is needed to communicate the exact intent, you should write instructional objectives or perhaps informational objectives with the conditions or the criterion added.

This concludes our formal discussion of the different types of objectives. Take a few minutes to complete Task 4.3.

✖ Classification of Objectives

Objectives are often classified as to the primary type of learning the instruction is trying to accomplish. The most commonly used system for classifying objectives is the taxonomy developed by Bloom, Engelhart, Furst, Hill & Krathwohl (1956) and Krathwohl, Bloom, & Masai (1964). This system is divided into three major categories or domains of learning: the cognitive, the affective, and the psychomotor. Each domain is arranged in hierarchical order from simple to complex. In spite of this, each level subsumes the previous level. That is, the objectives at one level make use of and build on behaviors found in the preceding level. Likewise, in reality the domains are interrelated. For example, when students are writing (psychomotor), they are also recalling information and thinking (cognitive), and they are likely to have some kind of emotional response to the task (affective).

Cognitive Domain

Objectives in the cognitive domain are concerned with imparting knowledge and thinking skills. The objectives can range from simple recall of information to complex synthesis and the creation of new ideas. This domain is concerned mainly with the subject matter content students are expected to learn.

Some performance verbs (arranged here according to the complexity of response) commonly associated with writing objectives in the cognitive domain include: *define, distinguish, identify, restate, explain, infer, apply, use, choose, classify, categorize, write, design, assess, compare,* and *contrast*. Examples of informational and instructional objectives include such statements as:

1. The student will define the terms *common noun* and *proper noun.*
2. The student will explain (in writing) the importance of mathematics in everyday life.

3. The student will design an experiment to test the effect of three different soaps on clothing.
4. Given various classes of music, the student will give (write) at least three effects each type of music had on society.
5. Given a sample of French prose, the student will verbally translate it into English with no more than two errors.

Affective Domain

Objectives in the affective domain are concerned with emotional development. Thus, the affective domain deals with attitudes, feelings, and emotions, and they vary according to the degree of internalization sought.

Since teachers must be concerned with the total development of students, not just their cognitive development, they need to consider attitudes, feelings, and emotions in their instructional planning. Yet most teachers do not, partly because it is difficult to write objectives for the affective domain. The reason for the difficulty is that it is hard to translate attitudes, feelings, and emotions into overt, observable behaviors. For example, the affective objective, "The student will like reading," is not properly written. The behavior *like* is not observable. Students must do something observable to show that they like reading. Replace the verb *like* with an observable behavior assumed to indicate liking, for example, "The student will volunteer to read in class." However, volunteering is only one of many possible indicators that the student likes to read. Some performance verbs, arranged from limited internalization to high internalization, often associated with writing objectives in the affective domain include: *to freely select, to respond positively to, to listen, to volunteer, to applaud, to support, to argue for (against), to complete,* and *to rate high (low)*.

When desired behaviors are related to the affective domain, you must observe the behaviors in a free-choice situation to obtain a true indication of student attitudes and feelings. If the situation is not free choice, students may exhibit the desired behaviors for a reward of some type or because they want to please you. For example, the affective objective, "The student will complete all mathematics assignments," would not be appropriate for showing a positive attitude toward mathematics. This objective must be rewritten for a free-choice situation. An example is, "The student will complete optional mathematics assignments with no extra credit given." Another technique often used to reveal attitudes and interests is the administration of attitude and interest inventories. These instruments will be discussed at length in Chapter 10.

To summarize, objectives in the affective domain must be written in overt, observable terms, and the behaviors must take place in free-choice situations. Other examples of informational and instructional objectives in the affective domain include:

1. The student will eagerly participate in class discussions of history-related topics.
2. Given an attitude survey at the beginning and end of the course, the student will rate science higher on the end-of-course survey.

3. When given the opportunity to select the class reading, the student will freely select poetry at least once during the semester.
4. The student will attend a music concert during the semester without receiving class credit for attendance.
5. Given the opportunity, the student will volunteer to stay after school to care for the classroom plants at least three times during the year.

Psychomotor Domain

Objectives in the psychomotor domain relate to the development of muscular and motor skills and range from beginning to expert performances. Some examples of performance objectives, from simple to complex muscle control, that can be used in writing objectives in the psychomotor domain are: *run, walk, measure, construct, type, play, align,* and *focus.* Examples of informational and instructional objectives in the psychomotor domain include:

1. The student will construct a table.
2. The student will type a paragraph.
3. Given a piano and the music, the student will play the piece with no more than two errors.
4. At the end of the year, the student will run a mile in less than eight minutes.
5. Given a meter stick, the student will measure the room within 5 percent of the correct value.

Most learning in the classroom will contain elements of all three domains. Nevertheless, in writing your objectives, your major emphasis is usually directed toward cognitive, affective, or psychomotor learning.

✖ Domain Taxonomies

Although objectives for a given instructional situation can be written at each taxonomic level, Mager (1984) suggests that this is a waste of time and effort. If you have completed a suitable analysis of instructional intent, you know the level at which you want your students to learn and thus you will automatically write objectives at those levels. There will be no need to write objectives at all levels.

Teachers often fall into the habit of writing objectives only for the lower taxonomic levels since objectives at the higher levels are more difficult to write. A working knowledge of the instructional intent of the various taxonomic levels helps prevent this pitfall. Thus, knowledge of the taxonomies should be used to formulate the best possible objectives for your teaching intent and to ensure that your intent is not overly focused on the lower levels.

A brief overview of the taxonomies for each of the three domains of learning follows. A more detailed description of each can be found by referring to one of the references listed at the end of the chapter. The cognitive taxonomy presented is adapted from the work of Bloom et al. (1956). However, Bloom's two highest levels, synthesis and evaluation, have been combined into a single "creative" level. The affective taxonomy presented here has been adapted from the work of Krathwohl et al. (1964), and it too combines the two highest levels, organization and characterization, into a single level labeled "commitment."

Levels of Cognitive Learning

Learning intent in the cognitive domain ranges from simple recall of facts to complex synthesis of information and the creation of new ideas. As adapted from the work of Bloom et al. (1956), five levels of learning are included in the cognitive learning taxonomy.

Knowledge learning refers to the simple recall of previously learned materials. This may involve the recall of terminology, basic principles, generalizations, and specific facts, such as dates, events, persons, and places. No manipulation or interpretation of the learned material is required. Knowledge-level objectives can be expressed with such verbs as *identify, define, list, match, write, state, name, label,* and *describe.* Knowledge-level examples include:

The student will spell at least 70 percent of the words in the third grade speller.
The student will list the names of 12 of the last 15 presidents of the United States.

Comprehension is the lowest level of understanding and may involve changing the form of previously learned material or making simple interpretations. Abilities include translating material to new forms, explaining and summarizing material, and estimating future trends. Comprehension-level objectives can be expressed with such verbs as *translate, convert, generalize, paraphrase, rewrite, summarize, differentiate, defend, infer,* and *explain.* Comprehension-level examples include:

After reading a short story, the student will summarize the major plot.
After studying the Civil War, the student will explain the conditions in the South and North that led to the war.

Application entails the use of learned information in new and concrete situations. It may involve the application of rules, general ideas, concepts, laws, principles, and theories. Application-level objectives can be expressed with such verbs as *use, operate, produce, change, solve, show, compute,* and *prepare.* Application-level examples include:

Using two different algorithmic forms, the student will solve two-digit addition problems.
The student will prepare a graph showing the United States's exports for the last 10 years.

Analysis entails breaking down material into its component parts so that it can be better understood. It may involve identification of components, analysis of relationships between parts, and recognition of organizational principles and structures. Analysis-level objectives can be expressed with such verbs as *discriminate, select, distinguish, separate, subdivide, identify,* and *break down.* Analysis-level examples include:

Given a sentence, the student will identify the major parts of speech.
The student will break down a story plot into various subplots.

Creation entails combining components to form a new whole or to produce an evaluation based on specified criteria. It may involve the making of a unique composition, communication, plan, proposal, or scheme for classifying information. The unique creation may require that a judgment regarding the value of material be made based on an internal or external criteria. Creation-level objectives can be expressed with such verbs as *design, plan, compile, compose, organize, appraise, compare, justify, conclude, criticize, explain,* and *interpret.* Creation-level examples include:

The student will compose an original story from an unusual situation.
Given the materials, the student will design a hat.

Levels of Affective Learning

Learning intent in the affective domain is organized according to the degree of internalization. That is, it is organized according to the degree to which an attitude, feeling, value, or emotion has become part of the individual. As adapted from the work of Krathwohl et al. (1964), four levels of learning are included in the affective taxonomy.

Receiving involves being aware of and being willing to *freely* attend to a stimulus (listen and look). Receiving-level objectives can be expressed with such verbs as *follow, select, rely, choose, point to, ask, hold, give,* and *locate.* Receiving-level examples include:

The student will listen for respect words (please, thank you, sir, madam, etc.)
    in stories read aloud in class.
When asked, the student will hold various science animals (snakes, rabbits,
    gerbils, etc.).

Responding involves active participation. It involves not only *freely* attending to a stimulus but also *voluntarily* reacting to it in some way. It requires physical, active behavior. Responding-level objectives can be expressed with verbs such as *read, conform, help, answer, practice, present, report, greet, tell,* and *perform.* Responding-level examples include:

The student will volunteer to help with a class mathematics project.
The student will report that poetry is enjoyable to read.

Valuing refers to voluntarily giving worth to an object, phenomenon, or stimulus. Behaviors at this level reflect a belief, appreciation, or attitude. Valuing-level objectives can be expressed with such verbs as *initiate, ask, invite, share, join, follow, propose, read, study,* and *work.* Valuing-level examples include:

When given a center choice, the student will ask to go to the science learning
    center.
The student will join at least one discussion of a school-related subject.

Commitment involves building an internally consistent value system and *freely* living by it. A set of criteria is established and applied in choice making.

Commitment-level objectives can be expressed with such verbs as *adhere, defend, alter, integrate, relate, synthesize, act, listen, serve, influence, use,* and *verify.* Commitment-level examples include:

The student will defend the importance of at least one governmental social
    policy.
The student will freely alter a judgment in light of new evidence.

Levels of Psychomotor Learning

Learning intent in the psychomotor domain ranges from acquiring the basic rudiments of a motor skill to the perfection of a complex skill. In this text three levels of learning are included in the psychomotor taxonomy.

Imitation refers to the ability to carry out the basic rudiments of a skill when given directions and under supervision. At this level the total act is not performed with skill, nor is timing and coordination refined. Imitation-level objectives can be expressed with verbs such as *construct, dismantle, drill, change, clean, manipulate, follow,* and *use.* Imitation-level examples include:

Given written instruction, the student will construct at least five geometric
    models.
The student will follow basic instructions for making a simple table.

Manipulation refers to the ability to perform a skill independently. The entire skill can be performed in sequence. Conscious effort is no longer needed to perform the skill, but complete accuracy has not been achieved. Manipulation-level objectives can be expressed with verbs such as *connect, create, fasten, make, sketch, weigh, wrap,* and *manipulate.* Manipulation-level examples include:

Given several different objects, the student will weigh each.
Given an oral description of an object, the student will sketch it.

Precision refers to the ability to perform an act accurately, efficiently, and harmoniously. Complete coordination of the skill has been acquired. The skill has been internalized to such an extent that it can be performed unconsciously. Precision-level objectives can be expressed by such terms as *focus, align, adjust, calibrate, construct, manipulate,* and *build.* Precision-level examples include:

The student will accurately adjust a microscope.
Given the materials, the student will construct a usable chair.

This concludes our formal discussion of the three domains of learning. Table 4.4 gives an overview of the taxonomies. Remember that the taxonomies can be a valuable tool for upgrading your writing of objectives. However, do not become a slave to the taxonomies. Base your objectives on the needs of the class. Use the taxonomies only as a guide and strive to incorporate the higher levels of each taxonomy in your learning experiences.

Now focus your attention for a few minutes on Task 4.4, which will check your understanding of the three domains and three taxonomies of objectives.

TABLE 4.4

The Three Educational Domains with Levels of Learning and Definitions

Domain and Level	Definition
Cognitive Domain	
1. Knowledge	Recall of factual information
2. Comprehension	Lowest level of understanding; giving evidence of understanding and the ability to make use of information
3. Application	Use of abstractions or principles to solve problems
4. Analysis	Distinguishing and comprehending interrelationships
5. Creation	Combining components to form a new whole
Affective Domain	
1. Receiving	Freely attending to stimuli
2. Responding	Voluntarily reacting to stimuli
3. Valuing	Forming an attitude toward a stimulus
4. Commitment	Behaving consistently with an internally developed, stable value system
Psychomotor Domain	
1. Imitation	Carrying out basic skill with directions and under supervision
2. Manipulation	Performing a skill independently
3. Precision	Performing a skill accurately

✂ Communication of Objectives

As stated at the beginning of this chapter, communicating objectives to students is absolutely necessary if you are to get maximum value from the objectives. The communication can be accomplished through the use of either verbal or written statements or through a combination of both.

With younger students or those who have limited reading abilities, it is usually wise to communicate your objectives verbally. This is usually accomplished during the introductory phase of your lesson by translating the written objectives into appropriate verbal statements which communicate your intent. Care should be taken, however, that the translated material is in a form that is understandable. This translation process is discussed in greater detail in Chapter 5.

With older students multiple objectives are usually shared at the beginning of a unit of study and are presented in written form. One useful format for presenting multiple unit objectives is to list each individual objective with only the performance verb and the product. For example:

T A S K   4 . 4

Identifying the Domains and Taxonomies of Objectives

Respond to the following items. Check your responses with those given at the end of the chapter.

1. Classify each of the following objectives according to its most prominent behavior: cognitive (C), affective (A), or psychomotor (P).

   _____ a. The student will correctly adjust the microscope.
   _____ b. The student will write an essay in which an argument for or against prayer in school is developed.
   _____ c. Given the materials and the picture of a sugar molecule, the student will create a model of a sugar molecule with 100 percent accuracy.
   _____ d. The student will voluntarily check out books related to art.
   _____ e. Given a story, the student will orally read for at least five minutes with no more than four errors.
   _____ f. Given a paragraph, the student will type at a rate of 50 words per minute with fewer than two errors per minute.
   _____ g. The student will argue for more science in the public schools.
   _____ h. The student will correctly write the sums for all the basic addition facts.
   _____ i. Given an attitude inventory, the student will rate social studies on the high end of the scale.
   _____ j. The student will correctly compute (write answer) the volume of a cube, cone, and pyramid.

2. List and define the three major domains for classifying objectives.

   a. _____
   _____

   b. _____
   _____

   c. _____
   _____

3. The creation of a unique entity from basic components would fall into one of the higher levels of cognitive learning.(True/False)

4. The ability to perform a skill accurately would indicate only lower-level psychomotor learning.(True/False)

Analysis and Reflections

This section has focused on three major categories or domains of learning. How important do you feel it is to include objectives in the affective domain at your grade level or in your subject area? Do you think all teachers should include affective domain objectives? Share your thoughts with the class.

After completing the unit, you should be able to:

1. Identify (write) percents illustrated with 100-part graph paper, with pie shapes, and with various rectangular shapes.
2. Illustrate (shade) numerical percents with 100-part graph paper, with pie shapes, and with various rectangular shapes.
3. Rewrite common fractions and decimal fractions as percents.
4. Rewrite percents as common fractions and decimal fractions.
5. Work simple percent problems.

Another useful format for stating multiple instructional objectives is to use an introductory statement to communicate common conditions and the criterion level. The remainder of each individual objective is then listed with the performance verb, the product, and specific conditions. For example:

After completing the unit Learning about Sentences, you should be able to perform the following objectives with 70 percent proficiency on the unit exam:

1. Define the terms *simple subject* and *simple predicate*.
2. Identify (underline) the simple subject and simple predicate in a given sentence.
3. Define a simple and a compound sentence.
4. Identify (check) simple and compound sentences.
5. Define the terms *compound subject* and *compound predicate*.
6. Identify (underline) the compound subject and compound predicate in a given sentence.
7. Diagram the simple subject and simple predicate in a given sentence.
8. Diagram the compound subject and compound predicate in a given sentence.

The exact format used to communicate your objectives to students is not critical. The important thing is that you communicate precise information regarding your instructional intent. In most cases using the more informal "you" in your objective introductory phrase rather than the formal "the student" is preferable when the objectives are to be read by the students. The "you" will personalize your objectives.

Our discussion of goals and objectives would not be complete without addressing outcome-based education and state and national standards. Let us now look at these two highly debated issues.

✄ Outcome-Based Education (OBE)

The last twenty years have seen a fundamental shift in the way we determine educational quality. Traditional educational practices center on "inputs." Students are exposed to a segment of curriculum over a specified time. At the end of the specified time, an examination is usually administered, and grades are assigned regardless of whether all students have achieved mastery of the material. In effect, quality is judged in terms of inputs: intentions and efforts, institutions and services, resources and spending.

In contrast to a content and time-based method, **outcome-based education (OBE)** specifies the "outcomes" students should be able to demonstrate upon leaving the system (Glatthorn, 1993). The focus is on outputs: goals and ends, products and results, with a focus on core academic subjects. The identified instructional outcomes are derived from a community vision of the skills and knowledge students need to be effective adults. OBE focuses instructional practice on ensuring that students master the identified outcomes, and it asserts that all students can learn.

There is no single, authoritative model for outcome-based education. However, the emphasis is on system level change; observable, measurable outcomes; and the belief that all students can learn. Various outcome-based education models have gotten increased attention in recent years because they promise far-reaching reform, offer a balance between school autonomy and accountability, and appear to deliver dramatic results.

Outcome-based education has drawn intense criticism from parent groups and others who fear that by focusing on outcomes, schools are inflicting values on students that are antithetical to the very nature of education (Berliner, 1997; McKernan, 1993). Moreover, many on the right vehemently oppose outcome-based education. Religious fundamentalists and others on the right generally unite behind one major objection. They believe that the traditional forms of education have always worked so are sufficient for children today. As such, schools need not and should not attempt to teach students to think critically, weigh evidence, reason analytically and independently, or reach conclusions. Many critics also argue that there is no hard evidence that OBE works. Others argue that OBE will "dumb down" the curriculum. They claim that school transformation to outcomes will result in lower standards because not all young people have the same innate ability to learn and achieve at high standards.

Outcome-based education will cost more, much more. Teachers will have to be retrained, curricula revised, and new tests developed to take the place of traditional tests. Critics suggest that these monies could be better used elsewhere.

⚔ Educational Standards

Raising educational standards shows up on almost all polls of the public's chief education concerns. Indeed, the call for raising standards has been taken up by the president, governors, state representatives, mayors, and city councils (Berlak, 1999). Education leaders at every level are developing standards to specify what students should know and be able to do in key subject areas. Oklahoma, for example, has established Priority Assessment Student Skills (PASS) for each grade level. These standards outline exactly what students should know and/or be able to do as a result of schooling. As such, Oklahoma teachers must link instruction to the PASS outcomes.

It is suggested that the establishment of standards is essential to correct the educational ills of this nation. The plan advocated widely by politicians and now being actively pursued by both state and federal governments is the establishment of educational standards that are linked to appropriate testing.

But don't we already have standards in education? In most instances we do. They have been established by textbook publishers and test constructors.

Web Search: Educational Standards

Access the following Internet URL site: **http://putwest.boces.org/standards.html.** Analyze the educational standards for your state and for your subject area. Are they useful for improving teaching and learning? Can they be used to enhance the opportunity to learn? Will the standards lead to higher student achievement? Share your conclusions with the class.

Unless standards have been established by the state or the subject area, publishers and test constructors will continue to determine what students should know and be able to do and the skill level for mastery. Has your state or subject area established standards that you should follow as a teacher? Complete Web Search: Educational Standards to answer this question.

This completes our brief discussion of outcome-based education and educational standards. Complete Task 4.5 to check your understanding of these topics.

T A S K   4 . 5

Outcome-Based Education and Standards

Respond to the following items. Check your responses with those given at the end of the chapter.

1. How does quality differ between traditional educational practices and outcome-based education?

   _____

   _____

2. Outcome-based education models put emphasis on _____,
   _____ , and _____ .

3. Four criticisms often voiced against outcome-based education are the following:

   a. _____

   b. _____

   c. _____

   d. _____

4. The plan often advocated by politicians to solve educational problems is to _____
   _____ .

Analysis and Reflections

Some critics claim that outcome-based education often focuses on the teaching of values. What are your thoughts relative to this claim? Write a short paper expressing your thoughts and submit it to your instructor.

Summary

- Stating objectives is one of the most crucial components of the planning process. They specify what your students should know and be able to do following instruction.
- Objectives should be stated in terms of terminal student behaviors that are overt and observable.

Value of Objectives

- Objectives dictate, to a large extent, your teaching approach. They demand certain learning environments and activity sequences.
- Objectives help establish an evaluation framework.

Goal and Objective Specificity

- Specification of learning intent varies from extremely broad educational goals to very narrow, specific objectives. The three levels of learning intent, in order of specificity, are educational goals, informational objectives, and instructional objectives.
- The more specific objectives should be subordinate to major educational goals.

Educational Goals

- The behaviors called for by educational goals are covert. The behaviors called for by informational and instructional objectives are overt.
- Educational goals and objectives may be written for the cognitive, affective, and psychomotor domains of learning.

Covert Versus Overt Behavior

- The purpose of schooling is to produce learning. Students should act differently after instruction.
- The change in students can be covert (not easily observed) or overt (observable).

Well-Stated Objectives

- Well-stated instructional objectives consist of four components: the performance, the product, the conditions, and the criterion.

Informational and Instructional Objectives

- Informational objectives specify only the performance and the product; the conditions and the criterion are usually not specified. Informational objectives usually suffice for communicating learning intent.

Classification of Objectives

- There are three major categories or domains of learning: the cognitive, the affective, and the psychomotor. Each domain is arranged in hierarchical order from simple to complex.
- The three domains of learning are interrelated.

Domain Taxonomies

- Objectives can be written at any of the levels within the three domains of learning. However, teachers tend to write objectives at only the lower levels.

- Mager suggests it is a waste of time writing objectives at all levels of the domains. The proper level will be written when a suitable analysis of instructional intent is carried out.

Communication of Objectives
- You should always communicate objectives to students. This communication can be in either verbal or written form.
- The communication of objectives should not have as an intent to limit learning only to those areas specified in objectives. Objectives are intended only to provide a minimum level of learning.

Outcome-Based Education
- Traditional education practices center on "inputs." Outcome-based education focuses on "outputs."
- There is no single, authoritative model for outcome-based education.
- Outcome-based education has drawn intense criticism. Many people on the right vehemently oppose outcome-based education.

Educational Standards
- Raising educational standards is one of the chief concerns of the public. The call for higher standards has been taken up by state and national politicians.
- The plan is to link established standards with appropriate testing.
- Today's standards have been established by textbook publishers and test constructors.

Activities

1. *Analysis of textbook objectives*   Review the teacher's edition of a textbook that lists the unit or chapter objectives for a topic from your area of specialization. Address the following questions in your review.
   a. Are educational goals presented? informational objectives? instructional objectives?
   b. Are objectives written for all three domains of learning?
   c. Are the objectives written at different levels within each of the learning domains?
2. *Writing goals and objectives*   Write an educational goal for an area in your specialization. Now write informational and instructional objectives that tell what students should do to show that the goal has been accomplished.
3. *Writing cognitive, psychomotor, and affective domain objectives*   Write ten cognitive and psychomotor domain objectives for the class of your choice. Make the objectives at various levels of sophistication. Now write five affective domain objectives at various levels for the same class. Submit the objectives to your instructor for analysis.
4. *Outcome-based education*   Outcome-based education has become a national issue. Research its impact on education in your state. Write a short paper on the impact and status of outcome-based education in your state.

Answer Keys

Task 4.1 Identifying Verbs
1. O   2. O   3. O   4. C   5. O   6. C   7. O   8. C   9. O

Task 4.2 Identifying the Components of Well-Stated Objectives
1. <u>Given</u> a <u>set</u> of <u>pictures</u>, the student will be able to ⟨place⟩ the [pictures in proper sequence] with <u>no</u> <u>more</u> <u>than</u> <u>one</u> <u>error</u>.
2. <u>Given</u> the <u>necessary</u> <u>materials</u> <u>and</u> the <u>dimensions</u>, the student will be able to ⟨construct⟩ [a polygon] <u>with</u> <u>all</u> <u>dimensions</u> <u>being</u> <u>within</u> <u>5</u> <u>percent</u>.
3. The student will be able to ⟨identify (select letter)⟩ on a <u>multiple-choice test</u> [the subplots of the poems read in class] with <u>100</u> <u>percent</u> <u>accuracy</u>.
4. <u>After</u> <u>completing</u> a <u>series</u> of <u>Spanish</u> <u>language</u> <u>tapes</u>, the student will be able to ⟨orally recite⟩ a given [Spanish dialogue] with <u>no</u> <u>errors</u> <u>in</u> <u>pronunciation</u>.
5. The student will be able to ⟨write⟩ a [300-word essay] on a given <u>social</u> <u>studies</u> <u>topic</u> with <u>no</u> <u>sentence</u> <u>fragments</u> <u>and</u> <u>no</u> <u>more</u> <u>than</u> <u>two</u> <u>errors</u> <u>in</u> <u>grammar</u>.

Task 4.3 Objective Concepts
1. a. Assists in determining appropriate teaching approach.
   b. Sets framework for evaluation.
   c. Assists in communicating learning intent to students.
2. *False* One should always share objectives with students. It takes the guessing out of learning.
3. a. Educational goals
   b. Informational objectives
   c. Instructional objectives
4. a. *The performance* The action to be carried out by the students.
   b. *The product* The end results of the performance.
   c. *The conditions* The conditions under which the performance will occur.
   d. *The criterion* The acceptable level of performance.
5. *False* Informational objectives usually contain only the performance and the product.

Task 4.4 Identifying the Domains and Taxonomies of Objectives
1. a. P   b. C   c. P   d. A   e. C   f. P   g. A   h. C   i. A   j. C
2. a. *Cognitive domain* This area is concerned with imparting knowledge and with the thinking process.
   b. *Affective domain* This area is concerned with emotional development.
   c. *Psychomotor domain* This area is concerned with the development of physical skills.
3. *True* It would involve thinking at the creation level of the cognitive domain.
4. *False* Accurate performance would indicate that higher-level psychomotor learning had taken place. In fact, accurate performance indicates psychomotor learning at the precision level.

Task 4.5 Outcome-Based Education and Standards
1. Traditional practices define quality in terms of "inputs" while outcome-based education defines quality in terms of "outputs."
2. system level change; observable, measurable outcomes; and a belief that all students can learn
3. a. Schools will inflict values
   b. No evidence OBE works
   c. OBE will "dumb down" curriculum
   d. Too costly
4. establish standards and link them to instruction

Theory and Research

Alberto, P. A., & Troutman, A. C. (1999). *Applied behavior analysis for teachers* (5th ed.). Paramus, NJ: Prentice Hall.

Bradfield-Krieder, P. (1998). Creating a performance-based classroom. *American Secondary Education, 26*(4), 15–21.

Cobb, N. (Ed.). (1994). *The future of education: Perspectives on national standards in America.* New York: College Board Publications.

References

Beane, J. A., Toepfer, C. F., Jr., & Alessi, S. J., Jr. (1986). *Curriculum planning and development.* Boston: Allyn and Bacon.

Berlak, H. (1999). Standards and the control of knowledge. *Rethinking Schools, 13*(3), 1–10.

Bloom, B. S. (Ed.), Engelhart, M. D., Furst, E. J., Hill, W. H., & Krathwohl, D. R. (1956). *Taxonomy of educational objectives, handbook I: Cognitive domain.* New York: David McKay.

Berliner, D. C. (1997). Educational psychology meets the Christian Right: Differing views of children, schooling, teaching, and learning. *Teachers College Record, 98*(3), 381–416.

Glatthorn, A. A. (1993). Outcome-based education: Reform and the curriculum process. *Journal of Curriculum and Supervision, 8*(4), 354–363.

Gronlund, N. E. (1970). *Stating behavioral objectives for classroom instruction.* New York: Macmillan.

Kibler, R. J., Barker, L. L., & Miles, D. T. (1970). *Behavioral objectives and instruction.* Boston: Allyn and Bacon.

Krathwohl, D. R., Bloom, B. S., & Masai, B. B. (1964). *Taxonomy of educational objectives, handbook II: Affective domain.* New York: David McKay.

Kryspin, W. J., & Feldhusen, J. F. (1974). *Writing behavioral objectives.* Minneapolis, MN: Burgess.

Mager, R. F. (1984). *Preparing instructional objectives* (2nd ed.). Belmont, CA: David S. Lake.

McKernan, J. (1993). Some limitations of outcome-based education. *Journal of Curriculum and Supervision, 8*(4), 343–353.

Selecting and Designing Instruction

Objectives

After completing your study of Chapter 5, you should be able to:

1. Identify and describe the three broad hierarchical levels of learning.

2. Define a concept and describe the two kinds of concepts and strategies for teaching and learning concepts at the different levels of difficulty.

3. Define thinking, and differentiate among the various categories of thinking skills.

4. Describe creativity, the four stages of creative thought, and the difficulties that can hinder the creative process.

5. Describe different approaches that can be used in teaching thinking skills and the eight behaviors that exemplify "nonthinking."

6. Describe the different kinds of planning and the various key components associated with each.

7. Differentiate between teacher-centered and student-centered modes of instruction and describe the fifteen different methods associated with these two modes.

8. Describe the four variables that should be considered in the selection of an appropriate instructional method.

9. Differentiate between the traditional and mastery learning models of instruction.

Most elementary and secondary school instruction, both formal and informal, is based on the teaching of facts and concepts. Recently, however, the importance of teaching basic thinking skills has surfaced. Because facts and concept formation set the foundation for higher level thinking processes, thinking skills cannot be taught in isolation (Marzano et al., 1988). Effective teachers plan their teaching around facts and concepts that are important for the development of thinking skills.

The presentations of effective teachers usually appear so spontaneous that no planning is apparent. However, in most cases, these teachers have indeed— formally or informally—carefully planned each daily lesson. They have likely mastered the lesson content and the related teaching skills so well that their delivery is poised, secure, and automatic.

Even experienced teachers spend time replanning the presentation of lessons that they have taught many times. In this way they continue to improve their presentations and avoid becoming stale and routine. However, no amount of planning can ensure success. The way a presentation is delivered counts for a great deal.

✳ Categories of Learning

Learning is hierarchical as shown in Figure 5.1. In general, you can classify learning into three broad hierarchical categories: (1) facts, (2) concepts and principles, and (3) thinking skills.

Category 1 learning represents the learning of verifiable information obtained through observing, experiencing, reading, or listening. This category includes the rote memorization of information and, in some cases, the meaning of the information. There is little teaching strategy involved when facts are taught. The teaching of factual information generally includes the use of "repetitious brute force." That is, the information is rehearsed until learned or students drill or practice the information until it is learned. However, the teacher must also be certain that the terms within the fact are familiar. The learning of factual information can be made more meaningful when embedded in the higher levels of learning.

Category 2 represents the learning of the mental image of the set of characteristics common to any and all examples of a class (concept) or two or more

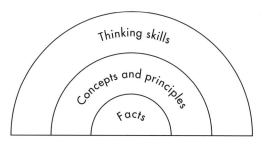

FIGURE 5.1 *Hierarchical Levels of Learning*

related concepts (principles). That is, strategies must be employed that will help learners establish in their minds a mental image (phototype) of the set of characteristics that makes something an example of a concept or principle.

Category 3 is learning to use facts, concepts, and principles in the thinking process. Strategies are provided to give students opportunities to engage in such operations as critical, analytical, and creative thinking. Essentially, it is the building of a repertoire of thinking skills such as explaining, predicting, comparing, generalizing, hypothesizing, and evaluating.

The teaching of facts, concepts, and thinking skills now entails a substantial portion of all elementary and secondary school instruction. The focus is on helping students understand their world and become responsible individuals with effective problem-solving skills. Let us now consider concept and thinking skills instruction in more detail.

⚔ Teaching Concepts

A **concept** is a category to which a set of objects, conditions, events, or processes can be grouped based on some similarities that they have in common. This category of things is then represented by a single symbol. Thus, concepts can be thought of as definitions. They mean what they mean because it is defined in a given way. For example, if several people were asked to explain the concept of a *tree*, the descriptions would be different in some respects, but all would have similar elements that we associate with "treeness." Basically the descriptions would be based on the individuals' experiences with trees. However, a tree can be defined in terms of the essential characteristics and can be represented by the symbol "tree." The list of concepts taught in schools is virtually endless, but additional illustrative examples of concepts include:

noun	*triangle*	*living organism*
democrat	*verb*	*car*
frog	*psychology*	*city*
library	*mammal*	*base*
government	*fascism*	*numeral*
student	*war*	*party*

This list of examples reveals that some concepts, such as *frog, car,* and *verb,* are simple and can be taught to young children, while others like *fascism, war,* and *democrat* require advanced and more sophisticated learners.

Concepts give meaning and order to our world. They enrich our psychological world. Basically, concepts benefit us in three ways. First, they reduce the complexity of learning tasks. Second, they give us a means to communicate with each other. Third, they help us better understand our environment.

Categorizing helps us to organize and relate information. For example, once we have learned what a bird is, we do not have to form a new category for each bird we encounter. We simply need to determine whether or not it has certain identifying characteristics and when it does we add it to the bird category.

Concepts speed up and make communication more efficient. Because people share similar concepts, they need not explain in great detail every object, event, or idea. Schooling and experience help us build new concepts on the pre-ceding ones which leads to better communication. Thus, when culturally diverse individuals understand the concepts associated with each other's cultures, communication is enhanced.

Our environment is very complex. Concept formation helps us function better in this environment. For example, some concepts, such as *table, airplane,* and *car,* are acquired for their functional value to us. Others, such as *algebra, shorthand,* and *drafting,* are acquired because they will be useful in the future.

Concept Learning

Concepts are abstractions. They can be categorized into two kinds: abstractions derived from concrete objects such as *table, rain, bird, car,* or *house;* and abstractions derived from conditions or processes such as *angry, verb, noise, music,* or *cold.* The learning process for the different abstractions can be quite different. Indeed, some concepts are learned through informal situations while others are learned through some type of systematic situation. Figure 5.2 presents a simple continuum of the formality that might occur for individuals in learning concepts.

Concepts are generally learned in one of two ways. The learning of object concepts such as *rock, chair,* or *car* can usually be accomplished through a classification process of finding the essential characteristics that define the concept, while the initial understanding of condition or process concepts such as *cold, noise,* or *freedom* requires some type of direct experience.

Many simple concepts, such as *horse* and *blue,* can be taught through observation and association. Many of these simple concepts are learned outside of school. For example, a child learns the concept *bicycle* by hearing certain objects referred to as *bicycles.* Initially, the child may include motorcycles or tricycles or other toys with wheels in the concept category of *bicycle,* but with time and experience, the concept is refined until the child can differentiate between *bicycle* and *nonbicycle.* In a similar way, the child learns the more difficult concepts of *happy, naughty, dirty,* and *fun* through observation and associations.

The more abstract concepts, such as *aunt* or *square root,* are typically learned through definitions and verbal explanations that involve more basic concepts. For example, an extremely difficult concept such as *aunt* is almost impossible to teach through observation and association alone. Children could make hundreds of observations of *aunts* and *nonaunts* and still not understand

Learning the concept *storm*	Learning the concept *fire fighter*	Learning the concept *longitude*
●————————————————————● ————————————————————●
Mainly informal learning	Partial informal partial systematic learning	Mainly systematic learning

FIGURE 5.2 *Formality of Concept Learning*

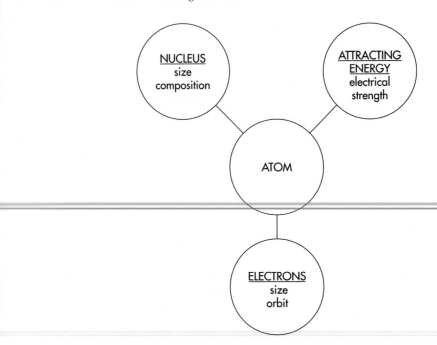

FIGURE 5.3   *Simple Web for Study of an Atom*

the concept of *aunt*. In this case, the concept is best taught by definition and verbal explanation after the child understands more basic concepts, such as *mother, father,* and *sister*. Following a definition and verbal explanation, instances and noninstances of *aunt* can be more readily differentiated. Finally, after the instances and noninstances, the definition and verbal explanation leads to even better understanding. Still more complex abstractions, such as *goodness* and *beauty,* may require a complex verbal explanation and the presentation of many positive and negative examples.

Diagrams, mappings, and webbings can often be employed as visual examples of abstract concepts. They can also aid the teacher in analyzing the concept for instructional decisions. Figure 5.3 offers a simple example of a webbing. The web is nothing more than a visual representation of a concept.

The writing of Lev Vygotsky (1978), a Russian psychologist, focused heavily on a social aspect to learning. He theorized that most human learning results from inner thoughts and interactions between people, both adult–child and child–child. Research on the social aspects of learning support the important role that verbal interaction can play in helping students learn.

An important concept resulting from Vygotsky's work is the notion of scaffolding. Scaffolding refers to the instructional support given to students to perform a skill. Teachers can provide instructional scaffolding in a number of ways, including summarizing main ideas, breaking complex skills into subcomponents, adjusting the difficulty of questions, providing examples and nonexamples, and offering prompts and cues. If necessary, teachers might provide additional scaffolding in the form of skeletal notes, study guides, or partial outlines.

Planning for Concept Teaching

Strategies employed to teach concepts will generally depend on their level of difficulty. According to Tennyson (1978), concepts are most efficiently learned when learners are provided with examples and a definition. Thus, teaching concepts can be simple or it can be very difficult depending on how difficult it is to illustrate the concept. Students may be given examples and nonexamples of a concept and later be asked to generate or infer a definition. Concepts can also be taught by giving students a definition and then asking them to give instances and noninstances. The first is called an inductive approach and the latter a deductive approach. Since both approaches can be used effectively, teachers should be skilled in the use of both.

The goal of the inductive approach is to provide direct experience to help students understand a concept. Although there are a number of variations of inductive concept teaching, they all involve presenting positive and negative examples with follow-up questions asking students to analyze and figure out how the positive examples are similar and how they are different from the negative examples. This procedure is generally time-consuming and sometimes results in digressions. However, inductive lessons often result in more incidental learning, greater motivation, and better time on-task.

The primary goal in using the deductive approach is to help the learner understand the concept by linking its definition to real-life examples. The essence of deductive-type lessons is for the teacher to first present a definition and then link subsequent examples to the definition. It closely parallels the process of deductive reasoning.

While there are relative merits associated with the inductive and deductive teaching approaches, no categorical claims for the superiority of either approach can be made for classroom instruction. Both approaches have a place in providing contrast for learning concepts. Some concepts lend themselves to being taught through the inductive approach, while others are best taught through the deductive approach. For the more complex concepts taught in schools, it is usually more advisable to state a definition, present several instances (and, if appropriate, noninstances), and then restate the definition, showing how the instances typify the definition. This latter pattern is often referred to as the *rule-example-rule* approach.

Eggen, Kauchak, & Harder (1979), on the other hand, maintain that concepts consist of four elements: (1) a concept name or label, (2) a definition, (3) examples and nonexamples, and (4) relevant and irrelevant attributes. They further suggest that any concept lesson should include all four components.

The verbal label or name, such as *boat* or *justice,* that identifies a concept is not the same as the concept itself. The label or name is important only for the purpose of communication but is entirely arbitrary. Knowing the label or name does not guarantee an understanding of the concept.

A definition gives clarity to the concept. It is a statement of the concept's defining attributes.

A concept will have distinctive features that define the concept. Indeed, as noted earlier, each concept will be represented by a prototype, a typical or standard example. An understanding of the essential characteristics of the prototype is a critical dimension of concept learning. Thus, certain examples of a concept may be more typical than others. Robins, for example, are viewed as more typical birds than are ostriches and penguins. In other words, whether an object, event, or idea fits into a concept category or not is a matter of degree.

Examples are important in teaching concepts. More examples are needed when teaching complex concepts and when working with less sophisticated learners. Indeed, examples and nonexamples (sometimes referred to as positive and negative instances) are usually used to make the concept boundaries clear. The examples should be chosen to develop students' understanding of the wide range of possibilities the concept includes. A good example will include the important characteristics or features of the concept. The learner must be able to see the characteristics or features of the concept in the examples. The nonexamples should be very close to the essential attributes of the concept but lacking in a few critical attributes.

Once students have learned facts, concepts, and related principles, what do they do with them? Another important goal of teaching is to help students manipulate these facts, concepts, and principles in order to develop and use various thinking skills.

❖ Teaching Thinking Skills

One of the primary purposes of education is to provide students with a sound education in basic concepts. A complete education, however, must also focus on those thinking skills that will enable students to be responsible and to be effective problem solvers.

Research (Sadler & Whimbey, 1985) has led many educators to suggest that **thinking skills** are the basis on which all other skills are developed. That is, a command of thinking skills required for remembering information, incorporating knowledge, learning and using motor skills, and developing values and attitudes is necessary if students are to successfully develop the skills necessary to become responsible, productive citizens. Many of these skills are generic and can be taught as general learning strategies, without reference to content. Furthermore, the research findings tend to confirm that when thinking skills become an integral part of the curriculum and instructional practice, test scores in academic areas increase.

It is generally agreed that students must assume much of the responsibility for developing desired thinking skills. They must take an active role in the learning process, but the teacher must provide opportunities for using thinking skills and not inhibit such activity.

Since responsibility is essential to the functioning of the broader dimensions of thinking, a brief look at this core thinking skill seems in order.

Responsibility

One of the primary functions of education is the development of a society of social and self-responsible individuals; in other words, to develop in people a state of being not only accountable or answerable for their actions, but able to meet obligations or act without direct guidance.

Teachers should help students develop responsible ways of thinking, believing, and acting. The goal is not to indoctrinate students, but to provide a climate of thoughtful examination where wise convictions regarding responsibility can be formed. A climate of responsibility will have six important characteristics:

1. It will be concerned with communication. It will inspire students to hold positive visions of their abilities. That is, it helps students foster the belief that they can be successful thinkers, problem solvers, and creators. Using different teaching and learning styles along with improved communication with students will help individual students find the styles that work well for them. Helping students become aware of their own learning styles can benefit them in dealing with the demands of critical and creative thinking. Thus, they are better able to take responsibility for their own learning and are better able to see new perspectives and increase their tolerance for each other's differences.
2. Nothing succeeds like success. Thus, the law of effect is used effectively in a responsible climate. Students tend to repeat those experiences that have proven satisfying. When new skills are tried and are quickly learned, the sky is often the limit on what they can and will do.
3. Teachers are the classroom models of responsibility. They should model and guide students in the formation of thinking skills. Students should be asked to duplicate observed responsible behaviors.
4. Responsible climates should be active not passive. Students should be part of the decision-making process. They should be provided experiences that will give them opportunities for testing their ideas and weighing the different options available to them.
5. A responsible climate provides experiences through which students make connections between what they learn and how it can be used in the thinking process. Too often students see no connection between what they must learn and how it can be used. Experiences must be provided that will show that learning is useful for decision making, that education means developing the capacity for making judgments and forming convictions.
6. Management of a classroom can be overwhelming, but remains the responsibility of the teacher. However, students can share some of the responsibilities.

You should convey to your students that you view them as responsible persons and help them view themselves as successful thinkers. So, you should nurture different ways in thinking, believing, and acting. Help students develop the vital sense of responsibility for their own accomplishments and capacity for finding solutions to complex problems.

Thinking Skills

What are thinking skills? How do you go about teaching them? Since all cognitive acts require thinking, these are difficult questions to answer. Indeed, there are as many definitions of **thinking** and ways to teach them as there are thinkers. While it is true that all cognitive acts require thinking, it is important to distinguish between the ability to simply reproduce memorized information and the ability to generate new information through the use of higher thinking skills. Most educators believe that it is possible to teach students the thinking skills that will enable them to produce the creative thoughts that lead to finding solutions to problems. Moreover, these educators view "thinking" as being more than the mere replication of information. In a 1990 Association for Supervision and Curriculum Development (ASCD) video, for example, David Perkins of Harvard University says that thinking is "problem solving, it's decision making, reading, reflecting, making predictions about what might happen." On the other hand, Ernest Boyer, president of the Carnegie Foundation, suggests that thinking cannot be separated from good language. Finally, Webster's Twentieth Century Dictionary, Unabridged, Second Edition, defines thinking as "a bringing of intellectual faculties into play; of making decisions, and the drawing of inferences; it is to perform any mental operation, or to reason, judge, conclude, to choose, hold an opinion, to believe, or to purpose, or to muse over, to mediate, to ponder, to reflect, or to weigh a matter mentally." While the different views of the operation of thinking have merit, it seems important to establish that there are many areas to approach in the teaching of thinking. For our purposes, however, we will define *thinking* as the act of withholding judgment in order to use past knowledge and experience to find new information, concepts, or conclusions. Let us now look at the different types of thinking in detail.

Categories of Thinking

What thinking skills are appropriate for your class? Your first task is to answer this question. In doing so, the maturity level of students along with the special needs of your content subject must be considered. It is usually better to teach a few skills well and thoroughly rather than many skills superficially.

Bloom's Taxonomy offers a guide to the various thinking levels that can be developed in the classroom. Thus, instruction can be provided at six levels of thinking: knowledge, comprehension, application, analysis, synthesis, and evaluation.

At the knowledge level, thinking tasks generally require that students manipulate key facts. Students are asked to be attentive to information, to repeat memorized information, to recite facts such as math rules and formulas. Activities that ask students to recite, recognize, practice drills, or identify concepts represent a few knowledge-level thinking tasks.

At the comprehension level, students translate, interpret, or explain given information. Comprehension-thinking tasks might involve interpreting graphs or diagrams or decoding words. Because students are not required to come up with new information, knowledge and comprehension levels are not representative of the higher-order thinking-skill levels. Instead, they are called on to translate the information that has been given.

Students at the application level can apply known information. They can think and decide how information can be applied to situations other than those presented. For example, students could be asked to transfer known skills to another area in solving a problem or to solve equations by applying a correct formula.

Students must think about how to divide a whole into component elements at the analysis level. This can include finding relationships between the parts to the whole concept and making comparisons. Students can be required to break down complex information or ideas into simpler parts, to identify the underlying structure of complex ideas or information, and to compare similarities and differences at this level.

Synthesis-level thinking requires that students take parts of previously learned information and create completely new products, or wholes. Inductive and deductive thinking and reasoning are included in this category. With inductive thinking, students are provided instances and noninstances and then asked to use thinking skills to develop concepts. Conversely, students using deductive thinking are given definitions and are asked to provide instances and noninstances relative to the concepts. Hypothesizing, predicting, and concluding are examples of deductive thinking.

Finally, at the evaluation level, thinking tasks include those in which students judge quality, credibility, worth, or practicality. Students are asked to provide evidence, logic, or values in support of their conclusions. Evaluation-level thinking also demands that students use all the previous levels of thinking. The key to this level is students' ability to withhold judgments until they are able to explain the logic or provide the evidence in support of their judgments.

Critical Thinking

Critical thinking is not the same as intelligence. It is a skill that can be improved in everyone (Walsh & Paul, 1988, p. 13). Moreover, educators differentiate between ordinary thinking and critical thinking (Meltzer & Palau, 1996). According to Lipman (1988), critical thinking is more complex than ordinary thinking. Also, ordinary thinking is usually simple and lacks standards, while critical thinking is based on standards of objectivity and consistency. Lipman further suggests that students must be taught to change their thinking (1) from guessing to estimating, (2) from preferring to evaluating, (3) from grouping to classifying, (4) from believing to assuming, (5) from inferring to inferring logically, (6) from associating concepts to grasping principles, (7) from noting relationships to noting relationships among relationships, (8) from supposing to hypothesizing, (9) from offering opinions without reasons to offering opinions with reasons, and (10) from making judgments without criteria to making judgments with criteria. Possible critical thinking questions could include "Can human beings live on Venus?," "Should we eliminate free public school education in the United States?," or "Why do you think such a high level of poverty exists in some parts of this country?"

Critical thinking generally requires higher levels of thinking; that is, more evaluation and synthesis than application or analysis. Indeed, it should be remembered that evaluation-level operations require use of the previous thinking levels as well.

Creative Thinking

All persons have the potential for creative thinking. It occurs as the result of learning beyond the gathering of rote information. However, before we can decide how we can develop creativity, we must decide what, exactly, is creativity.

Whenever a person assembles information to discover something not previously taught or understood, some degree of creativity is being used. For example, this may be the discovery of a new unknown relationship between two unlike concepts. This concept of creative thinking is often associated with creative thinking as a process.

When the result of creativity is the production of a new invention theory, the idea of creativity as a product is being embraced. This type of creative thinking usually results in the realization of an original concept. For example, the creation of a poem, a song, a game, or some unusual use for a common item.

Creative thinking is often equated with curiosity, imagination, discovery, and invention. Even though it is not possible for one person to teach another person these attributes, it is possible to provide activities that will enhance opportunities for thinking.

Creative thinking can be thought of as putting together information to come up with a new understanding, concept, or idea. Asking students to create a short story using given components, to devise techniques for improving the mathematics grades of the class, or to formulate inferences as to why a certain chemical reaction takes place represent creative thinking tasks. Generally there are four stages to the development of creative thought: preparation, incubation, illumination, and verification. These stages can be viewed as a ladder (Figure 5.4) that must be climbed one level at a time. A variety of thinking skills are used

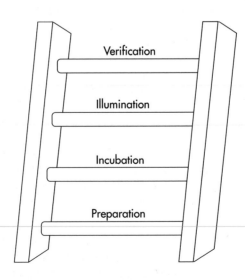

FIGURE 5.4   *Levels of Creative Thinking*

during each of these stages of the creative process. In fact, the greater the thinking flexibility at each stage, the greater the possibility for creative thinking.

The first stage, preparation, requires that creative thinkers collect information and examine it using many of the thinking processes previously mentioned. Creative thinkers will question and investigate until major relationships are found between events, objects, or ideas. The forming of a hypothesis of some sort in the thinker's mind, which causes the individual to ponder and meditate in a questioning manner, forms the second stage of creative thought, incubation. Sometimes an individual will spend quite some time allowing images from the subconscious to surface. At other times, this stage may be short-lived, moving the creative thinker into the "I've got it" or illumination stage. At this stage, the individual gains confidence in answering the initial questions and regains some degree of equilibrium, which can be followed by new questioning. Finally, the individual will seek out ways of verifying and testing the idea. This is called the stage of verification.

Creative persons have expressed frustration and disconcerting feelings while struggling with a puzzling concept that later led them to a discovery. Difficulties often encountered that hinder the creative process include the following (Torrance, 1983).

1.   Difficulty in finding the right words for describing original images is one of the frequently reported frustrations given by creative thinkers. Sometimes the images are too complex to be put into words.
2.   Inability to permit themselves to "let go" in childlike play even momentarily on a problem. The ability to relax, manipulate, and play with new ideas is an important characteristic of creative thought.
3.   Although analysis is often helpful during the early stages of creativity, synthesis is necessary in the full development of new, original ideas. A common mistake often made that can hinder creative thinking is a tendency to analyze rather than synthesize.
4.   Sometimes creative thinkers create "thinking blocks" which hinder consideration of possible solutions. These "thinking blocks" result from a tendency to synthesize before analysis of the facts is complete.
5.   Many creative individuals have communicated fears of expressing new ideas they were generating in their own minds. In effect, they are afraid to let others see their inventions and fear that their ideas will not be appreciated by others.
6.   Creative thinkers frequently complain that they get too many ideas at one time. This flood of ideas becomes a form of stress and gives the individual an "avalanche effect." Successful completion of one or more of these ideas will require the thinker to focus on what is needed for the moment rather than on all of the ideas.

If you can help students confront and overcome the above cited difficulties, they can be given opportunities for creative successes in the classroom. Moreover, you should avoid judging students' creative endeavors and provide support and encouragement for their attempts.

Thinking-Skills Instruction

Teaching thinking skills requires that you be open-minded. You must be willing to turn over every rock of information, explore every avenue of learning. You must be willing to question, take risks, and explore, otherwise, how can you lead others through the same processes?

Should you teach thinking skills separately or infuse them into the content being taught? Some suggest that you teach thinking skills by selecting and implementing only a few individual lessons, which focus on particular skills. Then, as students gain experience and confidence, you should consider extending the emphasis on thinking skills and integrate these skills into your content area. Conversely, others will argue that thinking skills should be infused directly into the content being taught. There are pros and cons to the separate and infusion approaches. Advocates of the separate approach maintain that thinking skills are similar to reading and writing in that they are enabling disciplines and deserve separate instruction (Lipman, 1988, p. 143). Conversely, those favoring the infusion approach feel that certain cognitive skills are specific to particular disciplines and should be taught in context (Ashton, 1988, p. 4). Therefore, perhaps the answer to this controversy is to use the separate instructional approach along with the infusion approach. Let's look at these two approaches in more detail.

The Separate Approach   Reuven Voyerstein (ASCD, 1990) points out that students sometimes lack the basic skills and abilities for seeing relationships or comparisons between ideas. He suggests that these students need separate instruction on thinking skills, that is, programs that focus on instruction on specific skills. Because of the difficulty for students who are unfamiliar with a skill to focus on the learning of a new skill and on learning of content at the same time, many educators prefer this separate approach when introducing a new skill.

Modeling is an important aspect of the separate approach. Indeed, you should always begin the teaching of a skill by modeling it when using the separate approach. When teaching students about problem solving, for example, you should demonstrate the skill by doing a whole class problem-solving activity. Although you may demonstrate how to solve problems, you would be wise to create a thinking exercise wherein students' answers diverge. Guidance can be provided, for instance, by presenting the steps that are followed on the overhead projector or chalkboard. For example:

1. Identify the problem and write a problem statement.
2. Develop possible solutions and propose testable hypotheses.
3. Collect applicable data.
4. Analyze and interpret data.
5. Obtain new data and test conclusions.

You should ask for whole class responses to each of these steps, which in turn will demonstrate that there are usually several correct responses to the problem-solving steps. Class input is one of the most important aspects of teaching problem solving as a thinking skill. As students make suggestions and learn to use the problem-solving steps, you need to gradually release responsibility to students by allowing them to arrive at answers. Afterward, students should give explanations to the logic that led to their answers. Once the initial practice has been carried out with the group, you should provide students an opportunity for practicing the skill on their own so their understanding of the skill modeled can be evaluated.

The Infusion Approach   The infusion approach calls for instruction of desired skills in conjunction with the regular school curriculum. In effect, the infusion approach requires that students transfer newly acquired skills to the regular content being studied. If you are teaching students the skill of problem solving, for example, after the skill has been taught, it would be applied to the regular curriculum. That is, once students are taught to solve problems through introductory activities, they are asked to apply problem solving to the content being studied. If necessary, direct them toward problems in your content area that need to be solved. Once another problem has been established, go through the whole class collaboration steps once again—using the skill in this new context. Afterward, the procedure of infusing the thinking skill into your content needs can be finalized by assigning students a problem situation in your content area in which they may apply the skill.

Thinking-Skills Activities

Direct and specific instruction is often useful in teaching thinking. Direct and specific instruction can be used to assist students in dealing with assumptions so that a more open-minded attitude toward new modes of thinking can be developed. Such instruction is needed for dismantling those truths our society has outgrown; for example, previously held conceptions about AIDS, racism, and sexism.

An important aspect of teaching thinking is the modeling of the open-minded attitude you hope to foster. This may not be possible if you are a dictator of your most comfortable ways of thinking and behaving. Indeed, you must provide opportunities for students to think about their views and the views of others. However, you must be sure to let students make final decisions. Without this atmosphere of respect for students as thinkers, it is impossible to model the concepts you desire to teach.

Having students work in small groups with a list of "loaded" statements is one good way of providing opportunities for students to examine assumptions (Verduin, 1996). The following statements are examples of loaded questions.

1. When we hear someone has AIDS, what do we generally think?
2. When we see a person who is wearing dirty, shabby clothes, what assumptions might we make about him or her?
3. When we see a picture of a movie star, what assumptions might we make about his or her lifestyle?

4. When we see a classmate get an F on his or her semester test, what assumptions might we make about him or her?

5. When we see an African American person running for the presidency of the United States, what assumptions might we have about his or her abilities?

The groups must gather responses to such statements from each member and then report their areas of agreement and disagreement during whole class discussions.

Raths, Wassermann, Jonas & Rothstein (1986) purport that classroom teachers frequently report the existence of eight nonthinking behaviors. These eight behaviors will have a negative impact on the development of thinking skills. As such, you must learn to diagnose and prescribe thinking activities that will enable your students to overcome the following nonthinking behaviors.

1. *Impulsiveness*   These students do not take time to consider the problem or alternatives. They try to respond before the question is completed. In effect, they "jump the gun" without adequate thought. These students often fail to consider consequences of their inferences, hypotheses, or decisions. They think, but blurt out answers without having enough information, or they impulsively base decisions on the first thoughts that enter their minds.

2. *Overdependence on the teacher*   Some students will raise their hands as soon as the teacher finishes explaining the assignment and assigns the independent seatwork. These students won't try the assignment, but rather say, "I don't understand this," before even attempting to follow the instructions. These students fail to pay attention during instruction and insist that the teacher provide individual instruction at their desks.

3. *Inattentive behavior*   These students don't stay on-task. They need constant prompting; their attention span is short and their attention constantly wanders. These students demonstrate a lack of self-motivation and rarely finish assignments.

4. *Restless rusher*   Restless rushers get very little meaning out of assigned tasks. They rush through their work and concentrate only on turning in the assignment. These students will finish their work first, but it will lack accuracy. When questioned about their assignments, they may reply, "I don't know." If the student is asked to redo the work he or she usually rushes through just as quickly the second time. These students differ from your impulsive students in that they will concentrate only on turning in the work, rather than basing their responses on past or similar experiences and jumping the gun as impulsive students will do.

5. *Dogmatic, assertive behavior*   Dogmatic students fail to consider others' points of view. They think their perceptions are the only correct ones. They see no reason for considering or listening for other possibilities because their views are already perfect.

6. *Rigidity, inflexibility of behavior*   These students are reluctant to use new strategies. They often fear giving up old strategies that have worked for them in the past, even when they prove inadequate in the new situation.

7. *Fearful, lack of confidence*   These students lack confidence in their own thinking and rarely respond to questions that require anything other than one right answer! They are reluctant to express their own views and opinions. These students are afraid to express themselves when asked to answer a question that calls for higher-order thinking skills or to voice their thoughts during a brainstorming activity.

8. *Responsibility forfeiture*   These students are afraid of taking risks or assuming responsibility. They want the teacher to provide one right way of accomplishing all learning tasks. These students are often grade-conscious individuals who frequently approach their teachers for specific guidelines. In doing so, they obligate the teacher and shift responsibility to the teacher and relieve themselves from thinking for themselves.

Often you will need to prescribe thinking activities that will alter the behaviors cited above and promote self-confidence. Brainstorming, flexible thinking, forecasting, inductive thinking, making inferences, logical thinking, deductive thinking, problem solving, and decision-making activities, for example, can often be used to foster thinking skills and correct faulty thinking habits. Complete Web Search: Thinking Skills to generate additional thinking-skills activities.

Once you decide what to teach, you must then decide how to teach it. Thus, planning is often the key to good teaching. However, before we look at the planning process, complete Task 5.1 to check your understanding of the material presented up to this point.

⚔ Planning Instruction

As shown in Figure 5.5, teachers engage in various levels of **planning.** Course and unit planning has much greater scope than weekly and daily planning. Your course and unit plans give the more specific daily plans their direction and determine in a general way what the impact of the entire curriculum will be.

No matter what your level of planning, decisions must be made with respect to student grouping, instructional materials, and the special needs of students. Therefore, before we look at the levels of planning in greater detail, let us focus our discussion on grouping for instruction, selecting instructional materials, and making provisions for students who have special needs.

Web Search: Thinking Skills

Conduct web searches relative to thinking-skills activities using search engine sites **http://www.altavista.com** and **http://www.yahoo.com** for the subject and grade level you plan to teach. Write brief descriptions of the appropriate activities. Share your descriptions with the class. Initiate a resource file and add these activities to your file.

T A S K   5 . 1

What to Teach

Respond to the following items. Check your responses with those given at the end of the chapter.

1. Describe the three broad categories of learning.

   a. _____

   _____

   b. _____

   _____

   c. _____

   _____

2. Define concept: _____

   _____

3. Concepts are abstractions that are derived from object concepts or conditions or processes.   (True/False)

4. When students are given instances and noninstances of a concept and then asked to analyze and figure out how the positive instances are similar and how they differ from the noninstances, the _____ approach is being used.

5. Define thinking: _____

   _____

6. Creativity can be viewed as a _____ or a _____ .

7. The teaching of thinking skills can take place through the _____

   or _____ approach.

8. Thinking skills are best taught through the use of open-ended activities. (True/False)

Analysis and Reflection

The teaching of thinking skills is becoming more important in our schools. Write a couple of paragraphs on how important it will be to teach thinking at the grade level you plan to teach. Submit your reflections to your instructor.

Grouping for Instruction

Organizing students into homogeneous classes or groups often makes the instructional process much easier (Tice, 1997). Probably the most common means of grouping students is to assign them to classes or groups according to an established criterion such as ability, interest, or skill. Basically this grouping can take place in two ways: between classes and within classes.

Course plans	General
Unit plans	
Weekly lesson plans	↓
Daily lesson plans	Specific

FIGURE 5.5   *Levels of Planning*

Between-Class Grouping   The formation of separate classes to which students are assigned on the basis of established criteria is called **between-class grouping.** For example, separate English classes can be formed for low-, middle-, and high-ability English students. Between-class grouping may take many forms. At the elementary level, for instance, students are normally assigned to a single, self-contained classroom, but they may be assigned to specific classrooms on the basis of reading ability, mathematics ability, and so on (Lemlech, 1997). On the other hand, in some middle schools, seventh grade high-ability students may be assigned to 7-1 classes, seventh grade average-ability students to 7-2 classes, and seventh grade low-ability students to 7-3 classes. In high schools, students may be "tracked" (assigned) into "college preparatory" courses or to a "general" track depending on their measured ability. Because of scheduling considerations, students are sometimes assigned to specific classes on the basis of their involvement in special activities such as athletics.

Special classes are often formed for students outside the normal range of individual differences. For example, many schools have special classes for students with serious learning problems or for students who are academically gifted and talented. Indeed, some districts are developing special schools, called **magnet schools,** which focus on special themes or curriculum areas. For example, one magnet school may focus on mathematics and science, while another may focus on music and the performing arts.

While between-class grouping has been used widely and with some success with better students, research (Good & Marshall, 1984; Oakes, 1985; Rosenbaum, 1980) does not support its use with poorer students. One reason for this is that poorer teachers tend to be assigned to lower-ability classes. For example, teachers of poorer students are often less organized and less enthusiastic, and they tend to emphasize the learning of facts. Moreover, most teachers do not like to teach low-ability students and tend to communicate low expectations for such students. Finally, perhaps the most damaging effect of between-class grouping is the negative messages it can communicate to poorer students. In short, students in lower tracks often feel humiliated and believe that they are the school "dummies."

Despite criticism about between-class grouping, teachers generally support its use because teaching homogeneous groups is comparatively easy. However, it is recommended that whenever possible heterogeneous grouping be used since it has proven beneficial to most students at all grade levels (Goodlad, 1984; Oakes, 1985).

Within-Class Grouping   The second means of adapting instruction to student differences is through within-class grouping. **Within-class grouping** calls for the formation of groups within a classroom to accommodate student differences. For example, science groups may be formed on the basis of interest in working on class projects. Within-class grouping is far more common at the elementary level than at the secondary. Indeed, grouping for reading, and frequently for mathematics, is almost universal at the elementary level. For instance, a second-grade teacher may create ability or interest groups with names such as "Bluebirds," "Stars," and "Rockets" and may have each group use a different reader. Teachers who form mathematics groups may use a different textbook with each of several groups, or may teach one lesson to the whole class and then work with individual groups while the others are doing seatwork.

At the secondary level, within-class grouping generally involves small-group activities. Examples include buzz groups, brainstorming groups, and task groups. The particular type of group used should be related to the lesson goals and objective. *Brainstorming,* for example, is a small-group activity used to generate ideas. The topics can be as simple as "What would be a good class project?" or as complex as "What can we do about the low class test grades?" All reasonable suggestions are accepted as possible solutions, and brainstorming usually results in a mood of delightful quest. *Buzz groups,* on the other hand, are work groups of relatively short duration. Such groups are established quickly and maintained for a short period of time, and their purpose is to share opinions, viewpoints, or reactions. Finally, *task groups* are used to solve problems or to complete assigned projects. Task groups are unlike other group activities in that they involve students in some kind of work and in that each group member has a role or assignment which is clearly defined to all group members.

Small-group instruction in the secondary school has several strengths, including the development of communication skills, leadership abilities, open-mindedness, persuasive arguing, and other interpersonal skills. In addition, the direct involvement offered by small-group work often leads to a stronger sense of personal commitment to group decisions than is the case with whole class or individual decisions. Finally, students involved in small-group work are usually given valuable opportunities for active verbal participation and, in some cases, for physical movement.

Secondary small-group instruction also has its limitations. One of the primary problems is the tendency for students to drift off-task quite quickly, with the result that the activity often disintegrates into wasteful bickering. Another problem is that the composition of groups sometimes leads to problems, as when students with very different viewpoints, backgrounds, or interests find it difficult to work together. For example, some group members may like to stay on-task until an assignment is completed, while others in the group will be easily sidetracked.

Instructional Materials

Surveying available media and preparing materials for instruction are essential to effective planning. Textbooks, audiovisual materials, supplementary reading materials, and supplies and equipment for group and individual projects should be procured and coordinated with your lesson. The time you spend on familiarizing yourself with what is available in the district will be time well spent. You should review printed materials, preview films, listen to records, and learn to use the latest technology.

The use of a wide variety of instructional materials and aids spices up a lesson and sharpens students' attention and interest. The use of videotapes in presenting examples and nonexamples of concepts, for instance, will act as an effective lesson stimulus. The effective use of other stimulus variation techniques will be covered in Chapter 9.

Students with Special Needs

Some of your students will be academically bright while others are slow; some will be socially skillful while others are inept. You must learn to modify your instruction to fit the individual needs and interests of your students. Examples of appropriate modifications include developing special worksheets to help teach difficult concepts, modifying assigned work, developing special study guides, changing grouping patterns to fit special needs, and obtaining and using special equipment for students with disabilities or gifted students.

Teachers with mainstreamed (handicapped) or special students must learn to give differentiated assignments. You can do this by varying the length or difficulty of assignments. For example, in a mathematics class, you might assign five problems to your slow students, 10 problems to the average students, and 10 more difficult problems to the better students. Similarly, you might require only half as much writing from children who experience motor difficulties.

Another approach is to vary the type of work students do. Some students should be allowed to complete and submit their written assignments on a word processor. Creative students may occasionally be allowed to create something instead of writing a report. Students might sometimes be allowed to assist each other.

Some general planning guidelines for working with students who have special needs include:

1. Learning about the nature of the exceptional student's difference and how that difference might affect the learning process.
2. Determining whether help is available from a special-education or resource expert.
3. Determining the exceptional student's equipment needs to allow him or her to function at an optimum level.
4. Considering how to adapt the curriculum and your teaching strategies to better serve the needs of the exceptional student.
5. Considering how to individualize the curriculum as much as possible.
6. Providing for the removal of barriers, both physical and psychological, that inhibit the exceptional student's full functioning.

Having looked at the planning of instruction, let us next look at the four planning levels in more detail.

⋊ Course Planning

The most general type of planning you will do as a classroom teacher is course planning. In most cases, the textbook will form the basic structure of your course plan, but it should not be the main premise of instruction. Beginning teachers should use their textbooks as instructional guides and should integrate supplementary material into the basic text structure. Experienced teachers, however, often structure their courses on the basis of experience and use the textbook to supplement the experience base.

When a textbook is used to structure a course for the year, you should lay out your instruction on the basis of the content included in the textbook. That is, you should outline and sequence the units of study for the year and make unit time allotments based upon the textbook content, as in the example below.

UNIT 1	The Birth of a Nation *(3 weeks)*
Chapter 1	The Immigrant Experience
Chapter 2	The Colonial Experience
Chapter 3	Of War and Revolution
UNIT 2	The Constitution *(3 weeks)*
Chapter 4	Framing the Constitution
Chapter 5	The Constitution of the United States
Chapter 6	The New Nation
UNIT 3	The New Nation *(4 weeks)*
Chapter 7	Crises of the New Nation
Chapter 9	American Life and Letters
Chapter 10	The Peculiar Institution
UNIT 4	The Divided Nation *(4 weeks)*
Chapter 11	Westward Expansion
Chapter 12	Sectional Conflict and the Gathering Storm
Chapter 13	The Civil War
Chapter 14	The War's Aftermath
UNIT 5	The Indivisible Nation *(6 weeks)*
Chapter 15	Farm, Forge, and Factory
Chapter 17	Imperial America
Chapter 18	The United States and World War I
Chapter 19	The Tired Twenties
UNIT 6	This Urban Nation *(4 weeks)*
Chapter 20	The City and Its People
Chapter 21	The Shame of the Cities
Chapter 22	The Cry for Reform
Chapter 23	The Culture of City Life
UNIT 7	The Great Depression *(2 weeks)*
Chapter 24	The Great Depression and the New Deal

Expansion Activity: Course Planning

Obtain the teacher's edition for a subject that you hope to teach. Using the text-book as a guide, structure two different course plans for a year. Outline the content units to be taught and unit time allotments for each plan. Write a brief rationale for each plan. Submit your course plans and rationales to the instructor.

UNIT 8	The Nation Comes of Age *(4 weeks)*	
Chapter 25	War Clouds Again	
Chapter 26	The United States in World War II	
Chapter 27	Uncertain Peace	
Chapter 28	Postwar Politics and Problems	
UNIT 9	A New Road for America *(4 weeks)*	
Chapter 29	The New Frontier at Home and Abroad	
Chapter 30	Toward the Great Society	
Chapter 32	The Worst or the Best of Times?	

Course plans should be flexible so that changes can be made during the year as the need arises. For example, plans often change due to bad weather, fire drills, pep rallies, class meetings, guidance needs, testing and so on. Also, as you select chapters to be assigned, recognize that not all chapters need to be covered, that the text sequence is not always the best for every class, and that not all chapters are of equal importance. Make time allotments based upon your intended methods and procedures and on the importance of the topic. For example, if you plan on taking field trips or if a library research project will be completed during a unit, make sure your unit time allotment reflects the extra time needed.

One of the chief values of course planning is that it permits you to gather more and better media and instructional materials (films, special equipment, computer programs, special books, etc.) by the time they are needed. Some school districts even require that all special materials be requested at the beginning of the year. In such districts, course planning is essential. Now complete Expansion Activity: Course Planning which will further develop your course-planning skills.

⚔ Unit Planning

Courses, as shown above, are usually divided into units of study that represent discrete segments of the year's work in a given subject. Each unit is organized around a specific topic, theme, or major concept. Thus, a unit is a series of many intended learning activities and experiences unified around the topic, theme, or major concept. More specifically, a well-constructed unit should include the following sections:

1. *A topic*   Presumably the topic will be suggested by the course outline, a textbook, or a curriculum guide.
2. *Goals and objectives*   A list of your learning intent in broad and specific terms.
3. *Content outline*   An outline of the content to be covered with as much detail as you feel is needed. This outline should help clarify the subject and help you with the organization.
4. *Learning activities*   The activities (for the teacher and for students) that will lead to the desired learning. They should include introductory, developmental, and culminating activities. The activities should be arranged into a series of daily lessons.
5. *Resources and materials*   A list of materials to be selected and prepared for the unit.
6. *Evaluation*   An outline of your evaluation procedure. It could include projects, homework, or tests. Tests and evaluative exercises should be planned and prepared prior to instruction.

The units can vary greatly in scope and duration depending on the grade level and subject. Generally they range in duration from one to six weeks. Other examples of typical units are community helpers in kindergarten, transportation in the second grade, the library in the sixth grade, astronomy in the eighth grade, and photosynthesis in high school biology.

⚔ Weekly Plans

Many schools ask that teachers submit weekly lesson plans so that, in the event that a teacher becomes ill, the substitute teacher will have some idea of what was to be covered that day. Weekly lesson plans vary greatly in detail from school to school. Essentially they are watered-down copies of the week's daily lesson plans written on special forms provided by the school or in a daily plan book.

Basically, weekly plans are a layout sheet on which the teacher shows what lessons will be taught during the week. Usually the form or book provides only a small lined box for each class period for each day of the week. These plans are useful only for outlining the topics, a very brief description of the activities, and the assignments projected for the week.

⚔ Daily Lesson Plans

The most specific type of plan is a daily lesson plan, which is simply the class activities for a single day. Thus, unit planning does not eliminate daily planning. However, since the objectives, general activities, experiences, and necessary materials have been specified in a well-done unit plan, the daily lesson plan flows naturally out of the unit plan. It should include the following sections:

1. *Objectives*   The specific learning intent for the day selected from the unit plan. For example, "The student will write the basic subtraction facts with at least 80 percent accuracy."

2. *Introduction (set induction)*   An activity to be used to begin the lesson. As an example: "As you know, there are 22 children in this class. We are planning to go to a movie next week. Three of you—Mary, Mike, and Cindy—have music practice and will not attend the movie until the weekend. How many tickets should we buy?"

3. *Content*   A brief outline of the content to be covered in the lesson. For example, the content outline for a lesson on the basic subtraction facts might include:
   a. Solve 11–6 and 11–8 types.
   b. Explain 20–5 and 20–10 types.
   c. Explain 22–10 and 22–15 types.

4. *Methods and procedure*   A list of the developmental activities. Here are some examples:
   a. Explain three different subtraction types, using the overhead projector. Using checkers as subtraction aids to represent numbers, have children do examples and other similar problems.
   b. Do several practice problems orally. Ask volunteers to use their checkers to help solve problems.
   c. Have children complete practice problem sheet.

5. *Closure*   The lesson wrap-up activity. For example, an activity could be: "Using the overhead projector, do practice problems while the children give input. Have the children score their own papers for formative feedback."

6. *Resources and materials*   A list of instructional materials needed for the lesson. For example, you might need the following: overhead projector, checkers, and subtraction practice sheet.

7. *Assignment*   The in-class or homework assignment to be completed for the next class period. For example, distribute a practice subtraction sheet to be completed and turned in.

As might be expected, teachers vary widely in their approach to daily planning. Some develop detailed daily plans, whereas others merely write out a few notes as reminders. Regardless of the amount of detail or general format, your daily plan should consist of three key ingredients: the set induction (cognitive set), the lesson itself (strategy and procedure), and the lesson closure.

Set Induction

Set induction is what you do at the outset of a lesson, that is, what you do to get students' undivided attention, to arouse their interest, and to establish a conceptual framework for the information that follows.

Student Attention   Until your students are prepared to listen (until they have a cognitive set), it is usually unwise to begin a lesson. Your opening remarks, frequently related to the homework assignment or some recent lesson, will have to be repeated if you have not gained their attention. On special days (holidays, "big-game" days, stormy days, etc.), you will find it particularly difficult to get and maintain their attention. On such days you must take special care with your introduction.

Teachers can use a variety of techniques to gain student attention. One of the most frequently used and most effective techniques is to do nothing. Simply stand silently facing the class. Soon the entire class will be drawn to the silence. The lack of customary teacher talk arouses students' interest and attention. This technique is especially effective when you have a small group within the class that is inattentive. Silence and an intense stare in the group's direction will soon get their undivided attention.

Another attention-getting technique is to begin speaking in a very low tone and gradually raise your voice to normal volume when the class is quiet and attentive. If used often, this technique can even become a signal to be quiet and pay attention. In a sense you will have conditioned the class to become attentive on the signal.

Gestures and teacher movement can also be effective attention getters. Students, like most people, are naturally drawn to any type of movement. For example, waving your hand, practicing your golf swing, or walking toward noisy students can direct attention to yourself. Experimenting with various movements will determine which ones are most effective with a particular class. Classes will differ based on such factors as course content, socioeconomic level, family background, motivation, grade level, and class size.

To summarize, silence, voice control, and movement can all be used effectively to gain student attention at the onset of a lesson. However, the establishment of cognitive set is not the only use of these techniques, as you will see in later chapters.

Student Interest and Involvement   The second purpose of the set induction is to establish student interest and involvement in the forthcoming lesson. Thus, your introduction should act as a lesson motivator. It should, insofar as possible, create an atmosphere that makes students feel, "Tell me more; this sounds interesting." Motivation can be quite difficult at times, for no matter what teaching strategies you employ, some topics are of little interest to students. However, regardless of the topic, you can always try to be creative.

One method of developing student interest is to begin the lesson by relating it to a topic of vital interest to the class. The topic itself need not even be closely related to the lesson. For example, interest in music can lead to a study of sound. School elections can serve as a lead to the U.S. political system. Or a discussion of home pets can be used to introduce a unit on animals. This technique is an art that needs to be practiced and refined. Listen to the conversations of your students for topics that you can use to start your lessons. A simple remark related to the topic will usually get the discussion started.

Suspense can also create interest and involvement. Begin the class with an interesting demonstration or a discrepant event. For example, demonstrate a volcano in earth science, show an airplane in flight when introducing a story on air travel in reading, or mix paints to form various paint colors in art. Make the demonstration or discrepant event as novel or surprising as possible. Even better, involve students in the introductory demonstration or in showing the event.

Models, diagrams, or pictures situated in visible spots are effective in capturing attention and interest. You might begin the lesson by soliciting student comments. For example, you might ask the class to guess the model's function or what the diagram or picture represents.

Questions and hypothetical cases are also effective in establishing sets. To be effective, however, they must stimulate student curiosity or interest. For example, questions such as, "What would happen if . . . ?" are excellent for gaining interest. When the right conditions are attached, hypothetical cases that deal with the unknown or the presentation of a puzzling situation are often successful. For example, ask what effect not going to school would have on their lives, show an ice cube sinking in a clear liquid that looks like water, or show a piece of wood that will not burn. However, if you decide to create sets by using questions or hypothetical cases, make sure they are strong. Too often, teachers use questions or cases that are ineffective and, consequently, weaken their chances for future success with this technique.

Establishing a Framework   Students learn more when they know what to expect from a lesson. Thus, to maximize learning, your introductory remarks should provide students with what Ausubel (1963) calls an **advance organizer.** That is, your opening remarks should give students a "what-to-look-for" frame of reference. In a sense, the concept of advance organizer is related closely to the establishment of student interest but is usually more specific in nature.

Advance organizers can be generalizations, definitions, or analogies (Orlich, Harder, Callahan, Kauchak, and Gibson, 1980). For example, a science teacher might start a lesson on animal life with a generalization about the major characteristics of life. A second-grade teacher might start a math lesson with definitions of the new vocabulary words. A social studies teacher might start a lesson on war by relating it to a tennis match. No matter what form it takes, the purpose of an advance organizer is either to give students the background information they need to make sense of the upcoming lesson or to help them remember and apply old information to the lesson. Thus, the organizer acts as a kind of conceptual bridge between the new and old information.

Many teachers use a verbal statement of one or more lesson objectives as the advance organizer. However, in using this technique you must take care to translate the written objectives into a form that is both understandable and interesting to students. An example of this technique is:

Objective   The students will be able to correctly calculate the impact speed of a dropped object.

Translation   [Teacher holds an object overhead.] When I drop this object, watch it closely. [Teacher drops object.] There was a continuous increase in the object's speed as it fell. But it fell so fast that the increase was impossible to detect. What was its speed upon impact? [Silence.] That's what we're going to find out today.

To summarize, you must set the stage for the learning process. If you fail to arouse student attention and interest, the remainder of the lesson is often

Web Search: Sets

Access the lesson plans at URL web sites **http://www.lesson-planspage.com** and **http://www.connectedteacher.com/lessonplans/lesson-plans.asp.** Locate five lesson plans relative to the subjects you plan to teach. Analyze and modify the sets to make them more effective for your future students. Add these plans to your resource file.

wasted. In addition, a framework for the lesson must be established in order to achieve maximum learning. Therefore, in most cases, your introductory remarks (set) should consist of two parts: the attention getter or motivator and the advance organizer.

Let us now apply the set induction concepts from this section. Complete Web Search: Sets which will let you develop some set inductions of your own.

Delivering Instruction

A lesson consists of the content to be taught as well as the instructional strategy to be employed in teaching it. This section of your plan should contain, in the order of implementation, a list of the topics, skills, and activities that you want to cover during the instructional period. The details included in this section will vary between individuals. However, the information should be detailed enough to serve as a memory jogger. Thus, you should include all the information needed to remind you of your plan of action. Perhaps a few brief notes will suffice, or a detailed description of content, activities, and questions may be needed. The details are entirely up to you. After all, you will be the one using the plan.

The **instructional strategy** consists of two components: the methodology and the procedure. The instructional strategy is the global approach to teaching a particular lesson. It can be viewed as being analogous to an overall plan for winning a football game or tennis match.

The **methodology** "sets the tone" of the lesson and acts as the student "motivator." It consists of patterned behaviors that are definite steps by which the teacher influences learning. The methodology should be selected and planned so that it captures and holds the attention of students and involves them as much as possible in the learning situation.

The **procedure** differs in that it is the sequence of steps that has been designed to lead students to the acquisition of the learning objectives. For example, you may decide on the following sequence for a lesson on Japanese history:

1. Present a short introductory lecture on the history of Japan.
2. Show a film on Japanese history.
3. Conduct a summary discussion on the content of the film.
4. Conduct a question-and-answer session on major points covered in the lecture and in the film.

As you see, the procedure consists of the sequenced teacher and student activities used to carry out the lesson.

Your instructional strategy is the actual presentation of the lesson content—that is, how you will give students the information. This requires that you choose from a wide variety of methods and learning experiences that you feel will best lead to the desired learning (Ornstein, 1999).

Methodology Selection

Some instructional methods influence students directly through focused, teacher-directed instruction, while others influence them indirectly by involving them actively in their own learning (Pigford, 1995). Thus, there are two basic instructional types: teacher-centered and student-centered. Comparisons of these two methods of instruction are given in Table 5.1. The teacher-centered instructional approaches are the more "traditional" or didactic ones in which students acquire knowledge by listening to the teacher, by reading a textbook, or both. In such an approach, the student is a passive recipient of information. In contrast, student-centered approaches to instruction provide a learning environment that invites students to actively participate in and help shape their own learning experiences. Either of the two instructional approaches can be used effectively to bring about learning. Concepts in science, for example, can be taught through a teacher-centered approach such as the Socratic method or through a student-centered approach such as discovery learning. Let us now take a brief look at some of these methods.

TABLE 5.1

Comparison of Teacher-Centered and Student-Centered Methodologies

Method	Amount of Teacher Control	Intent and Unique Features
Teacher-Centered Instructional Approaches		
Exposition teaching	High	Telling technique. Authority presents information with little or no student interaction.
Lecture	High	Telling technique. Teacher presents information without student interaction.
Lecture-recitation	High to moderate	Telling technique. Teacher presents information and follows up with question-and-answer sessions.
Socratic	Moderate	Interaction technique. Teacher uses question-driven dialogues to draw out information from students.

Continued on next page

TABLE 5.1

Comparison of Teacher-Centered and Student-Centered Methodologies (*Cont.*)

Method	Amount of Teacher Control	Intent and Unique Features
Demonstration	High to moderate	Showing technique. Individual stands before class, shows something, and talks about it.
Modeling	High	Showing technique. Teacher or other model behaves in way desired of students. Students learn by copying actions of model.

Student-Centered Instructional Approaches

Method	Amount of Teacher Control	Intent and Unique Features
Discussion	Low to moderate	Interaction technique. Whole class or small group interact on topic.
Panel	Low	Telling technique. Group of students present and/or discuss information.
Debate	Low	Telling technique. Competitive discussion of topic between teams of students.
Role playing	Low	Doing technique. Acting out of roles or situations.
Cooperative learning	Low	Doing technique. Students work together in mixed-ability group on one or more tasks.
Discovery	Low to moderate	Doing technique. Students follow established procedure in an attempt to solve problems through direct experiences.
Inquiry	Low	Doing technique. Students establish their own procedure for solving a problem through direct experiences.
Simulations, games	Low	Doing technique. Involvement in an artificial but representative situation or event.
Individualized instruction	Low to moderate	Telling and doing technique. Students engage in learning designed to fit their needs and abilities.
Independent study	Low	Telling and doing technique. Learning is carried out with little guidance.

Teacher-Centered Instruction

This section will focus on the major direct modes of instruction: exposition teaching, exposition with interaction teaching, Socratic teaching, and demonstration teaching. These are modes of instruction with which you should have had much experience in your own past schooling.

Exposition Teaching   **Exposition teaching** is most often used to communicate large amounts of information in a relatively short period of time. Exposition techniques include those methods in which some authority—teacher, textbook, Internet, videotape, or microcomputer—presents information without overt interaction between the authority and the students.

The **lecture** is probably the most widely used exposition teaching method in our schools. Virtually every teacher uses it to some degree, and some secondary teachers use it almost exclusively. However, the lecture does possess some strengths. It is an excellent way of presenting background information when building a unit frame of reference or when introducing a unit. Moreover, a short lecture can set a lesson atmosphere, focus student activities, or wrap up a unit, activity, or lesson. Finally, the lecture is time efficient, that is, planning time is devoted to organizing content, rather than to devising instructional procedures. However, it is a passive form of learning, with very low student involvement.

Exposition with Interaction Teaching   The **exposition with interaction** or **lecture-recitation** technique is an instructional method in which the teacher presents information in some form and follows up with question-and-answer sessions at periodic intervals. In effect, questions are used to summarize the content of the lecture and to help students consolidate and organize the presented information. The lecture-recitation method is often time efficient in terms of time flexibility and learning while actively involving students in the lesson. Its basic structure of—teacher talk/teacher question/student response/teacher talk—makes questioning the key component of the method (see Chapter 8).

Socratic Teaching   The **Socratic method** is a technique that uses a questioning-and-interaction sequence which has been designed to draw information out of students, rather than pouring it into them. This is a purely verbal and interactive method. The Socratic method can be quite effective, and works best in small-group sessions and in tutorial sessions.

Demonstration Teaching   The **demonstration method** is a technique in which the teacher or another designated individual stands before the class, shows something, and tells what is happening or what has happened or asks students to discuss what has happened. The demonstration can be viewed as a process of teaching by means of using materials and displays, but the only person directly involved with the materials is the teacher or individual conducting the demonstration.

Student-Centered Instruction

This section will focus on the major indirect modes of instruction: the discussion, cooperative learning, discovery learning, inquiry learning, simulations and games, and individualized strategies. These strategies are typically less teacher-directed, but more time-consuming.

Discussion   A **discussion** is a carefully structured exchange of ideas directed toward a specific goal. Two kinds of classroom goals are conducive to using the discussion method. First, subjects that pose questions with no simple answers. For example, is there a simple answer to the rising cost of medical care? What can be done about the growing world population? Questions of this type are open to debate. Through discussion of issues from government, science, literature, history, or societal issues, students develop an understanding of the issues, rather than simply receiving and rehearsing factual information.

The second type of goal that lends itself to the discussion method involves situations in which issues from the affective domain are addressed. A discussion relative to drug use, for example, would likely tap into students' attitudes. Similarly, discussions on issues such as poverty, types of music, voting, and art can lead to the establishment of such attitudes as civic duty, patriotism, and a commitment to the arts.

Cooperative Learning   An emerging approach to grouping which is proving effective at both the elementary and secondary level is **cooperative learning.** Generally, cooperative learning requires that mixed-ability students work together to accomplish a set of tasks. Students are placed in task groups composed of high, middle, and low learners. The percentage of each level that is represented in the group generally approximates the percentage of that level in the whole class. Rewards to individual students are usually based on the performance and accomplishment of the whole team rather than on that of individual team members, which provides an incentive for students to work together productively. Advantages associated with cooperative learning include: (1) higher academic achievement than is generally achieved with other commonly used approaches, (2) development of better interpersonal relationships, (3) increased time on-task, and (4) development of more positive attitudes toward the subject and classroom.

Discovery Learning   **Discovery learning** is a means by which students develop knowledge or skills while engaging in problem solving. Discovery learning can be viewed as intentional learning through supervised problem solving following the scientific method of investigation. Thus, students follow a well-defined sequence of problem-solving steps: identify a problem, develop possible solutions, collect data, analyze and interpret data, and test conclusions. Discovery learning can take place at three levels, depending on the level of problem solving. At level I, discovery learning is carefully guided (guided discovery); at level II, a moderate amount of guidance is administered (modified discovery); at level III, it is very casually supervised (open discovery).

Inquiry Learning   **Inquiry learning** is basically a problem-solving technique. The emphasis is placed on the process of investigating a problem, rather than on reaching a correct solution. Unlike discovery learning, no established pattern is followed in inquiry learning. Indeed, different students may use different strategies in obtaining information related to a problem. As with discovery learning there are three levels to inquiry learning: guided inquiry, modified inquiry, and open inquiry. Thus, the teacher may want to identify the problem and then decide how to investigate it (guided inquiry); the teacher may want to identify the problem and then have students decide how to go about finding out about it (modified inquiry); or the teacher may want the students to identify the problem and then design ways for obtaining information (open inquiry). The inquiry approach is flexible yet systematic. It is systematic in that a basic, three-step problem-solving procedure is followed: identify the problem, work toward solutions, and establish solutions.

Simulations and Games   **Simulations** and game activities can be very useful as teaching tools. The only distinction between simulations and games is that games are played to win, whereas simulations need not have a winner.

Simulations are presentations of artificial situations or events that represent reality. There are two basic types of simulations: human simulations and person-to-computer simulations. Human simulations are usually conducted in the form of role playing and sociodramas, whereas person-to-computer simulations often take the form of simulation games.

Simulations and educational games involve students in decision-making roles. Thus, educational games should reflect society; they should offer students the opportunity to experience roles that are common in life.

Individualized Strategies   Students do not, in general, learn or master skills uniformly. Therefore, individualization is often required to maximize the potential of each student. Individualization can take two different forms: individualized instruction and independent study.

Individualized instruction can take several forms. Ideally, **individualized instruction** engages students in learning plans tailored to meet their interests, needs, and abilities. Accordingly, you might vary one or more of the following: (1) the instructional objectives, (2) the learning pace, (3) the teaching/learning method, or (4) the learning materials.

There is no reason for the teacher to do what students can do for themselves. As such, students can often be involved in independent study. **Independent study** can be defined as any educational activity carried out by an individual with little or no guidance. In effect, independent study is self-directed learning.

With all these possible methods, how do you decide which is best? Experience often provides the best basis for selection; however, your lesson procedure, as well as other factors, often must be considered in your selection of methods. Indeed, Orlich et al. (1980) identify four variables that affect the selection of the appropriate instructional method for a particular lesson. These variables include the content and objectives of the lesson, teacher characteristics, learner characteristics, and the learning environment.

Every lesson must have purpose. What is the purpose of your lesson? Are you trying to teach in the cognitive, affective, or psychomotor domains? Obviously your selection of methodology and experiences will be related to the teaching domain. In addition, the methodology should be related to such factors as goals, specific learning objectives, and content. For example, if you are trying to teach problem solving or a psychomotor skill, the lecture method is not a desirable approach.

Every teacher has a unique set of personal experiences, background knowledge, teaching skills, and personality traits that make him or her more comfortable and effective with certain methodologies than with others. Obviously most teachers select the methods that have proved most successful in the past. Because people are inclined to select the methodology that makes them feel most comfortable, it is easy to get into a teaching rut. Be prepared to experiment with different methods. You cannot become familiar and comfortable with methods you have not used. Remember that you too are a learner.

The particular methodology selected must also match the maturity level and experiences of your students (Hunt, Touzel, & Wiseman, 1999). You would not use the lecture method with very young children or with students who have trouble paying attention to verbal messages. Students, like teachers, feel comfortable and learn better when the method fits their abilities, needs, and interests. Always keep in mind that when the method is mismatched with your students, learning will not take place at the maximum level. Thus, effective teachers select the best possible method for a particular class.

Obviously, the selected method may not always be the best one for every student in the class, but it should be the best fit for the class as a whole (Ornstein, 1999). To truly fit the abilities, needs, and interests of every student in a class, you must individualize the instruction. However, individualizing instruction does not mean that you should rely solely on individual seatwork. You should always use direct instruction (active teacher-centered instruction) to some extent even when individualizing. After all, you, the teacher, are still responsible for organizing the content and directing the learning process. This point cannot be overemphasized.

Finally the environment and related factors should be taken into account when you are selecting your methodology. Such factors as space available, time of day, and weather can influence a lesson and should be considered in selecting the methodology. For example, one should not select a method that requires a high level of concentration and little activity late in the school day or on a day when there has been a drastic weather change. Another example is that, if you have little space and a large class, the discovery approach may not be appropriate.

Finally, how much time should be devoted to each of the two approaches to instruction? This is a complex question. Suffice it to say that this decision will vary depending on the subject, the grade level, the amount of time that students have available for the lesson, the materials available, and the philosophy of the teacher and school. Indeed, whenever possible, you should vary your method and become skilled in combining various methods into a total lesson strategy.

Let us now turn our attention to the selection of the procedures component of the instructional strategy.

Procedures Selection

As noted earlier, the lesson procedure is the "outline" for implementing the lesson. In effect, it is your model of instruction, and it will generally take one of two basic forms: the traditional model or the mastery learning model. Both models are group approaches to teaching.

The Traditional Model   Figure 4.1 (on p. 79) shows the traditional model, which involves all students in all activities at the same time. Instruction begins with identification of your objectives, and this is followed by your presentation of the primary instruction to the entire class. The primary instruction may come in the form of lectures, reading, individualized instruction, simulations, discussions, media presentations, seatwork, or some combination of such activities. After all students have completed the primary instruction, the teacher evaluates their achievement of the lesson objectives.

The Mastery Learning Model   The mastery learning model, through its diagnostic-corrective-enrichment activities, provides a high degree of individualization because it enables students to learn at different paces and to use different materials. The **mastery learning model** which is depicted in Figure 5.6 and discussed below, is essentially a five-step pattern.

As with the traditional model, step 1 in using the mastery model is to identify your unit objectives. However, before the primary instruction is delivered, preassessment (step 2) is carried out. The purpose of this second step is to determine where students are with respect to the unit objectives. Students who lack prerequisite skills will need to work on these skills prior to receiving the primary instruction. Other students may have already mastered the unit objectives and should be directed to enrichment activities or to the next unit.

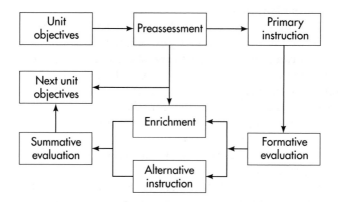

FIGURE 5.6   *The Mastery Model of Instruction*

Step 3 in the mastery learning model is to deliver the primary instruction. This instruction, as with the traditional model, involves all students except those who have demonstrated mastery, and is presented through lectures, discovery, discussions, reading, and so on.

The mastery learning model, unlike the traditional model, provides for a formative evaluation (progress check) after the primary instruction. The purpose of this check (step 4) is to determine which students have achieved the desired mastery level and which are in need of further instruction. Those at the mastery level are directed to enrichment activities, while those below the mastery level are involved in further objective-related activities. These enrichments and alternatives can be structured as group or individual activities. Further formative evaluations should be an integral part of the alternative instructional sequence. After the initial alternative activities have been completed, student progress should be checked once again; this cycle is repeated until mastery is achieved. At this point, all students are given a final or summative evaluation (step 5).

The basic structure of the mastery learning model can take two forms. In the first, the enrichments and alternatives parallel each other with the summative evaluation providing closure for the unit. As students achieve mastery, they are routed to the enrichment component until the class is ready for the formal evaluation. In the second form, step 5, the summative evaluation is administered to students at different times. In this form, students are tested when the formative evaluation indicates that mastery has been achieved. Those students who achieve mastery early can be involved in other types of individualized strategies or can work on the next set of unit objectives on an individualized basis.

The evidence supporting the value of mastery learning is mixed. When programs provide corrective instruction in addition to regular class instruction, research (Block & Burns, 1976; Bloom, 1984) suggests that the mastery learning approach does lead to higher student achievement. Such approaches, however, when they are used as the only method of instruction, have not proved more effective than traditional methods. Mastery learning tends to leave students on their own too much. Only the most motivated and self-directed students stay on-task for extended periods of time. Most students therefore waste much time. Another drawback is that most students lack skill in analyzing and thinking reflectively about study materials. They often need the direct teaching and explanations that can be provided by a teacher. However, if mastery learning is carefully designed and monitored, it can be effective at providing needed remediation or enrichment.

No matter how much detail you include in your written lesson plan or what instructional strategy you employ, the lesson must be well structured to be successful. The structure should include techniques that will keep students interested and motivated. Henson (1981) suggests several techniques:

1. Actively involve students in the lesson through meaningful activities.
2. Make the content as relevant as possible.
3. Keep the instructional atmosphere as informal as possible.

Web Search: Methodology

Access the lesson plans at URL web sites **http://www.pacificnet/~man-del/index.html** and **http://ericir.syr.edu/Virtual.** Locate two lesson plans relative to the subjects you plan to teach. Analyze and adapt the lesson for different instructional strategies. Add the adapted plans to your resource file.

4. Be enthusiastic about the material you are teaching.
5. Keep students challenged by pointing out problems, inconsistencies, and contradictions throughout the lesson.
6. Share your goals and procedures with students so that they will know where they are going and how they are going to get there.
7. Use the ideas and opinions expressed by students so that they will feel you value their input.

Attention to these suggestions and to the factors that should be considered in selecting an instructional strategy will lead to more effective instruction. The result should be enhanced learning by your students. Complete Web Search: Methodology to apply your knowledge of instructional strategies.

Closure

Once your lesson has been concluded, the main points and concepts must be pulled together so that they will be organized and integrated within the students' existing cognitive structure. This is accomplished in your **lesson closure.**

Closure should be more than a quick review of the points covered in the lesson. It should enable students to organize the new material in relation to itself and to other lessons. Closure is as vital to the teaching-learning process as are set induction and the lesson itself.

Sometimes you may want to achieve closure during the course of a particular lesson. Shostak (1982) suggests that closure is appropriate in the following situations:

1. To end a long unit of study
2. To consolidate the learning of a new concept
3. To close a group discussion
4. To follow up a film, record, play, or TV program
5. To summarize experiences of a field trip
6. To summarize the presentation of a guest speaker
7. To end a science experiment

These situations represent only a few activities that might call for closure. An important part of instruction is being able to judge when closure is needed.

Allen, Ryan, Bush, and Cooper (1969) suggest five different ways in which closure can be accomplished. First, you can organize your content around a central theme, generalization, or model. Either the teacher or the students can then relate the material covered back to the organizing theme, generalization, or model. Examples include such statements as "The characteristics of this play make it an excellent example of a tragedy," "These proofs support our original generalization that a negative number times a negative number results in a positive number," and "This form of government fits our model of a democracy."

Second, you can achieve closure through the use of cueing. This can take the form of an outline on the chalkboard, which helps students to organize the material by outlining the major points covered, or you can simply use a cueing statement such as "The main parts are as follows . . ." or "There are three important points to remember. First, . . ." Cueing can be effectively used at any point in a lesson and is often used at several points when new concepts are being developed.

Third, you can draw attention to the completion of the lesson through the use of summary questions. A question such as "What were the four major points covered in today's lesson?" or "Anne, can you summarize today's lesson?" or "Can you draw any conclusions from our discussion?" can be used effectively to close a lesson.

Fourth, connecting new and previously learned material helps students to achieve closure. A structured statement can be used, such as "Let's relate this to yesterday's study of addition," "This form of government is similar to the other forms of government we have studied," or "Can we relate this example to examples we have studied in the past?"

Fifth, a commonly used and effective way to achieve closure is to let students demonstrate or apply what they have learned. If the new concept or skill cannot be demonstrated or applied, it has not been learned. Examples of this technique include such teacher questions or statements as "Can you give me other examples of nouns and pronouns?" or "Let's diagram the two sentences at the top of page 56 as we did these examples," or "Let's do the oral exercises in the book together." Demonstrating or applying the new information at the conclusion of the lesson has the added advantage of providing immediate feedback to the students. Many teachers have students do worksheets or in-class assignments to achieve closure by application and to provide immediate feedback to the students.

It is important that all students in your class achieve closure on a lesson. Just because one student demonstrates closure does not necessarily mean that

Web Search: Closure

Conduct a web search for lesson plans using search engine sites **http://www.northernlight.com** and **http://www.searchopolis.com** relative to the subject and/or grade level you plan to teach. Select, analyze, and modify the closures of five lesson plans so they are more effective for your future students. Add the plans to your resource file.

all have achieved it. Now plan some closure activities of your own by completing Web Search: Closure.

Team Planning

Team planning is relatively new in most schools. In most cases, it centers around interdisciplinary instruction. These teams often consist of a mathematics teacher, science teacher, language arts teacher, and social studies teacher. In some schools special teachers (special education, gifted, reading, etc.) may be part of a team. These teachers plan together for a common group of students. Thus, students are given the opportunity to see the connectedness of the content being studied. Moreover, assignments can be planned to enhance student understanding and thinking skills.

Team planning gives teachers opportunities to engage in critical thinking and analysis of the learning intent and to engage in reflections related to the different aspects of the curriculum. A team approach gives teachers the opportunity to critically analyze the content of their respective courses in order to merge the concepts into one unified, workable whole. Teaming, however, requires careful attention to details so that each member of the team knows what to do, how to do it, and when to do it. It also requires that student evaluation be carefully planned, that the evaluation be executed properly, and that the evaluation accomplish its intended function. A team of teachers working effectively together can accomplish much more than any one teacher alone.

Interdisciplinary teams offer social, emotional, and physical benefit to the students being taught by the team. In a sense, the group becomes a community—students and adults—in which a climate of learning and development is created. Students learn to work together. The teachers who work and plan together get to know the strengths and weaknesses of the students, as well as problems that may affect their performance. Classroom management is often more efficient with common routines, rules, and expectations implemented and enforced by the entire team of teachers.

Teacher-Student Planning

Some students can also be engaged in the planning process. The extent to which students participate in the planning of their own learning activities varies greatly from classroom to classroom. In most classrooms, the only involvement is the selection of class projects, reports, and outside readings. However, by involving students in the planning process, you can gain valuable insights into student interests and areas of weakness and strength.

Teacher-student planning can promote "ownership" of the curriculum. If your students resist studying something they believe they already know, they could be tested on the material. If, in fact, they do have mastery of the material in question, then valuable instructional time and resources could be reallocated to other areas.

Task 5.2 further refines your skill at determining how to teach. Complete it before you continue.

T A S K   5 . 2

How to Teach

Respond to the following items. Check your responses with those given at the end of the chapter.

1. The four levels of planning, in descending order from most general, are

   _____ , _____ , _____ , and _____ .

2. Grouping of students can be _____ or _____ .

3. For each statement below, indicate whether the technique would be effective for gaining student attention and interest (A) or for providing students with a framework for the lesson (F). If you feel that the example would be ineffective as a set induction technique, leave it blank.

   _____ a. "Today we're going to learn to subtract decimal fractions. The procedure is very much like the procedure we learned for subtracting common fractions."

   _____ b. "John, come up and show us with this model how you think our solar system works."

   _____ c. "Let's get to work on today's lesson."

   _____ d. "Have any of you noticed the strange diagram on the board? What do you suppose it is?"

   _____ e. "Let's go over our new vocabulary words and their meanings before we read the story."

4. The two components of a lesson's instructional strategy are the _____ and _____ .

5. Describe the student-centered approach to instruction.

   _____

   _____

6. Classify the following as teacher-centered (T) or student-centered (S) methods of instruction.

   _____ a. Role playing   _____ d. Simulations
   _____ b. Demonstration   _____ e. Discovery
   _____ c. Modeling   _____ f. Lecture

7. Explain the purpose of the preassessment step in the mastery learning model: _____

   _____

8. For each example below, indicate whether the teacher used a closure technique that was appropriate (A) or not appropriate (NA).

   _____ a. As the bell rings the teacher gives the students an assignment that requires application of the lesson content.

   _____ b. "Let's now review the major concepts we have studied in today's lesson."

   _____ c. With 10 minutes left in the period, the teacher has the students work on the homework assignment so that he can assist them as needed.

Continued on next page

T A S K 5 . 2 C o n t i n u e d

_____ d. "Are there any questions on how to write a declarative sentence?"
_____ e. "John, can you tell us how the material we covered today is similar to the material we covered in the lesson we had last week?"

9. Describe team planning. _____

_____

_____

Analysis and Reflections

There are two basic instructional formats: teacher-centered and student-centered. When is it appropriate to use teacher-centered methods and when is it appropriate to use student-centered methods? Taking into account the objectives and purpose of the instruction, as well as the students themselves, write a few paragraphs relative to when to use the different instructional formats. Submit your paragraphs to your instructor.

This completes our formal discussion of techniques for planning. Complete Task 5.3 which will check your understanding of the concepts presented in this chapter.

T A S K 5 . 3

Planning Concepts

Respond to the following items. Check your responses with those given at the end of the chapter.

1. Explain how teachers determine what should be taught in their classrooms.

_____

_____

_____

2. List and describe four levels of teacher planning.

a. _____

_____

b. _____

_____

c. _____

_____

d. _____

_____

Continued on next page

3. Name and describe the three ingredients of a well-planned presentation.

a. _____

_____

b. _____

_____

c. _____

_____

4. Describe the three purposes of a set induction.

a. _____

_____

b. _____

_____

c. _____

_____

5. Name the four variables that affect the instructional method you choose to employ in a lesson.

a. _____

_____

b. _____

_____

c. _____

_____

d. _____

_____

6. Describe five ways to achieve closure in a lesson.

a. _____

_____

b. _____

_____

c. _____

_____

d. _____

_____

e. _____

_____

Analysis and Reflections

A lesson plan serves as an organizational tool that ensures that you cover the material you wanted to. Develop a lesson plan format that will best fit your teaching philosophy and style. Share your format with your instructor. Add your personal lesson plan format to your resource file.

Summary

- The importance of teaching basic thinking skills has recently surfaced. However, they cannot be taught in isolation.
- The presentations of effective teachers appear spontaneous. However, they have planned carefully.
- No amount of planning can ensure success.

Categories of Learning

- Learning can be classified into three broad hierarchical categories: facts, concepts and principles, and thinking skills.
- The learning of facts includes the rote memorization and, in some cases, the meaning of the information.
- Concept and principle learning include the learning of the mental images of the set of characteristics common to any and all examples of concepts or two or more related concepts (principles).
- Thinking-skills learning is learning to use facts, concepts, and principles in the thinking process.

Teaching Concepts

- A concept is a category to which a set of objects, conditions, events, or processes can be grouped based on some similarities that they have in common.
- The learning of concepts reduces the complexity of learning tasks, gives us a means to communicate, and helps us better understand our environment.
- Concepts are abstractions. They are learned in two ways. First, simple concepts are generally learned through observation and association. Second, abstract concepts are typically learned through definitions and verbal explanations.
- Some educators maintain that concepts consist of four elements: a name or label, a definition, examples and nonexamples, and relevant and irrelevant attributes. These educators suggest that concept lessons should include all four elements.

Teaching Thinking Skills

- Thinking can be defined as the act of withholding judgment in order to use past knowledge and experience to find new information, concepts, and conclusions. This act requires individual responsibility.
- Teaching students to think and be responsible is a primary goal of education.
- Because all activities call on people to use their own thoughts, the misconception is often voiced that all activities teach thinking. But thinking at a level other than that where factual information is recalled demands practice.
- Bloom's Taxonomy offers six levels at which thinking can take place: knowledge, comprehension, application, analysis, synthesis, and evaluation. The most appropriate level for a specific class will depend on the maturity of the students and the needs of the content area.
- Commonly taught thinking skills are critical thinking and creative thinking.

- Thinking skills can be taught separately (separate approach) or by infusing them into the content (infusion approach).
- Direct and specific instruction often proves useful in fostering critical and creative thinking skills.
- Eight nonthinking behaviors have been identified that often negatively impact the development of thinking skills—impulsiveness; overdependence on the teacher; inattentive behavior; restless rusher; dogmatic, assertive behavior; rigid, inflexibility of behavior; fearful, lack of confidence; and responsibility forfeiture.

Planning Instruction
- Planning is essential to effective teaching. Therefore, teachers must plan, and plan well.
- Organizing for instruction sometimes requires between-class or within-class grouping.
- Assigning students so that classes are homogeneous (between-class grouping) or forming working classroom groups (within-class grouping) often make the instructional process easier.

Course Planning
- Course planning is the most general type of planning.
- Beginning teachers often use a textbook as their guide in planning a course. Experienced teachers often structure their course on the basis of experience.
- A course plan should outline the sequence of the units of study for the year and the unit time allotments.

Unit Planning
- Units represent discrete segments of the year's work. Each unit is organized around a specific topic, theme, or major concept.
- Well-constructed units should include six sections: a topic, goals and objectives, a content outline, learning activities, a listing of resources and materials, and the evaluation procedure.

Weekly Plans
- Weekly plans are watered-down copies of the week's daily plans written on special forms or in a daily plan book.
- Weekly plans usually contain the topic, a brief description of activities, and the projected assignments.

Daily Lesson Plans
- The planning of your daily lesson presentation should be viewed as a major tool for effective teaching. If your daily lessons are not leading to high-quality learning, you should review and revise your techniques.
- A strong beginning (set induction) is crucial for any activity or lesson. It establishes the tone and sets a conceptual framework for the coming activities. It should be planned so that the immediate attention of every student is captured.
- The lesson instructional strategy consists of your methodology and procedure. The method used forms the heart of your lesson and should be chosen with care.

- Methodology can be teacher-centered or student-centered. In making this decision a teacher must take into account the objectives, personal abilities, the intended learners, and the environment.
- Lessons must be organized according to one of two models: the traditional model or the mastery learning model. While the traditional model emphasizes teacher-directed instruction, mastery learning provides for a high degree of individualization.
- Lessons should also have definite endings. This can be done with a summary, a recapitulation of what was covered, a series of open-ended questions, or student application of the covered concepts.
- Team planning consists of several teachers planning together for a common group of students.
- Interdisciplinary teams offer social, emotional, and physical benefits to the students being taught by the team.
- Some students can be engaged in the planning process. Involving students in planning gives valuable insights into student interests and areas of weakness and strength.

Activities

1. *Classroom observation*   Make several school observations. Collect data relative to the following questions.
   a. What type of learning is being emphasized?
   b. What strategies are employed to teach concepts?
   c. What type of thinking is emphasized? Are responsibility, critical thinking, and creative thinking rewarded?
   d. What type of classroom environment would be conducive to developing responsibility? critical thinking? creative thinking?
   e. Is cooperative learning used? If so, how?
2. *Teaching methods and procedures*   What teaching methods and procedures can be used to improve students' sense of responsibility? critical thinking abilities? creative thinking abilities?
3. *Investigating textbook concepts and thinking skills*   Obtain the teacher edition of a textbook for any grade level and subject that you plan to teach. Analyze the concepts and thinking skills included. Are the concepts appropriate for the grade level? Are thinking skills taught? If so, which ones?
4. *Listing of methods*   Make a list of the instructional methods you feel are appropriate for the grade level you plan to teach. Give a valid rationale for your selections.
5. *Set induction techniques on television*   Watch the beginnings of several television programs, and notice how the concept of set induction is used to get viewers interested in the upcoming program. Can the same techniques be used by a teacher in a classroom environment?
6. *Closure techniques on television*   Watch the endings of several television programs, and notice whether closure is achieved. If so, how?

7. *Planning a lesson*   Plan a complete lesson presentation for the topic of your choice from your area of specialization. Include in the plan the three key ingredients that make up a lesson presentation.

Answer Keys

Task 5.1 What to Teach
1. a. The learning of verifiable information or facts.
   b. The learning of the mental images of the characteristics associated with concepts and principles.
   c. Learning to use facts, concepts, and principles in the thinking process.
2. A concept is a category to which a set of objects, conditions, events, or processes can be grouped based on some similarities that they have in common.
3. *True*   Concepts can be categorized into object abstractions and condition or process abstractions.
4. inductive
5. Thinking is withholding judgment in order to use past knowledge and experience in finding new information, concepts, or conclusions.
6. process, product
7. separate, infusion
8. *True*   The best activities for developing thinking skills are those that have more than one answer.

Task 5.2 How to Teach
1. course, unit, weekly, and daily
2. between classes or within classes
3. a. *F* A framework is established for the subtraction of decimal fractions.
   b. *A* Student attention and interest should be gained.
   c. *[Ineffective]*
   d. *A* The diagram should gain student attention.
   e. *F* A framework is established through the use of an advance organizer.
4. methodology and procedure
5. Students are actively involved in their own learning in the student-centered approach.
6. a. *S*   b. *T*   c. *T*   d. *S*   e. *S*   f. *T*
7. The preassessment step determines where students are with respect to the lesson or unit objectives.
8. a. *NA*   Immediate feedback is missing.
   b. *A*   Major concepts are reviewed.
   c. *A*   In-class application and feedback are provided.
   d. *NA*   The question is not directed to an individual student.
   e. *A*   The material is related to previous learning.
9. Team planning is usually centered around interdisciplinary instruction with a group of teachers planning together for a common group of

students. Instruction and assignments are planned to enhance student understanding and thinking skills.

Task 5.3 Planning Concepts

1. A textbook can be used to form the basic structure of a course. Supplementary material can be integrated into the basic textbook structure.
2. a. *Course planning*   Course planning is long-range planning in which instruction for the year is laid out.
    b. *Unit planning*   A unit plan is a segment of the year's work organized around a specific topic, theme, or a major concept.
    c. *Weekly planning*   A weekly plan is a collection of daily plans for the week.
    d. *Daily lesson planning*   A daily lesson plan is the presentation for a single day.
3. a. *Set induction*   Set induction is what you do at the outset of a lesson to get students' attention, to trigger their interest, and to establish a conceptual framework.
    b. *Lesson*   A lesson is the content to be taught and the instructional strategy used to teach it.
    c. *Closure*   This is the summing up of the lesson. The new material is tied together and tied to previous learning.
4. a. To get student attention.
    b. To get students interested and involved.
    c. To establish a framework for the content to be taught.
5. a. The content and objectives of the lesson.
    b. The personality and characteristics of the teacher.
    c. The characteristics of the learner.
    d. The environment.
6. Responses may vary considerably. However, five possible closure techniques are:
    a. Relate material to a central theme, generalization, or model.
    b. Outline major points on the overhead projector or on a chalkboard.
    c. Use a series of summary questions.
    d. Relate material to previously learned material.
    e. Have students demonstrate or apply the new material.

Theory and Research

Brooks, J. G., & Brooks, M. G. (1993). *In search of understanding: The case for constructivist classrooms.* Baltimore, MD: Association for Supervision and Curriculum Development.

Eggen, P. D., & Kauchak, D. P. (1996). *Strategies for teachers* (3rd ed.). Needham Heights, MA: Allyn and Bacon.

Jones, D. (1998). *Exploring the internet using critical thinking skills.* New York: Neal-Schuman Publishers.

Marshak, D. (1998). Key elements of effective teaching in block periods. *The Clearing House, 72*(1), 55–57.

References

Allen, D. W., Ryan, K. A., Bush, R. N., & Cooper, J. M. (1969). *Creating student involvement.* Stanford, CA: General Learning Corporation.

Ashton, P. (1988). *Teaching higher-order thinking and content: An essential ingredient in teacher preparation.* Gainesville, FL: University of Florida.

Association for Supervision and Curriculum Development. (1990). *Teaching thinking skills* (Video). Alexandria, VA: Author.

Ausubel, D. P. (1963). *The psychology of meaningful verbal learning: An introduction to school learning.* New York: Grune and Stratton.

Block, J. H., & Burns, R. B. (1976). Mastery learning. In L. S. Shulman (Ed.), *Review of research in education,* vol. 4. Itasca, IL: F. E. Peacock.

Bloom, B. S. (1984). The 2 sigma problem: The search for methods of instruction as effective as one-to-one tutoring. *Educational Researcher, 13,* 4–16.

Eggen, P. D., Kauchak, D. P., & Harder, R. J. (1979). *Strategies for teachers: Information processing in the classroom.* Englewood Cliffs, NJ: Prentice Hall.

Good, T., & Marshall, S. (1984). Do students learn more in heterogeneous or in homogeneous groups? In L. C. Peterson & M. Hallinan (Eds.), *The social context of instruction: Group organization and group process* (pp. 15–38). New York: Academic Press.

Goodlad, J. I. (1984). *A place called school.* New York: McGraw-Hill.

Henson, K. T. (1981). *Secondary teaching methods.* Lexington, MA: D. C. Heath.

Hunt, G. H., Touzel, T. J., & Wiseman, D. (1999). *Effective teaching.* Springfield, IL: Charles C Thomas.

Lemlech, J. K. (1997). *Curriculum and instructional methods for the elementary and middle school.* Englewood Cliffs, NJ: Prentice Hall.

Lipman, M. (1988). Critical thinking—What can it be? *Educational Leadership, 46*(1), 38–43.

Marzano, R. J., Brandt, R. S., Hughes, C. S., Jones, B. F., Presseisen, B. Z., Rankin, C. S., & Suhor, C. (1988). *Dimensions of thinking: A framework for curriculum and instruction.* Alexandria, VA: Association for Supervision and Curriculum Development.

Meltzer, M., & Palau, S. M. (1996). *Acquiring critical thinking skills.* Philadelphia, PA: W. B. Saunders.

Oakes, J. (1985). *Keeping track: How schools structure inequality.* New Haven, CT: Yale University Press.

Orlich, D. C., Harder, R. J., Callahan, R. C., Kauchak, D. P., & Gibson, H. W. (1980). *Teaching strategies.* Lexington, MA: D. C. Heath.

Ornstein, A. C. (1999). *Strategies for effective teaching* (3rd ed.). Boston, MA: McGraw-Hill.

Pigford, A. B. (1995). Involving students: Strategies which effective teachers can plan and employ. *Education Digest, 61*(4), 17–18.

Raths, L. E., Wassermann, S., Jonas, A., & Rothstein, A. (1986). *Teaching for thinking.* New York: Teachers College Press.

Rosenbaum, J. (1980). Social implications of educational grouping. *Review of Research in Education, 8,* 361–401.

Sadler, W. A., & Whimbey, A. (1985). A holistic approach to improving thinking skills. *Phi Delta Kappan, 67*(3), 199–203.

Shostak, R. (1982). Lesson presentation skills. In J. M. Cooper, et al. (Eds.), *Classroom teaching skills: A handbook* (2nd ed.). Lexington, MA: D. C. Heath.

Tennyson, R. (1978). Pictorial support and specific instructions as decision variables for children's concept and rule learning. *Educational Communication and Technology Journal, 26,* 291–299.

Tice, T. N. (1997). Research spotlight: Grouping students. *Education Digest, 63*(1), 47–49.

Torrance, E. P. (1983). *Creativity in the classroom.* Washington, DC: Library of Congress.

Verduin, J. R., Jr. (1996). *Helping students develop investigative, problem solving, and thinking skills in a cooperative setting.* Springfield, IL: Charles C Thomas.

Vygotsky, L. (1978). *Mind in society: The development of higher psychological processes* (M. Cole, V. John-Steiner, S. Scribner, and E. Souberman (Eds.). Cambridge, MA: Harvard University Press.

Walsh, D., & Paul, R. (1988). *The goal of critical thinking: From educational ideal to educational reality.* Washington, DC: American Federation of Teachers.

Implementing Instruction

Once planned, your lessons must be implemented, and this requires that you master a variety of teaching skills. First, you must be able to communicate effectively. Second, you must be able to establish and maintain student attention. Third, you must be able to elicit responses from your students so as to keep them involved and to examine the results of your teaching. Finally, you must be an effective classroom manager.

Part II will assist you in the development and refinement of these skills. Chapter 6 addresses the most important skill—communication. It looks at techniques associated with both verbal and nonverbal communications and examines the often overlooked but important skill of listening. Chapters 7 and 8 address the skills that will assist you in keeping students involved in their lessons; the topics covered in these chapters are reinforcement and questioning, respectively. Chapter 9 discusses classroom management. It focuses on getting students involved in their own learning. It addresses motivation from the intrinsic as well as the extrinsic perspectives. In addition, Chapter 9 will look at leadership and classroom atmosphere and their effect on behavior.

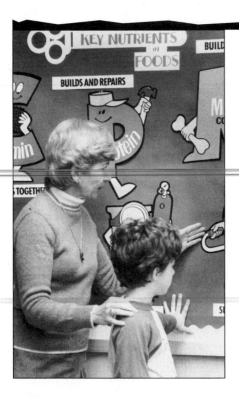

Communication

Objectives

After completing your study of Chapter 6, you should be able to:

1. Explain the importance of the communication process.

2. Differentiate between the verbal and vocal components of a message.

3. Identify variables associated with the verbal and vocal components of a message.

4. Explain the role nonverbal communication plays in the communication process.

5. List and describe various nonverbal behaviors that are commonly used in teaching-learning situations.

6. Explain the importance of and techniques for establishing communication links with the community and parents.

7. Explain the importance of listening as part of the communication process.

8. Identify and describe variables that interfere with the listening process.

9. Define and explain the reflective listening process.

10. Explain the importance of feedback in the communication process.

Without communication, teaching and learning could not occur. Teachers, therefore, are intimately involved in the communication process as they interact with students on a daily basis. Teachers continually send messages to students and receive messages from them (see Figure 6.1).

As shown in Figure 6.1, communication can be viewed as a four-phase process. The sender first encodes (composes) a message into a form which will, it is hoped, be understood by the receiver and then transmits this message. The transmitted message is received and decoded by a receiver, who then encodes some form of reaction to the message. The reaction is often nonverbal and is used to communicate whether the message was understood or not. The receiver sends the encoded reaction back to the sender, who then decodes and reacts to the feedback. The sender's reaction to the feedback may be to continue with new information, to clarify the original message, or to repeat the message.

A typical classroom situation serves to illustrate the communication process. Suppose you want to communicate the importance of a specific point to your students, and you encode and send a message such as "This is a point worth remembering." The transmitted message is received and decoded by students as meaning that the information will probably be on the next exam. They add it to their notes. Since you see (feedback) the information included in the students' notes, you feel you have communicated the importance of the information and continue with new information. However, if you see that the students do not add the information, you might want to encode and send another message such as "This point is so important that I think I will repeat it!" This example shows the importance of encoding your messages so that they are decoded accurately by students, and it shows the importance of feedback in the communication process. Noise and interference are usually present during the communication process. They must be overcome if messages are to be received and decoded accurately.

Messages may be sent or received through verbal, vocal, physical, or situational stimuli (Trenholm, 1998). As a teacher you must be skilled at sending and receiving messages through all these modes. Your ability to decode messages

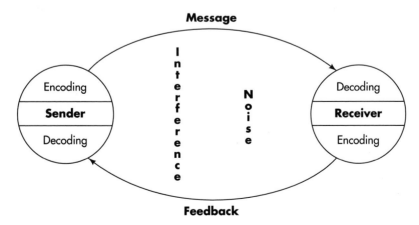

FIGURE 6.1 *The Communication Process* A four-phase process.

(feedback) transmitted by students depends directly on your skill at observing and listening. We will discuss making accurate observations in Chapter 11. The three skills that we will examine here are verbal communication, nonverbal communication, and skill at listening.

Most teacher preparatory programs stress reading and writing in their communication curriculum. Little emphasis is put on speaking, and almost no attention is given to nonverbal communication and the skill of listening. However, the most persuasive and effective teachers do not rely exclusively on reading and writing; they talk, they observe, and they listen with equal skill.

❧ Verbal Communication

Teachers talk in order to convey information. Unfortunately, learning does not always result from teacher talk. Nonverbal variables often determine whether or not something is learned.

Hennings (1975, p. 3) breaks spoken messages into verbal and vocal components. The **verbal component** includes the actual words spoken and their meanings, while the **vocal component** includes such variables as voice firmness, modulation, tone, tempo, pitch, and loudness. We shall now take a closer look at each of these two components.

Verbal Learning

What is learned in a verbal interaction depends on the meanings attached to the spoken words by the learner. The meanings vary according to the unique experiences through which each learner filters the words. For example, a discussion of the importance of school or a discussion of dentists will have varying meanings for students depending on their past experiences. Despite language conventions and formal definitions, you must make sure that your verbal instruction is related as much as possible to the unique experiences of your students. This calls for an assessment of what your students bring to the learning situation, for example, intelligence, prior experiences, and learning ability. This assessment may show that the verbal aspects of your messages are outside the experience base of your students. (A word of caution: Do not let your assessment of students color your expectation of their ability. Students tend to perform up or down to their teacher's expectations.)

Hurt, Scott, & McCroskey (1978, p. 76) suggest several other variables that are related to the verbal component of a message and that may have some effect on whether the message is learned. These variables include:

1. *Organization*   Good or well-organized verbal information tends to be learned better. Also information presented at the beginning or end of a message tends to be retained better.
2. *Message sidedness*   Two-sided messages, that is, messages that present opposing views, tend to be learned best.
3. *Language intensity*   Verbal information that deviates from a neutral position appears to be learned better.

Expansion Activity: Verbal Communication

There is generally wide agreement on what common physical objects are. However, when we talk about abstract qualities, like "school," "trust," "discipline," "right," "wrong," and so forth, will people have the same understanding of meaning? Is meaning related to culture? Is communication related to class or culture? As the world grows increasingly smaller will communication become a problem? Submit a short paper to your instructor related to these issues.

4. *Concreteness and ambiguity*   The more concrete a message, the better it is learned. However, the message must not be made so concrete that the basic concept is lost.

Generally such variables as those discussed earlier and those suggested by Hurt et al. tend to increase the attention of the learner and thereby increase learning. Complete Expansion Activity: Verbal Communication to further address issues related to the verbal components of a message.

Vocal Learning

The human voice can bring words to life. Changes in voice loudness, pitch, inflection, tone, and rate not only affect the emphasis within messages but can actually change the meaning of words. For example, "Come here!" or "Sit down!" can convey different meanings depending on voice loudness, pitch, and tone.

Although not everyone is endowed with a strong voice that projects well, teachers must learn to interact with groups and to emphasize points with their voices. It is essential that you learn to vary the strength of your voice and to project it so that it can be heard by all members of the class. This takes practice but is well worth the effort. Simple exercises that involve talking over a little distance or consciously inhaling and exhaling air will improve both the strength and projection of your voice. These exercises are available in most speech and communication handbooks.

The rate at which you speak is important as well. When someone speaks rapidly, it often conveys the unintended message that the subject is not really important and should be completed as soon as possible. In contrast, words spoken at a slower rate often communicate their importance and invite careful attention. This is important to remember since you might be required to teach subjects in which you have little personal interest or for which you are not well-prepared. With such subjects you must take care to watch your rate of presentation.

The tone, inflection, and pitch of the voice often affects a message. Tone or inflection can communicate word seriousness or validity. For example, your tone and inflection will communicate your seriousness when you make such statements as, "I mean it! Sit down!" or "I am losing my patience with this class!" Moreover, as Hennings (1975, p. 17) points out, "The high-pitched voice can grate on a decoder's nerves so that the listener turns off to words spoken; the very deep voice can distract from the message." You must, therefore, guard against using a tone, inflection, or pitch that detracts from your message.

Voice loudness, rate, tone, inflection, and pitch can also send emotional messages. Loudness, fast rate, and uneven pitch communicate excitement or enthusiasm, whereas a slow rate and even pitch sometimes communicate disinterest. Joy, eagerness, anger, wonder, awe, displeasure, determination, and indecisiveness are communicated through variations in the voice. Skill in using your voice can greatly assist you in keeping students on task, in maintaining a

T A S K   6 . 1

Verbal Communication

Observe a conversation between several people around you or on a television talk show. Listen to both the verbal component (the words) and the vocal component (the manner in which they are spoken) of participants in the conversation, and note below any discrepancy between the two. Also record below any vocal messages (excitement, interest, fear, etc.) you observe being sent and the voice qualities (tone, pitch, rate, etc.) used to send these messages.

The recorded observations for this task will vary considerably. However, some possible observations are listed at the end of the chapter.

Differences between Verbal and Vocal Communication

1. Difference _____

2. Difference _____

3. Difference _____

4. Difference _____

5. Difference _____

Vocal Messages Communicated

Vocal Messages	Voice Qualities Used

Analysis and Reflections

Choose a specific school situation (meeting with parents, visiting with the principal, disciplining a student) and select words that would be appropriate and words that would not be appropriate in the particular situation. Share your situation and words with your instructor and the class.

positive classroom environment, and in preventing a loss of student attention. Practice the effective use of your voice and, above all, watch your students for feedback. It will pay dividends.

To reinforce your understanding of how the voice can affect communication, complete Task 6.1.

✄ Nonverbal Communication

Not all communication is audible (Galloway, 1976; Trenholm & Jensen, 1996). Of special importance to teachers is nonverbal communication, which, according to the estimates of some researchers, accounts for over 80 percent of our total communication.

We constantly send messages through our postures, the way we look, stand, move, use our voice, dress, and use space, as well as the way we use words. These nonverbal messages can reinforce, modify, or even contradict our verbal messages as, for example, when a vacant, half-hearted smile accompanies a rote welcome such as, "Hello. It's so nice to see you." In fact, sometimes the nonverbal part of communication is more important than the verbal part. We often use the nonverbal information we receive in deciding what our reaction or role will be in a certain situation. For example, your host may ask you to stay longer, but his posture, look, and voice suggest that he would much rather you leave. Actions do often speak louder than words.

Nonverbal communication can be accidental, or it can be planned and managed. Either way, nonverbal cues influence perceptions and attitudes. Rather than taking them at face value, we often use them as the basis of inferences we make about each other or situations. Teachers and students often unwittingly reveal attitudes and feelings toward each other and school in general through nonverbal cues. You must be aware of your nonverbal expressions and the effect they can have on students. Awareness is the first step toward controlling nonverbal expressions, a difficult but manageable task. We will now look at some nonverbal languages.

Facial Language

According to Miller (1981), the face is second only to words in communicating internal feelings. Miller further suggests that facial expressions can be readily visible or fleeting, involuntary or voluntary. Whatever the type, it should be remembered that facial expressions can reinforce, modify, or even contradict the spoken word.

Readily visible facial expressions are usually intentional. They are used to send a message (e.g., a smile indicating pleasure) or to mask our true feelings (e.g., a poker face hiding displeasure). These expressions are formed by movement of the facial muscles as, for example, wrinkling the forehead to communicate deep thought, lifting the eyebrows to reveal wonder or surprise, sneering to show anger, and jutting the chin to show firmness. Fleeting facial expressions, on the other hand, are often unintentional and are quickly covered up with other expressions. For example, we may feel sudden disgust, anger, or dislike for someone which we do not want to communicate to the individual. We quickly mask our true feelings with other expressions.

Involuntary facial expressions usually take place under highly emotional circumstances in which we are fearful, angry, happy, or surprised. In learning environments these expressions are often fleeting and are quickly covered up with other expressions. However, under certain circumstances you may want to retain these expressions to convey a message to students. For example, teachers often use expressions of anger to control misbehaving students and expressions of humor to relieve tension or to improve student attention.

Teachers have learned to use certain expressions to convey specific messages. Familiar examples include the smile of approval and the frown of disapproval.

The use of the eyes is probably the most meaningful channel of nonverbal communication available to us. As Miller (1981, p. 14) points out, our eyes "can be shifty and evasive, conveying hate, fear, and guilt, or they can express confidence, love, and support." Also with eye contact we can open communication, prolong communication, or cut off communication.

Teachers often use eye contact to control interaction in the classroom. When they want a student to speak, they make direct eye contact with him or her. Conversely, when they want to continue talking they avoid direct eye contact with anyone who may want to speak. In addition, teachers sometimes use eye contact to determine which students may not be able to answer a question, which students have not completed their homework, or which students may be lying. The stereotype has it that when we have not done as we should or when we are lying, we avoid direct eye contact. However, this stereotype has not been proved by research.

Direct eye contact—a stare—can also be used to change behavior. A stare used in conjunction with silence can be quite useful in gaining the attention of misbehaving or inattentive students. The stare alone often results in appropriate student behavior.

Body Language

Gestures with the head, arms, hands, and other body parts are pervasive nonverbal communicators. Gestures may describe, as when we form a model in the air with our hands; they may reinforce, as when we nod our head when someone is speaking; they may emphasize a point, as when we tap something we have written on the chalkboard; they may gain attention, as when we rap the desk or stomp our foot. Each of these actions physically communicates some type of information. However, you should take care not to overuse gestures. When a speaker uses too many gestures, the listener cannot really tell what is important in the message. Overuse can also result in a listener's attending to the gestures rather than the message. In short, watch your students and ask questions. If students appear to be attending more to your gestures than to your messages, curtail the use of some gestures.

Your stance and general posture can also communicate information. A tense body tends to communicate closeness and insecurity. A relaxed torso or relaxed limbs tend to denote strength, openness, and friendliness. The orientation of a speaker's body, that is, the degree to which the speaker's body faces the listener, can also communicate information. A more direct orientation suggests a liking for the audience and a feeling of security in the communication process.

The use of touch is a very powerful nonverbal communicator. However, for teachers, communication through touch is directly related to the age of the student. It is usually a necessary communicator with primary age children but inappropriate with upper elementary and secondary age students.

Younger children in the primary grades have a strong need for touch and physical contact with the teacher. The physical contact is needed to form a sense of belonging, security, and a caring relationship. Withholding contact can communicate rejection or dislike for a child. Remember that a hug or a pat on the back is a good reinforcer for the young child.

With secondary students touching should usually be avoided. However, a pat on the back for a job well done can sometimes be appropriate even with students at this age. Although it is usually unwise for a teacher to touch a student of the opposite sex, it can sometimes be used effectively. You should use your best judgment about whether to communicate by touch with older students or with students of the opposite sex.

The Language of Space and Motion

How you use space and arrange your learning environment can also communicate a message. Significant factors in the learning environment include where and how you choose to move within the confines of the learning environment and how you arrange objects within that environment.

Learning environments are often territorial. The teacher's desk forms the teacher's territory, and each student's seat or desk forms the individual student's territory. In such an arrangement, it is often understood that neither is to invade the other's territory. This arrangement too often restricts classroom interaction and feelings of openness and may lead to a feeling of separation between teacher and students.

Teacher movement during interaction can aid or hinder the communication process. Teacher movement toward a speaker conveys a message of interest, whereas teacher movement away from a speaker communicates lack of interest. This movement, then, can result in termination of the communication process or can prolong the process.

The physical makeup of the learning environment creates moods and affects the interaction within the environment. These findings are pointed out by Miller (1981, p. 24) in his summary of research related to student reactions in ugly and beautiful classrooms. He reports that "subjects in the ugly room had reactions of monotony, fatigue, headaches, irritability, and hostility, while subjects in the beautiful room responded favorably with feelings of comfort, pleasure, importance, and enjoyment for completing the assigned tasks." These findings tend to suggest that a well-decorated, pleasing environment is more conducive to open communication and learning.

The Language of Time

How a teacher decides to use class time communicates important information. Spending little time on a topic or passing it by often communicates that the topic is unimportant or that the teacher has little interest in it. Unless care is taken, this same attitude can unintentionally be instilled in students.

Pauses represent another way time can be used to enhance communication. Pausing just before or just after a specific point is presented signifies the importance of the topic. The teacher's pauses can cue students that an important point is going to be made or that the last point was important and the students should think about it. Long pauses, however, can reflect anxiety or an attempt to mask uncertainty or fear.

Teachers ask students many questions in the course of a day's instruction. However, teachers often find it difficult to wait a sufficient time for student responses. Too often, teachers expect instant answers to their questions and, when these are not forthcoming, tend to answer the questions themselves. If these teachers were to increase the time they wait for a response (wait time), they would find improved communication in the classroom. The subject of wait time is further developed in Chapter 8.

The Language of the Voice

As noted earlier, we often send messages vocally, that is, through voice intonations. Intonations subtly reveal many things about a speaker, such as hidden prejudices, strong emotions and beliefs, and, often, background information about the speaker, such as socioeconomic background, level of education, and place of birth.

The adage, "It's not what we say, but how we say it that counts," is true. If a teacher responds to a student statement with "Very good!" (with rising intonation), it conveys a different message from a simple, monotone "Very good." The latter response conveys the message that it really was not that good. As pointed out earlier, when such contradictions occur between a verbal and a vocal message, the latter is usually believed.

Clearly, different vocal intonations communicate different meanings. A message can be changed by varying loudness and softness, using high pitch or low pitch, or varying the tone or quality of speech. You must understand and pay attention to the effect these voice intonations have on the meaning of your messages. You must learn to speak so that there is congruence between your verbal and vocal messages.

Task 6.2 gives you more experience at identifying the various methods and messages that can be communicated through nonverbal communications. Complete the task and discuss your observations with fellow observers.

This concludes our discussion of verbal and nonverbal communication. However, before we proceed, complete the Expansion Activity: Communication Strengths and Weaknesses to check your communication skills.

A discussion of communication would not be complete without giving some attention to communicating with the community and parents. Effective teachers are quite aware of the influence that community and parent communication and support can have on what teachers and schools are trying to accomplish.

TASK 6.2

Nonverbal Communication

Watch and listen to an interaction episode between several people around you or on a television talk show. Note examples of nonverbal communication that fall into each of the categories listed, and briefly describe the meaning of each. Although the responses will vary considerably, possible examples are given at the end of the chapter.

	Nonverbal Examples	**Example and Message Sent Nonverbally**
Facial expressions		
Eyes		
Gestures		
Stance and posture		
Touch		
Space		
Motion		
Time		

Analysis and Reflections

Make note of some occurrences of nonverbal communication around you. Make a list of these occurrences and share them in class.

Expansion Activity: Communication Strengths and Weaknesses

Assess your own communication strengths and weaknesses. Rate your ability to understand others. How does your behavior impact others and the ways others respond to you? How could you improve your communication skills? Write a short paper relative to your communication skills. Share your thoughts with your instructor.

Community and Parental Links

The overall quality of instruction will be improved when a school has a "concordant relationship" among the students, teachers, administrators, parents, and the community as a whole. This relationship will help schools create a climate that fosters the development of the whole child. In addition, a harmonious relationship will help build trust and promote respect (Krall & Jalongo, 1999).

At a time when schools are being urged to solve many of society's problems, community links are imperative. Community outreach programs should be developed that will provide supportive and nurturing home, school, and community environments in which the academic and affective needs of students are effectively addressed. The National Network of Partnership Schools was established in 1995 to assist in the development of such programs. The National Network of Partnership Schools uses Epstein's framework of six types of involvement: (a) parenting, (b) communicating, (c) volunteering, (d) learning at home, (e) decision making, and (f) collaborating with the community to improve and expand connections with students, communities and families (Epstein, Coates, Salinas, Sanders, & Simon, 1997). School meetings, back-to-school night, opening the school grounds and buildings for community use, meeting the teacher or principal for coffee, newsletters, student performances and presentations, student buddy systems, involving parents in school policy-making, team teaching, offering adult courses in the evenings, developing a senior mentoring program, and using community guest speakers are just a few ways to link the community with the school. This takes an open school-community communication system. Although it is important to link the whole school and community, bringing parents into the equation is still essential (Ludwig, 1999).

An effective parent communication system is essential to effective teaching and learning. Indeed, many colleges and universities are now requiring coursework that prepares teachers and administrators to work more productively with parents as partners (Epstein, 1991). Many public schools are also putting more thought into and developing better communication with parents. Schools now realize that initial contacts can make or break relationships with parents and that first contacts often affect later communication.

Opening communication lines with parents should be a high teacher priority at the beginning of each school year. Parents can represent a great deal of potential help and support for teachers and schools. However, this help and support is too often locked up by insecurity, ignorance, timidity, and apathy, as well as a hands-off attitude toward schools by many parents.

Organized systems that consistently advise parents result in extremely positive attitudes from parents (Charles, 1981). Therefore, it behooves the teacher to find ways to unlock the reluctance of parents to become involved in the education of their children. This takes communication, and it must be initiated by you, the person in charge of the classroom. Sadly, this contact between teachers and parents usually comes only when their children have upset the apple cart.

Establishing effective communication systems requires a variety of techniques and devices that will convey messages to parents. Newsletters, notes, phone calls, weekly folders home, daily reports home, and parent conferences represent some commonly used forms of communicating with parents. Weekly and daily reports home may appear to be impossible to teachers with large numbers of students. However, short-term communication checklists are useful when addressing specific improvement goals with students (see Figure 6.2) and weekly calendars on which students list their daily assignments in each class are good ways to keep parents informed.

This student is on a daily home progress report system. At the end of each class period he/she will ask teachers to place a check mark in the boxes below to indicate behavior, work production, and homework for the day. Teachers will sign with their initials and add comments if needed. This report is to be signed by a parent each night and brought back to the first hour teacher each morning.

Student Name: _____   Date: _____

CLASS HOUR	LIST YOUR CLASSES BELOW	BEHAVIOR ACCEPTABLE	BEHAVIOR UNACCEPTABLE	WORKED IN CLASS		HOMEWORK		TEACHER'S INITIALS
				YES	NO	YES	NO	
1.								
2.								
3.								
4.								
5.								
6.								

Teacher Comments: _____
_____
_____
_____

Class	Homework Assignment (Student Completes)	Teacher Signature

Parent's Signature: _____   Date: _____

Parent's Comments: _____
_____
_____
_____

FIGURE 6.2   *Short-Term Communication Checklist*   Daily progress report

Although there are many techniques for communicating with parents, person-to-person communication is best. Well-planned parent-teacher conferences and home visits are most productive in removing barriers and establishing healthy parent-school relationships. While it is true that parent-teacher conferences can be one of the most productive techniques to get parents involved in school, they can be a discouraging waste of time—or even turn into ugly confrontations. In addition to the five helpful steps to planning and holding parent conferences offered in Chapter 10, the following tips will make your parent-teacher conferences more productive and successful.

1. *Encourage both parents to attend conferences*   Misunderstandings are less likely when both parents are involved in the discussions of the student.
2. *Make early contact with parents*   Send a note or letter home with all your students and let parents know you'll be happy to meet with them at any time.

3. *When parents come to the school building meet them at the entrance they will use* And above all get the name right. Do not assume Michael Alport's mother is Mrs. Alport.

4. *When visiting with parents, do not sit behind your desk and squeeze parents into children's desks* Arrange to have a conference room and table available.

5. *When parents arrive, review the agenda of the conference—the why, what, how, and when of the conference* However, you should remain flexible.

6. *Avoid educational jargon* Avoid terms such as flexible scheduling, criterion-referenced testing, least restrictive environment, and outcomes-based assessment.

7. *Occasionally you will run into parents who are abusive and hostile* Try not to be rude to these parents.

8. *Watch your nonverbal communication* Smile, nod, and make eye contact to show you are interested in the conference proceedings.

9. *Remember that parents may not share your attitudes and values* Do not be judgmental. Do not try to assign blame.

10. *Before the conference ends summarize the discussion* Outline future plans and actions.

11. *If you run out of time, arrange another meeting* Do not rush to a conclusion because of time constraints.

12. *Keep a record of the conference discussion* Make some brief notes as soon as possible after the conference, while details are fresh.

Attention to the steps offered in Chapter 10 and the tips cited above will make your conferences and home visits more valuable and productive.

It is difficult to design a system of communication that will be appropriate with all parents. Factors such as parents' preference for reading, listening, speaking, and writing; time available to devote to school activities; parents' level of comfort in working with teachers, administrators, and counselors; and parents' level of literacy will influence communication. Furthermore, community ethnic diversity, cultural beliefs, and past school involvement will have an effect on teacher-parent communication.

Communicating with parents requires skill and tact. Parents expect teachers to be friendly but professional. They do not want you to be their pals or buddies. They expect teachers to be knowledgeable and businesslike. That is, they expect teachers to state information in a brief and clear manner. Jargon and terminology should be translated into familiar and comfortable language for parents. Teachers should be optimistic, have high expectations, and feel confident that by working together both parents and teachers can make a difference.

Teachers often need communication resources. Complete Web Search: Communication Resources which will help you identify some sites that will give you resource assistance.

This concludes our discussion of communication and communicating with parents. In the next section, we consider another important topic related to the communication process—the art of listening. However, before going on, check your understanding of the communication material presented by completing Task 6.3.

Web Search: Communication Resources

Access resources for those who work with parents at Internet URL site **http://npin.org/reswork/workorgs.htm.** Review the various organizations and their services. Do you feel they would be useful to teachers? Write a brief summary of your findings and share it with your class and instructor.

T A S K   6 . 3

The Communication Process

Respond to the following items. Check your responses with those given at the end of the chapter.

1. As a teacher your major concern related to communication should be with the encoding and sending of information.   (True/False)

2. The two components of the spoken word are the_____ and the_____ .

3. We tend to send various messages through the manner of our spoken word. (True/False)

4. Define nonverbal communication.

   _____

   _____

5. Teachers sometimes communicate undesirable messages through their expressions and mannerisms.   (True/False)

6. Briefly describe five nonverbal languages that can be used to convey messages and information.

   a._____

   _____

   b._____

   _____

   c._____

   _____

   d._____

   _____

   e._____

   _____

7. Explain the importance of an effective school-community link. _____

   _____

   _____

Continued on next page

8. Describe techniques that can be used to effectively communicate with parents.

_____

_____

_____

_____

Analysis and Reflections

How can e-mail and technology be used to improve communication within a school? With parents? Share your ideas with classmates.

✵ Listening

Listening is an art. We have all known someone in our life who, no matter what was being said, really listened. Real listening is hard work, harder than talking. The natural tendency of most people is to talk rather than listen. Although the art of listening takes effort and discipline, all teachers should develop and refine the skill since, once mastered, it pays handsome dividends both inside and outside the classroom (Wolvin & Cookley, 1979).

The first step in learning to listen is to cut down on talking. Most of us have learned this to some extent. Although as children we tend to go on and on, oblivious to the reactions of those around us, we soon learn from adults that this is unacceptable behavior. But cutting down on talking is only the start of becoming a really active listener.

Listening is an active process that can be divided into three sequential steps. The three steps form a continuum in which attention is the first phase, understanding the middle phase, and evaluation the final phase. The first step, attentiveness, is the key to the whole process.

The Attention Process

The attention process involves focusing on the speaker and the message being transmitted (Friedman, 1983, p. 5). To listen, you must "put on the stops," that is, you must stop talking, stop fidgeting, stop letting your mind wander, and lock in on what the speaker is saying. In short, you must learn to block out everything else around you.

Blocking out is not an easy task and may not always be a desirable behavior for teachers, who must be aware of everything that is happening in the classroom. However, as a teacher you must learn to pay strict attention to your students when the situation calls for it.

Attentiveness to a speaker is directly related to the relevance of the message as well as to its intensity, concreteness, duration, and the setting in which it is delivered. In some cases you may not like what the speaker is saying or you may not see its importance, but you will never know unless you listen. You must sit it out. Often you will be unable to control all the variables that affect listening, but an awareness of the variables is a step toward controlling them.

The way one views a speaker also affects listening. If someone is described as being very intelligent or very important, we tend to listen more intently. This also applies to speakers who are attractive or who hold values, beliefs, and attitudes similar to our own. Other factors such as size, dress, and name may also affect our tendency to listen. All such variables must be controlled to the best of our ability in order to truly listen.

Listening, as well as talking, consists of both a verbal and a nonverbal component. What reaches us through words is only one aspect of listening. We also gain information through nonverbal means, that is, through the interplay of gestures, feelings, body movements, and so on, which are always present when people interact. A person sometimes erroneously believes that he or she is sending a planned verbal message whereas actually his or her voice, choice of words, and gestures all indicate a completely different message.

Sokolove, Sadker, & Sadker (1986, p. 232) identify four nonverbal cues that affect communication. They suggest that communication and attentiveness can be improved by giving special attention to:

1. *Eye contact* Focusing your eyes directly on the speaker shows interest. However, be careful that the direct eye-to-eye contact does not make the speaker uncomfortable.
2. *Facial expressions* Your expressions show that you are really listening. Expressions give feedback (positive and negative) to the speaker as to whether the message is being communicated. If not, the speaker can make changes to assist you in your listening.
3. *Body posture* A relaxed listener is a better listener. If the listener is relaxed, the speaker also tends to relax, and to be stimulated in the direction of further self-expression. A listener who is relaxed and leans toward the speaker communicates interest and involvement.
4. *Physical space* Move to a position that provides a comfortable space between you and the speaker. Avoid being too close or too far away.

Although much of the nonverbal information we receive is on a conscious level, much is also received at the subconscious level. For example, you may dislike someone on sight for "no reason at all." Or you may know that a friend has a problem even though there is no way you *could* know. This subconscious information plays an important role both in the decoding process and in forming an overall impression of the message. Sometimes we draw inaccurate inferences about people based on subconscious information.

The Understanding Process

Understanding involves mentally processing the information received. In this phase, the listener actively selects and organizes information based on judgments regarding its relevance and worthiness (Friedman, 1983, p. 5). You judge the information and decide, "Am I really interested?" The judgment is based on your perceptions of what is being said. But have you really understood? Listening is more than public relations, that is, pretending to understand. To really listen you must sometimes seek clarification, since true comprehension is always the ultimate goal.

The Evaluation Process

The last phase of the listening process is evaluation. In this phase, one "is weighing the message against beliefs, questioning the speaker's motives, challenging the ideas presented, suspecting the validity of the message, holding the speaker's ideas up to standards of excellence, wondering what has been omitted, thinking how the message could have been improved, and in other ways evaluating what is being said" (Friedman, 1983, p. 5). Such evaluation is based upon the internal beliefs and values one holds. Thus, to really listen, one must learn to evaluate information on its own merit. You must guard against modifying messages to better fit the beliefs and values you hold. This ability is difficult, and it takes self-discipline. However, it is well worth the effort, especially to teachers.

Effective listening then is more than just being silent. It requires comprehension, the ability to grasp the main ideas of what is heard. Active listening, like thinking, is an intense, dynamic process that involves "listening between the lines." You must adjust to the pace of the speaker and actively process what is being said. It takes concentration and discipline.

Past experiences and internal feelings often have an effect on what we hear. We all have emotional filters that may block certain words or phrases or, conversely, may allow others to rush in and overwhelm us. They may at times even change what we hear, as in the case of such loaded words as *lice, yankee, test,* and *radical.* Listening, like observing, is always selective to some degree. Task 6.4 should reveal some of your filters.

T A S K   6 . 4

Identifying Personal Listening Filters

Write down all the things that have impaired your ability to listen at some time in your life; that is, record words or experiences that have made it difficult for you to receive and decode messages accurately. These filters can be physical, social, or emotional. Compare your list with others. Are the lists identical? Is your list composed of items in only one area?

Although the lists will vary among individuals, possible responses are found at the end of the chapter.

Analysis and Reflections

Diversity in our schools is growing. Do you think personal listening filters are related to culture? What can teachers do to address such filters? Can listening filters be detrimental to working with other teachers or administrators? Discuss your thoughts and ideas with classmates.

Nichols and Stevens (1957, pp. 102–103) offer three guidelines for reducing the effects of your listening filters. They include:

1. *Withholding evaluation until the total message has been received*   Again this requires self-discipline.
2. *Hunting for negative evidence related to the message*   Do not take what you hear at face value. Look for evidence that disputes what you hear.
3. *Making a realistic self-analysis of what you hear*   Test the message against your own biases, values, and feelings.

Nichols and Stevens also suggest that some people are poor listeners because they have developed bad listening habits. These bad habits include:

1. *Faking attention*   One who is faking attention appears to be listening, but in reality is thinking about other things.
2. *"I-get-the-facts" listening*   For some reason, many people listen only for the facts in a message. However, memorizing facts is not the way to really listen. An understanding of the main ideas that contain the facts is the most important component of listening.
3. *Avoiding difficult listening*   Some of us avoid listening when it takes mental exertion to understand what is being said. If you have such a habit, make special efforts to practice listening to difficult information.
4. *Premature dismissal of subject as uninteresting*   Some people automatically cease to listen when the message is of little interest. They equate interest with value. The fallacy in this habit is that the message is often worth hearing.
5. *Criticizing delivery and physical appearance*   This involves associating the importance of the message with the way it is delivered or the appearance of the speaker. However, it should be remembered that the content of most messages is more important than the method of delivery or the appearance of the speaker.
6. *Yielding easily to distraction*   You must learn to concentrate on the speaker and mentally shut out distractions to be a good listener.

In most cases an awareness of the preceding guidelines and pitfalls will automatically help you overcome their effects. However, you must actively practice the guidelines and avoid the bad habits if you want to become a really good listener.

Thinking can also affect listening. It is a well-established fact that listeners can process incoming information faster than speakers can deliver it. Consequently, listeners often drift off on mental tangents that interrupt their listening. To be a good listener you must learn to keep your thought processes harnessed to what is being said.

⚔ Reflective Listening

Reflective listening is listening with feeling as well as with cognition. It is an earnest attempt to vicariously identify with the speaker's experiences and to respond to that experience. It calls for careful attention to both the verbal and nonverbal cues given by the speaker. The listener puts these cues together into a statement that reflects the full meaning of the speaker's message, both its content and associated feelings.

The response portion of reflective listening is an attempt to avoid misinterpreting the speaker's message or to further clarify it. Sokolove, Sadker, & Sadker (1986, p. 230) note that a teacher's response in reflective listening involves holding up a mirror to the student's words, feelings, and behaviors. Thus, the teacher provides direct feedback regarding the success of the student's communications. This response can take the form of simple paraphrasing of the speaker's words or can be the listener's interpretation of the message as reflected in the verbal and nonverbal behaviors. For example, your response to a student who tells you that he hates coming to school might be, "I believe you are saying that coming to school upsets you for some reason."

Listener responses can reflect either the content or the emotional components of the message. For example, to reflect the content of a message, the listener might respond with a statement such as "Are you saying . . . ?" or "I believe that you are saying . . ." To reflect the affective component of a message, one might respond with "I think you are feeling . . ." or "You appear to feel . . ."

In summary the importance of good listening to the teaching-learning process is more recognized and accepted today than ever before. Listening skill

```
T  A  S  K      6 . 5
```

The Listening Process

Respond to the following items. Check your responses with those given at the end of the chapter.

1. All good talkers are good listeners.   (True/False)

2. Listening is an active process.   (True/False)

3. Listening is an easy task for most people since it requires only the use of the ears. (True/False)

4. Briefly describe the three components of the listening process.

   a. _____

   _____

   b. _____

   _____

   c. _____

   _____

5. Reflective listening is concerned only with the affective component of a message. (True/False)

Analysis and Reflections

Reflective listening can be an effective tool for teachers. How could it be used to establish a more positive learning environment? Share your ideas with classmates.

is now viewed as being directly related to teacher effectiveness. All teachers need the skill.

Take a few minutes to complete Task 6.5, which will check your understanding of the listening process.

⚹ Feedback

The communication process requires that a specific message be encoded and transmitted by one person and received and accurately decoded by a second person. This is a continuous, two-way process in any interactive encounter. The listener is continuously decoding the information being sent and returning a message that is often nonverbal.

Listeners are continuously sending nonverbal messages conveying understanding or uncertainty, agreement or disagreement, liking or distaste, concern or lack of concern, attention or inattention. This feedback, when received by the speaker, should be used to modify or clarify the original message. Perceptive teachers respond to feedback from students by reexplaining, using further examples, or changing their mode of instruction.

T A S K   6 . 6

Identifying Feedback

Observe a discussion period in one of your courses or a conversation among several people. Note any nonverbal feedback sent from the listener to the speaker and note whether the speaker responds to the feedback. Record your observations below. Possible observations and reactions can be found at the end of the chapter.

Nonverbal Feedback to Speaker	Speaker's Response to Feedback
1.	1.
2.	2.
3.	3.
4.	4.
5.	5.
6.	6.
7.	7.
8.	8.
9.	9.

Analysis and Reflections

The use of feedback is important to effective teaching. Since language is sometimes vague and misleading, how can you make your feedback interpretations more in line with the reality of the sender? Submit a short paper to your instructor relative to your ideas.

Identifying and responding to feedback is a skill all teachers should learn. Task 6.6 gives you further practice in identifying feedback.

Although responding to feedback in the learning environment is an effective way to improve instruction, many teachers rarely, if ever, use feedback as part of their teaching strategy. The most effective teachers know that feedback is too valuable to be avoided or ignored.

Summary

- Teachers communicate with students to bring about learning.
- Teacher interactions consist of both a spoken and a nonverbal message, with the spoken message having a verbal and a vocal component.

Verbal Communication
- The verbal component of a message is the actual words spoken.
- The vocal component of a message is the meaning attached to the words, depending upon the voice loudness, pitch, inflection, tone, and rate.

Nonverbal Communication
- Not all communication is audible. Special importance should be given to nonverbal communication.
- Although most teachers understand the importance of verbal communication, many underestimate how much students learn from a teacher's facial language, body language, use of space and motion, use of time, and use of the voice.

Community and Parental Links
- A concordant relationship among students, teachers, administrators, parents, and community will improve the quality of instruction.
- Schools are being urged to solve many of society's problems. This task calls for links between schools and communities.
- Opening communication with parents is essential to effective classroom instruction. This communication should be initiated at the beginning of the school year.

Listening
- Both teachers and students should acquire listening skills. They are essential to both teaching and learning.
- It is impossible to learn without skill in listening.
- Better listening on a teacher's part will result in more effective teaching. Teachers must learn to control the bad habit of talking too much and actively listen.

Reflective Listening
- Teachers need to practice the art of reflective listening.
- Teachers must learn to listen with feeling as well as with cognition.

Feedback
- Teachers generally talk too much. They have not learned to use nonverbal communication effectively.

- Teachers have not learned to really listen to students and to use the feedback students continuously send regarding lesson understanding.
- It is essential that teachers develop an understanding of and a skill in all facets of the communication process.

Activities

1. *Classroom observation*   Complete several observations in different level classrooms. Plan your visits to collect viable data related to the communication process. Collect observational data regarding:
   a. the effective use of verbal communications.
   b. the different types of nonverbal communications used by the teachers.
   c. the teachers' skill as effective listeners.
2. *Listening in your present setting*   Using the Listening in Your Present Setting Worksheet on page 179, record all that you hear in your present setting for five minutes. When finished, compare what you heard with others in the same setting. Consider the following questions in your comparisons:
   a. Were the same things heard?
   b. Does past experience affect what is heard?
   c. Do internal feelings affect what is heard?
3. *Vocal communications*   Play a tape of an instructional episode with no video. List any information you note being sent through vocal communications.
4. *Nonverbal communications*   Play the tape in Activity 3 with video but no audio. List any information you see being sent by the teacher or the students through nonverbal communication.
5. *Community-school links*   Research suggests that it is important to have strong family involvement in school learning. Access Internet URL site **http://ericweb.tc.columbia.edu/families/strong/index.html** for ways to involve families in school learning. Briefly describe techniques that you feel would be effective at the grade level you want to teach.

Answer Keys

Task 6.1 Verbal Communication
Possible observations of differences between verbal messages and vocal messages include:
1. "I really enjoy my work." A monotone voice with no variation in pitch or tone conveys a neutral attitude or a dislike for work.
2. "He is such an interesting person." A voice with no variation or reflections could indicate dislike of the person.
3. "I'm not too excited about next week." A fast voice rate and higher pitch could indicate excitement about the next week.
4. "Good idea." Steady tone with no variation could indicate that the idea was not so good.

5. "I wasn't a bit afraid!" Quiver in voice, fast rate, and high pitch would indicate fear.

Possible observations of vocal messages and voice qualities include:

1. *Excitement*   High voice tone, fast rate.
2. *Thinking*   Slow rate, hesitant with words.
3. *Happiness*   High voice tone, high pitch, fast rate.
4. *Interest*   High pitch, reflection at word endings.
5. *Anger*   Loud voice with high pitch, voice variation.

Task 6.2 Nonverbal Communication
Observed nonverbal message possibilities include:

1. *Raised eyebrows*   Surprise at something being said
2. *Wink*   A joke on a group member
3. *Rigid posture*   Discomfort about something being discussed
4. *Looking at watch*   In a hurry to leave
5. *Backing away from individual*   Dislike of individual
6. *Fist hit into palm of other hand*   Stressing a point
7. *Hard stare*   Disapproval
8. *Pat on back*   Approval for doing something good
9. *Eyes looking away from speaker*   Not really interested in what is being said
10. *Continuous movement*   Restlessness

Task 6.3 The Communication Process
1. *False*   You should also be concerned with receiving and decoding feedback.
2. verbal component, vocal component
3. *True*   The manner in which something is said will sometimes convey a message. Often this nonverbal message is more important than the verbal.
4. Nonverbal communication is communication without words, communicating through the way we speak and use our bodies.
5. *True*   These messages are nonverbal in nature.
6. a. *Facial language*   The use of facial expressions that communicate.
   b. *Body language*   The use of the body and its parts to communicate.
   c. *Space and motion language*   The use of space and movement in the environment to communicate.
   d. *Time language*   The use of time to send information.
   e. *Voice language*   Using voice intonation to communicate.
7. The whole community is often needed to foster the development of the whole child.
8. Newsletters, notes, phone calls, weekly folders home, daily reports home, parent conferences, and home visits are a few effective techniques for communicating with parents.

Task 6.4 Identifying Personal Listening Filters
Possible filters include:

1. Words such as: Republican, Democrat, hick, AIDS, Jew, communist, venereal disease, party, and school

2. Worry about someone
3. A special occasion
4. Just after an accident
5. An upcoming date
6. Past dislike for a subject or person
7. A fight with someone
8. A fight between parents
9. Hunger
10. An upcoming job interview

Task 6.5 The Listening Process

1. *False*   Often people who talk too much are poor listeners.
2. *True*   Good listeners must think.
3. *False*   True listening requires one to think.
4.   a. Attention to the speaker and the message.
     b. Understanding, that is, selecting and organizing the information sent.
     c. Evaluation, that is, judging the worth of the information against personal beliefs, values, and attitudes.
5. *False*   Reflective listening involves the content of the message and its associated feelings.

Task 6.6 Identifying Feedback

Possible nonverbal feedback and responses include:

1. *Yawning*   Speaker speeded up presentation.
2. *Looking out the window*   Instructor moved to a new position and raised voice loudness.
3. *Reading book or newspaper*   Speaker paused, gave student a hard stare, and continued.
4. *Writing letter*   Instructor moved closer to individual.
5. *Talking*   Instructor stopped speaking.

Theory and Research

Benson, P. L. (1997). *All kids are our kids: What communities must do to raise caring and responsible children and adolescents.* San Francisco: Jossey-Bass.

Gettinger, M., & Guetschow, K. W. (1998). Parental involvement in schools: Parents and teacher perceptions of roles, efficacy, and opportunities. *Journal of Research and Development in Education, 32*(1), 38–52.

Youngerman, S. (1998). The power of cross-level partnerships. *Educational Leadership, 56*(1), 58–60.

References

Charles, C. (1981). *Education for dignity and rapid achievement.* Washington, DC: ERIC Reports. Document 170. SP016751.

Epstein, J. L. (1991). Paths to partnership. *Phi Delta Kappan, 72* (5), 344–349.

Epstein, J. L., Coates, L., Salinas, K. C., Sanders, M. G., & Simon, B. (1997). *School, family, community partnerships: Your handbook for action.* Thousand Oaks, CA: Corwin Press.

Friedman, P. G. (1983). *Listening processes: Attention, understanding, evaluation.* Washington, DC: National Education Association.

Galloway, C. (1976). *Silent language in the classroom.* Bloomington, IN: Phi Delta Kappa Educational Foundation, Fastback 86.

Hennings, D. G. (1975). *Mastering classroom communications—What interaction analysis tells the teacher.* Pacific Palisades, CA: Goodyear.

Hurt, H. T., Scott, M. D., & McCroskey, J. C. (1978). *Communications in the classroom.* Menlo Park, CA: Addison-Wesley.

Krall, C. M., & Jalongo, M. R. (1999). Creating a caring community in classrooms: Advice from an intervention specialist. *Childhood Education, 75*(2), 83–89.

Ludwig, S. (October 1999). Working with parents. *Teaching K–8,* 60.

Miller, P. W. (1981). *Nonverbal communications.* Washington, DC: National Educational Association.

Nichols, R. G., & Stevens, L. A. (1957). *Are you listening?* New York: McGraw-Hill.

Sokolove, S., Sadker, D., & Sadker, M. (1986). Interpersonal communication skills. In J. M. Cooper (Ed.), *Classroom teaching skills* (3rd ed.). Lexington, MA: D. C. Heath.

Trenholm, S. (1998). *Thinking through communication: An introduction to the study of communication* (2nd ed.). Boston: Allyn and Bacon.

Trenholm, S., & Jensen, A. (1996). *Interpersonal communication* (3rd ed.). Belmont, CA: Wadsworth Publishing.

Wolvin, A. D., & Cookley, C. G. (1979). *Listening instruction.* Urbana, IL: ERIC Clearinghouse Reading and Communications Skills.

Listening in Your Present Setting Worksheet (5-Minute Time Limit)

Setting _____

Date _____ Time: from _____ to _____

Listener _____

List of what is heard.

1. _____
2. _____
3. _____
4. _____
5. _____
6. _____
7. _____
8. _____
9. _____
10. _____
11. _____
12. _____
13. _____
14. _____
15. _____
16. _____
17. _____
18. _____
19. _____
20. _____

Reinforcement

Objectives

After completing your study of Chapter 7, you should be able to:

1. Describe the attributes of reinforcement theory and the theories of Pavlov, Thorndike, and Skinner.

2. Differentiate between positive and negative reinforcement.

3. Describe the different types of reinforcement that can be used in the classroom.

4. Describe the characteristics and components of a reinforcement system.

5. Describe the effects of different reinforcement schedules on the patterns of response.

6. Explain procedures that can be used to identify effective classroom reinforcers.

7. Differentiate between praise and encouragement, and explain the effects of each.

Actions that bring pleasure tend to be repeated. This is human nature. When a student works to obtain something, that "something" (object, action, event, etc.) acts as a reinforcer for that student. However, what reinforces one student may not reinforce another. Remember that reinforcement always increases the strength of some behavior. For example, students who repeatedly ask to stay in from recess are being reinforced in some way. You should keep in mind that any repeated behavior, appropriate or inappropriate, is somehow being reinforced.

Reinforcement, or the rewarding of desired student behavior, is a long-recognized and essential skill for classroom teachers. Once learned and refined, it will make you much more effective in the classroom. Too often, however, teachers unconsciously overuse the same reinforcers, which leads to a loss in their effectiveness. Moreover, teachers sometimes unwittingly reinforce undesirable student behaviors, making their teaching less effective. Since reinforcement is so important in the classroom, let's take a brief look at the theory behind its use.

⚔ Reinforcement Theory

The one theory of influence almost every teacher knows about is reinforcement theory, often referred to as stimulus-response (S-R) theory by theorists. And if you know only one theory, this would be a good candidate. It works in many situations, it can be simply applied, and it has just a few basic ideas. In fact, reinforcement theory boils down to the point that: Consequences influence behavior. This means that people do things because they know other things will follow. Thus, depending upon the type of consequence of an action, people will produce some behaviors and avoid others. Simply stated, reinforcement theory or stimulus-response (S-R) theory suggests that consequences influence behavior. Classical conditioning, connectionism, and operant conditioning are three forms of reinforcement or S-R theory.

Classical Conditioning

Classical conditioning is perhaps the oldest model of change. The essence of classical conditioning comes from the work of Russian physiologist Ivan Pavlov (1849–1936). Pavlov developed what is called classical conditioning in his experiments with salivating dogs. When meat powder was placed on a dog's tongue, the dog salivated. This process was repeated several times, with one difference. Pavlov preceded the meat powder by half a second or so with the sounding of a bell on each occasion. After pairing the meat powder and bell several times, Pavlov sounded the bell but did not follow the bell with the meat powder. Still the dog salivated. The dog had learned to salivate in response to the bell. Thus, conditioning takes place when you start with two things that are already connected with each other (food and salivation). Then you add a third thing (bell) for several trials. Eventually, this third thing becomes so strongly associated that it has the power to produce the old behavior.

Classical conditioning does not address rewards and punishments which are key terms in reinforcement theory. Classical conditioning is built on creating strong relationships by associations formed over various numbers of trials.

This type of influence is commonly found in everyday life. If you have a pet and you feed it with canned food, what happens when you operate the can opener? Sure, the pet comes running even if you are opening a can of corn. Your pet has associated the sound of the opener with its food. Some people confuse classical conditioning with reinforcement theory. To keep them separated just look for the presence of rewards and punishments.

Perhaps the strongest application of classical conditioning involves some form of emotion. Common experience and careful research both confirm that human emotion conditions very rapidly and easily. Particularly when the emotion is intense or negatively directed, it will condition quickly. For example, several years ago a car coming toward me swerved over into my lane resulting in a head-on collision. I was hurt quite severely in the collision. This event happened at night with the car headlights shining in my eyes and for a long time thereafter, I was extremely apprehensive at night when a car came toward me with its headlights shining in my face.

Clearly, classical conditioning can have a strong impact on behavior in our world. It is a natural feature of all humans and it is relatively simple and easy to accomplish.

Connectionism

The work of Thorndike represents the original S-R framework of behavioral psychology: Learning is the result of associations or connections formed between stimuli and responses. Such connections or "habits" become strengthened or weakened by the nature and frequency of the S-R pairings. The original pattern for S-R theory was trial-and-error learning in which certain responses come to dominate others due to rewards. The proof of **connectionism** was that learning could be adequately explained without referring to any unobservable internal states.

Thorndike's theory consists of three primary laws: (1) law of effect—responses to a situation which are followed by a reward will be strengthened and become habitual responses to that situation, (2) law of readiness—several responses can be linked to satisfy some goal which will result in annoyance if blocked, and (3) law of exercise—connections become strengthened with practice and weakened when practice is discontinued. A corollary to the law of effect is that responses that reduce the likelihood of achieving a rewarding state (i.e., punishments, failures) will decrease in strength.

Connectionism theory suggests that transfer of learning depends upon the presence of identical elements in the original and new learning situations; that is, transfer is always specific, never general. The concept of "belongingness" was introduced in later versions of the theory. The belongingness concept suggests that connections are more readily established if the person perceives that stimuli or responses go together.

Operant Conditioning

Decades after Thorndike published his theory, another American psychologist, B. F. Skinner, extended and formalized many of Thorndike's ideas. The theory of

B. F. Skinner is based upon the idea that learning is a function of change in overt behavior. Changes in behavior are the result of an individual's response to events (stimuli) that occur in the environment. A response produces a consequence such as solving a math problem, making a good basketball shot, or spelling a word. When a particular stimulus-response (S-R) pattern is reinforced (rewarded), the individual is conditioned to respond. The distinctive characteristic of **operant conditioning** relative to previous theories is that the organism can emit responses instead of only eliciting response due to an external stimulus.

Skinner introduced the term *operant* or *operant response* to distinguish the responses in operant conditioning from those in classical conditioning. An operant is a response that has some effect on the world, it is a response that *operates on* the environment. For example, when a student says, "Mrs. Jones, I can't work this problem." and is then helped, the student has made an operant response that determines when help will appear.

Reinforcement is the key to Skinner's S-R theory. A reinforcer can be anything that strengthens the desired response. It could be a good grade, free time, or a good feeling of increased accomplishment or satisfaction. The theory also covers negative reinforcement. Before we look at reinforcement in more detail, complete Task 7.1 which will check your understanding of this section.

T A S K   7 . 1

Reinforcement Theory

Respond to the following reinforcement theory items. Check your responses with those given at the end of the chapter.

1. The main point of reinforcement theory is _____ .

2. According to reinforcement theory, why do people do things? _____

   _____

   _____

3. Match the theory characteristic on the left with the theorist on the right.

   ___ a. Individual can emit responses for a   1. Pavlov
          desired award.

   ___ b. New connection learned from pairing   2. Thorndike
          new desired connection with an existing
          connection.

   ___ c. The law of effect.   3. Skinner

Analysis and Reflections

Classical conditioning often comes from some kind of strong emotion. Can the ideas associated with classical conditioning be applied to the classroom? If so, how can they improve learning? Can you identify examples (past experiences or projected ideas) of the effective classroom use of classical conditioning? Form groups of four or five and discuss the answers generated to these questions.

✗ Positive Versus Negative Reinforcement

Reinforcement in the classroom can occur in two different ways (Woolfolk, 1987). **Positive reinforcement** occurs when teachers use a rewarding stimulus to motivate some action or behavior. The reward may be something tangible or intangible, such as grades, free time, praise, being named class leader, or even being made to stand in the hall. Sometimes an event (such as being made to stand in the hall) is a positive reinforcer for a student, even though it may not seem rewarding to the teacher. Many times positive reinforcement of inappropriate behavior occurs unintentionally in the classroom because teachers have a limited understanding of what students find rewarding. You should be conscious of this fact and try to diagnose the hidden reinforcers when an undesirable behavior persists.

Negative reinforcement involves removing students from an unpleasant stimulus, such as detention or the threat of punishment. Students are allowed to escape the unpleasant situation by behaving appropriately. Examples are sitting in their seat until they are ready to participate appropriately during an activity, staying in at recess until work is completed, or going to a time-out area until they are ready to settle down. Note that with the use of negative reinforcement, the student is in control. The negative situation can be escaped when the student chooses to perform the appropriate behaviors. Negative reinforcement is often confused with punishment, which gives the student no choice.

Positive or negative reinforcement is a powerful tool for motivating students and should result in an increase in some desired behavior. Moreover, when teacher reinforcement is withheld, undesirable behaviors will often desist.

✗ Types of Reinforcement

Several types of reinforcement are typically used in the average classroom (Cooper et al., 1994). The most effective type in any given situation depends on such variables as the grade level, individual student, learning activity, and teacher.

Verbal Reinforcement

Verbal reinforcement occurs when the teacher follows a student action or response with some type of positive comment. The most common verbal reinforcers are one-word comments or phrases such as "Good," "Excellent," "Correct," or "That's right." One should take care not to overuse these brief reinforcers or they will lose their effectiveness. Likewise, if *all* student comments are followed by verbal reinforcement, the comments will soon lose their effectiveness. Therefore, do not overuse verbal reinforcements, and vary them so that they remain fresh and meaningful.

Another commonly overlooked form of verbal reinforcement is the use of student ideas. This technique can be used by applying, comparing, or building on contributions made by students during a lesson. Incorporating student ideas shows that what they say is important and usually increases the degree of student participation.

Nonverbal Reinforcement

Nonverbal reinforcement refers to the use of some physical action to send a message of approval for some student action or response. The physical action can be in the form of eye contact, a nod, a smile, movement toward the student, a relaxed body, or some positive gesture. Do not overlook the use of nonverbal reinforcement in the classroom; it may be even more powerful than verbal reinforcement. Research suggests that when verbal and nonverbal messages differ, students tend to respond to the nonverbal message.

Vicarious Reinforcement

People learn by observing others. If they observe others being reinforced for certain actions or behaviors, they tend to act in the same way if the reinforcement is desirable. This is termed **vicarious reinforcement.** For example, if student A is praised for a certain action and student B desires the same teacher praise, student B will model the reinforced action. Such teacher statements as, "I like the way Mary raises her hand before talking," "Mike's science report was excellent," and "Cindi always gets right to work on her assignments" are examples of the effective use of vicarious reinforcement. Vicarious reinforcement is usually more effective with younger students; however, it can also be used effectively with older students when the reinforcers are carefully chosen.

Vicarious reinforcement is usually efficient in that the desired behavior has already been modeled and consequently does not have to be taught. With properly chosen reinforcers and appropriate application, vicarious reinforcement can be used to teach new behaviors, encourage old behaviors, or strengthen or weaken inhibitions.

Delayed Reinforcement

Teachers usually reinforce students immediately following desired actions. However, it is also possible and sometimes desirable to reinforce students for some earlier action. For example, a class question can be directed to a student who has shown prior knowledge in the subject area. This reinforcement of earlier action is referred to as **delayed reinforcement.** Through delayed reinforcement you show that actions or contributions are not forgotten but have continuing importance. It also reveals to students the importance you attach to earlier student actions.

Qualified Reinforcement

When student actions are only partially acceptable, you may want to reinforce the student in a manner that will motivate continued attempts at the desired action. In such situations you should use the technique of qualified reinforcement.

Expansion Activity: Reinforcement

We have discussed various types of reinforcement. Which type(s) do you feel would be most effective for use with students at the grade level you plan to teach. Write a paragraph or two outlining the rationale for your selection(s). Submit your work to the instructor.

Qualified reinforcement occurs when you reinforce only the acceptable parts of a student action or the attempt itself. For example, when a student gets a problem wrong at the chalkboard, you could reinforce the fact that the procedure used was correct, or you could reinforce the student's good effort. Or a student could be reinforced for presenting an interesting idea even though it was not related to the topic being discussed. Qualified reinforcement is an effective technique that can be used to get shy and less able students more involved in class discussions.

This completes our discussion of reinforcement types. Complete Expansion Activity: Reinforcement to apply these concepts to the grade level you plan to teach.

✷ Reinforcement Systems

You may sometimes want to use a more formal system of reinforcement (Woolfolk, 1987). One program that has been highly successful is the **token reinforcement system,** in which students earn tokens by performing teacher-desired actions or behaviors. These actions can be related to academics or to classroom behaviors. Tokens may be in the form of points, chips, holes punched in a card, stars, checks, play money, or anything else that seems appropriate. The tokens are exchanged periodically for rewards. The rewards can be such things as free time, less homework, food, tangible objects, being named class leader, games, free reading, or anything appropriate that is desired by the students.

One can also offer a menu of rewards in a token reinforcement system. Students then purchase the rewards for different numbers of tokens. It is usually wise to offer some less desirable rewards for only a few tokens and the most desirable rewards for a larger number of tokens. This way students will work for the higher number of tokens to get the more desirable rewards. For example, with young children you might offer five minutes of free time for a few tokens and a little toy for several tokens. With older students you might offer being excused from a homework assignment for a few tokens and being allowed to listen to music in class for several tokens.

One advantage to using a formal reinforcement system is that no students are inadvertently overlooked and excluded from receiving reinforcement. In addition, reinforcement systems have proved to be successful at both the elementary and the secondary level, as well as in special classrooms.

The types of reinforcement used by a teacher depend on the situation. However, all types can be effective if used appropriately. Try your skill at categorizing the different types of reinforcement by completing Task 7.2.

T A S K   7 . 2

Identifying Reinforcement Types

Classify the following reinforcement types as specified. Check your responses with those given at the end of the chapter.

1. Identify each of the following statements as an example of positive reinforcement (P) or negative reinforcement (N).

    _____ a. "Steve, you can read your book when you finish the assignment."
    _____ b. "James, please sit down until you can behave appropriately."
    _____ c. "This paper is excellent, Maria! You made some very valid points. Keep up the good work."
    _____ d. "Frank, go to the time-out area until you calm down!"
    _____ e. "Mary, since you raised your hand before talking, I want you to be class monitor next week."

2. Classify each of the following examples of reinforcement as verbal reinforcement (VR), nonverbal reinforcement (NR), vicarious reinforcement (VIR), delayed reinforcement (DR), qualified reinforcement (QR), or a reinforcement system (RS).

    _____ a. "I like the way Susan got right to work on the assignment."
    _____ b. Kenny received three checks today for not talking out in class.
    _____ c. The teacher nods her head as a student talks.
    _____ d. "Excellent answer, John!"
    _____ e. The teacher makes good eye contact as a student answers a question.
    _____ f. "That's an important point, Jane, but it doesn't really answer the question."
    _____ g. "I believe Helen can answer that question since she gave an excellent report on the topic last month."
    _____ h. "Mary's paper certainly is neat."
    _____ i. "That's a good point, Joe."
    _____ j. An hour of free time on Friday is earned if all homework is completed for the week.
    _____ k. "That's a good attempt at the problem, Edna, but the solution is incorrect."
    _____ l. The teacher writes a student response on the board.
    _____ m. "You're right, Alan, in that the disease is transmitted by an insect, but it isn't a fly."
    _____ n. "Good point, Mike. Elaborate on it."
    _____ o. "Sally, can you add to Ellen's point from your earlier study?"

Analysis and Reflections

Write a short paper that addresses the pros and cons of using positive and negative reinforcement at the grade level you plan to teach. Submit your paper to the instructor.

If you had trouble with Task 7.2, reread the last three sections on types of reforcement.

Reinforcement Schedules

Timing and frequency of reinforcement are extremely important in reinforcement theory. Students are more likely to repeat an action if they are reinforced immediately after the action occurs. The longer you delay reinforcement following a desired student behavior, the less likely the student is to repeat the behavior. Therefore, if a teacher wishes to encourage a certain student action, that action should be followed *immediately* by reinforcement.

Students learn faster when they are reinforced after each occurrence of a desired action, or what is referred to as a **continuous reinforcement schedule.** Generally, a continuous reinforcement schedule should be used in the early stages of learning. However, once the desired behavior has been established, it is best to use an **intermittent reinforcement schedule,** that is, to reinforce often but not following each occurrence of the desirable behavior.

An intermittent reinforcement schedule can be administered on either a ratio or an interval basis. If a student is reinforced only after a certain number of desired actions, a **ratio reinforcement schedule** is being used by the teacher. For example, the teacher might praise a student after every third question is answered correctly. However, if the teacher praises a student after a certain amount of time, an **interval reinforcement schedule** is being used. Reinforcing students after every five minutes of time spent on an assigned task or in a cooperative learning situation is an example of this method.

Ratio and interval reinforcement schedules can be further subclassified into fixed and variable schedules. A **fixed reinforcement schedule** is being used if the reinforcement is given after a fixed number of the desired behaviors (fixed ratio) or after a fixed amount of time (fixed interval). A fixed ratio schedule is being used when a teacher gives a student a gold star, say, after every fifth assignment is completed. However, if the student receives the gold star every second day for completing all the assignments, a fixed interval schedule is being used.

In a **variable reinforcement schedule,** no predetermined number of actions or length of time is used in administering the reinforcement. For example, a variable ratio schedule is being used when a student is given praise for raising his or her hand before speaking after three times, then ten times, then five, fifteen, and so on. If the student receives the praise after five minutes, then ten minutes, then two, fifteen, and so on, a variable interval schedule is in operation.

Generally it takes longer to establish a desired action through intermittent reinforcement. However, one major advantage of intermittent reinforcement is that extinction is slower. Slow **extinction** means that the desired action will continue without reinforcement for a longer period of time. Moreover, variable ratio and variable interval schedules are more resistant to extinction than are fixed ratio and fixed interval schedules, because the students never know when reinforcement will come. The hope of reinforcement lasts longer when its application has been unpredictable. For example, students working on a group project in the library or completing seatwork are more inclined to stay on-task when the teacher checks their progress on an unpredictable basis. If teacher visits are predictable, students will be tempted to work only when the teacher is due. Since the ratio schedule is based on output while the interval schedule is more concerned with being on-task, it is best to use fixed or variable ratio schedules if you desire production. If your goal is to keep students on-task, fixed or variable interval schedules usually work best.

Table 7.1 summarizes the different kinds of reinforcement schedules, gives an example, and lists the major advantage and disadvantage of each. An examination of the table suggests that, if possible, you should use a continuous reinforcement schedule in establishing a new desired behavior. This schedule generally works fastest. However, once the new behavior has been mastered,

TABLE 7.1

Reinforcement Schedules

Schedule	Definition	Advantage	Disadvantage
Continuous	Reinforce every correct behavior.	Behavior rapidly established	Very rapid extinction
Intermittent			
Fixed ratio	Reinforce after fixed number of correct behaviors.	Slow extinction	Behavior established slowly
Fixed interval	Reinforce after fixed time interval following correct behaviors.	Slow extinction	Behavior established slowly
Variable ratio	Reinforce after various numbers of correct behaviors (second, fifth, tenth, fourth, etc.).	Very slow extinction	Behavior established very slowly
Variable interval	Reinforce after various time intervals following correct behaviors (5 min., 10 min., 8 min., etc.).	Very slow extinction	Behavior established very slowly

you should switch to an intermittent variable schedule of reinforcement since it resists extinction better once reinforcement is discontinued.

Because the effective use of reinforcement can greatly facilitate student learning, it is extremely important that you understand the different types of reinforcement and reinforcement schedules. Task 7.3 checks that understanding.

T A S K   7 . 3

Reinforcement Concepts

Respond to the following items. Check your responses with those given at the end of the chapter.

1. Classify the following examples of reinforcement schedules as being continuous (C), fixed ratio (FR), fixed interval (FI), variable ratio (VR), or variable interval (VI).

   _____ a. Ralph is praised every half hour if he has stayed in his seat.

   _____ b. Liz is praised every time she raises her hand before speaking.

   _____ c. The class is occasionally given an hour of free time for being quiet when told to do so.

   _____ d. Joe is given a token for every fifth neat paper he hands in to the teacher.

   _____ e. Students in Ms. Smith's class are praised when they answer a question correctly.

   _____ f. At various times throughout the day, Mr. Harmon gives his students five minutes just to relax and talk.

   _____ g. Tammy is sometimes allowed to go to the library when her math assignments have been completed correctly.

   _____ h. Mr. Franklin allows his students time to discuss any topic they wish if there has been no class misbehavior for a week.

   _____ i. Students in Ms. Anderson's class receive an extra point on their final grade for every two optional assignments they complete.

   _____ j. Ms. Holt occasionally grades her students' progress on the term paper they have been assigned.

2. Established behaviors usually result from some type of reward.   (True/False)

3. Positive and negative reinforcement occur when a desirable stimulus is presented for an appropriate behavior.   (True/False)

4. List and briefly describe the five types of reinforcement.

   a. _____

   _____

   b. _____

   _____

   c. _____

   _____

   d. _____

   _____

Continued on next page

e. _____

_____

5. A reinforcement system that uses tokens is most effective in the special education classroom.   (True/False)

6. When used, reinforcement should always immediately follow the desired student action.   (True/False)

7. An intermittent reinforcement schedule requires reinforcement after each occurrence of a desired behavior.   (True/False)

8. A fixed interval reinforcement schedule is being used when the student receives reinforcement once a week (on Fridays) for appropriate behavior during the week. (True/False)

9. A variable ratio reinforcement schedule is being used when the student receives reinforcement after 2 desirable actions, then 6 desirable actions, then 1, 4, 15, and so on.   (True/False)

10. Generally one should establish desirable behaviors by using intermittent reinforcement.   (True/False)

11. Extinction of desirable behaviors is slowest when a fixed schedule of reinforcement is used.   (True/False)

Analysis and Reflections

Plan a reinforcement system that you think will be effective at the grade level you plan to teach. Form groups of four or five and discuss your system. Write a short report on the final version of your reinforcement system and submit it to your instructor.

❈ Selecting Reinforcers

Teachers must use care in selecting appropriate reinforcers for use with individual students (Boules, 1981; Hall & Hall, 1998). As noted earlier, what is viewed as a reinforcer by one student may not be a reinforcer for another. Thus, the best reinforcers for students are the ones selected by the students themselves.

There are various ways in which a teacher can identify student reinforcers, for example, through student observation, by simply asking the students, or through the use of student questionnaires.

Teacher attention is, for most students, an effective reinforcer. The attention can be either verbal or nonverbal; that is, it can be in the form of verbal statements or gestures that show you approve of the student's action. However, care must be taken in giving students attention. Remember that even criticism is a form of teacher attention, and that some attention-hungry students will misbehave in order to receive negative attention.

A useful guide in choosing the most effective reinforcement is the **Premack principle,** which states that a preferred activity is an especially effective reinforcer for a less preferred activity (Premack, 1965). Simply stated, the rule says: First do what I want you to do, and then you can do what you want to do. Too often teachers reverse this procedure and allow students to do what they want with the promise that they will do what the teacher wants later. Of course, they seldom get around to doing what the teacher wants. For example, visiting among students should not be allowed until seatwork has been completed. Do not accept the students' promise that they will do the work later.

Teachers use many different reinforcers in their daily interaction with students. They can grant privileges, give tangible rewards, grant free time, allow talking, grant exemption from assignments or tests, allow students to read magazines or play games, or simply give praise for a job well done. Whatever method is used to choose rewards for students, you must remember the importance of reinforcement and select reinforcers carefully.

⚔ Misuse of Reinforcement

Reinforcement must be used with care, and it does not always bring about the desired learning or the desired student actions. Misused reinforcement can actually be detrimental to the learning process.

As mentioned earlier, one way teachers misuse reinforcement is to rely totally on one or two favorite types. These overused reinforcers soon lose their effectiveness. In fact, once students note their overuse and begin looking for them, these teacher behaviors can distract from the learning process. Perhaps the most commonly overused reinforcers are "Okay" and "All right." You should guard against their overuse.

Another way in which reinforcement can be misused is to reinforce virtually all student responses. Too often teachers feel that students should always be reinforced for their contributions, and thus, they reinforce students even when the response is not appropriate. Incorrect responses should *never* be reinforced; only the attempt or any part of the response that was on the right track (qualified reinforcement) should be reinforced. A similar misuse occurs when a teacher reinforces unworthy responses or actions of their high-achievement students. Since these students are too often viewed as being superior, it is assumed that their responses *must* be superior and thus must warrant praise.

Given too quickly, reinforcement can detract from the learning process by blocking or interfering with the complete development of student ideas. One must take care that the student has finished before providing reinforcement for the ideas presented. Also, frequent reinforcement can interfere with student-to-student interactions by focusing attention back to the teacher with each new reinforcer. Thus, a two-way student-to-student interaction pattern can unwittingly be transformed into a three-way student-teacher-student pattern. You must learn to wait before applying desired reinforcement. After all students have finished, you can provide individual or group reinforcement.

Finally, some criticism has been voiced regarding the use of reinforcement. It is argued that its use weakens or slows the development of **intrinsic motivation**

Web Search: Intervention Portfolios

Access Internet URL site **http://www.usd.edu/usdspa/discipline. html** relative to intervention reinforcement strategies to discourage inappropriate behaviors or to reinforce appropriate behavior. Analyze at least two portfolio sets (preschool and grades K–2, Grades K–2 and 3–5, or Grades 6–8 and 9–12) and write a short paper on the appropriateness of the suggestions for the grade level you plan to teach. Form groups of four or five and discuss your conclusions.

(motivation from within) and leads students to depend on **extrinsic motivation** (motivation from without). In other words, it teaches students to do things only for the external reward received rather than for internal satisfaction. However, if reinforcement is used appropriately and with care, this criticism can be avoided. Reinforcement should be used only with students who need the extra incentive or when the desired behavior is unpopular or difficult. The reinforcement can then be phased out when the appropriate time seems to have come—that is, when the students are behaving as desired. Complete Web Search: Intervention Portfolios which will let you examine possible reinforcers.

⚔ Encouragement

Teachers often use praise as a reinforcer in the classroom. However, one should use care in reinforcing with praise, because praise rewards the individual and tends to address the self-worth of the student. For example, praise statements such as "Good answer!" or "Good boy (or girl)!" tend to convey the message that the person is worthy only if he or she knows correct answers. This is not to say that praising a student's actions or responses should be avoided. We all like to receive praise at times, but we also like to receive encouragement. In fact, sometimes we need encouragement to complete a task before we can receive praise for a job well done.

Encouragement differs from praise in that it stimulates the efforts and the capacity of the individual. Examples include, "How nice that you figured that out yourself," "Keep trying," "Don't give up," "I am sure you can solve the problem," "I'm sure you can handle it," or "You certainly are a hard worker!" These responses encourage students to continue trying and not to give up.

Praise and encouragement are effective teaching tools when used with care. Teachers must know their students well enough so that they can praise or encourage them on an individual basis.

Take a few minutes to complete Task 7.4, which checks your understanding of the selection and use of reinforcements.

T A S K   7 . 4

Reinforcement Selection and Use

Respond to the following items. Check your responses with those given at the end of the chapter.

1. Describe three techniques you can use to identify student reinforcers.

   a. _____
   _____

   b. _____
   _____

   c. _____
   _____

2. Teacher attention can be used as an effective reinforcer.   (True/False)
3. State the Premack principle.

   _____
   _____

4. It is always good to use reinforcement in the classroom.   (True/False)
5. Praise and encouragement are basically the same thing; that is, they are reinforcers. (True/False)

Analysis and Reflections

Praise and encouragement can be used as reinforcement. Which do you feel would be best for use with students at the grade level you plan to teach? Why? Share your conclusions with the class.

Summary

- Actions that bring pleasure tend to be repeated. Any repeated student behavior is being reinforced.
- Teachers sometimes unwittingly reinforce undesirable student behaviors.

Reinforcement Theory

- Reinforcement theory boils down to the point that: Consequences influence behavior.
- Classical conditioning is perhaps the oldest model of change. Conditioning takes place when a new association is made by pairing it with an existing association.
- The strongest application of classical conditioning involves some form of emotion.
- Thorndike's work represents the original S-R theory: Learning is the result of connections formed between stimuli and response.
- Thorndike's theory consists of three primary laws: (1) law of effect, (2) law of readiness, and (3) law of exercise. A corollary to the law of effect is that

responses that reduce the likelihood of achieving a rewarding state will decrease in strength.
- Skinner extended and formalized many of Thorndike's ideas in developing the theory of operant conditioning.
- Skinner suggests that behavior is the result of an individual's response to events (stimuli) that occur in the environment. The distinctive characteristic of operant conditioning is that the individual can emit responses instead of only eliciting response due to an external stimulus.
- Reinforcement is the key to Skinner's S-R theory. A reinforcer can be anything that strengthens the desired response.

Positive Versus Negative Reinforcement
- Teachers can either apply a rewarding stimulus (positive reinforcement) or remove an unpleasant stimulus (negative reinforcement) to motivate students to some action or behavior.
- Positive or negative reinforcement is a powerful tool for motivating students and should result in an increase in some desired behavior.

Types of Reinforcement
- Reinforcement can be a verbal comment, a nonverbal action, a vicarious experience, a delayed comment, or a qualified comment.
- Teachers should base selection of reinforcement types on the grade level, the individual student, and the learning activity.

Reinforcement Systems
- A formal system of reinforcement is sometimes needed. One highly successful program is the token reinforcement system. Students are given tokens for performing teacher-desired actions or behaviors.
- Menu of rewards can be used in a token reinforcement system.
- An advantage to using a formal reinforcement system is that no students are inadvertently overlooked and excluded from receiving reinforcement.

Reinforcement Schedules
- Use continuous reinforcement to establish desirable behaviors, and switch to an intermittent schedule to maintain the behavior.
- An intermittent reinforcement schedule can be administered on either a ratio or an interval basis. When reinforcement is given after a certain number of actions, a ratio schedule (fixed or variable) is being used, whereas when reinforcement is given after a certain time interval, an interval schedule (fixed or variable) is being used.

Selecting Reinforcers
- Use care in selecting appropriate reinforcers for use with individual students. The best reinforcers are the ones selected by the students themselves.
- Use the Premack principle as a guide: First do what I want you to do, and then you can do what you want to do.

Misuse of Reinforcement
- Reinforcement should be used with care. It does not always bring about the desired learning or action.

- Avoid using one favorite reinforcer. It soon loses its effectiveness.
- Avoid reinforcing all student responses.
- Avoid giving reinforcement too quickly.

Encouragement
- Do not overuse praise as a reinforcer. Praise tends to reward the self-worth of the individual.
- Some students will benefit from the use of encouragement.

Activities

1. *Classroom observation*   Complete several observations in different teaching-learning environments. Plan your visits to collect viable data related to reinforcement. Collect observational data regarding:
   a. The use of positive and negative reinforcement
   b. The different types of reinforcement used by teachers
   c. The different reinforcement schedules used in the learning environment
   d. The use of praise and encouragement
2. *Microteaching*   Teach a 20-minute mini-lesson to a group of students or peers. Try to use as many of the different types of reinforcement as possible in your teaching. If possible, videotape the lesson.
3. *Microteaching analysis*   Study the videotape you made in Activity 2. Record your uses of reinforcement and reinforcement schedules. Draw conclusions about your use of positive and negative reinforcement, reinforcement types, and reinforcement schedules.

Answer Keys

Task 7.1 Reinforcement Theory
1. consequences influence behavior
2. People do things for what will follow their actions; that is, for the reward it gives them.
3. a. 3 b. 1 c. 2

Task 7.2 Identifying Reinforcement Types
1. a. P   b. N   c. P   d. N   e. P
2. a. VIR   d. VR   g. DR   j. RS   m. QR
   b. RS   e. NR   h. VIR k. QR   n. VR
   c. NR   f. QR   i. VR   l. NR   o. DR

Task 7.3 Reinforcement Concepts
1. a. FI   c. VR   e. C   g. VR   i. FR
   b. C   d. FR   f. VI   h. FI   j. VI
2. *True*   Almost all established behaviors are a result of some reward.
3. *False*   A positive stimulus is presented when using positive reinforcement, but negative reinforcement involves the removal of an undesirable stimulus following appropriate behavior.

4. a. *Verbal reinforcement*   A verbal comment of acceptance or satisfaction.
   b. *Nonverbal reinforcement*   The use of a physical action to send a message of approval or satisfaction.
   c. *Vicarious reinforcement*   Learning proper behaviors by seeing others being reinforced for those behaviors.
   d. *Delayed reinforcement*   Reinforcing an earlier response or action.
   e. *Qualified reinforcement*   Reinforcing only the correct portion of a response or action.
5. *False*   Reinforcement systems can be effective in any classroom when used appropriately.
6. *True*   The longer one waits, the less effective the reinforcement.
7. *False*   An intermittent schedule requires that you reinforce often, but not following each occurrence of the desired action.
8. *True*   The time interval between reinforcements is fixed (constant).
9. *True*   The number of desirable actions between reinforcements is variable.
10. *False*   Desired behaviors are usually best established through the use of continuous reinforcement.
11. *False*   Extinction of desirable behaviors is slowest when a variable schedule is used.

Task 7.4 Reinforcement Selection and Use
1. The responses will vary. However, possible responses are:
   a. Ask students what they want or will work for.
   b. Observe students during free time for ideas on what they like to do.
   c. Use a student questionnaire to elicit suggestions.
2. *True*   Teacher attention can be an effective reinforcer, but care must be taken not to reinforce negative behaviors.
3. First do what I want you to do, and then you can do what you want to do.
4. *False*   The overuse of reinforcement can be detrimental to the learning process.
5. *False*   Praise is a reinforcer, whereas encouragement is a stimulator or motivator.

Theory and Research

Domjan, M. (1995). *The essentials of conditioning and learning.* Pacific Grove, CA: Brooks/Cole.
Wallace, W. (1993). *Theories of personality.* Needham Heights, MA: Allyn and Bacon.

References

Boules, A. (Ed.). (1981). *Crossroads . . . A handbook for effective classroom management.* Oklahoma City: Oklahoma State Department of Education.
Cooper, J. M., Garrett, S. S., Leighton, M. S., Martorella, P. H., Morine-Dershimer, G. G., Sadker, D., Sadker, M., Shostak, R., TenBrink, T. D., & Weber, W. A. (1994). *Classroom teaching skills* (5th ed.). Lexington, MA: D. C. Heath.

Hall, R. V., & Hall, M. L. (1998). *How to select reinforcers.* Austin, TX: PRO-ED.

Premack, D. (1965). Reinforcement theory. In D. Levine (Ed.), *Nebraska symposium on motivation* (vol. 13). Lincoln, NE: University of Nebraska Press.

Woolfolk, A. E. (1987). *Educational psychology for teachers.* Englewood Cliffs, NJ: Prentice-Hall.

Questioning

Objectives

After completing your study of Chapter 8, you should be able to:

1. Explain the importance of questioning to the teaching process.

2. Explain the importance of using different levels of questions.

3. Identify and differentiate between convergent and divergent questions.

4. Identify and differentiate among factual, empirical, productive, and evaluative questions.

5. Explain the importance of using different types of questions.

6. Identify and differentiate among focusing, prompting, and probing questions.

7. Define *wait time 1, wait time 2, halting time,* and *silent time.*

8. Explain the importance of and benefits derived from the use of redirecting, wait time, halting time, silent time, and reinforcement.

9. Identify guidelines that should be followed in effective questioning.

Research indicates that in most classrooms someone is talking most of the time. Generally it is the teacher who talks and the students who listen. One way to switch from teacher-centered instruction to student-centered instruction is through the use of questions. Thus, skill in questioning becomes a vital component of effective teaching (Brown & Wragg, 1993; Wilen, 1991).

✕ The Art of Questioning

Questioning is basic to good communications. However, proper questioning is a sophisticated art, one at which few people are proficient despite having asked thousands of questions in their lifetimes. Questioning lies at the heart of good, interactive teaching. Questions must be at the appropriate level, be of the appropriate type, and above all, be worded properly. Moreover, refining the art of questioning requires that teachers master techniques for following up on students' responses or lack of responses. We will now look at the different levels at which questions can be asked.

✕ Levels of Questions

Questions may be categorized as narrow or broad. Narrow questions usually require only factual recall or specific, correct answers. Broad questions, however, can seldom be answered with a single word and often do not have one correct answer. Broad questions usually require that students go beyond simple memory and use the thinking process to formulate answers. Although both kinds of questions are useful in the learning process, teachers traditionally rely too heavily on narrow questions at the expense of broader, thought-provoking ones.

Effective teachers adapt the level of questions to their teaching objectives (Dillion, 1983, 1990). If learning specific information is the objective, then narrower questions are appropriate. If thinking processes are the objective, then broader questions are needed. Since thinking can take place at several levels of sophistication, it is important that teachers be able to classify and ask questions at these levels.

There are many classificational systems for describing the different levels of questions. Most of them are useful only to the extent that they provide a framework for formulating questions at the desired level within a classroom environment. Consequently, some teachers may want to use only a two-level classificational system, while others may want to use a more detailed system.

One of the most extensive systems for classifying educational objectives (see Chapter 4 for a modified version) and classroom questions is that devised by Benjamin Bloom (Bloom, Englehart, Furst, Hill, & Brathwohl, 1965). His system consists of six levels of cognitive thought, five of which can be further divided into sublevels, making it possible to classify questions to an even greater degree.

Although Bloom's Taxonomy is extensive and very useful for classifying questions, most teachers find it too complex to use in the classroom. Instead of using Bloom's Taxonomy, we will focus our attention on two alternative systems that will benefit you more. The first is the system of classifying questions as convergent or divergent; the second categorizes questions according to the mental operation involved in answering them. This second system was created by the author as a simplified version of the question types presented in Bloom's Taxonomy and is correlated with Guilford's Structure of the Intellect model (Guilford, 1956).

The classification systems that are presented and discussed in this chapter are only two of the many systems that can be used effectively in the classroom. By using these or another system of questioning, you will significantly improve the quality of your questions and the quality of classroom interaction and learning.

Convergent and Divergent Questions

One of the simplest systems for classifying questions is to determine whether they are convergent or divergent. **Convergent questions** are those that allow for only one right response, whereas **divergent questions** allow for many right responses. Questions about concrete facts are convergent, while questions dealing with opinions, hypotheses, and evaluations are divergent.

Questions about concrete facts (who, what, when, and where questions) which have been learned and committed to memory are convergent. Examples are:

Who is President of the United States?
What is 5 + 3?
Where is Austria located?
What was the major cause of the Depression?

Convergent questions may also require students to recall and integrate or analyze information to provide *one expected* correct answer. The following questions are also convergent:

Based on our discussion, what was the major cause of the stock market crash of 1929?
Combining the formulas for a triangle and a rectangle, what would be the formula for finding the area of a parallelogram?
Based on our definition of war, can you name any countries that are now engaged in war?

Most alternate-response questions, such as those that can be answered yes or no, or true or false, are also classified as convergent, since student response is limited. Some examples of alternate-response questions are:

Is $x + y = 3$ a quadratic equation?
Is this a picture of a farm animal or a house pet?
Are the results what we expected from this experiment?
Is this logic statement true or false?
Is this statement an observation or an inference?

Conversely, questions calling for opinions, hypotheses, or evaluations are divergent, since there are many possible correct responses. Examples include:

Why do you suppose we entered World War I?
What would be a good name for this story?
Can you give me an example of the use of this word in a sentence?
Why is it important that we continue to explore space?
Who do you consider the greatest scientist that ever lived?

Divergent questions should be used frequently because they encourage broader responses and are, therefore, more likely to involve students in the

T A S K   8 . 1

Convergent and Divergent Questions

Respond to the following items. Check your responses with those given at the end of the chapter.

1. Classify each of the following questions as convergent (C) or divergent (D).

   _____ a. What can you tell me about Africa?
   _____ b. Which of these plants is tallest?
   _____ c. Mary, can you define a noun?
   _____ d. Do we have sufficient information to answer this question?
   _____ e. What do you suppose will happen to the lost dog?
   _____ f. What can we possibly make from these things?
   _____ g. What holiday do most people celebrate in November?
   _____ h. What would it be like to live in China?
   _____ i. Based on what you read in the textbook, what causes the different seasons of the year?
   _____ j. Given a length of 15 centimeters and a width of 25 centimeters, what is the area of this rectangle?

2. Write two questions that are convergent. You will not find an answer key for this question. You must decide by rereading the last section whether you have written acceptable questions.

   _____
   _____
   _____

3. Write two questions that are divergent. You will not find an answer key for this question. You must decide by rereading the last section whether you have written acceptable questions.

   _____
   _____
   _____

Analysis and Reflections

When questioning students, does the teacher need to be concerned with how children from different cultures might respond to certain types of questions or to the teacher's questioning technique? Write a short response to this question and submit it to your instructor.

learning process. They require that students think. However, convergent questions are equally important in that they deal with the background information needed to answer divergent questions. In the classroom it is generally desirable to start with convergent questions and move toward divergent questions.

In summary, convergent questions limit student responses to only one correct answer, whereas divergent questions allow for many possible correct responses. To check your ability to differentiate between and to write convergent and divergent questions, complete Task 8.1.

Mental Operation Questions

In the late 1950s, J. P. Guilford (1956) published his Structure of the Intellect, a model that classified all mental operations into five major groups: cognitive, memory, convergent thinking, divergent thinking, and evaluative thinking. Based on this model and the six levels of Bloom's Taxonomy, the Mental Operation System for classifying questions was developed. Table 8.1 shows the relationship between the Mental Operation System, Bloom's Taxonomy, and Guilford's Structure of the Intellect model. The Mental Operation System is basically a four-category system that combines four of Bloom's categories into two categories. In addition, the system combines the cognitive and memory categories of the Guilford model into a single factual category. The four categories of questions that make up the Mental Operation model are factual, empirical, productive, and evaluative.

Factual questions test the student's memory. Answering a factual question requires the simple recall of information through the mental processes of recognition and rote memory. Students simply recall information, or recall and translate information. Factual questions are the narrowest of questions. Some examples include:

Who invented the automobile?
Nick, can you define the short story?
Mary, what did we do and see at the zoo yesterday?

TABLE 8.1

Categories of Questions

Mental Operation Questions	Bloom's Taxonomy	Guilford's Structure of the Intellect
1. Factual	Knowledge or comprehension	Cognitive or memory processes
2. Empirical	Application or analysis	Convergent thinking
3. Productive	Synthesis	Divergent thinking
4. Evaluative	Evaluation	Evaluative thinking

Which side of the room is the longest?

What is the formula for the volume of a cone?

Empirical questions require that students integrate or analyze remembered or given information and supply a predictable answer. The question may call for a lot of thinking, but once thought out, the answer is usually a single, correct answer. That is, information must be applied correctly to arrive at a single answer, or the logical evidence of analysis must lead to a single valid conclusion. Empirical questions are also often narrow questions. Some examples are:

Based on our study of Germany, what conditions in that country led to World War II?

Given this triangle with a height of 4 centimeters and a base of 5 centimeters, what is its area?

What is the most economical source of energy?

Which of these two forms of government is the most democratic?

Note that these questions require that students recall learned information and use it to arrive at the correct answer to the question. However, there is only one correct answer.

Productive questions do not have a single correct answer. They are open-ended, and it is usually impossible to predict what the answers will be. They call for students to use their imagination, to think creatively, and to produce something unique. Productive questions are broad and require that students go beyond the simple recall of information. However, students need the basic related information in order to answer the question. Some examples are:

How can we improve our performance in mathematics?

What changes would we see in the attitude of society if we were to elect a woman president?

What are some possible solutions to the unemployment problem?

What do you suppose was the author's intent in writing this story?

Evaluative questions require that students make judgments or put a value on something. Like productive questions, they are often open-ended. However, they are often more difficult to answer than productive questions since they require the use of some internal or external criteria; that is, some criteria must be established for making the judgment. The responses to evaluative questions can often be confined to a limited number of choices. For example, the question "Which of these two paintings is better?" limits the responses to two, whereas the question "What is the best automobile made today?" allows a number of responses. Other examples of evaluative questions include:

Who was our greatest president?

How would you rate our success in controlling hunger in this nation?

Do you think the author of the book developed the main character sufficiently?

Were the Indians treated fairly by the white man?

TABLE 8.2

Levels of Classroom Questions

Category	Type of Thinking	Examples
Factual	Student simply recalls information.	Define . . . Who was . . . ? What did the text say . . . ?
Empirical	Student integrates and analyzes given or recalled information.	Compare . . . Explain in your own words . . . Calculate the . . .
Productive	Student thinks creatively and imaginatively and produces something unique.	What will life be like . . . ? What's a good name for . . . ? How could we . . . ?
Evaluative	Student makes judgments or expresses values.	Which painting is best? Why do you favor this . . . ? Who is the best . . . ?

These questions require that students make a judgment based on some internal criteria. Therefore, it is often good practice to follow an evaluative question with an empirical or productive question asking for the reasons behind the stated judgment or value.

The Mental Operation System of classifying questions will give you the needed framework for improving your questioning skill. You should be asking questions at all levels of the system instead of at only the factual level, as many teachers tend to do. It is especially important that you ask more productive and evaluative questions than is common practice. These questions give students the opportunity to think.

Table 8.2 offers a review of the Mental Operation System for classifying questions. Study it carefully and complete Task 8.2, which will check your understanding of the system.

We have looked at two different systems for classifying questions. Either system can be used to improve your questioning skill. However, the Mental Operation System offers a greater degree of differentiation without the complexity attached to Bloom's Taxonomy. We will use the Mental Operation System in the remainder of this chapter.

⚔ Types of Questions

Effective teachers must also ask the right type of questions; that is, you must adapt the type of question to your lesson objectives (Falkor & Moss, 1984; Sadker & Sadker, 1982; Wassermann, 1992). For example, you may want to ask questions to determine the level of your students' learning, to increase their

T A S K   8 . 2

Mental Operation Questions

Respond to the following items. Check your responses with those given at the end of the chapter.

1. Classify each of the following items as factual (F), empirical (EM), productive (P), or evaluative (EV).

    _____ a. Calculate the area of this circle.
    _____ b. What is your opinion of our court system?
    _____ c. According to the text, what was the main cause of the Depression?
    _____ d. What do you predict will happen to the automobile in the next 20 years?
    _____ e. Who was the father of mathematics?
    _____ f. John, compare the work of Steinbeck with that of Hemingway.
    _____ g. How can we as a nation better meet the changing needs of our society?
    _____ h. Why do you favor the American form of government over the British form?
    _____ i. What does this story mean to you?
    _____ j. How do mammals differ from fish?

2. Write two questions at each of the four levels of the Mental Operation System for classifying questions. No answer key is provided for this task; you must decide whether your questions are acceptable by studying Table 8.2 and rereading the last section.

    a. Factual

    _____

    _____

    _____

    _____

    b. Empirical

    _____

    _____

    _____

    _____

    c. Productive

    _____

    _____

    _____

    _____

    d. Evaluative

    _____

    _____

    _____

    _____

Continued on next page

T A S K   8 . 2   C o n t i n u e d

Analysis and Reflections

Questions should be asked not just to assess student learning but to promote it. What does this mean? Write a short response to this statement and submit it to your instructor.

---

involvement and interaction, to clarify understanding, or to stimulate their awareness. These purposes all call for different types of questions.

Focusing Questions

Focusing questions, which may be factual, empirical, productive, or evaluative, are used to focus student attention on the day's lesson or on material being discussed. They may be used to determine what students have learned, to motivate and arouse student interest at the start of or during the lesson, or to check understanding during or at the close of a lesson.

Did students read the assigned chapter? No use discussing the material if it was not read! Did the students learn and understand the material assigned? Can students apply the information? Focusing questions provide the answers to such questions. Factual questions can be used to check on basic knowledge at the beginning of or during a lesson. Empirical questions prompt students to figure out correct solutions to assigned problems and issues. Productive and evaluative questions motivate and stimulate student thinking and interest in a topic.

When you ask a question to open a lesson or discussion, it is good practice to use a productive or evaluative question, since they tend to arouse students' interest and thinking. For example:

What do you suppose would happen if I were to combine these two solutions?
How could we test the hypothesis presented in the text?
Should the United States assume the role of world peacekeeper?

Questions of this type should then be followed with questions at all levels to develop understanding and to maintain interest.

Prompting Questions

What do you do when a student fails to answer a question? Most teachers answer the question themselves or move on to another student. This tactic gets the question answered, but it fails to involve the original student in the discussion. It leaves that student with a sense of failure which, more than likely, will result in even less future participation. A better way to address an unanswered question is to use a prompting question as a follow-up.

Prompting questions use hints and clues to aid students in answering questions or to assist them in correcting an initial response. A prompting question is usually a rewording of the original question with clues or hints included. The following dialogue includes a prompting question:

"What is 5 plus 7, Pat?"
"I don't know."
"Well, let's see if we can figure it out. What is 5 plus 5?"
[Pause.] "10."
"Right. Now, we want 5 plus 7. How many more than 5 is 7?"
[Pause.] "2."
"Good. So, if 5 plus 5 is 10 and we add 2 more, what is 5 plus 7?"
[Pause.] "12."
"Very good, Pat."

Note that in this example a series of questions is used to develop the prompting question: "So, if 5 plus 5 is 10 and we add 2 more, what is 5 plus 7?" This need not always be the case, as we see next:

"What is the chemical formula for water, Henry?"
[Pause.] "I don't know."
"Well, if a water molecule consists of two atoms of hydrogen and one atom of
    oxygen, what is its chemical formula?"
[Pause.] "H_2O."
"Right."

Students often respond to questions incorrectly. As a teacher you cannot let incorrect answers pass. Of course you could give the correct answer or have another student give it. However, a better tactic is to have the student analyze his or her initial response for the error. The following sequence shows the use of prompting questions to correct an initial student response:

"Can you give me a noun, Randy?"
[Pause.] "Go."
"Let's look at that answer. What is a noun?"
[Long pause.] "A person, place, or thing."
"Is 'go' the name of a person, place, or thing?"
[Pause.] "No."
"Good. Can you give us another example?"
"New York."
"Very good."

Note that in this example the teacher asks the student to examine the initial answer and then assists the student in arriving at a correct response through the use of prompting questions.

The use of prompting questions should give students a sense of success when they finally answer correctly. These successes should act as reinforcers to students, which should result in even greater participation.

Probing Questions

Focusing questions are used to determine the level of learning and to increase student participation, whereas prompting questions are used when no response is forthcoming. Another situation arises when student responses lack depth. In such cases you should ask students to supply additional information through the use of probing questions.

Probing questions force the student to think more thoroughly about the initial response. They are used to develop clarification, develop critical awareness, or refocus a response.

You may want to probe for clarification. Students sometimes give answers that are only half-answers or that are not well thought out. These responses should be followed up with probing questions to force the student to think more thoroughly and to firm up the response. Examples of such probing questions are:

What do you mean by that?
What do you mean by the term . . . ?
Would you rephrase that?
Could you elaborate on that point?
Can you explain more fully?

You may sometimes want students to justify their answers, that is, to develop their critical awareness. This can be accomplished through the use of probing questions, as in the following examples:

What is your factual basis for this belief?
Why do you say that?
What are you assuming?
What are your reasons for that statement?
Are you sure there isn't more?

Finally, you may want to probe to refocus a correct or satisfactory response to a related issue. Examples of such questions are:

Let's look at this answer with respect to . . .
Can you relate this answer to . . . ?
What implications does your answer have for . . . ?
Apply your solution to . . .
Can you relate Mike's earlier answer to the issue . . . ?

The different types of questions are invaluable teaching tools. They can increase student participation and involve students in their own learning. You should become proficient in their use. Task 8.3 will help you do that.

✵ Questioning Techniques

There are certain techniques associated with asking questions that tend to increase the quantity and quality of the students' responses (Hunkins, 1994; Hyman 1979). In this section we will look at four such techniques.

Redirecting

Redirecting is a technique in which you ask several students to respond to a question, in light of the previous responses. It is an effective way of building

T A S K   8 . 3

Identifying Types of Questions

Read the following anecdote and identify the teacher's questions as focusing (F), prompting (PT), or probing (PB). Check your responses with those given at the end of the chapter.

_____ 1. "We've been studying polygons this week, and I want to review what we've studied to this point. What is a polygon?" [Pause.] "Sandy?"
"A closed figure with three or more sides."

_____ 2. "Good, Sandy. Can you name one way that we use polygons in everyday life?" [Pause.] "Mike?"
"Road signs have the shape of different polygons."

_____ 3. "Right. What do we call a four-sided figure?" [Pause.]
"Helen?"
"A square."

_____ 4. "You're right in that a square has four sides, but there are many figures with four sides. What do we call all four-sided figures?"
[Pause.] "A parallelogram."

_____ 5. "That's another example of a four-sided figure. Do you remember what the prefix *quad* means?"
"Yes, four."

_____ 6. "So, a four-sided figure would be a quad . . . ?"
"Quadrilateral!"

_____ 7. "Can you name the quadrilateral that has only two sides parallel and no sides equal? Sam?"
[Long pause.] "I don't know."

_____ 8. "Does this help?" [Teacher draws trapezoid on the board.]
"A trapezoid."

_____ 9. "Very good, Joe, name the triangle that has two sides of equal length."
"Isosceles triangle."

_____ 10. "Okay. Do you see an example of an isosceles triangle in this room, Mary?"
[Long pause.] "Yes, the easel."

_____ 11. "Right. What is a regular polygon? Jan?"
"A polygon with all angles of equal size."

_____ 12. "Good. What else can you tell me about a regular polygon?"
"All the sides are of equal length."

Analysis and Reflections

Write a brief dialogue, using realistic teacher and student responses, that illustrates a sequence of related questions that prompt student responses. Submit your dialogue to your instructor.

broader participation in classroom discussions. Since there must be several correct responses, the question must be divergent, productive, or evaluative. The following is an example of how you might use the redirecting tactic.

"We have now studied the contributions of several great men and women of
    science. Which scientist do you think made the greatest contribution?"
    [Pause. Several hands go up.]
"Carol?"
"Albert Einstein."
"Mary?"
"Marie Curie."
"Mike, your opinion?"
"Thomas Edison."

Notice that in using the redirecting tactic, you do not react to the student
response. Your function is simply to redirect the question to another student.
Thus student participation and involvement are increased, which should lead
to greater learning and increased interest.

The redirecting technique can also be used effectively with students who
do not volunteer to answer questions. It is important to involve nonvolunteers
since, as noted earlier, participation leads to more learning and stimulates interest. The following is an example of how to use the redirecting technique to
involve nonvolunteers:

"We've been discussing atomic energy as a source of power. However, there
    are dangers associated with its use. The question is, should we develop
    it as a power source?" [Long pause. Several hands go up.] "Bob?"
"Yes, I think we should. We can build them with a lot of safeguards."
"Okay. What do you think, Helen?"
[Long pause.] "I don't think we should. It's just too dangerous. We couldn't
    put in enough safeguards to make it really safe."
"Would you like to make a comment, Billy?"
[Long pause.] "I agree with Bob. I think we could make it safe to use."

It is important to note that, in this last example, the nonvolunteers are not
forced to answer. Rather they are given the opportunity to make a contribution
to the discussion. In addition, note that they are given time to consider a response. This time is referred to as *wait time,* which we will discuss next.

Wait Time

Students need time to think, time to ponder the responses they will give to your
questions. However, research (Rowe, 1974a, 1974b, 1978) has shown that teachers
on the average wait only about *one second* for students to answer questions. Further
research by Rowe revealed that when teachers learn to increase the time they wait
following a question to between three and five seconds, the following things occur:

1. The length of student responses increases.
2. Failure to respond decreases.
3. Questions from students increase.
4. Unsolicited responses increase.
5. Confidence of students increases.
6. Speculative thinking increases.

There are two types of wait time. **Wait time 1** is the initial time provided for the first student response to a question. **Wait time 2** is the total time a teacher waits for all students to respond to the same question or for students to respond to each others' responses to a question. Wait time 2 may involve several minutes. If you wish to raise student involvement, you must learn to increase your wait time tolerance so that students will have more opportunities to think about their answers.

The pattern of questioning that is all too typical in the average classroom is:

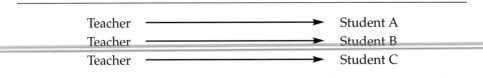

It is nothing more than a question-and-answer period. The teacher asks a question of an individual student, receives an answer, moves to the next student, asks a question, receives an answer, moves to the next student, and so on. Students are often given little time to think and express themselves and no time to react to each others' comments. In fact, most of the questions are typically at the factual level. Appropriate use of high-level questions and wait time can often change this sequence to:

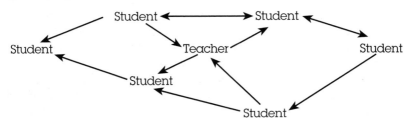

Rather than a question-and-answer session, you have a real discussion. Students give extended responses, comment on other students' responses, and ask questions. There is real interest and involvement. Thus, extending the time you wait following a question to between three and five seconds and giving students time to react to other students' responses is well worth the added effort.

Halting Time

Halting time is similar to wait time in that the teacher pauses during what he or she is saying to give students time to think. However, no questions are asked, and no student comments are elicited. Halting time is particularly useful when you are presenting complex material or directions.

In using halting time, you present some of the complex material or directions and then stop so that students have time to think or carry out the directions. During the halt, you visually check with the class to see whether they appear to understand what you are trying to communicate. If the students do appear to understand, you continue. If, on the other hand, students appear to be confused, you may want to ask questions or redo the explanation or directions.

Listening

Learn to listen to your students. Listen to what they have to say, and when they have finished, and only then, formulate further questions or comment on their answers. Too often teachers are busy focusing on themselves while students are speaking. They are formulating the next question, the next explanation, or the next activity. In fact, teachers are often so eager to continue that they interrupt or cut off students before they have finished.

Develop the use of silent time. **Silent time** is the time taken after a student has finished speaking before you reply or continue. Research indicates that teachers wait on the average only about one second following a student response. Silent time, like time after asking a question, should be increased to between three and five seconds to prevent you from cutting off students and to allow time for other students to interject their comments.

Reinforcement

Once you have asked a question and an acceptable response has been given, you must decide how to react. Should you offer praise or approval, or should you merely accept the response without comment and continue with the lesson? How you react—that is, your pattern of reinforcement—has a powerful effect on the direction of the interaction in the classroom.

Reward and praise following student responses to a teacher's questions are effective in encouraging students to participate. Responses like "Good," "Great," "What an outstanding idea," and "Super" may be used to effectively reward a student's correct answer. A detailed discussion of reinforcement techniques was given in Chapter 7. You may want to review these techniques at this point.

Although some reinforcement is good, the too-frequent application of reinforcement negates the benefits derived from wait time. Wait time is used to give students time to think and to give other students the opportunity to respond. However, if you reinforce students early in an answering sequence, other students may decide not to respond because they fear their answer could not be as good as the earlier response. After all, you did say the earlier response was "super."

Rather than giving reinforcement after the initial response to a question, you should allow as many students as possible to respond, then reinforce all of them for their contributions. You can return to the best answer for further comment.

This concludes our discussion of various techniques that can be used to improve questioning skills. Apply the concepts addressed up to this point in Expansion Activity: Teacher Intent.

The next section gives some general guidelines on questioning. Before you continue reading, however, complete Task 8.4, which involves questioning techniques.

Expansion Activity: Teacher Intent

Being asked a question can be a punishment as well as a reward.

Form groups of four or five and react to this statement. Generate ways teacher questions can be a punishment and ways questions can be a reward. Share your group's conclusions with the class.

T A S K   8 . 4

Questioning Techniques

Respond to each of the following items that deal with the use of various questioning techniques. Check your responses with those given at the end of the chapter.

1. Label the following definitions as wait time 1 (W1), wait time 2 (W2), halting time (HT), or silent time (ST).

   _____ a. The time you wait following a student response before you continue
   _____ b. The time you allow all students in class to respond to a question
   _____ c. A pause used to give students time to think and ponder
   _____ d. The time you wait for the initial response to a question

2. The appropriate use of wait times will usually lead to greater student participation. (True/False)

3. Student question responses should always be reinforced.   (True/False)

4. The redirecting tactic requires that a student respond to a question in light of another student's response.   (True/False)

5. Teacher silent time should be about _____.

6. The use of halting time requires that you be proficient at asking higher-level questions.   (True/False)

7. Wait time 1 may be as long as _____.

8. The redirecting tactic may be used successfully with nonvolunteers.   (True/False)

Analysis and Reflections

The criteria for effective *oral* questions generally apply equally to written questions as well, but there are some exceptions. Try to identify other criteria that are applicable only to written questions. In what important ways do written and oral questions differ? Share your criteria with the class.

✴ Questioning Guidelines

Asking good questions is an art that can be mastered with practice (Hyman, 1979). The following guidelines will be helpful as you refine your skill at questioning.

1. *Ask clear questions*   Questions should ask something definite in simple, clear language that students can understand. Avoid ambiguous, confusing constructions and excess verbiage.
2. *Ask your question before designating a respondent*   Ask the question, wait for the class to think about it, and then ask someone for an answer. As usual, there are exceptions to this rule. When you call on an inattentive student, it is often better to call the name first so that the question will be heard. Similarly, you should call the name first when you address slow or shy students, so that they can prepare themselves.
3. *Ask questions that match your lesson objectives*   When facts are wanted, ask factual and empirical questions. When you want to stimulate student thinking, ask productive and evaluative questions. Use different levels of questions.
4. *Distribute questions about the class fairly*   Avoid directing all questions to a few bright students. However, also avoid developing a mechanical system for asking questions. Students soon catch on to such systems as going by alphabetical order or row by row, and they will pay attention only when they know it is their turn.
5. *Ask questions suited to all ability levels in the class*   Some questions should be easy and some should be difficult, so that all students will have a chance to respond to some questions correctly.
6. *Ask only one question at a time*   Asking two or three questions at once often confuses students. Multiple questions permit no time to think and, since several questions were asked, students are not sure which question to answer first.
7. *Avoid asking questions too soon*   It is usually much more effective to establish a knowledge base before initiating a questioning sequence. This is especially true when higher-level questions are to be asked.
8. *Pause for at least 3 seconds following each question*   A three-second pause gives students time to think and to formulate their answers.
9. *Use questions to help students modify their responses*   Use prompting and probing questions to help students to think more thoroughly about their responses. This keeps students involved in the lesson, develops better thinking skills, and reinforces the idea that students can be successful.
10. *Avoid too many questions that give away answers, and avoid one-word-answer questions*   These questions do nothing to stimulate student thinking. When used too often, they lead to boredom.
11. *Reinforce student answers sparingly*   Remember that the reinforcement of every student response can kill a discussion. Students often fear that they will be unable to compete with the preceding reinforced responses.
12. *Listen carefully to student responses*   Wait at least three seconds following an answer to give the student time to make further comments and to allow other students time to react to the first response.

This list of guidelines is not all inclusive. Complete Expansion Activity: Guidelines to generate some guidelines of your own.

Expansion Activity: Guidelines

Form groups of four or five. Generate additional do's and don'ts in asking questions. Share your lists with the class.

Summary

- Someone is usually talking in the classroom. The teacher does most of this talking.
- Questions can help switch from teacher-centered instruction to student-centered instruction.

The Art of Questioning

- Questioning is basic to good communication.
- Questions are at the heart of good, interactive teaching. However, these questions must be appropriate.

Levels of Questions

- Asking good questions involves more than simply asking students clear questions about specific content. You must adapt questions to your lesson intent.
- Questions may be categorized as narrow or broad. Factual recall of information requires the use of narrow (convergent) questions, whereas the desire to stimulate thinking calls for the use of broad (divergent) questions.
- A more detailed system for classifying questions is sometimes needed. Your instructional purpose may require different levels of questions, from simple factual, to empirical, to productive, to evaluative.

Types of Questions

- Effective teachers ask the right types of questions. They fit their purpose.
- Effective instruction may require the use of focusing, prompting, and probing questions.

Questioning Techniques

- Redirecting your questions, using wait time and halting time, listening well, and using reinforcement will enhance your skill as a teacher.
- Proper questioning techniques can widen student participation and improve the quality of student responses.

Questioning Guidelines

- There is no end to the degree of sophistication your questioning skills may attain.
- Practice and modify your questioning behavior in order to improve student learning and the social-emotional climate of your classroom.

Activities

1. *Classroom question analysis*   Construct an instrument to analyze questioning in an observational setting. Use your constructed instrument in several observational settings and analyze the results. Consider the following in your instrument construction and analyses:
   a. What levels of questions are used most often?
   b. Are questions clear?
   c. Is time used effectively?
   d. Is reinforcement used effectively?
   e. Are various types of questions used?
2. *Microteaching*   Teach a 20-minute mini-lesson to a group of students or peers. Try to use different levels of questions, different types of questions, and the various techniques discussed in this chapter. Record the lesson.
3. *Microteaching analysis*   Study the recording of your miniteaching experience made in Activity 2. Use the instrument you constructed in Activity 1 to analyze the experience. What conclusions can you draw regarding your questioning proficiency?
4. *Investigating textbook questions*   Obtain the teacher and student editions of a textbook for any grade level and subject. Choose one unit within that textbook and analyze the questions contained in the student text and the questions suggested by the teacher edition. What levels of questions are most frequently used?

Answer Keys

Task 8.1 Convergent and Divergent Questions
   a. *D*   Many responses possible
   b. *C*   Limited predictable responses possible
   c. *C*   Only one correct response possible
   d. *C*   Yes or no response
   e. *D*   Many responses possible
   f. *D*   Many responses possible
   g. *C*   Limited predictable responses possible
   h. *D*   Many responses possible
   i. *C*   Limited to information from the textbook
   j. *C*   Only one correct response possible

Task 8.2 Mental Operation Questions
   a. *EM*   One correct response
   b. *EV*   Judgment required
   c. *F*   Recall of textbook information
   d. *P*   Many possible correct, unpredictable responses
   e. *F*   Simple recall of information
   f. *EM*   An analysis of recalled information required

g. *P*   Many possible correct, unpredictable responses
h. *EV*   Values expressed
i. *P*   Many possible correct, unpredictable responses
j. *EM*   Analysis of recalled information required

Task 8.3 Identifying Types of Questions
1. *F*   Used to see whether student has learned material
2. *F*   Used to stimulate thinking
3. *F*   Used to see whether student has learned material
4. *PT*   Hint given to correct response
5. *PT*   Clue given to correct response
6. *PT*   Clue given to assist student
7. *F*   Used to see whether student has learned material
8. *PT*   Clue given to help student arrive at correct answer
9. *F*   Used to see whether student has learned material
10. *F*   Used to see whether student can apply the concept
11. *F*   Used to see whether student has learned materials
12. *PB*   Probe for additional information

Task 8.4 Questioning Techniques
1. a. ST   b. W2   c. HT   d. W1
2. *True*   The appropriate use of wait times 1 and 2 has been shown to lead to greater student participation.
3. *False*   Although the use of reinforcement may increase student involvement, overuse may be detrimental to student interaction.
4. *True*   This is the basic purpose of the redirecting tactic.
5. between 3 and 5 seconds
6. *False*   No questions should be asked during halting time.
7. between 3 and 5 seconds
8. *True*   The use of the redirecting tactic with nonvolunteers may get them involved in the lesson.

Theory and Research

Carlsen, W. S. (1991). Questioning in classrooms: A sociolinguistic perspective. *Review of Educational Research, 61*, 157–178.

Pizzini, E. L., Shepardson, D. P., & Abell, S. K. (1992). The questioning level of select middle school science textbooks. *School Science and Mathematics, 92*(2), 74–78.

Wilen, W. (1991). *What research has to say to the teacher: Questioning techniques for teachers* (3rd ed.). Washington, DC: National Education Association.

References

Bloom, B. S. (Ed.), Engelhart, M. D., Furst, E. J., Hill, W. H., & Brathwohl, D. R. (1965). *Taxonomy of educational objectives, handbook I: Cognitive domain.* New York: David McKay.

Brown, G., & Wragg, E. (1993). *Questioning.* London: Routledge.

Dillion, J. (Ed.). (1990). *The practice of questioning.* New York: Routledge.

Dillion, J. T. (1983). *Teaching and the art of questioning.* Bloomington, IN: Phi Delta Kappa.

Falkor, L., & Moss, J. (November 1984). When teachers tackle thinking skills. *Educational Leadership,* 4–9.

Guilford, J. P. (July 1956). The structure of intellect. *Psychological Bulletin, 53,* 267–293.

Hunkins, F. P. (1994). *Effective questions, effective thinking* (2nd ed.). Needham, MA: Gordon Publishing.

Hyman, R. T. (1979). *Strategic questioning.* Englewood Cliffs, NJ: Prentice Hall.

Rowe, M. B. (1974a). Wait time and rewards as instructional variables, their influence on language, logic, and fate control: Part 1, Wait time. *Journal of Research in Science Teaching, 11*(2), 81–94.

———(1974b). Relation of wait time and rewards to the development of language, logic, and fate control: Part 2, Rewards. *Journal of Research in Science Teaching, 11*(4), 291–308.

———(1978). *Teaching science as continuous inquiry.* New York: McGraw-Hill.

Sadker, M., & Sadker, D. (1982). Questioning skills. In J. M. Cooper (Ed.), *Classroom teaching skills* (3rd ed.). Lexington, MA: D. C. Heath.

Wassermann, S. (1992). *Asking the right question: The essence of teaching.* Fastback 343. Bloomington, IN: Phi Delta Kappa.

Wilen, W. W. (1991). *Questioning skills for teachers.* Washington, DC: National Education Association.

Classroom Management

Objectives

After completing your study of Chapter 9, you should be able to:

1. Define the concept of motivation from the cognitive and stimulation points of view.

2. Discuss student attitudes, needs, self-esteem, and natural motives and their motivational effect on learning.

3. Differentiate between deficiency and growth needs as well as their relation to student motivation.

4. Describe various techniques that can have a positive influence on student motivation.

5. Operationally define stimulus variation and its appropriate use.

6. Identify and categorize six teacher behaviors that can be used to vary the stimuli in the teaching-learning environment.

7. Describe incentives that can be used to motivate students.

8. Define *classroom management* and discuss control techniques that are commonly used by effective classroom managers.

9. Identify and discuss various teacher-tested guidelines for effective motivation and classroom management.

10. Describe the importance of parent involvement in discipline endeavors and the importance of parent-teacher conferences.

This is a book about teaching, but effective teaching requires that you also be a motivator and manager. Are you able to get students' cooperation, maintain their involvement in instructional tasks, and carry out the business of the classroom smoothly? If so, you are an effective motivator and manager. Many teachers have trouble with these aspects of teaching, essential as they are.

People have physiological, psychological, and social needs and interests that direct and focus their energies (Franken, 1998). As a result, individuals will be attracted to those activities that they view as having the potential to meet unmet needs and that appear interesting. Moreover, young people in our media-oriented society have grown up with television, special-effects movies, and highly stimulating music. They are consequently accustomed to high levels of stimulation on a daily basis, and too often they expect similar experiences when they enter the classroom. Classroom life, which rarely offers such stimulation, is perceived as dull and lifeless by many students, a perception that often limits their motivation to learn.

A highly important aspect of motivation and management is discipline, which perennially appears as a major concern on surveys of teachers, parents, and administrators. Discipline should not be equated with punishment. Whereas punishment is the reaction to disruptive behavior, discipline is concerned with the prevention of disruptive behavior as well as reactions to it. Therefore, discipline is concerned with what you do to prevent behavior problems as well as what you do when problems occur. As a teacher, you should be skilled in both the prevention and the reaction aspects of discipline.

It is almost impossible to deal with behavior or misbehavior without addressing both motivation and discipline. Indeed, experienced teachers will tell you that there is usually little misbehavior in classrooms when students are highly motivated. Classroom management, then, consists of two major related components: motivation and discipline. We will look at each of these in the following sections.

✵ Motivation

Most experienced teachers will undoubtedly agree that motivation is a very important factor in classroom learning. But what is motivation, and more important, how do you go about motivating students to learn? Unfortunately, even a simple definition of motivation is hard to give and there is no surefire method for motivating students. Techniques that work in one situation or with one group of students may be totally ineffective in other situations or with other groups.

Many scholars have proposed theories to explain why we behave as we do (Petri, 1996). The ideas of these thinkers fall into three general views: cognitive, behavioral, and humanistic. Cognitivists explain motivation in terms of a person's active search for meaning and satisfaction in life. They believe that people respond to their internal perceptions of environmental events. Many cognitivists would say that there is a biological basis to motivation. Thus, motivation is considered internal by cognitivists, and the teacher's role is to diagnose and guide self-activated learners.

Behaviorists, on the other hand, explain motivation in terms of external stimuli and reinforcement. The physical environment and the actions of the teacher are of prime importance to this school of thought. This is not to imply that behaviorists totally discount the effects of internal factors on motivation. Indeed, some behaviorists extend motivation to include such internal factors as anticipations, self-evaluations, expectancies, and intentions. Finally, humanists stress the need for personal growth and, like the cognitivists, emphasize aiding the development of intrinsic needs. They place a great deal of emphasis on the total person, along with the related needs of personal freedom, choice, and self-determination.

Essentially, the sources of motivation can be classified as being either internal or external. Effective teaching requires that both of these sources be addressed.

Intrinsic Versus Extrinsic Motivation

Motivation can be defined as forces or drives that energize and direct us to act as we do. Some **primary motives,** such as hunger, thirst, and sex, are inborn. However, most of the motives you will deal with in the classroom are learned or **secondary motives**—that is, motives that are learned through their association with primary motives. The association, for example, of affection with food is a commonly learned motive. Obviously, motivational influences can come from within or outside the individual. **Intrinsic motivation** is what learners bring to the learning environment, that is, their internal attributes: attitudes, values, needs, and personality factors. This emphasis on internal factors can be viewed as a **cognitive approach** to motivation, one which is concerned with the unique internal attributes that direct our actions. In contrast, **extrinsic motivation** originates outside the individual and is concerned with external, environmental factors that help shape students' behaviors. Teachers, being one of the most important elements in the classroom environment, can have considerable influence on student motivation through their choice of teaching strategies. For example, permitting direct student involvement in the learning process or the granting of free time for work well done often provides positive motivation to students. This emphasis on external factors can be viewed as a stimulation approach to motivation. In short, the **stimulation approach** places emphasis on factors in the environment that students find exciting, enjoyable, or interesting.

Intrinsic motives are often difficult to change, and when change does occur, it usually occurs slowly. Indeed, even elementary teachers who are with their students most of the day often lack the time to bring about change in individual students. Thus, given the limited time you have to interact with individual students, the likelihood of changing their internal motivational patterns will be slim at best. In short, you must learn to work with the motivational attributes that already exist.

Intrinsic, or cognitive, and extrinsic, or stimulation, motives are interrelated; they interact with one another. Figure 9.1 shows how these two viewpoints interact to influence student motivation. In extrinsic motivation, the external incentives and rewards that are used to get students to learn or work—

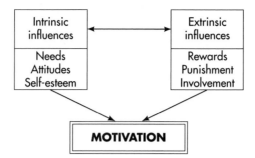

FIGURE 9.1 *Motivational Interactions*

modify or change their actions—are artificially devised techniques. Ideally, once extrinsic motivation has been used to help develop intrinsic motivation, it should be phased out. Elementary teachers, for example, can attempt to develop an intrinsic enjoyment of reading by giving children rewards for reading and can phase out the rewards as the year progresses. Complete Expansion Activity: Behavior to further address the concept of motivational sources.

Students, in general, have a tendency to react and behave according to their perception of events. Differing perceptions will result in differing actions because of variations in students' attitudes, need structures, curiosity levels, task interests, satisfaction with learning, sense of well-being, self-esteem, the classroom environment, instructional variables, and so on.

Students' Attitudes

Students' feelings range from loving school to hating it. These predetermined attitudes are the results of prior experiences with school and with teachers which, in most cases, had nothing to do with you. Some will love school and learning because they find it interesting or easy, while others will hate school and learning because they find it boring or difficult. One of your responsibilities as a teacher will be to deal with negative attitudes and to try to make them positive. Since you cannot force students to like school, or you, or learning, this will not be an easy task. In short, you cannot force students to change their attitudes against their will. Your best bet is to entice them to change by using innovative motivational strategies.

Expansion Activity: Behavior

Form groups of four or five. Discuss the virtues of the cognitive, behavioral, and humanistic concept of behavior. Which is most applicable to the classroom? Does the related intrinsic or extrinsic motivation do a better job of explaining classroom behavior? Share your group's conclusions with the class.

Often your first task as a teacher will be to reverse students' negative mind-sets regarding school and learning. You must show them that school is worthwhile and important to the development of life skills. In other words, concepts should be applied to the real world. For example, at the elementary level, class stores can be established and operated, or the local newspaper can be used in various reading lessons, or road sign shapes can be studied in geometry. At the secondary level, job applications can be completed, or checking accounts can be balanced, or state and federal income tax forms can be filled out. Another way relevance can be shown is to invite respected business and community leaders to visit the classroom to discuss the importance of school and learning.

Since students are concerned about subject relevance, you should be prepared to respond to those age-old questions, "Why do we gotta learn this stuff?" and "What good is this stuff gonna do me?" If you cannot respond convincingly, perhaps you should reevaluate what you are teaching and why you are teaching it. In general, the more you involve students in their own learning and stimulate their interest, the more likely they will be to see the importance of school and, in the process, to develop more positive attitudes toward school, learning, and you as their teacher.

Students' Needs

A *need* is often defined as some kind of deficiency in the human organism or the absence of anything the person requires, or thinks he or she requires, for overall well-being. Obviously, students in your class will have a wide variety of needs. Indeed, Maslow (1970) suggests that human beings function on seven hierarchical needs levels. The first four lower-level needs, called **deficiency needs,** are for survival, safety, belonging, and self-esteem, while the three higher-level needs, called **growth needs,** are for intellectual achievement, aesthetic appreciation, and self-actualization. Unlike the deficiency needs, growth needs are never truly satisfied. In other words, meeting the growth needs only motivates individuals to seek further fulfillment.

Maslow's suggested needs hierarchy can provide valuable insight into why students behave as they do. In effect, students' desire to fulfill lower-level needs may sometimes interfere with your desire to have them achieve higher-level goals. The desire, for example, to maintain self-esteem and belong to a peer group may interfere with your desire to maintain order in the classroom. Indeed, students may sometimes openly defy a teacher simply in order to get recognition from peers. Furthermore, needs are not static and the intensity with which various needs are felt often varies from individual to individual and even changes within the same individual over time or in differing circumstances.

The need for security has important ramifications for teachers. Indeed, the extent to which students believe they will be successful or are likely to fail are important motivational influences. The hope for success can be equated with achievement motivation, while the fear of failure is often referred to as **anxiety.**

Achievement motivation (the need to achieve) refers to the degree to which a student wishes to do well on school tasks. Generally, students with a high need to achieve tend to receive higher grades and are far more likely than high-fear-of-failure (highly anxious) students to respond to repeated failure by persisting and working harder on assigned tasks. However, care must be taken that the natural tendency to persist not be allowed to become excessive. Likewise, highly anxious students who tend to respond to repeated failure by quitting must be encouraged to persist.

Anxious students are those who expect to fail, who view the classroom as threatening, and who lack confidence in their own abilities. Figure 9.2 shows the relationship between anxiety and performance. As shown in the figure, high levels of anxiety can impede performance and school achievement. In fact, people with a high fear of failure are generally attracted to either very easy tasks or very difficult ones, because they can be certain of success on the simple tasks whereas failing on the difficult tasks was expected and therefore is not too upsetting.

Care must also be taken with students who lack confidence so that **learned helplessness** is not taught. That is, the perception that, no matter what the student does, he or she is doomed to failure must be avoided. Learned helplessness is often voiced in such statements as "Nothing I do matters, it will be wrong!" or "I failed because I'm dumb!" or "I'm not smart enough to do this assignment." Such learned helplessness will sometimes develop because of a teacher's overuse of sarcasm or because of the unpredictable use of rewards and punishments. However, it can often be avoided by making sure that students have as many successes as possible, by giving them constructive feedback, and, most important, by communicating to them your positive expectations.

As shown in Figure 9.2, anxiety can have an adaptive, positive influence as well as a detrimental, negative influence, depending on its intensity. Therefore, the removal of all anxiety from the learning environment is not a desirable goal. For example, moderate levels of anxiety can motivate students to better prepare for examinations. However, since students find it more difficult to learn when they feel insecure, you should avoid the overuse of anxiety as a motivating device. In other words, limited amounts of anxiety can be used to motivate your students, but you should avoid shaming them and making them fearful, because these feelings can have a negative effect on learning. Also, you should

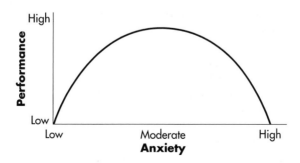

FIGURE 9.2   *The Relationship between Anxiety and Performance*

avoid an overemphasis on tests and grades and remember that not all students are motivated by grades.

Students also have a need to feel personally competent. Indeed, all humans have a need to achieve and a need to avoid failure. Consequently, there will be an overall tendency to take some risks in order to achieve but, at the same time, to avoid threatening situations that might lead to failure. In other words, how students size up their chances for success at an assigned task represents a strong motivational factor. Students' view of the potential difficulty of a task is related to the nature of the task, the amount of support they feel can be expected from the teacher, the adequacy of their perceived preparation for the task, and the expected amount of work time needed for completion of the task.

Finally, in planning, consider which of your students have high achievement needs, which have low achievement needs, and which have a fear of failure. Such information can be gleaned through careful observation of students and their work habits. With this information you can, on the one hand, provide challenging optional assignments for students with high achievement needs, while, on the other hand, providing encouragement and reinforcement for students with a high fear of failure. Moreover, when making assignments, you should take care to clearly explain to students what they are to do, and you should communicate your belief that they are capable of performing the task. With regard to length, you must make your assignments reasonable and you must convince students that the time needed to complete an assigned task is reasonable. Convincing all students that they will have enough time will not be easy, since perceptions of the time needed to complete a job vary greatly among students.

Natural Motives

Intellectual curiosity is often a motivator for students. People are naturally curious and have a desire for action and adventure. Most students come to class the first day full of wonder about what lies ahead. They have interests to nourish, ideas and beliefs to test, and informational gaps to fill. These natural desires should be harnessed when you plan learning activities. The use of suspense, educational games, computers, and simulations, for instance, are strategies that often appeal to the natural motives of students. Insofar as feasible, select activities that will give individual students the opportunity to be directly involved in their own learning. For example, class questions can be turned into library research projects or class science investigations. Finally, whenever possible, give students the opportunity to pursue their own interests and desires.

Student needs will set up drives. The specific way in which the need is satisfied and the drive reduced is determined in large part by learning. It is therefore imperative that teachers have a good understanding of their students' needs. Before you proceed, complete Expansion Activity: Student Needs to further refine your understanding of student needs.

Expansion Activity: Student Needs

Make no mistake: Understanding student needs is a foundation for handling behavior successfully. Ignoring these needs can cause teachers to overlook the first essential step in changing unacceptable behavior to acceptable behavior. Write a short paper on what you think are the primary needs of students at the grade level you plan to teach. Submit your paper to your instructor.

Classroom Environment

The school and the classroom environment set the tone for learning. Indeed, the environment can often make the difference between a motivated learner and a bored, reluctant learner.

An attractive room is conducive to learning and is motivational. Will your classroom be attractive and colorful, or will it be bleak and drab? Again sadly, many classrooms, especially at the secondary level, tend to be on the bleak side.

Bulletin boards and displays can add much to the attractiveness and atmosphere of a classroom. They should be designed to be both informative and colorful, and when student work is prominently displayed, they can be quite motivational. Having students design and construct classroom bulletin boards and displays gives added meaning to the classroom environment; it becomes their room, a place to be proud of and to be cared for.

The classroom is a social setting in which the **affiliation motive,** the desire to be with others, can serve as an effective motivator when taken into account in arranging your classroom. For example, at the elementary level, isolation areas can be established for students who do not follow directions or who constantly bother other students. Likewise, at the secondary level, seating or work arrangements based on friendship patterns can be quite effective as a means of developing group cohesiveness and motivation. Even more effective is affording students an occasional opportunity to rearrange their own seating. Finally, always keep in mind that a part of the teacher's job in motivation is to help build relationships among students so that they will come to care about each other. Giving students the opportunity to assist each other with in-class assignments, for instance, often results in the development of a more cohesive and positive classroom environment.

Good communication definitely affects motivation. Often you must be able to convince students that the material they are about to study is both interesting and important. Also, communication patterns should be more than the old "teacher talks—students listen" routine. Effective communication is an open, two-way exchange of ideas; you talk, but you also listen. Give students the opportunity to provide input into all phases of classroom life—lessons, classroom rules and routines, and motivational problems. In short, you must strive to listen with an open mind and to consider the ideas, feelings, and opinions of your students.

Finally, make your classroom as stimulating as possible. Students are constantly searching for new and interesting things to do, for challenge and variety. They prefer settings that are fast-paced and novel. In short, students will find environments rich in stimuli and change more motivating than monotonous and dull environments. Without periodic changes in their learning environment, students often lose interest. Thus, to keep students' motivation high and to keep their attention directed toward the lesson, you should vary your classroom behaviors and teaching strategies. In effect, you should consciously incorporate stimulus changes into your lessons for the purpose of gaining, maintaining, and increasing student involvement and interest.

Modeling

Modeling is the technique of using the behavior of admired persons to demonstrate the values and behaviors you want students to acquire. Teachers are probably the most notable models in most classrooms. As such, the enthusiasm and sense of wonder that you show for your subject will often infect your students and make them anxious to find out what is so interesting. However, the relationship between teacher enthusiasm and student achievement seems to be directly related to the age of the students. Teacher enthusiasm is often less important with young children than it is with older children and adolescents.

Teacher movement and eye contact as students talk can also act as a motivator. Movement toward the student, for example, will often communicate your interest in their message, while movement away from the speaker often communicates a lack of interest or even a lack of confidence in a speaker's ability.

At times, students serve as role models to each other. In other words, when certain desirable behaviors in respected or admired peers are observed, these behaviors will sometimes be adopted. Thus, the use of peer modeling in group work will sometimes result in the transfer of desirable behaviors. Moreover, students who role-play, or who observe others role-play, musicians, scientists, poets, and political leaders sometimes develop similar or related interests.

Instructional Strategies

Group activities and student-centered teaching strategies such as cooperative learning can be motivational since they build upon the need for recognition and belonging (Rogers, Ludington, & Graham, 1998). In contrast, teacher-centered teaching strategies that rely heavily on competition are often criticized for discouraging students from helping one another, for setting up a classroom pecking order, and for discouraging low-ability students who have little chance for success. Students should gain needed recognition and a sense of belonging when they work together toward a common goal. The interaction and sharing in cooperative learning represents a form of social motivation that greatly enhances students' sense of recognition and belonging.

The use of individualized instructional strategies can also be highly motivational. Exploring concepts and their environment on their own initiative can help students to acquire an increased sense of competence (that is, it can satisfy their intrinsic need to cope with the environment) and to raise their level of aspiration. The use of strategies that maximize student self-direction in learning may well stimulate a sense of competence and accomplishment. This is especially true when students help to select and plan their own activities. Consequently, most forms of individualized instruction are effective techniques for motivating students because they allow students to work at their own pace and on their own level.

As mentioned earlier, students desire variety, action, excitement, and novelty. Therefore, they respond better to active, fast-paced teaching techniques such as inquiry, discovery, simulation, and group work than to slow-moving, passive ones such as lectures, recitation, and demonstrations. Moreover, students prefer techniques that are new or represent new experiences rather than techniques that are routine or familiar. Computer-assisted instruction (CAI), for example, often arouses a great deal of interest and excitement. Finally, you should try to add life to your lessons by keeping them lively and by introducing interesting, stimulating materials.

Stimulus Variation

All of us seek stimulation. We are constantly looking for interesting things to do, for variety and challenge to enliven our daily existence. In other words, we are constantly motivated to seek stimulus variation. We prefer settings that provide stimuli rather than settings that are monotonous and dull. Stimulating environments arouse in us a state that is, within reasonable limits, a pleasant one. In short, doing something, no matter how trivial, is motivating and is generally more interesting than doing nothing. Likewise we tend to prefer stimuli that are new, novel, or fast-paced to that which is routine, familiar, and slow-paced.

The human need for stimulation and its relation to motivation have important implications for the teaching-learning environment. The typical learning environment is under continuous bombardment from such external stimuli as street traffic, hall traffic, schoolyard activities, and weather conditions. All these stimuli interfere to some degree with the learning process and force the teacher to compete for students' attention. If external stimuli are more interesting or novel to students than the classroom learning activity, attention will more than likely be directed toward the external stimuli.

Students, especially younger children, have very short attention spans. If some new or changing stimulus does not occur in the learning environment after a certain period of time, they lose interest. Most of you have undoubtedly had the same experience—for instance, with an untrained speaker who stood rigidly behind a podium and put you to sleep with his or her monotonous voice. Unless you were extremely interested in the message, your attention soon turned to external stimuli or to your own inner thoughts.

Effective teachers consciously vary their behaviors and their learning activities so that students receive new or modified stimuli that keep their attention directed toward the learning process. These refocusing skills eventually become second nature to the experienced teacher. They become an essential part of the teacher's lessons.

Six simple behaviors or behavior patterns can be used to vary the stimuli offered to students. These behaviors and patterns include using gestures, focusing attention, varying interaction styles, using pauses, shifting sensory channels, and using teacher movement.

Gestures   Gestures are effective attention-getting devices. In a crowd of people, your attention is usually directed to the person who is making some sort of gesture. The message received is that "This is where the action is." In classrooms a snap of the fingers or a nod of the head will focus student attention on you as you teach. Moreover, you can add emphasis through various general movements of the hands, head, and body.

You can effectively use gestures to refocus student attention or to emphasize a point in a lesson presentation. As students' attention wanders, a tap on the chalkboard or desk, a hand gesture, or a change in body position is often all that is needed to refocus attention on the lesson. These gestural movements represent a change in stimuli that usually results in directing student attention back to the teacher.

Focusing Attention   Focusing may be the most common attention-getting technique used by teachers. Essentially it consists of directing students' attention to what you have said or will say through the use of either verbal statements or gestures.

Verbal focusing can be used to direct attention to certain specifics in a lesson or to redirect students' attention when it begins to wander. Refocusing students' attention is often necessary when the teacher has been speaking for a long time. Commonly used verbal focusing statements are, "That was an important point, Jane," "This is a major issue," "Pay close attention to this point," "This should be included in your notes," "Know this diagram well," and "That statement is important enough to be repeated." Learn to use such statements, and gradually build your own personal repertoire of similar statements.

Gestures are also effective in focusing attention. You are using this technique when you bang a desk, tap a map, use a pointer, use hand gestures, or make sudden movements with your body. The gestures represent new stimuli to students and will usually result in better attention.

An even better attention-focusing technique is to combine a verbal focusing statement with some form of gesture. Essentially the combination increases the intensity of the stimulus change. Examples of this technique include such combinations as:

[Teacher taps statement on chalkboard.] Remember this statement!
[Teacher slams one hand into the other.] This is a very important point!
[Teacher pats student on the back.] Great idea, Sam!
[Teacher simulates an explosion with hands.] An explosion can result if you
    aren't careful with these chemicals.

The imaginative use of such combinations can provide an effective stimuli change that results in increased attention and learning.

Varying Interaction Styles   There are four basic interaction styles that can be used in the average classroom: teacher-group, teacher-student, student-student, and student-group. You can use any one or a combination of these styles in the course of a lesson. The style or combination you choose depends to a large degree on the content and objectives of the lesson.

The teacher-group interaction style should be used when you want to address the class as a whole, as when you are giving a lecture or demonstration that covers new content. If questions are asked during the course of the lecture or demonstration, they are usually directed to the total group.

When you choose to address or question a specific student, the teacher-student interaction style is being used. This type of interaction is referred to as the *Ping-Pong style* since it usually goes teacher-student, teacher-student, teacher-student, and so on, with the teacher addressing or questioning different students in the group. Used wisely, this style enhances student involvement in the lesson.

Under certain circumstances you may wish to redirect a student comment or question to another student for a response or for clarification. This is the student-student interaction style and is frequently used to acknowledge some student's accomplishment in the discussed area or to redirect an inattentive student back to the lesson. An example of student-student interaction is, "John, you did a report on France last week. Can you answer Mary's question?" Student-student interaction should be encouraged in class discussions since students often learn best from each other.

At times you may want to transfer the leadership of a lesson to one of your students. For example, after redirecting a question or a request for clarification to one of your students, you might briefly withdraw from the discussion. This style should be used with care and only with students who can assume a central role in the group. Try to avoid putting your students in uncomfortable situations, since some of them cannot take the pressure of leadership roles.

You can often provide the stimulus necessary to maintain student attention simply through changes in the patterning of these interaction styles. For example, you could intersperse a lecture with individual questions, have other students react to student comments, or withdraw almost entirely from a discussion by giving students leadership over the group discussion.

Using Pauses   As mentioned in the discussion of set induction, silence can be a powerful force. A sudden and unexpected silence can often put a stop to the most animated conversation. When background noise suddenly ceases, more than likely you are drawn to the silence and begin searching for cues that explain it.

This same principle can be used to focus or redirect student attention to a lesson presentation. This is particularly true when you have been speaking for an extended period of time and your words have lost their ability to stimulate the students. At such times appropriate pauses serve to refocus student attention to the message being communicated. In essence, you deliberately reduce the stimuli in order to force students to strain for stimulus cues.

Many teachers appear to be afraid of silence and consequently do not use pauses. These teachers too often feel that for learning to take place there must be some form of continuous oral communication. They rush to fill in any silences that might occur. The result is often loss of student attention.

Teacher pauses can serve functions other than stimulus variation. Possible related uses include:

1. To break the lesson content up into smaller units so that it is more easily understood by students
2. To serve as a cue to students to search for direction in the lesson
3. To prepare students for the next statement to be made by the teacher

As a teacher technique, pauses or silence has much to offer teachers. Contrasting sound with silence provides alternating stimuli to students and usually results in better attention and hopefully in more and better learning.

Shifting Sensory Channels   Although most communication in the average classroom revolves around teacher talk, there are four other sensory channels—seeing, touching, tasting, smelling—through which learning can take place. Consequently you can provide stimulus variation by shifting between these sensory channels. The shifts require that students make a corresponding shift in reception modes. This results in their refocusing attention toward your presentation.

The use of the overhead projector is a typical example of refocusing by shifting sensory channels. Students are required to shift their primary reception from aural to visual. To make the shift even more effective, you could ask that students acquire some information through visual means alone, that is, without any oral comment.

Tactile (touch), gustatory (taste), and olfactory (smell) senses can be used when appropriate learning materials are available. Sampling or manipulating such materials in conjunction with oral discussion requires refocusing attention on the lesson presentation.

Teacher Movement   Any physical movement by the teacher, who is normally the most significant person in the classroom, naturally draws students' attention. You can effectively refocus student attention by incorporating into your lesson simple movements that require some aural and visual adjustments on the part of students. The possible movements available to you include:

1. Moving to the left or the right
2. Moving to the back or the front
3. Moving among the students

Rather than remaining stationary (hiding) behind a podium or desk, teachers should activate the environment with their movement. Lateral movement is frequently used to draw attention to something in the environment or on the chalkboard. Movement to the back of the room or among the students allows the teacher to become less conspicuous and permits better student-student interaction.

Although stimulus variation techniques are quite useful in motivating and maintaining student attention, these same techniques, if overused, can draw attention away from the learning situation. If they are overdone, students may become more interested in the novelty of your presentation than in its content. This is especially true when the lesson content is familiar, ordinary, or less than exciting.

The overuse of any behavior, even a desirable one, can result in focusing attention away from the learning situation. Such common occurrences as the continual use of "uh" or "okay," silence used too often, continually pacing around the room, or tapping a pencil can detract from a lesson, as can an overly enthusiastic teacher. That is, hyperactive or excessively emotional teacher behavior results in focusing student attention on the behavior rather than the lesson. One of the skills associated with stimulus variation, then, is to monitor your own behaviors so that they do not interfere with the learning process.

Teacher Expectations

Students tend to perform at a level that is consistent with teacher expectations. Furthermore, they tend to perform better and feel more competent when teachers establish high expectations and hold them to these expectations (Good & Brophy, 1987). These findings, often referred to as the **self-fulfilling prophecy,** allow teachers to influence student motivation by communicating high (but not unreasonable) expectations. Essentially, teachers who have high expectations are telling students that they have confidence in the students' abilities; this, in turn, helps to create a personalized and positive teacher-learner relationship.

Studies on classroom interaction suggest that teachers tend to favor students they perceive as high achievers (Allington, 1980; Good & Brophy, 1987). High achievers have more frequent and higher-quality interactions with their teachers than do poorer students. For example, they are usually given more time to answer questions, and they receive more positive feedback when they respond correctly. Cooper and Good (1983, p. 10) suggest several other differences in the ways teachers respond to high- and low-achieving students.

1. Low-expectation students (or "lows") are often seated farther from the teacher than are high-expectation students (or "highs").
2. Less attention is paid to lows in academic situations (this includes less eye contact and fewer nods, winks, and smiles).
3. Lows are called on less often to answer classroom questions and are given less wait time to answer questions.
4. Lows are criticized more frequently for incorrect classroom responses and are praised less frequently for correct responses.
5. Lows are praised more frequently than highs for marginal or inadequate classroom responses.
6. Lows are given less accurate and less detailed feedback than highs.
7. Less work and less effort are demanded from lows than from highs.
8. Lows are more frequently interrupted during performance.

These findings reveal that, too often, teachers give extra support to students whom they view as being especially capable and that, as a result, the interactions between such students and their teachers tend to be more positive and supportive. In order to avoid such classroom bias, teachers must learn to give similar support to low-ability students. Moving closer to them and waiting longer for their responses, maintaining eye contact, and smiling are examples of simple but effective ways of communicating high expectations and improving motivation. However, you should be aware that any teacher action that is overly used with either low- or high-ability students can create labeling and become counterproductive.

To a considerable extent, students' aspirations and self-concepts will be affected by your projected expectations and your actions toward them. When you hold low expectations for certain students, you may unconsciously give them less encouragement, less time to answer questions, and less attention. As this pattern continues throughout the year, students often move closer and closer to your projected expectations. In summary, you should be aware that students use your views and actions as a mirror of themselves. You can help them by holding realistic expectations up to them. You can communicate your belief in their abilities—and you can mean it!

Be aware, then, that your perceptions and student actions can be influenced by a halo effect or Hawthorne effect, respectively. It is possible that your view or assessment of a student can be influenced by a halo effect—that is, by the tendency to view particular aspects of a student based on a general impression, either positive or negative (Murphy, Jako, & Anhalt, 1993). For example, a very pleasant student who seems to work hard and cause little trouble may be given the benefit of the doubt. A second kind of bias can come from a Hawthorne effect. This bias comes from the fact that students will sometimes behave differently when they know they are being watched. As a teacher, you must guard against these two forms of bias.

Feedback as Motivator

Three techniques are commonly used to provide feedback to students: praise, knowledge of results, and grades. However, to be effective motivators, these feedback techniques must be carefully and systematically applied. Simply handing out positive feedback to all students will, in time, destroy its effectiveness as a motivator. Used appropriately, your feedback should be contingent on the desired action, should specify clearly the action being reinforced, and should be believable. In other words, feedback should be the sincere recognition of well-done student work or behavior.

Experienced teachers have long acknowledged and recognized the power of praise as a motivator. Indeed, praise is often more powerful than other techniques because it generally calls for teacher attention and energy beyond the use of the standard one-word or short-phrase response ("Good!", "Okay," or "Fine answer."). For example, a teacher might say, "John, that's an excellent idea! Let's discuss what might happen if you implemented it," rather than simply saying, "Good idea, John." Remember, however, that what is praise to one student may not represent praise to another. A teacher's smile, for example, might be taken as praise by one student but as ridicule by another student. Finally, praise can lay the foundation for lasting internal change because it works to improve students' self-esteem. Although it should be used with all kinds of students, praise seems especially effective with young children and in classrooms with many low-ability students.

Used too often or inappropriately, however, praise can easily become manipulative and seem underhanded, as when it is used to reinforce mediocre work. Moreover, students are sometimes suspicious of teachers' praise, especially when they perceive it as dishonest or when it is closely followed by criticism. In addition, praise can be mistaken by students to mean "I'm a good person today because I know the answers!" Likewise, when the praise is withheld, students may feel, "I'm a bad person today because I don't know all the answers!" Thus, praise should be used sparingly and should be directed to specific actions or behaviors, so as to avoid the pitfalls associated with its use. Encouragement, on the other hand, can be used with greater frequency and, combined with the selective use of praise, can help to establish and maintain a positive learning environment.

Knowledge of results can also serve as a powerful motivator. The communication of successful results naturally leads to renewed vigor, while an indication of needed corrective measures communicates specific means for achieving success. To use knowledge of results effectively and to make sure that students benefit from its motivational effects, you must return papers and tests to them immediately, with more feedback than a simple grade. To provide the maximum incentive, each paper should be personalized with comments about strengths and weaknesses. Brief notes written at the top of the page or in the margins should be sufficient to offer students needed guidance.

Teachers have always considered grades and test results as motivating students to learn. Unfortunately, this belief is not always supported. In truth, tests typically motivate students only to cram for tests. Tests and grades are primarily motivational to better and older students, while offering only limited incentive to young and low-ability students. Grades are given too infrequently to be useful as feedback or to allow most young children to associate them with their daily work. Therefore, don't make grades your primary source of motivation. Instead, appeal to students' intrinsic motives and rely on cooperative strategies, which are more likely to be motivational to students, especially to younger and lower-achieving students.

Motivation and Incentives

This discussion of student motivation would not be complete without a look at the use of incentives in the classroom. Motivation is closely related to reinforcement principles which state that behaviors are controlled by their consequences. Students who are rewarded with good grades, for example, may be motivated to study, while those who receive low grades may be unmotivated to study. In some instances, peer pressure may operate against good grades by turning good grades into a form of punishment. This example shows the complexity of motivation. In short, you must choose incentives with care because what you consider a reward may be viewed differently by students. In other words, rewards and punishment are often unique to the individual; what is rewarding to one person may represent punishment to another. The motivational value of a reward cannot be assumed; motivation is influenced by many factors.

Table 9.1 lists examples of incentives that teachers have traditionally used to motivate students. Some of these are used frequently, while others are seldom used. For example, praise and teacher attention are used daily to keep attention directed toward a lesson, whereas grades are generally used less frequently as incentives. The concepts associated with incentives and reinforcement were discussed at length in Chapter 7.

Motivation Guidelines

How then should teachers go about motivating their students? Unfortunately, as pointed out earlier, techniques that work in one situation or with one group of students may be totally ineffective with other situations or groups. There are, however, several general guidelines that may prove useful in motivating students.

1. *Expect the best from students*   Research reveals that students tend to live up (or down) to their teacher's expectations. Teacher expectations, then, can be used to motivate students. If you expect and demand the best from your students, you will often get it.

2. *Model desired behavior*   Modeling is a process of teaching through example. By following your example, students will change their behavior. For instance, you can model enthusiasm about what you are teaching. If your students see that you are excited about your subject, they will be, too. Remember, enthusiasm is highly contagious. Once it infects students, the learning gains can be amazing.

3. *Share expectations*   Share your goals and objectives with students, as well as the procedures for reaching them. In fact, whenever possible you should involve students in the development of class goals, objectives, and procedures. This sharing gives students a sense of responsibility for

TABLE 9.1

Classroom Incentives

Frequently Used		Infrequently Used	
Daily	**Weekly**	**Monthly**	**Yearly**
Praise	Quiz grades	Six-week grade	Final grades
Attention	Positive notes	Desired activities	Honor roll
Feedback	Recognition	Free day	Promotion
Smiles	Privileges	Free talking	Graduation
Interest		Change in seating	Recognition
Involvement			Prizes

their own learning and a sense of real accomplishment when the goals and objectives are successfully met.

4. *Establish a positive atmosphere*   From the beginning, establish a friendly but businesslike atmosphere. Communicate the fact that the class has a job to do. Show that each student is special to you, and give each as much personal attention as possible.

5. *Actively involve students*   Since students are naturally active, you should make them active participants in the learning process. The wise teacher attempts to use lively rather than passive activities.

6. *Make learning seem worthwhile*   Communicate the value of every lesson to your students. Otherwise they may be reluctant to participate.

7. *Cultivate self-esteem*   Everyone wants to feel important and respected. Try to plan and assign work so that every student can experience some success. Remember that repeated failure soon ends the desire to try.

8. *Capitalize on student interest and prior knowledge*   Whenever possible, relate learning to students' prior experiences and interests. Generally, students pay closer attention and become more involved when the topic relates directly to their experiences and areas of interest. These can improve their attitudes toward school and even carry over into later life.

9. *Capitalize on student ideas*   Often students will willingly carry out activities that they themselves generate. Whenever possible, you should use student ideas in planning instructional activities.

10. *Capitalize on curiosity*   Because people are naturally curious, adding a little puzzle or suspense can improve your lessons. For older students the use of well-constructed questions can serve the same purpose.

11. *Challenge students*   Easy tasks soon become boring. One way to avoid boring your students is to make learning tasks challenging but not discouraging. Some students skip their schoolwork because it is too easy; it is busywork. This is especially true for bright students. Assigning challenging work gives students the opportunity to test themselves and to really accomplish something. On the other hand, you should take care not to make the tasks so difficult that students will become frustrated.

This concludes our discussion of motivation. Use Task 9.1 to check your understanding of the concepts in the last two sections.

T A S K   9 . 1

Motivation

Respond to the following motivation concept items. Check your responses with those given at the end of the chapter.

1. Define motivation: _____

_____

Continued on next page

T A S K   9 . 1   C o n t i n u e d

2. Match the definition on the left with the proper term on the right.

_____ a. Motivation is a result of external stimuli. 1. Cognitivists
_____ b. Motivation is related to personal growth   2. Behaviorists
             and the total person.   3. Humanists
_____ c. Motivation is the response to internal
             perceptions.

3. Describe achievement motivation: _____

_____

4. Maslow's two categories of needs are _____ and _____ .

5. Describe modeling: _____

_____

6. Label the following stimulus variation techniques as examples of gestures (G),
   focusing attention (FA), varying interaction styles (VIS), using pauses (P), shifting
   sensory channels (SSC), or teacher movement (TM). Check your responses with those
   given at the end of the chapter.

_____ a. "That's an interesting question, Jenny. Could you answer it, Mark?"
_____ b. "Make special note of this issue! It was one of the most important of
             the Civil War."
_____ c. The teacher pauses for a few seconds following a statement, then
             continues.
_____ d. In the class discussion of other lands, Ms. Smith shows the children
             pictures of the country being discussed.
_____ e. The teacher uses a pointer to emphasize a statement in the textbook
             by tapping the book.
_____ f. As he speaks, Mr. Emerson moves toward the back of the room where
             two students are talking.

7. List the six teacher behaviors or behavior patterns that can be used to vary stimuli to
   students.

a. _____

b. _____

c. _____

d. _____

e. _____

f. _____

Analysis and Reflections

Too often our thinking is totally in terms of student adjustments when problems develop in the classroom. What kinds of adjustments should the teacher make relative to motivation when classroom problems continue to take place? How important is it to provide students with fulfillment rather than frustration?

⚔ Control Techniques

Every classroom teacher must eventually develop his or her own approach to classroom management and discipline. Your total management approach will be based on your philosophy related to teaching, learning, motivation, students, and schooling.

Only you can develop an overall approach to discipline that is appropriate for your classroom. However, several control techniques appear to be characteristic of effective classroom managers. We now look at some of these techniques.

Setting Limits

Students need and want limits (rules). They want to know what is expected of them and why. Teachers who try to avoid setting limits and imposing necessary structure will often find that chaos results, particularly when dealing with younger children.

Clarity and consistency are vital in the establishment of rules. You should explain why certain rules are needed or, even better, involve students in a discussion about why certain rules are necessary. Your rules should always reinforce the basic idea that students are in school to study and learn. Moreover, you should avoid making too many rules, unnecessary rules, and above all, unenforceable rules. When no longer needed, a rule should be discarded or changed. However, so long as they are retained, rules must be enforced.

It is often better to have a few general rules (five or six) that cover many specifics rather than trying to list all the specifics. But if specific actions represent a problem area, then a rule should cover the specific problem. Examples of appropriate general classroom rules include:

1. Be polite and respectful.
2. Take care of your classroom.
3. Do not hit, shove, or hurt others.
4. Follow directions.
5. Obtain permission before speaking or leaving your seat.
6. Be prepared with books, paper, pencil, and so on when you come to class.

Your rules should always be discussed with students. Specific behaviors that are included and excluded in each general rule should be explained and discussed. With younger children you should post the rules, whereas it is wise to have older students record the rules for future reference. You should also consider sending parents a copy of your classroom rules.

As soon as you decide on your rules, you must consider what to do when a student breaks a rule. It is too late to make this decision after the rule has been broken. For many classroom infractions, a logical consequence is to have the students correct their mistakes. Incomplete papers can be finished or redone; messes can be cleaned up. For other infractions you may want to form a graduated series of consequences, such as:

First infraction: Name on board
Second infraction: Lose lunch recess

Third infraction:	Teacher conference
Fourth infraction:	Conference with principal
Fifth infraction:	Parent conference

When infractions occur, avoid, if at all possible, a direct classroom confrontation. Instead, ask the student to refrain from the behavior. If the student responds negatively and continues the behavior, ask him or her to leave the room and wait outside until you are free to have a private conference. At this conference address the undesired behavior, the consequences of that behavior, and the student's responsibility as a member of the class. If the behavior continues after the conference, you should seek the principal's assistance.

Once you have determined the rules for your classroom and the consequences for breaking the rules, you have taken the first step toward having a well-managed classroom. You must now get the year started right.

Getting Started

The first few weeks of the school year are of prime importance with regard to management. They set the stage for the year and establish your credibility. In fact, it can be predicted from what you do during the first few weeks both how well you will manage your classroom and the extent of student engagement in learning tasks.

What do effective managers do during those first critical weeks? Based upon our discussion to this point and related research, to be an effective manager you should develop and establish an efficient organizational system and supporting classroom procedures. For example, you must arrange student seating and storage of materials, establish procedures for starting and ending class, establish lesson procedures, and set up homework procedures and policies. The classroom focus during the first few weeks of school should be teaching your system and procedures. You should establish a positive classroom environment, establish rules and consequences, and above all, plan well and make your content meaningful to the students. It is also important to communicate your expectations to your students and to establish an atmosphere of free exchange. Invite students' cooperation. Develop self-discipline by having students analyze their own behavior. Finally, be firm, organized, and consistent in your expectations of students.

What about the problem of the teacher who enters a class after the beginning of the term and does not have access to early focus on an organizational system and supporting classroom procedures? Again, the first task is to establish credibility. Communicate your expectations to students, discuss changes in classroom procedures that are needed to support the expectations, and, above all, be firm and consistent with regard to the expectations.

Likewise, what about new students who enter a class during the term? Here again, the student must be made aware of your expectations, organizational system, and classroom procedures. This task can often be accomplished in a private conference, with appropriate reminders given as needed in class.

Ripple Effect

Any time a student is publicly corrected or punished for misbehaving, the impact is felt not only by the student but also by other students in the class. Although at times this impact, which is called the *ripple effect,* can help to establish the ground rules of your classroom, it can at other times be harmful to the overall classroom atmosphere.

When a student tests your enforcement of the rules (and there will always be at least one student who will) you cannot ignore it. If you do, the fact that the student got away with something "ripples out" to other students and encourages them to test you. Conversely, when you stand firm and consistently apply your rules and consequences, this action too will ripple out to other students. They will be less likely to try you in the future.

Care must be taken in correcting students. Some students become nervous and fearful when someone is treated harshly. They may lose their desire to learn. Therefore, you should use care in correcting student behavior in front of the class. Correct misbehavior in an unobtrusive manner if at all possible, using the least force necessary for getting the job done. In addition, address the problem behavior itself rather than ridiculing the student or putting him or her down as a person. Be direct, fair, open, and respectful with students when correcting their behavior.

Criticism

Avoid criticism; it just provokes hostility. The student may blow up and say something unintentional or may even give up trying. To put a student down in front of his or her peers is probably one of the most damaging things you can do.

Students react more favorably if your criticism is in the form of a suggestion. Better yet, take the student aside, out of earshot of others, and deal with the problem in a matter-of-fact manner.

Rewards

All behavior must have some kind of payoff (reward, reinforcer, etc.). The reward can be anything that causes the behavior to increase in frequency. For some students the payoff is intrinsic, the inner satisfaction of doing well or doing the right thing. However, some students need extrinsic rewards for behaving properly. You would be wise to establish rewards for following the rules. Such rewards could be stickers, free time, a popcorn party, toys, or anything that is desirable to your students.

Some people feel that granting rewards is tantamount to bribing students. However, bribing is defined as "receiving money or favors for doing something immoral or illegal." Helping a student to learn or to achieve self-control does not fit this definition.

This concludes our discussion of the various control techniques that can be used in the classroom. Let us now look at some general guidelines related to effective management.

⚔ Management Guidelines

Managing a classroom is a difficult but essential task that you must perform well in order to teach effectively. The discussion thus far has been based on the theory and research of classroom management scholars. Sometimes, however, experience is the best teacher when it comes to learning to manage a classroom. The following are teacher-tested suggestions for managing a classroom and preventing behavior problems.

1. *Begin class on time*   When the bell rings, require that everyone be in his or her seat. Require that all talking stop.
2. *Set up procedures for beginning your class*   You should have a set routine or activity that automatically occupies the first four or five minutes of class.
3. *Set up procedures for dismissing class*   Require that all students be in their seats and quiet before they are dismissed. This prevents most problems that develop as students rush to leave.
4. *Keep desks and storage areas clean*   Set aside a particular time to clean out desks and storage areas.
5. *Stop misbehavior immediately*   Send nonverbal cues (making eye contact, moving in that direction, pointing toward his or her work) to the offender. Tell the student the correct procedure or rule in a clear, assertive, and unhostile manner.
6. *Make transitions between activities quick and orderly*   Give all directions before any movement begins or before materials are passed out. Students should know where they are expected to go and what they are expected to do when they get there.
7. *Direct your talk to the class, not to the chalkboard*   Make eye contact with your students as you talk. It is usually unwise to turn your back to the class for long periods.
8. *Be polite to students and reinforce their politeness*   Communicate to the class that you expect their cooperation. Never use sarcasm in communicating your desires to students.
9. *Be firm and consistent*   If a rule is broken, warn students only once; then follow through with the consequences. Do not let yourself be talked out of a position you have taken, and do not back down on the consequences for breaking a rule.
10. *Do not threaten*   Do not take a position or make a threat that you cannot hold or carry out. Do not make threats; make promises.
11. *Be with-it*   Move around the room and know what is going on in all areas. Do not become engrossed with a few students and forget that you are in charge of a class.
12. *Use nonverbal signals*   The use of nonverbal signals and body language is one of the best ways to prevent discipline problems. Examples are a frown, a nod, movement toward the student, an intent look, and a raised hand.
13. *Be helpful, not hurtful*   Show students that you want to support their best behaviors and help them develop their own self-discipline.

Web Search: Classroom Discipline Techniques

Access the following two Internet URL sites: **http://users.aol.com/church-ward/hls/techniques.html** and **http://users.aol.com/churchward/hls/back-fire.html.** Review and analyze the eleven techniques for better classroom discipline and the techniques that often backfire. Write a short paper on techniques that will and will not work with the age group of students you plan to teach. Submit your analysis to the instructor.

14. *Use corporal punishment only as a last resort*   Try other approaches first, as corporal punishment generally does not work well.
15. *Plan well*   You should enter your classroom every day with well-planned lessons that involve all students in activities that have specific, clear-cut goals.
16. *Use verbal reprimands with care*   Avoid nagging and the use of sarcasm, ridicule, and loud, frequent reprimands. They are ineffective. Instead, use calm, firm reprimands and, as a rule, deliver your reprimands in private.
17. *Always set a good example*   Remember, you are a model for classroom behavior. Do as you would be done to. Do not take yourself too seriously. Develop a sense of humor.

Attention to these guidelines will result in a smoother running classroom. Indeed, if you can successfully carry out the guidelines cited above, it will prevent most of the problems you will encounter in your classroom. Complete Web Search: Classroom Discipline Techniques for additional management techniques.

Parent involvement can also positively influence the climate of a classroom. Before we conclude our discussion of classroom management, let's look at parent involvement in classroom management.

Parents as School Disciplinarians

All parents want their children to be successful in their endeavors. School is no different! Parents want their children to learn and be accepted by their peers and teachers. Consequently, they want their children to behave at school. Indeed, it would be strange to hear a parent say, "I hope my kid causes trouble at school today."

Even though occasionally you may find parents who seem to interfere negatively and criticize your efforts, it is safe to assume that most parents will be supportive of school efforts. The Gallup poll repeatedly reports that parent attitudes toward schools and teachers continue to be positive year after year. This is not to say parents don't criticize those things they feel are not in the best interest of their children.

The key to gaining parental support in your undertakings is to learn to take criticism seriously without taking it personally. Hopefully, you will find criticism your friend rather than your enemy. In fact, you should consider criticism taken personally as a warning signal that you might be assuming too much responsibility. This is frequently a source of teacher stress and burn out. After all, the teacher's legal role has always been "in loco parentis." The bottom line is that parents have primary responsibility for their children. You are simply offering parents your service as a professional in educating their children. As with most business relationships, you may have to sell your ideas. It is unlikely that you would buy everything you hear about and see; neither will parents. However, parents like most people are more apt to buy something when there are a number of things (or ideas) to choose from. For this reason, it is important to guide families into understanding your role as a provider of a professional service, and also to use your professionalism to establish co-partnerships with parents.

Parents as Co-Partners

When parents are perceived as friends and co-partners in the education of their children, discipline efforts can be maximized. When enlisting parents for support in discipline endeavors always follow a well-planned conference schedule (see Chapter 10). Establish a positive, team-like atmosphere between yourself and parents. Remember, you're in this together as co-partners! Maintain your professionalism without sacrificing the warmness and compassion that should be felt toward students. Keep the conference short and sweet, and stick to the subject. Keep in mind it is possible that parents sometimes will not have the necessary parenting skills needed to deal with problem children. You must be the professional in these situations and be prepared to offer suggestions, and possible solutions for parents to try.

The opening remarks in a parent-teacher conference should be communicated to accomplish three goals: (1) establish a co-partner relationship, (2) relate the seriousness of the meeting, and (3) confirm you have their child's best interest at heart. For example, immediately after the formal introductions, you might say, "Jamie is having some problems at school and I'd like to try some things to help her." Or you could start with, "I'm going to need your help to be able to help Jamie be more successful in the classroom." Statements of this nature invite parents to comment and immediately become involved. Parent hostility, anger, and/or frustration often indicate that parents feel inadequate in dealing with school problems. After all, most parents cannot be at school all day. Sometimes it will be necessary to allow parents a few minutes to vent their frustrations but be prepared to get the conference back on the subject as soon as possible. Opening the conference in this manner will help to explain that school problems are serious and require working together to ensure success. However, it is crucial that you provide specific ways parents can assist you with student problems. Of course, you could assign consequences to be carried out by the school, but this does not involve parents. To involve parents, you must sell your plans in such a way that they will want to buy.

With regard to discipline, parents need to know four things: (1) exactly what is expected of students, (2) how those expectations are going to be enforced,

(3) how students are doing, and (4) what they (the parents) can do to help. Once you have established your intent to deal with a student problem as a co-partner with the parent, you may want to follow these four easy steps to reach your discipline goals.

When discussing exactly what is expected of students, it is important to keep expectations as few in number as possible to cover the immediate problem. The expectations should be briefly communicated in easily understood language.

How you would like to enforce your expectations will reflect your leadership style to some degree. However, if you are going to involve parents, it may be necessary to adjust your style to a more democratic approach. For instance, often teachers can lead parents in brainstorming activities that will yield in-school and at-home solutions and/or consequences for misbehavior. Many parents will lack the skills needed for solving problems and will be unable to contribute ideas. In these situations you need to have a list of suggestions ready for parents to consider.

When discussing how students are doing, you should examine with parents a list of things that demonstrate the student's skills and abilities. This will also be a good time to examine the student's strengths and weaknesses and use these as a link in finding ways to motivate and/or change the undesired behavior(s). When communicating about strengths you might choose to share specific assignments in which the student performed well. Perhaps the student performed well in completing a poster assignment on baseball. Baseball could become a source for motivation.

One way to involve parents in providing solutions for behavior problems is to ask their support in providing needed resources. For example, parents could be asked to provide baseball cards to use as reinforcements when their child performs appropriately. Although it might seem easier for you to just buy the cards and try these strategies on your own, an important element becomes lost—parent involvement and support! The value of these elements should not be underestimated. Helping parents assume responsibilities as co-partners benefits the student because it gives the student a perception of parents who are modeling the importance of education to the family.

Explaining what parents can do to help is undoubtedly a vital element to gaining their support in discipline. For example, if the student refuses to do his or her class assignment day after day, you could ask the parents to attend class with the student. Most older students would rather die than admit their behavior is showing immaturity and requires their parents attend school with them. However, a request of this nature should never be made to humiliate a student but rather to communicate your feelings that the student will not receive an education if allowed to continue on his or her present path. Of course, the age of the child will be important to consider. Younger children might enjoy having their parents present in the classroom so much that the bad behavior would be reinforced. Instead, parents of young children might be asked to require students to read their lessons onto a cassette tape recorder every night until work starts to be completed during class time. Frequently, working

---

Web Search: Discipline Problems

Access Internet URL site **http://www.disciplinehelp. com/behindex/de-fault.htm.** The site gives a list of 117 problem behaviors and suggestions for handling the problems. Select five of the problems that you think will cause you great concern at the grade level you want to teach. Analyze the website advice for the five problems and write a summary of your conclusions. Present your five problems and analysis to the class and the instructor.

---

parents will have no way of knowing whether the child has homework assignments or not. However, parents could be instructed to require 20 minutes of oral cassette taped reading in needed subjects each night. Through parent involvement of this type you are able to set reasonable standards for working parents to be involved in the education of their children. This will help to foster the co-partnerships needed between parents and teachers.

Even though parents don't always support teachers in every endeavor, it is important not to get a one-sided view about the role parents can play in shaping your classroom efforts. It is a rewarding experience when teachers and parents pool their abilities and resources to bring about positive student change. Even though it will require some time to plan appropriate ways to involve parents, the time will be worthwhile.

Students will misbehave. How you handle the misbehavior will impact to some degree how smoothly your classroom will function. Complete Web Search: Discipline Problems which will let you address some of the problems you may encounter as a teacher.

T A S K   9 . 2

Management Techniques and Guidelines

Respond to the following management items. Compare your responses with those given at the end of the chapter.

1. Rules should always be stated specifically; never state a rule in general terms. (True/False)

2. Should teachers be firm or lenient at the start of the school year? Why? _____

_____

3. The use of sarcasm, criticism, ridicule, and harsh or humiliating punishments can be effective as management techniques.   (True/False)

4. One should avoid giving students a reward for desired behavior since it amounts to bribery.   (True/False)

Continued on next page

5. Is corporal punishment an effective management technique for teachers to use in managing a classroom? _____

_____

_____

6. The key to gaining parent support in discipline is _____

_____ .

7. When conducting a parent-teacher conference to enlist parent support, the three goals to be accomplished should include:

a. _____

b. _____

c. _____

Analysis and Reflections

The first few weeks are critical to a smooth running classroom. What would you do to start the year to accomplish this task? How would you communicate your expectations to students? How would you make sure they understood your expectations?

This concludes our discussion of classroom management control techniques, discipline guidelines, and parent involvement in classroom management. Take a few moments to complete Task 9.2, which will check your understanding of the material presented in the last three sections.

Summary

- Motivating students is perhaps the most difficult task facing teachers today. Students are influenced by internal factors and external factors.
- There is no surefire method that will motivate all students. Techniques that work with one student may be totally ineffective with another.

Motivation

- Motivation is a key to effective instruction and management.
- Intrinsic motivation originates within an individual, and extrinsic motivation originates outside the person.
- Intrinsic motivation is associated with the individual's attitudes, needs, personality factors, and values. Extrinsic motivation is the result of environmental stimuli.
- Students are motivated by their perception of events. These perceptions are often related to such internal factors as attitudes, needs, curiosity, interests, and sense of well-being.

- Appropriate models can also be motivating. Students often develop attributes similar to those they perceive in admired individuals.
- Various stimulus variation techniques that can be used to gain and maintain student attention include (1) the use of gestures, (2) focusing attention, (3) varying interaction styles, (4) the use of pauses, (5) shifting sensory channels, and (6) teacher movement.
- Students usually react to your expectations. The best should be expected from students.
- Teacher perceptions can sometimes be influenced by a halo effect. Student actions can sometimes be influenced by a Hawthorne effect.
- Knowledge of results or feedback is a long-recognized technique for motivating students. The nature of the feedback is critical if it is to be motivational.
- Do not rely on grades as your principle means of providing feedback; they are too general and they are given too infrequently to be effective with most students. Praise and verbal knowledge of results tend to be more effective.
- Incentives can serve as effective motivators. Students tend to repeat behaviors that are rewarded.

Control Techniques

- Start your year with a bang. Plan your classes well.
- Establish class rules, with student input if possible. Plan consequences for breaking the rules.
- Be sure that everyone understands the need and the reasons for the rules and consequences.
- Be consistent and fair in the enforcement of rules. Be firm at the beginning of the year; you can be less strict later on.
- Keep in mind that students want structure and need limits. It is your responsibility to provide leadership, to provide classroom structure, and to set classroom limits.
- Parents want their children to be successful. Teachers should enlist the support of parents in establishing a positive classroom environment.
- Parental support is generally established by setting up and carrying out a positive, well-planned conference.

Activities

1. *Classroom observation* Complete several school observations. Plan your visits to collect motivational data related to:
   a. The use of different types of teaching techniques
   b. Different bulletin board arrangements used for motivation
   c. Different forms of modeling observed in the classroom
   d. The different types of stimulus variation utilized by the teachers
   e. Examples of teacher enthusiasm
   f. Examples of teacher expectations displayed
   g. Examples of teacher feedback
   h. The use of praise and encouragement

2. *Microteaching*   Teach a 20-minute mini-lesson to a group of students or peers. Use as many stimulus variation techniques as you can. If possible, videotape the lesson.
3. *Microteaching analysis*   Study the videotape you made in Activity 2. List your stimulus variations and determine how proficiently you used them.
4. *Motivational menus*   Develop a list of motivational incentives that could be used in your subject area. Arrange them in ascending order of value.
5. *Teacher enthusiasm*   List the characteristics of an enthusiastic teacher. Recall the general characteristics of past teachers you have had that were enthusiastic. When finished, compare your list of characteristics with others' lists.
6. *Management profile*   Access Internet URL site **http://education, indiana.edu/casltt/vli2/what.html.** Follow the directions provided to determine your management style. Is your style what you want? If not, what will you do to adjust to a new style?
7. *Causes of misbehavior*   Think back over the classes you have observed and attended in which there have been disciplinary incidents. List all the possible causes for the student misbehavers. How might knowledge of the causes of these misbehavers influence a teacher's action? Some behavior problems are teacher-created. Can you think of some examples?
8. *Behavior observation*   Complete several observations in various classrooms at different levels. How do the observed teachers control behavior? Do the teachers use signals, warnings, nonverbal messages, or other subtle measures to prevent discipline problems from arising? Which techniques seem most successful? Do all students respond the same way? Does there appear to be a difference in effectiveness at the various grade levels?
9. *Planning*   Plan a first day for a class you may teach. What introductory activities would you use? What rules and consequences would you introduce and discuss? What would you do to motivate your students?

Answer Keys

Task 9.1 Motivation
1. Motivation is a force or drive that energizes and directs individuals to act as they do.
2. a. 2   b. 3   c. 1
3. Achievement motivation is the degree to which a student wishes to do well.
4. deficiency needs; growth needs
5. Modeling is using a person admired by students to demonstrate desired behaviors.
6. a. *VIS*   Teacher redirects question to another student.
   b. *FA*   Verbal statement is used to focus attention.
   c. *P*   Pause is used to focus attention.
   d. *SSC*   Children are required to use both aural and visual receptors.
   e. *G*   Gesture is used to emphasize a statement.

   f. *TM*   Teacher uses movement to refocus attention and proximity as a control technique.
 7. a. gestures
   b. focusing behaviors
   c. interaction styles
   d. pauses
   e. shifting sensory channels
   f. teacher movement

Task 9.2 Management Techniques and Guidelines

1. *False*   It is often best to have a few general rules. The specifics of these general rules should be discussed with students.
2. A firm, businesslike start is usually best. It communicates to students that they are in class to learn.
3. *False*   Sarcasm, criticism, ridicule, and harsh or humiliating punishment should be avoided. These techniques often provoke hostility and a desire for revenge.
4. *False*   It is not bribery to help someone improve his or her achievement or self-control.
5. Corporal punishment has not proven to be an effective management technique. Corporal punishment should only be used as a last resort.
6. to take parent criticism seriously without taking it personally.
7. a.   Establish a co-partner relationship.
   b.   Relate the seriousness of the meeting.
   c.   Confirm you have their child's best interest at heart.

Theory and Research

Kasten, R., & Weintraub, Z. (1999). Rating errors and rating accuracy: A field experiment. *Human Performance, 12*(2), 137–153.
Porro, B. (1996). *Talk it out: Conflict resolution in the elementary classroom.* Alexandria, VA: Association for Supervision and Curriculum Development.
Wong, H. K., & Wong, R. T. (1997). *The first days of school: How to be an effective teacher.* Alexandria, VA: Association for Supervision and Curriculum Development.

References

Allington, R. (1980). Teacher interruption behaviors during primary-grade oral reading. *Journal of Educational Psychology, 71,* 371–377.
Cooper, H., & Good, T. L. (1983). *Pygmalion grows up.* New York: Longman.
Franken, R. E. (1998). *Human motivation* (4th ed.). Belmont, CA: Wadsworth Publishing.
Good, T. L., & Brophy, J. E. (1987). *Looking in classrooms* (4th ed.). New York: Harper and Row.
Maslow, A. H. (1970). *Motivation and personality* (2nd ed.). New York: Harper and Row.
Murphy, K. R., Jako, R. A., & Anhalt, R. L. (1993). Nature and consequences of halo error: A critical analysis. *Journal of Applied Psychology, 78*(2), 218–225.

Petri, H. L. (1996). *Motivation: Theory, research, and applications* (4th ed.). Pacific Grove, CA: Brooks/Cole Publishing.

Rogers, S., Ludington, J., & Graham, S. (1998). *Motivation and learning: A teachers guide for building excitement for learning and igniting the drive for quality.* Evergreen, CO: Peak Learning Systems.

Assessing Instruction

Eventually, teachers must evaluate the effectiveness of instruction. To this end, you must have a clear understanding of the assessment process. Chapters 10 and 11 focus on an understanding of the assessment process and on the collection of assessment data.

Chapter 10 focuses on the role of evaluation in the instructional process, sources of information, and various evaluative instruments. Authentic and performance assessment and the development and use of rubrics will also be a major focus of this chapter.

Observations often provide needed data for ongoing planning and evaluation processes as well as for managing the interactive dynamics of the classroom. Hence, Chapter 11 provides a framework for making accurate observations to be used in planning, evaluation, and during the instructional process.

Planning the Evaluation

Objectives

After completing your study of Chapter 10, you should be able to:

1. Explain the dual role served by the evaluation process.

2. Explain the importance of evaluation in the learning process.

3. Explain why evaluation should be a continual process.

4. Explain the importance of evaluation in the affective domain.

5. Compare and contrast diagnostic, formative, and summative evaluation.

6. Describe the six sources of evaluative information.

7. Identify limitations associated with the different data collecting sources.

8. Identify and describe various evaluative instruments that can be used in the evaluative process.

9. Identify advantages and disadvantages associated with the different evaluative instruments.

10. Discuss the different types of teacher-made tests as well as the common types of test items associated with each.

11. Discuss the use of performance assessment and portfolios in student evaluation.

All teachers must evaluate in order to determine where students are with respect to targeted learning objectives. If students have not mastered the intended material, reteaching must be planned. Viewed in this context, evaluation performs a dual role in the teaching-learning process. It gives the teacher information regarding the level of student learning, and it provides information that can be used in planning future lessons.

Being able to identify learner difficulties is a basic skill that successful teachers must possess. No matter how well you plan and implement your lessons, some students will probably experience difficulty in achieving the desired learning outcomes. Without proper identification and remediation, these difficulties may compound until the student becomes frustrated and turns off to learning altogether. Thus, evaluation and measurement are essential components in the teaching process.

Evaluation is the process of making a judgment regarding student performance; **measurement** provides the data for making that judgment (Hills, 1981). Thus, evaluation often involves more than simply measuring academic achievement. It can be related to how well students carry out specific actions (performance) or to what they can produce (product). Sometimes you will be more interested in a student's performance than in the end product. This is particularly true in the teaching of psychomotor skills. For example, you may want to evaluate how well your students participate in group work, how well they stay on an assigned task, or how they go about adjusting a microscope in an experiment. Also, since attitudes and feelings often have a tremendous effect on learning, you should address such factors in your teaching and in your evaluation.

You teach to bring about learning. Consequently the ultimate question in the instructional process is whether or not your students have learned what they were supposed to learn (Ahmann & Glock, 1981). Can they display the outcomes specified in your original objectives? More specifically, do they meet the acceptable level of performance as specified in the criterion of your objectives? These objectives will call for the evaluation of cognitive skills, performance skills, and in some cases attitudes or feelings. Thus, evaluation can be required in the cognitive, psychomotor, and affective domains. These differences call for different evaluation techniques.

Evaluation in the three domains of learning requires the collection of different types of information. However, before we focus on the gathering of evaluation information in these three domains, let's look at the different evaluation types and the different sources of evaluation information.

⚔ Evaluation Types

Teachers need continuous feedback in order to plan, monitor, and evaluate their instruction. Obtaining this feedback may involve the use of any one of three different types of evaluation: diagnostic, formative, and summative (see Table 10.1). These three primary types of evaluation differ mainly in terms of their chronological position in the instructional process.

TABLE 10.1

Relationship between Diagnostic, Formative, and Summative Evaluation

	Diagnostic	Formative	Summative
Purpose	To identify problems and group students	To promote learning	To derive a grade
Nature	Many questions related to general knowledge	Few questions related to specifics	Many questions related to specific and general knowledge
Frequency of administration	Once—usually before instruction	Frequently—before or during instruction	Once—usually at conclusion of instruction

Diagnostic Evaluation

Diagnostic evaluations are normally administered before instruction in order to assess students' prior knowledge of a particular topic. Their purpose is to anticipate potential learning problems and, in many cases, to place students in the proper course or unit of study. Two examples of diagnostic evaluation are (1) placement of certain elementary children in special reading programs based on standardized testing and (2) assignment of high school students to basic mathematics courses based on entrance assessment. Such evaluation is sometimes referred to as *preassessment* because it is often designed to check the ability levels of students in designated areas so that instructional starting points can be established. Diagnostic evaluation can provide valuable information to teachers about the knowledge, attitudes, and skill of students when they enter courses and can be used as a basis for remediation or special instruction. They can be based on teacher-made tests, standardized tests, or observational techniques.

Diagnostic information gives educational planners invaluable information regarding the appropriateness of the curriculum being taught. Unfortunately, it is most frequently used to check on established levels of achievement rather than to evaluate the curriculum. Assessment of achievement test scores, for example, is too often confined to making comparisons of district group scores with national norms, whereas it could be used to make needed curriculum changes and to renew instructional emphasis on areas found to be below the national norms.

Diagnostic information also provides information needed for the correct placement of students in curricula tracks, courses, and ability groups within courses. One critical piece of diagnostic information needed by all teachers is reading ability and comprehension. If your students have reading difficulties, remedial instruction must be planned to address these deficiencies.

Formative Evaluation

Formative evaluation is carried out during the instructional process to provide feedback to students and teachers on how well students are learning the material being taught. Whatever diagnostic information there was should be revised as additional information is gleaned from students' performance on oral and written work. This permits teachers to modify their instruction as needed. As individual student deficiencies are noted, remedial work should be planned to bring the slower-learning students up to the level of their peers. Some students may require more assistance than you can provide. When this occurs, you should seek outside assistance from an appropriate specialist. Finally, the information gained from formative evaluation can be used to vary the pace of instruction or to correct any general misconceptions that might be observed.

Formative evaluation usually focuses on small, comparatively independent pieces of instruction and a narrow range of objectives. Essentially, formative evaluation asks, "How are we doing?" and uses pretests, checkup tests, homework, seatwork, and classroom questioning to answer the question. The results of formative evaluation should be used to adjust instruction or the curriculum rather than to determine grades.

Summative Evaluation

Summative evaluation is primarily aimed at determining student achievement for grading purposes. Grades provide the school with a rationale for passing or failing students and usually are based on a wide range of accumulated behaviors, skills, and knowledge. As the term implies, *summative evaluation* provides a summing up of students' accomplishments. It is most frequently based upon cognitive knowledge as expressed through test scores and written work and rarely takes into account such areas of learning as values, attitudes, and motor performance.

Examples of summative evaluation include end-of-chapter tests, homework grades, completed project grades, and standardized achievement tests. Summative evaluation asks, "How did we do?" and can be used to judge not only student achievement but the effectiveness of a teacher or a particular school curriculum as well. The data collected, data collection method, and instrumentation will differ depending on the type of summative evaluation being conducted.

Although such evaluative devices as homework and tests are most often used in summative evaluation, they can also be used to diagnose learning problems and to promote learning. Thus, some devices serve a triple function: to diagnose learning problems, to promote learning, and to derive a grade. For example, homework can be analyzed to identify learning difficulties (that is, it can be used to diagnose problems), feedback comments can be written in the margins (to promote learning), and a grade can be recorded (to derive a grade). Likewise, tests should be analyzed to determine problem areas; then they should be returned to students and discussed to promote learning; and finally, grades should be recorded.

Evaluation should be a continual process that includes diagnostic as well as formative and summative goals. Many times you can gain valuable information regarding achievement, motor skills, or attitudes prior to or during the course of instruction. Difficulties may be noted, and if they are noted, on-the-spot feedback can be provided to remedy the situation. For example, lack of response to questioning can reveal that a concept is misunderstood. Trouble with a piece of lab equipment may suggest that students need further instruction on its use. A spot check of children's papers during seatwork might reveal problem areas.

Clearly, if teachers are to make accurate judgments about student performance, they need a high degree of confidence in the data they collect. In other words, they must use measurement devices that provide reliable and valid information.

⚹ Measurement Accuracy

Reliability and validity are two qualities that every measurement device should possess. If a teacher-made test reveals that 50 percent of a fourth grade class are below grade level in mathematics comprehension, should the teacher be concerned? The answer depends on the reliability and validity of the test, that is, the ability of the test to consistently measure what it is supposed to measure. A brief description of these two essential characteristics of measurement follows.

Reliability

Reliability refers to the consistency with which a measurement device measures some target behavior or trait. In other words, it means the dependability or trustworthiness of the measurement device. For instance, a reliable bathroom scale would give identical (or nearly identical) weights for each of five separate weighings in a single morning. If, on the other hand, some of the five weighings differed from others by 10 pounds, the scale would not be very reliable. Likewise, a multiple-choice test that is so ambiguously worded that students are forced to guess would probably yield different scores from one administration to another, and would thus be extremely unreliable.

Any measurement device, whether it is a standardized test, a teacher-made test, or an observation instrument, must provide reliable information if it is to be of value in decision making. Measurement, however, always involves some error. For example, (1) the characteristic being measured may vary over time (trait instability), (2) poor instrument or test construction could affect the score (sampling error), (3) inaccuracies in scoring or recording data will affect scores (scoring error), and (4) things such as motivation, fatigue, health, and luck in guessing can cause variance. The extent to which these errors can be minimized will determine the reliability of the measurement device.

How can teachers make their measurement devices more reliable? Basically, the reliability of measurement instruments can be improved by following the suggestions listed on the following page when you are constructing tests.

1. *Increase the number of evaluative items*   Reliability is improved when the amount of data collected is increased because you have a larger sample of the trait being evaluated. Thus, a test of 50 items is more reliable than one of 25 items.
2. *Establish optimum item difficulty*   Reliability is increased when the items being used (test or observational) are of moderate difficulty, because a test made up of such items spreads the information over a greater range than does a device composed mainly of difficult or easy items. In the case of observational data, an observational item with a five-point scale would yield more reliable information than one with a seven- or three-point scale because it would give more consistent results than would an item with a larger or smaller scale.
3. *Score objectively*   Reliability is greater when objective data are collected. With subjective data, even when the recorder is the same, identical responses or behaviors can be scored differently on different occasions due to internal differences within the scorer.

Validity

Validity is the degree to which an evaluative device measures what it is supposed to measure. For instance, if a test is supposed to measure scientific content knowledge, students' scores should not be based upon their reading ability. If it is supposed to measure second grade arithmetic skills, it should not measure fourth grade arithmetic skills or reading ability. In order for a measurement device to be valid, it must first be reliable. For example, if you cannot get consistent weight measures from a bathroom scale, you cannot expect it to be accurate. However, the weight measurements might be very consistent (reliable) but not accurate (valid). Clearly, if a measurement device is to be used to make decisions, it is essential that the information be both reliable and valid.

Although there are several types of validity, the simplest and most important one to teachers is content validity. **Content validity** is established by determining whether the instrument's test items correspond to the content that the students are supposed to learn. In the case of standardized tests, this inspection is carried out by subject experts. Similarly, to evaluate the content validity of a teacher-made test, items should be inspected regarding their correspondence to the teacher's stated objectives. However, this inspection alone will not guarantee content validity. For example, the objectives themselves may be obsolete or they may have been prepared by leafing through a book and writing objectives at random rather than carefully matching objectives to actual classroom instruction. In short, content validity requires that a teacher's test items match what was actually taught in the classroom.

Any type of measurement device, whether it is a test or an observation instrument, must be valid to give usable information. However, an instrument is not valid or invalid per se; it is a matter of degree, with each instrument having low, satisfactory, or high validity. Thus, the adequacy of an instrument involves a judgment about how useful the information it provides will be to future decision making. Although most teachers lack the time and the access to measurement experts to do extensive validity checks, they can at least check to see whether their test items match their stated learning objectives.

❈ Information Sources

Evaluation requires that a judgment be made, and this judgment requires accurate information. Therefore, it is essential that you be familiar with the different sources of evaluation information (TenBrink, 1982).

Cumulative Record

Cumulative records hold all the information gathered on students over the years. These records are usually stored in the main office or guidance center office and contain such things as vital statistics; academic records; conference information; health records; and family data; as well as scores on tests of aptitude, intelligence, and achievement. Cumulative records may also contain anecdotal and behavioral comments from past teachers. These comments often prove useful in understanding the reasons for students' academic and behavior problems.

It is important that the comments of past teachers be used with great care. You must avoid letting their comments color your judgment or expectations. Indeed, it is strongly suggested that you not consult students' cumulative records without good reason. The information contained in students' files may affect your own observations and lead to the formation of inaccurate judgments. Moreover, care should be exercised in interpreting student tests. Sadly, most teachers misinterpret test scores due to insufficient training.

Test scores reported in cumulative files are usually from standardized tests. As such, student scores will be reported in the form of standard scores such as percentiles, stanine, Z scores, or T scores. In addition, students' scores will be given in terms of how they compare with a large (usually national) group of students used to establish norms for the test.

It is important to recognize that an individual score or a group of scores may vary from established norms for many reasons. For example, the important knowledge, concepts, and skills of a course may be different from those addressed in the selected standardized test, or the test may be inappropriate to an individual or a group in terms of reading level, clarity of instruction, and so forth. Therefore, when a standardized test is to be used to collect evaluative information, a test that is appropriate for the group being evaluated must be selected—which isn't always an easy task.

Federal legislation permits the records of any student to be inspected and reviewed by parents. Parents also have the right to challenge any information contained in the file. As a result, many teachers are reluctant to write file statements or reports that may be considered controversial or negative. Sometimes this reluctance leads to the omission of important information.

Personal Contact

Much information can be gathered as you interact with students on a daily basis. Your observations of students as they work and relax and your conversations with students provide valuable clues that will be of assistance in planning your instruction. In fact, observing your students not only tells you how well they are doing in specific areas but also allows you to provide them with immediate feedback. Observational information is continuously available in the classroom as you watch and listen to students in numerous daily situations. A few such situations are:

1. *Oral reading*   Is the student having reading problems?
2. *Responding to questions*   Does the student understand the concepts?
3. *Following directions*   Does the student follow the given instructions?
4. *Group or seatwork*   Does the group stay on-task?
5. *Interest in subject*   Does the student participate eagerly?
6. *Using resource materials*   Does the group use materials correctly?

Accurate observations are needed to help you answer questions such as: Are students ready for the next lesson? Should I plan more activities for this concept? Are individual students having reading comprehension problems? Are individual students in need of special assistance? Based upon your observations related to these issues, certain conclusions about the academic and social progress of students can be made. Your observation during seatwork, for instance, might reveal that certain students have trouble staying on-task, or appear to need special help, or need additional help on lesson concepts. Therefore, watch your students closely and be alert as they go about their daily activities. In fact, you may want to develop devices such as checklists or rating scales to make your observations more accurate. The development and use of an anecdotal record form such as that shown in Figure 10.1 can prove useful for recording observations and conversations.

Students themselves can often provide valuable evaluative information if you simply ask them how they feel, what they like or dislike, what they think, or how they did. In short, information about student problem areas can often be gleaned from casual conversations before and after class. Indeed, conversations, formal and informal, with students may be one of the best techniques for gaining diagnostic and formative evaluative information. Therefore, you should pay close attention to students' comments when they want to talk about academic concerns, tests, and the desire for help. Such exchanges and questions, whether during individual seatwork or class sessions, give you the opportunity to gain valuable information not readily available from other sources. Of course, the reliability of the responses may be questionable since students, like most people, tend to tell you what they think you want to hear. Consequently, open inquiry should be used with care. A good way to improve reliability is to use observational skill in conjunction with inquiry.

Many educators criticize the use of informal observation and interaction information in making evaluative judgments. They claim that it is too subjective and that the record keeping associated with such sources is too time-consuming. However, once teachers have refined their observational skills, these criticisms have little basis, for two reasons. First, concern about subjectivity applies to all evaluation. Even pencil-and-paper tests involve subjectively choosing items for the test. The objectivity of personal-contact information can also be greatly enhanced through the use of appropriate instrumentation. (We

---

Student: _____ Date: _____

Description of environment: _____

_____

_____

_____

_____

Description of observation/interaction: _____

_____

_____

_____

_____

_____

Reported by: _____

FIGURE 10.1   *Anecdotal Record Form*

will address this issue later in the chapter.) Second, the time committed to personal-contact record keeping can be kept under control by opening a portfolio for each student and adding a few descriptive phrases periodically. Examples might include such phrases as "Larry has difficulty remembering his multiplication facts," "Alice must be continuously reinforced to stay on-task," and "Ron has trouble with fine motor adjustments in physics lab."

Analysis

Teachers grade or evaluate students' work on a regular basis; that is, they analyze it for possible errors. Such an analysis gives teachers much information about students' attitudes and achievement. The analysis can take place either during or following instruction and, like the other techniques we have discussed, has the advantage of not being a formal test with its accompanying pressures. However, analysis is often more formal than personal contact.

Analysis is important in that it provides early identification of learning difficulties. For this reason, a good rule is not to assign work unless it is going to be graded immediately by the teacher, another student, or the student himself or herself. Immediate feedback can then be provided to remedy the identified difficulties. A science teacher might analyze and correct a student's lab techniques, an art teacher a student's painting technique, a second grade teacher a student's math seatwork, and a fifth grade teacher a student's written report. Whatever the nature of the work, you would be wise to file samples of students' work for discussion during student-and-parent conferences.

Open-Ended Themes and Diaries

Teachers have long been aware of the influences that home background and out-of-school activities have on classroom learning. Therefore, knowledge about the emotional and social climate in which students live and learn can be indispensable in the evaluation process. This information will make it possible to adjust the curriculum to better address differences in students' backgrounds.

One technique that can be used to provide information about students is simply to ask them to write about their lives in and out of school. You might ask students to react to questions such as these:

1. What things do you dislike about school? What things do you like?
2. What do you want to do when you grow up?
3. What accomplishment in your life are you most proud of?
4. What persons in your life do you find it hardest to get along with?
5. Which school subjects do you like least? Why? Which do you like best? Why?
6. How do you feel about the students in this class?

The comments and judgments expressed in students' writing may be distorted to some extent; nevertheless, students' views of reality will often be revealed when the work is analyzed.

The use of diaries is another method for obtaining viable evaluative information. A diary can consist of a record, written every three or four days, in which students write about their ideas, concerns, and feelings. Thus, an analysis of students' diaries often gives valuable evaluative information. Under conditions of good rapport, students will often communicate openly and freely.

Conferences

Many times, conferences with parents will be needed, to gather evaluative information. Parents often have information that will shed light on students' academic problems. To be beneficial, however, parent conferences should be well-planned. Samples of the student's work and anecdotal observations (see Figure 10.1) should be discussed. Table 10.2 offers five helpful steps to planning and holding conferences. A parent conference should not be a time to lecture parents. Indeed, you should be cautious about giving too much advice on the home life of the student. The overall atmosphere should be unrushed and positive.

Useful information can often be obtained from other teachers who have had your students in their classes. Often such colleagues can describe difficulties students had in their classes, as well as the techniques that were tried to correct them. Conferences with other teachers, like conferences with parents, should be well-planned so that sufficient time will be available for productive meetings.

Finally, guidance counselors and other support personnel are often an excellent source of information. For example, counselors often will be able to shed additional light on test results, as well as on personality factors that might affect student performance.

TABLE 10.2

Steps to a Successful Conference

Step 1. *Plan ahead*   Establish your purpose. Plan what you intend to say, and what information you want to obtain from parents and share with them. What are your concerns about the student?

Step 2. *Start the conference*   Be positive. Establish a sharing atmosphere. Begin the conference with a positive statement.

Step 3. *Hold the conference*   Establish and display a positive attitude. Be an active listener. Be accepting with regard to input and advice. Establish a partnership so that all concerned can work toward a common goal.

Step 4. *End the conference*   End the conference with a positive comment. Communicate your belief that working together will lead to achievement of common goals.

Step 5. *Conduct follow-up contact*   Keep all parties informed. Send notes and make telephone calls to share successes, concerns, and other matters.

Expansion Activity: Conferences

You must be prepared if a parent/student/teacher conference is to be successful. Develop an agenda for such a conference. How would you involve students in the conference? Share your agenda and student involvement ideas with the class.

Parent/student/teacher conferences are assuming an important role in today's schools. However, conferences take planning. Complete Expansion Activity: Conferences which will let you experience planning a parent/student/teacher conference.

Testing

Brown (1971, p. 8) defines a test as "a systematic procedure for measuring an individual's behavior." This definition implies that a test must be developed systematically (using specific guidelines) and must provide a procedure for responding, a criteria for scoring, and a description of student performance levels. However, as noted earlier, if tests are to give useful information, they must be reliable and valid. Moreover, they must be usable. **Validity** refers to the degree to which a test measures what it is meant to measure. Test **reliability** is the consistency with which the test measures what it measures, that is, the consistency of scores obtained by the same person when retested with the identical or an equivalent form of the test. Finally, **usability** refers to practical considerations such as cost, time to administer, difficulty, and scoring procedure. For example, a two-hour exam would not be very usable for a one-hour exam period.

Although most tests are developed to measure cognitive achievement, some are used to measure attitudes, feelings, and motor skills. However, due to problems associated with reliability, validity, and usability, one must use extra care in selecting tests that measure attitudes and motor skills.

Testing, like other evaluative techniques, has certain limitations. Too often tests fail to provide information that is most important in the evaluation of students. For example, most tests do not measure student motivation, physical limitations, or environmental factors. In addition, teachers must guard against tests that are improperly constructed, poorly administered, and vulnerable to student guessing. Also by their very nature, pencil-and-paper tests are more likely to test knowing rather than thinking abilities, verbalizations rather than doing, and teacher wants rather than true attitudes or feelings. However, with care, tests can be developed to assess thinking ability. The problem is that most teachers lack either the time or the expertise to construct proper tests. Consequently, you must often use other devices, which will be discussed later in this chapter, to supplement formal pencil-and-paper tests.

Testing is probably the most common measurement technique used by teachers, but it may not be the most important. Testing should be thought of as only one of several techniques that you can use to obtain information about student progress.

Table 10.3 gives a comparison of the various evaluative information sources discussed earlier. Study the table, and then complete Task 10.1.

T A B L E 10.3

Comparison of Sources for Information Collecting

	Kind of Information Obtainable	Objectivity
Cumulative record	Factual information Cognitive and psychomotor skills Affective outcomes	Objective but can contain subjective information.
Personal contact	Factual information Performance Affective attributes Social skills Behaviors Opinions and feelings	Subjective but can be objective if instruments are used.
Analysis	Learning outcomes Cognitive and psychomotor skills Affective outcomes	Objective but not stable over time.
Open-ended themes and diaries	Cognitive and psychomotor skills Affective outcomes	Subjective but valuable information can be obtained through careful examination.
Conferences	Factual information Affective outcomes	Subjective but can obtain objective information.
Testing	Attitude and achievement Cognitive outcomes	Most objective and reliable.

T A S K   1 0 . 1

Collecting Information

Respond to the following items. Check your responses with those given at the end of the chapter.

1. Match the definition on the left with the term on the right.
   ___ a. Evaluation that ascertains   1. Formative
            the level of student
            achievement   2. Summative
   ___ b. Evaluation that normally
            precedes instruction   3. Diagnostic
   ___ c. Evaluation used to check
            learning during instruction

2. Summative evaluation is most often used to determine grades.   (True/False)

3. To provide useful information, measurement devices should be _____ and _____ .

4. Validity is _____
   _____ .

5. Describe six sources that can be used to obtain evaluative information.

   a. _____
      _____

   b. _____
      _____

   c. _____
      _____

   d. _____
      _____

   e. _____
      _____

   f. _____
      _____

6. Students' views of reality can often be gleaned from their writing.   (True/False)

7. Guidance counselors can be an excellent source of information about students.
   (True/False)

8. The most objective and reliable information is obtained through testing.   (True/False)

9. Following is a series of questions that requires you to collect information. Indicate the best source for the information: cumulative record (CR), personal contact (P), analysis (A), open-ended themes and diaries (O), conferences (CF), and testing (T).

   _____ a. Why is Mark's group always last in finishing assigned tasks?
   _____ b. What are the common errors on the algebra assignment?
   _____ c. Does the class like the poetry we have been studying?
   _____ d. Has the class learned what was taught about foreign lands?

Continued on next page

T   A   S   K   1 0 . 1   C o n t i n u e d

_____ e.   Has Mary always had trouble with science?
_____ f.   Can the students correctly write a research paper?
_____ g.   Which students are having trouble with social skills?
_____ h.   Which students know all their spelling words?
_____ i.   What are the class problem areas on pronouncing the new vocabulary words?
_____ j.   What would the students like to study next semester?
_____ k.   Is Joe having problems at home?
_____ l.   Have the class members learned to appreciate the place of science in our society?

Analysis and Reflections

Teachers must report student progress to parents. What methods should be used to report students' progress to their families? How frequently should progress reports be issued? Write a short summary of your reflections on these issues and submit it to your instructor.

⚔ Evaluative Instruments

Most sources of evaluative information require the use of some form of data recording instrument. Since evaluation is, ideally, a continual process in which information is systematically gathered from several sources, you should not rely on just one device to gain information about your students' progress. Consequently, we will discuss in this section the general characteristics of six commonly used evaluation devices. Whereas the specific guidelines for constructing the devices are beyond the scope of this book, we recommend that you take a course or read a basic textbook that deals with the construction of evaluation instruments. Let us now examine some of the evaluative options.

Standardized Tests

Ebel and Frisbie (1991) define a **standardized test** as one that has been constructed by experts with explicit instructions for administration, standard scoring procedures, and tables of norms for interpretation. Explicit instructions mean that the same questions are administered to students with the same directions, the time limit for taking the test is the same for everyone, and the results are scored using a carefully detailed procedure.

The procedure for development of a standardized test is quite complex. First, specialists write a series of questions about a particular subject or battery of subjects; the questions should be answerable by the well-informed student at a particular grade level. Next, the questions are tried out on a representative sample of students at that grade level from all kinds of schools in all parts of the country. Based on feedback from the representative sample, the test is revised and arranged in the final version of the exam. The exam is then administered to a sample of students that is larger and more carefully selected to represent the target grade level. These students form the **norming group** against which all subsequent scores are compared. Finally, a testing manual is prepared which explains how the test is to be given, scored, and interpreted. The development procedure for standardized tests makes it possible to compare the performance of a particular student against a large group of students or to compare the performance of one group of students against another group. Thus, you could compare school districts, compare a single school district's students with all students in a state, or compare students in a state with all students in the nation. For example, suppose a student scored 83 percent on a reading test. For most purposes, this is sufficient information for evaluation purposes, but at times, you might want to know how 83 percent compares to the scores of other students in the school, district, state, or nation.

Standardized tests come in several forms. Some are used to measure knowledge in specific areas, such as arithmetic, reading, English, social studies, or chemistry. These tests are usually referred to as **achievement tests,** since they measure how much a student has learned in a particular area or battery of areas. Other standardized tests are designed to measure students' aptitudes or abilities for performing certain activities. These tests are designed to measure a person's potential in a given field, such as science, mathematics, drafting, auto mechanics, or law, and are given a variety of labels including *scholastic aptitude tests, general ability tests,* and *intelligence tests.*

The major reason for using standardized achievement tests in the classroom is to supplement teacher evaluation. The tests can give valuable information on how well your students are doing in comparison with other local or national student groups.

There are also certain limitations associated with the use of standardized tests. First, they are expensive to administer. Second, their validity is questionable in situations in which they do not measure what was taught; that is, they may not be consistent with the teacher's goals and objectives. Finally, a standardized test is likely to have some cultural bias, which means that the test may discriminate against certain cultural groups that lack prerequisite language, background experience, or testing experience.

Teacher-Made Tests

Teacher-made tests are the most popular of all evaluative instruments. They differ from standardized tests in that they are constructed by the classroom teacher to meet particular needs and, if properly constructed, are usually consistent with classroom goals and objectives. In addition, they are much less expensive to administer.

Offsetting these advantages, however, is the fact that many classroom teachers lack the skill to design valid tests or write appropriate test items. Although the validity of many teacher-made tests is questionable, they are an important part of the instructional process. Consequently, you should develop and refine skill in test construction.

There are basically two types of items used by teachers in the construction of classroom tests: objective and essay. Objective items include multiple-choice, true/false, matching, and completion. Essay items, on the other hand, are supply items. They can be written either as brief- or extended-essay items, that is, the students must supply brief or extended responses. The brief form requires that students write a sentence or paragraph, solve a problem, or give a proof, while the extended form requires that students write at length. Which item type or types should be used in the construction of a test depends mostly on your objectives and the nature of the behaviors being measured. A common misconception is that objective items test only for facts or knowledge-level behaviors. In truth, any type of test item, objective or essay, can be used to measure instructional outcomes at any level. Although it is often difficult to write objective items at the higher levels, it is also difficult to write high-level items of any kind.

Your instructional objectives often suggest a particular type of test item. An objective, for example, that involves solving mathematics problems would probably be best evaluated through the use of short-answer items. On the other hand, knowledge of the definitions of terms would probably be best evaluated through the use of multiple-choice or matching items. In general, however, when objectives lend themselves to more than one type of test item, most teachers prefer multiple-choice items over other types because of their scoring ease and reliability.

Generally, tests should not contain more than two item types—or only one with younger students. Students, especially young children, may have trouble when they must shift to different types of responses. Therefore, such shifts should be kept to a minimum. In short, if your objectives can be evaluated by one or two different test types, then limit your test to these types.

Although student mastery can be measured through various types of test items, one overall principle applies to writing all test items: Every item should separate students who have mastered the objectives from those who have not. Students who do not know the material should not be able to guess or bluff their way to success on a test. Moreover, "test wiseness" (the ability to answer questions through the use of clues from the question) should never be rewarded with test success. Let us now briefly consider the various types of test items commonly used by classroom teachers.

Multiple-Choice Items   Probably the most widely used form of test item is the multiple-choice item. Undoubtedly, the major reason teachers and professional test developers use the multiple-choice format is its versatility. It can be used to measure different kinds of content and almost any type of cognitive behavior from factual knowledge to the analysis of complex data. Moreover, it is an easy kind of item to score.

In format, a multiple-choice item is composed of an introductory stem, which sets up the problem or asks a question, and a number of alternative answers or responses (usually three to five). One of the responses is the correct answer; the other alternatives are called *distractors* or *foils*. Writing good multiple-choice items is not the easy task that many beginning teachers believe it to be. It takes a substantial amount of time, patience, and creative ability; a thorough understanding of the mental processes; and thorough knowledge of the content and objectives being tested.

The goal for multiple-choice item construction is to write clear, concise, unambiguous items. Consider the following example:

Poor: The most serious disease in the world is
       A. mental illness.
       B. AIDS.
       C. heart disease.
       D. cancer.

The correct response depends on what is meant by "serious." Thus, since heart disease leads to more deaths, mental illness affects more people, and AIDS is a growing worldwide problem, there are three possible correct answers. However, the question could be reworded as follows, for example:

Better: The leading cause of death in the world is
       A. mental illness.
       B. AIDS.
       C. heart disease.
       D. cancer.

Additional guidelines that can be followed to write more effective multiple-choice items follow.

1. Each item should be clearly stated, with the central issue or problem in the stem. It should be in the form of a question or an incomplete statement, and there should be no ambiguity in terminology.
2. Avoid poor layout, such as having the beginning of a question at the end of one page and the continuation of it on the next, or placing choices in a linear sequence or paragraph.
3. Do not provide grammatical or contextual clues to the correct answer. For example, the use of *an* before the choices indicates that the answer begins with a vowel. Instead, use the form *a(n)*, which means "either *a* or *an*."
4. Keep the amount that students must read in a question to a minimum. This means that you should write concise stems and precise choices. Use language that even the poorest readers will understand.
5. Write appropriate answers and decoys. Write a correct or best answer and then write several distractors that are as plausible as possible, including common errors, errors that are likely, and erroneous commonsense solutions.
6. Make sure that items are grammatically correct. For example, the use of *is* or *are* can often eliminate choices, allowing students to guess the correct response. Each alternative response, or distractor, should fit the stem, in order to avoid giving clues to its incorrectness.
7. Avoid the use of negatives (such as *not*, *except*, and *least*) and double negatives. Negatives tend to make items difficult and confusing. If negatives must be used, they should be emphasized by capitalizing them and putting them as near the end of the stem as possible.

8. Avoid giving structural clues—for example, routinely having the correct response longer (or shorter) than the others or failing to use certain alternatives for the answer.
9. Use "all of the above" and "none of the above" sparingly. Use such responses only when they will contribute more than another plausible distractor. "All of the above" is a poorer response than "none of the above" because items that use it have three or four correct answers.
10. Avoid using items directly from the textbook. Test for understanding, not memorization.

Once a pool of multiple-choice items has been developed on a topic, it is generally easy to modify the items based on feedback data. Compared to true-false items, multiple-choice items are relatively insensitive to guessing. However, they are more sensitive to guessing than are items in which students have to create their own answers.

Alternate-Choice Items   If there are only two possible responses to a stem, the item is alternate-choice. Alternate-choice items are really just a branch of multiple-choice items. The true/false format is a form of alternate-choice item. Variations on the basic true/false item include yes-no, agree-disagree, and right-wrong items.

Alternate-choice items tend to be popular because they seem easy to write. Unfortunately, writing good alternate-choice items requires skill, in order to avoid triviality. Writing good true/false items, for example, is difficult because there are few assertions that are unambiguously true or false. Also, alternate-choice items are sensitive to guessing.

Most of the guidelines for multiple-choice item construction also apply to alternate-choice items. However, it is especially crucial that alternate-choice items be stated as clearly as possible since they are particularly sensitive to ambiguity. For instance, consider the following:

Poor: Normal human body temperature is 98.6.   T   F

This is normally true, but there are exceptions; some individuals have a lower normal body temperature. To be totally true, the item could be rewritten as follows:

Better: For the majority of people, normal body
            temperature is 98.6.   T   F

Although most of the guidelines for multiple-choice item construction also apply to alternate-choice items, it is important to avoid the following additional pitfalls.

1. Avoid the use of negatives. To disagree (to answer "false") with such a statement essentially creates a double negative.
2. The portion of an item that makes a statement false should be an important piece of information. For example, a statement should not be false because an individual's seldom-used first name is incorrect. In other words, avoid trick items that appear to be true but are false because of an inconspicuous word or phrase.

3. Don't make your true items more lengthy than your false items. If it is necessary to have a few lengthy true items, you should make sure that there are approximately the same number of lengthy false items.
4. Watch for item construction patterns. Generally, the proportion of true and false items should not be too different. Similarly, guard against correct-response patterns—such as T F T F T F . . . or T F F T F F T F F . . . —that could help students to achieve a misleading number of correct answers.
5. Be especially sensitive to the use of specific determiners. Words such as *always, all, never,* and *none* indicate sweeping generalizations which are associated with false items, whereas words like *usually* and *generally* are associated with true items.
6. Write each item first as a true statement with no more than one idea. You can then make the statement false by changing a word or phrase.
7. Avoid quoting exact statements from the textbook. Use of exact quotations could make students think that you prefer rote learning.

Like multiple-choice items, alternate-choice items permit teachers to take a broad sampling of behaviors in a limited amount of time. Moreover, the scoring of alternate-choice items tends to be simple and reliable. However, some kinds of content and learning cannot be easily evaluated through the use of alternate-choice items. For example, problem-solving situations and complex learning are often difficult to evaluate using alternate-choice techniques.

Matching   Matching questions are designed to evaluate students' ability to identify pairs of matching phrases, words, or other related facts from separate lists. Although quite different in appearance, a matching item is essentially an efficient arrangement of a series of multiple-choice items with all stems (sometimes called *premises*) having the same set of possible alternative responses. Thus, matching items can be used anywhere multiple-choice items can be used. They are best suited for measurement of verbal, associative knowledge—that is, knowledge such as inventors and their inventions, titles and authors, or objects and their characteristics.

The chief advantage of matching items is their efficiency. They permit taking a relatively large sample of behaviors in a limited space. Indeed, multiple-choice items with the same, similar, or with overlapping responses can be converted to matching items with a resultant saving of space. Conversely, the chief disadvantage is the limited scope of knowledge that can be measured.

A common problem associated with matching items is the tendency for one part of the exercise to give away the answer to another part. Consider, for example, the following:

Poor: 1. Herman Melville   A. Hamlet
          2. William Shakespeare   B. New Atlantis
          3. Henry Thoreau   C. Paradise Lost
          4. Francis Bacon   D. Walden
          5. John Milton   E. Billy Budd

Since there are exactly five premises and five responses, and if each statement is to be used once and only once, when students have correctly answered four of the premises, the fifth response is correctly identified for the last premise. It is better to use extra responses or to have each response used more than once. For example:

Better: 1. Herman Melville   A. Hamlet
           2. William Shakespeare   B. New Atlantis
           3. Henry Thoreau   C. Utopia
           4. Francis Bacon   D. Billy Budd
           5. John Milton   E. Paradise Lost
                                     F. Walden

To write sound matching items, you should think of matching items as a set of multiple-choice items with the same set of alternatives. Then each response is appropriate for each premise. In addition, following the guidelines listed below will lead to composition of better matching items.

1. Give clear directions that indicate the basis for matching the premises with the responses.
2. Be sure the entire matching exercise is on one page. In other words, don't put the premises on one page and the responses on the back or on the next page.
3. Avoid including too many premises on one matching item. The more premises, the more difficult it is to avoid giving inadvertent clues.
4. Put premises and responses in a systematic order. That is, be sure that premises and responses are easy to find.
5. Be sure there is a high degree of homogeneity in every set of matching items. Both the premises and the responses should be in the same general category.
6. Minimize reading time. Premises or responses composed of one or two words should be alphabetized.

Completion Completion items require that students associate an incomplete statement with a word or phrase recalled from memory. Usually, each completion test item contains a blank which the student must fill in correctly with one word or a short phrase. Since the student is required to create rather than choose a correct response, the completion item is a form of supply item. Skill is needed to write such items so that there is only one correct response. These items are most useful for the testing of specific facts. Like essay questions, they require that students write responses in their own handwriting. However, they are less powerful than essay items in terms of the kinds of thinking they can evaluate.

Placement of the blank is of prime importance in writing completion items. For example, consider the following:

Poor: The _____ of a _____ is found by multiplying one-half the base times the height.

As a general rule, it is best to use only one blank in a completion item and it should be placed near or at the end of the sentence. Thus, the example should be rewritten as follows:

Better: Multiplying one-half the base times the height yields the area
            of a _____ .

Other guidelines associated with writing better completion items include the following.

1.   Give clear instructions indicating whether synonyms will be correct and whether spelling will be a factor in grading.
2.   Be definite enough in the incomplete statement so that only one correct answer is possible.
3.   Avoid the use of direct statements from the textbook with a word or two missing. Such usage encourages students to memorize the text.
4.   If more than one blank is used, make sure that all blanks for all items are of equal length and that they are long enough to accommodate the longest response.

Essay   Essay items are designed to give students the opportunity to answer questions in their own words. Students are asked to recall information from memory and to create responses based on that information. Essay test items come in two forms: brief and extended. The brief-essay item usually requires a limited amount of writing or requires that a problem of some sort be solved, whereas the extended-essay item requires from several paragraphs to many pages of writing. Because of time constraints, the extended essay is seldom as useful in the classroom as other types of items.

The brief-essay item is usually structured to ask a specific problem for which the student must recall proper information, organize it in a suitable manner, derive a defensible conclusion, and express it within the limits of the posed problem. The question should specify response limitations to guide the student in responding and to provide evaluation criteria for scoring. For example:

> List the major similarities and differences between a short story and novel. Be sure to consider such factors as structure and character development. Limit your response to one page. Your score will depend on accuracy and organization.

As shown in the above sample, brief-essay questions are generally structured to assess skills that have been broken down into discrete parts.

Essay items continue to be used extensively by teachers because they take much less time to write than do objective items. Indeed, essay questions seem so easy to write that teachers sometimes prepare them too hastily. Consider the following example:

Poor: Discuss the problems that led to the Civil War.

This request is unclear. Do not tell students to simply discuss; tell them what to discuss, and tell them in descriptive terms such as "describe three economic reasons" or "analyze political reasons." Notice that the following phrasing makes the students' task much clearer.

Better: Analyze the political situation in the South that led to the start of the Civil War. Limit your response to one page. Your score will depend on accuracy and organization.

Careful consideration must be given to the construction of essay questions so that students will know what is required for a satisfactory response. The following guidelines should be of further assistance in writing better essay questions.

1.   Be explicit in giving directions for students' responses. If spelling and grammar are to be considered in grading, tell the students; if organization, creativity, and content are to be considered, this information also should be shared with your students.
2.   Be sure that students have ample answering time. If more than one essay question is to be answered in a period, you might want to set a time limit for each.
3.   Give students a choice of questions. A choice of two or three questions avoids penalizing students who may know the subject as a whole but happen to have limited knowledge in the particular area of a single question.
4.   Determine the worth of each question as you are writing the test, and establish how much weight will be given to components of each question. Include this information in the test instructions, and grade accordingly.

Another problem associated with essay tests is content coverage. Because of the time needed for students to respond to essays, adequate content coverage is often difficult. Typically, only a few items can be included on a given exam.

Essay items usually require both the recall and use of information in the demonstration of higher-level knowledge. Consequently, essay items are difficult to score. There is no single right answer to a question. Because of this tendency, essay items generally tend to be less valid and less reliable than other tests. Despite these drawbacks, such unrestricted items are usually required to evaluate higher-order knowledge.

Quizzes   Teachers also develop and use classroom quizzes to evaluate student progress. Teacher quizzes differ from regular teacher-made tests in that they are usually short (three to five questions) and limited to the material taught in the immediate or preceding lesson. The main purpose of teacher quizzes is to find out what concepts from the preceding lesson or from assigned homework the students have not grasped or perhaps have misunderstood. Short quizzes are rather easy to develop, administer, and grade, thus providing prompt evaluation to both students and teacher.

Quizzes encourage students to keep up with assignments, show students their strengths and weaknesses in learning, and help teachers to improve instruction. Errors identified through the use of quizzes serve as early warning signals of learning problems. Early identification allows the teacher to address problems before they worsen.

Rating Scales

As noted earlier, observations can be an effective evaluative technique. However, they often lack reliability and validity. For example, teachers can view students differently, let the time of day affect their observation, or allow their perceptions to change with time. These defects can be overcome to some extent through the use of rating scales, checklists, or other written guides to help objectify observations. Let us look first at the design and use of rating scales.

Rating scales can be extremely helpful in judging skills, products, procedures, social behaviors, and attitudes. A rating scale is nothing more than a series of categories that is arranged in order of quality. For example, a scale for using the backhand in tennis might have five steps, with the lowest category labeled inadequate and the top labeled proficient. It might look like this:

•———— • ———— • ———— • ———— • ———— •
0   1   2   3   4   5
Inadequate   Proficient

The rater would develop the criteria for what to look for in the proper use of the backhand and mark students on their use of it. Other scales might be prepared for effective use of the forehand, the serve, the lob, and the ability to volley. The total instrument might be similar to the one shown in Figure 10.2.

Scales similar to those presented in Figure 10.2 can be developed for observations of a student product, of social behaviors, or of attitudes. One need only change the attributes being judged and perhaps change the low and high scale classification. If applicable, you might want to change the zero-to-five scale values shown in Figure 10.2 to a more appropriate scale value, such as this:

•—————— • —————— • —————— • —————— •
Poor   Fair   Good   Very   Excellent
                                                            good

Rating scales allow observers to separate a total performance into various subskills and, with appropriate scale judgments, the quality of a student's performance can be better determined. The results are more valid and reliable observations. However, some uncertainty will still exist.

Checklists

A checklist differs from a rating scale in that it indicates the presence or absence of specified characteristics. A **checklist** is basically a list of the criteria upon which a student's performance or end product is to be judged. You use the checklist by simply checking off the criteria items that have been met.

The type of response for each entry on a checklist can vary. It can be as simple as a check mark indicating that a listed action has occurred. For

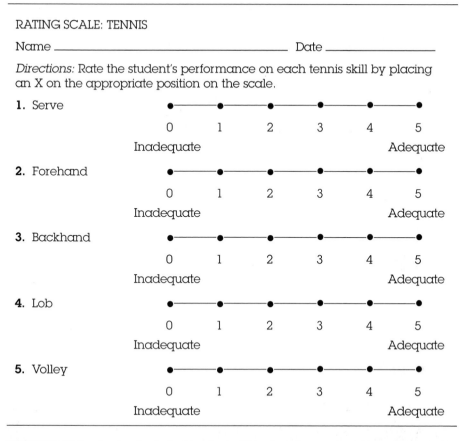

RATING SCALE: TENNIS

Name _____ Date _____

Directions: Rate the student's performance on each tennis skill by placing an X on the appropriate position on the scale.

1. Serve

      0   1   2   3   4   5

   Inadequate   Adequate

2. Forehand

      0   1   2   3   4   5

   Inadequate   Adequate

3. Backhand

      0   1   2   3   4   5

   Inadequate   Adequate

4. Lob

      0   1   2   3   4   5

   Inadequate   Adequate

5. Volley

      0   1   2   3   4   5

   Inadequate   Adequate

FIGURE 10.2 *Rating Scale for Tennis* An X is placed on each scale to represent the student's skill on the attribute.

example, a checklist for observing student participation in group work might look like this:

____ 1. Starts work promptly.

____ 2. Displays interest in work.

____ 3. Cooperates with others.

____ 4. Makes worthwhile suggestions.

The rater would simply check the items that occurred during group work.

    Another type of checklist that is sometimes used requires a yes or no response. The yes is checked when the action has been performed in a satisfactory manner; the no is checked when the action has been unsatisfactory. An example of this type of checklist used in a speech class is shown in Figure 10.3.

PERFORMANCE CHECKLIST: SPEECH

Name _____Date _____

Directions: Check Yes or No as to whether criterion level is met.

Did the student:	Yes	No
1. Use correct grammar.	____	____
2. Make clear presentation.	____	____
3. Stimulate interest.	____	____
4. Use clear diction.	____	____
5. Show poise.	____	____
6. Reveal enthusiasm.	____	____
7. Use appropriate voice projection.	____	____

FIGURE 10.3   *Performance Checklist for a Speech Class*

The rater would check the appropriate column on each item to indicate whether the performance level has been met.

The development and use of checklists sensitizes the observer to the various parts of desired actions. By getting reliable data on the component parts, the observer is able to evaluate the overall performance.

Questionnaires

Attitudes, feelings, and opinions are admittedly difficult to evaluate. For some attitudinal goals, long-time observation may be needed since representative behaviors may not occur on a daily basis. A common technique for overcoming this difficulty is the use of a pupil **questionnaire,** which requires students to examine themselves and react to a series of statements about their attitudes, feelings, and opinions. The author of the questionnaire decides what information is wanted and then designs statements or questions that will elicit this information.

The response style on questionnaires can vary from a simple checklist–type response to open-ended statements. Whenever possible you should design questionnaires so that they call for short answers only.

The checklist–type response usually provides students with a list of adjectives for describing or evaluating something and instructs them to check those that apply. For example, a checklist questionnaire on the attitude of students in a mathematics class might include such statements as:

1. This class is   ____   exciting.

                        ____   boring.

                ____ interesting.

                ____ unpleasant.

                ____ informative.

2. I find mathematics   ____ fun.

                ____ interesting.

                ____ a drudgery.

                ____ difficult.

                ____ easy.

The scoring of this type of test is simple. You subtract the number of negative statements checked from the number of positive statements checked. The result is the positiveness of the attitude.

     A second type of response cycle that can be used on questionnaires is often referred to as the semantic differential. A **semantic differential** is usually a seven-point scale that links an adjective to its opposite. The semantic differential response is designed so that attitudes, feelings, and opinions can be measured by degrees, from very favorable to highly unfavorable. Examples from a questionnaire that could be used to check students' attitudes toward science might look like this:

Science is

Interesting ___ : ___ : ___ : ___ : ___ : ___ : ___ Boring

   Pleasant ___ : ___ : ___ : ___ : ___ : ___ : ___ Unpleasant

      Good ___ : ___ : ___ : ___ : ___ : ___ : ___ Bad

The composite score on the total questionnaire is determined by averaging the scale values given to all items included on the instrument.

     One of the most frequently used response styles in attitude measurement is the **Likert scale,** which is usually a five-point scale that links the options "strongly agree" and "strongly disagree" as follows:

| Strongly agree | Agree | Undecided | Disagree | Strongly disagree |

The students respond to statements by checking the options that most closely represent their feelings about the statements. An example of this type of instrument is shown in Figure 10.4. The Likert scale is generally scored by assigning a value between 1 and 5 to the available options. The value 5 is usually assigned to the option "strongly agree" and 1 to the option "strongly disagree." These assigned values are usually reversed when the statement is negative. The composite score is then determined by adding all the scale values.

ATTITUDE SCALE: THE METRIC SYSTEM

Name _____ Date _____

Each of the statements below expresses a feeling toward the metric system. Rate each statement on the extent to which you agree. For each you may strongly agree (A), agree (B), be undecided (C), disagree (D), or strongly disagree (E).

```
 ●————————●————————●————————●————————●
Strongly    Agree    Undecided  Disagree  Strongly
 agree                                    disagree
```

____ **1.** The metric system is fun to use.

____ **2.** I don't like the metric system. It scares me to use it.

____ **3.** The metric system is easy to understand.

____ **4.** In general I have good feelings toward the metric system.

____ **5.** I approach the metric system with hesitation.

____ **6.** I feel at ease in using the metric system.

____ **7.** The metric system makes me feel uncomfortable, irritable, and impatient.

____ **8.** I feel a definite positive reaction to the metric system.

FIGURE 10.4   *Attitude Scale for Determining Students' Attitudes toward the Metric System*

Another type of response style that can be used on questionnaires is sentence completion. Partial sentences are presented, and students are asked to complete them with words that best express their feelings, for example:

I find biology to be _____.

This class is _____.

The responses are then scored as to content for each respondent.

The advantages of using questionnaires are that they can be administered in a relatively short period, they can often be used to help students improve their vocabulary, they can help students to clarify their feelings, and they are generally easy to score. However, there are also disadvantages. One cannot be absolutely sure that true feelings are being expressed, and they are often too complex for young children.

This concludes our discussion of the most commonly used types of evaluation instruments. However, before we leave the topic of evaluation instruments we need to briefly address the recent focus on performance assessment and the use of portfolios in evaluation.

⚔ Authentic and Performance Assessment

Teachers encounter many classroom situations in which the traditional pencil-and-paper test is inappropriate for gathering needed evaluation information. As a result, educators are trying to redesign school assessment so that it reflects changing world conditions. To this end, much attention is being directed toward "authentic" assessment and "performance" assessment (Herman, 1998; Tombari & Borich, 1998).

Authentic Assessment

Authentic assessment measures the student's ability on "real-life" tasks and in "real-life" situations. Thus, it is designed to resemble real tasks as closely as possible (Baron & Boschee, 1995). For example, students' ability to use a specific piece of science equipment would be tested by requiring students to perform a series of tasks using the equipment, rather than asking them to answer questions about the equipment. In language arts, the students' ability to write would be assessed by asking them to write on a real-life topic or a series of real-life topics (Meyer, 1992). The growing interest in authentic assessment can be linked to the move toward outcome-based education (Clark & Clark, 1998), where the emphasis is on the learning that students can demonstrate, rather than on inputs to the educational process (curriculum, credit hours, teacher efforts, etc.). The term *educational outcomes* refers to observable student behaviors that result from schooling.

Advocates of authentic assessment say that this type of assessment is more likely to motivate students to excel than are standard pencil-and-paper tests. The various forms that authentic assessment may take depend on the subject area and the age of the student. Some common forms include performances (dances, demonstrations, or presentations), portfolios, hands-on experiments, culminating exhibitions (artwork, demonstration of skill, or oral and written presentations), computer simulations, open-ended experiences (real-life tasks performed), writing sampling, open-ended questions, and integrated projects.

Experts also suggest that since authentic assessment involves students in real-life situations teaching and assessing become one in the same. Thus, it sets the stage for linking instruction and assessment.

Performance Assessment

The terms authentic assessment and performance assessment are often used interchangeably, but, the two do not mean exactly the same thing (Schurr, 1999). In authentic assessment, the student is required to perform specific behaviors in a real-life situation. In performance assessment, the student is required to perform specific behaviors to be assessed, the situation doesn't necessarily have to be real-life. Thus, **performance assessment** can be viewed as assessment in which students create an answer or a product that demonstrates their acquisition of knowledge or skill (Airasian, 1993). Possible types of activities that could be used to assess performance are (1) simulations, including simulated performance tests;

(2) performance tests, including actual work samples, identification tests, teacher and peer ratings, and self-assessments; (3) observational assessments; (4) oral assessments; (5) pencil-and-paper assessments, including essay tests, written reports, and design problems; and (6) personnel records, including transcripts, portfolios, and internships. In effect, performance assessment assesses students' ability to translate knowledge and understanding into an action or a product of some kind. With performance assessment, students must demonstrate the behaviors that the assessor wants to measure (Meyer, 1992). For example, if the desired behavior is typing, students type; if the desired behavior is identification of geometric figures, they draw or locate geometric figures; or if the desired behavior is a social skill such as leadership, they are given and observed in leadership roles. Performance assessment gives students the opportunity to show what they know or can do in real situations (Airasian, 1993).

With performance assessment, teachers must evaluate the levels of student performance. To carry out this evaluation of performance the teacher gathers observational evidence and makes judgments regarding each student's actual performance or product. According to Airasian (1993), there are four essential features to any formal performance assessment. They include:

1. Having a clear purpose which gives the reasons for the performance assessment.
2. Identifying observable and measurable attributes of the student's performance that will be judged by the assessor.
3. Providing an appropriate setting for making an accurate judgment of the performance or product.
4. Establishing a scoring or rating criteria and necessary instrumentation prior to the evaluation.

The reliability and validity of the formal performance assessment process can be improved through the use of anecdotal records, rating scales, checklists, questionnaires, and through the use of portfolios.

Portfolios

Portfolios are becoming increasingly popular with teachers and school districts in performance assessment (Farr & Tone, 1998; Mills, 1997). Samples of students' work are compiled for evaluation with the selection of items for assessment of performance being done by students, the teacher, or both. These items are then accumulated in portfolios. Thus, a portfolio can be thought of as a systematic, organized collection of evidence designed to illustrate a person's accomplishments and to represent progress made toward reaching specified goals and objectives. Artists collect their best artwork; professional models collect photographs of their best work; and composers collect their compositions. In school situations, teachers collect samples of each student's work and put them in a file folder with that student's name on it. However, a portfolio is more than a folder of student work; it is a deliberate, specific collection of accomplishments (Paulson, Paulson, & Meyer, 1991). It is not a one-time collection of examples; it is generally a collection over a specific time period. The purpose is to gain more accurate understanding of students' work and growth. Portfolios can be used to help students assess their progress, assist teachers in making instructional decisions, communicate with administrators and the public, and help teachers assess their progress toward curricular goals. Some teachers will collect samples related to a single subject area such as writing; others will establish mathematics portfolios that contain only worksheets and tests; and some will have behavior portfolios with observed student behaviors and students' reflections on these behaviors.

Basically teachers use several different kinds of portfolios depending on their purposes and uses. The four commonly used types are best piece portfolios, descriptive portfolios, process portfolios, and accountability portfolios. Best piece portfolios require students to select samples (sometimes with help from the teacher) that they consider to be their best efforts. They are popular because they encourage students to become more reflective about and involved in their own learning. Descriptive portfolios, on the other hand, enable teachers to gather a wide variety of measures on the students they teach. For example, these portfolios may contain documents related to writing, mathematics, science, and self-concept. Portfolios related to the writing process are labeled process portfolios. They generally contain samples related to how students have grown as readers and writers. Finally, accountability portfolios require that a satisfactory portfolio be presented at specific points in the educational process (for example, fourth, eighth, and twelfth grades). They generally include a table of contents and a representative sampling of the "best pieces" of work along with a letter explaining why each piece was selected as one of the best.

Portfolios enable students to display their best work or day-to-day accomplishments for examination by others. However, purpose is central to the contents of portfolios. They may be kept for a long period of time (a year) or a short period of time (duration of a unit, a term, or a semester). Writing or mathematics samples collected at the beginning of the year, for example, can be compared with those collected periodically throughout the year to show the growth and development of students' writing and mathematics abilities over the year. For a unit on the environment, samples of students' work, including homework, quizzes, pictures, videotaped presentations, and tests can be collected in a portfolio to document students' accomplishments during the unit.

Some teachers ask that students provide a reflection on their skills and accomplishments as part of their portfolios. This gives the teacher insight as to the students' perceptions about what they have learned and not learned. In effect, these reflections become a window into the student's head. As such, they can be used to encourage students to take charge of their own learning.

The contents of a student's portfolio must also be evaluated as part of the performance assessment process. The criteria for this evaluation should be set up prior to the accumulation of student materials.

Rubrics

Rubric scoring is becoming a common form of assessment. A **rubric** can be viewed as a scoring tool that lists the criteria for a piece of work, or "what counts" (for example, purpose, details, voice organization, and mechanics often count in a writing sample); it also articulates gradations of quality for each criterion, from excellent to poor (Goodrich, 1997). A sample scoring rubric that can be used to assess a research paper is shown in Figure 10.5. As shown in the example, the criteria are usually listed in the column on the left and the four columns to the right of the criteria describe varying degrees of quality. As concisely as possible, the columns explain what makes a good piece of work good and a bad one bad. A rubric is incomplete unless it contains all of these elements. Generally, there are two types of rubrics: holistic rubrics and analytic rubrics. A holistic rubric makes assessment decisions based on a global look at something. An analytic rubric examines only certain components. For example, we might take an overall global look at a portfolio or an analytical look might examine the portfolio artifacts.

Constructing a rubric is not an easy task. A clearly defined purpose is essential as each component is developed. With this in mind, the following steps should be followed.

Step 1: Review the standards that the product or performance is meant to address.

Step 2: Establish or review the criteria that will be used to judge the student's product or performance and make sure they match the standards.

Step 3: Design a frame by deciding on the major categories the rubric will address.

Criteria	Exceptional (4)	Excellent (3)	Acceptable (2)	Unacceptable (1)
Purpose	Explains the key purposes of paper in detail.	Explains all key purposes of paper.	Explains some of purposes but misses key purposes.	Does not refer to the purposes.
Content	The student is extremely knowledgeable about the topic.	The student has a good understanding of the topic.	The student demonstrates some knowledge and understanding of the topic.	The student shows no knowledge or understanding of the topic.
Organization	Well organized and easy to follow.	Good organization and fairly easy to follow.	Somewhat organized but hard to follow in places.	Not organized at all and difficult to follow most of time.
The Point	Reveals profound insight about topic.	Reveals insight about topic.	Doesn't show a central insight about topic.	Doesn't show any insight regarding subject.
Mechanics	There are few or no minor errors. Few careless mistakes.	There are some minor errors. Overall the student's writing is adequate.	There are numerous major and minor errors, but meaning is still clear.	Errors are so numerous and serious that they interfere with communication.

FIGURE 10.5 *Scoring Rubric for Research Paper*

Web Search: Rubrics

Access and analyze the rubrics on the following Internet URL sites: **http://west.pima,edu/~bfiero/105Rubrc.html, http://cresst96.cse.ucla.edu/ CRESST/pages/Rubrics.htm,** and **http://www.odyssey.on.ca/~elaine.coxon/ rubrics.htm.** Using the information gleaned from your analysis of the Internet rubrics, develop a rubric for a student project or activity of your choice. Share your rubric with the class.

Step 4: Describe the different levels of performance that match each criterion. Be sure to choose words or phrases that show the actual differences among the levels. Make sure they are observable.

Step 5: Test the rubric with students to make sure it is understandable.

Step 6: Revise the rubric as necessary.

A well-designed rubric enables students to understand what is expected of them. Furthermore, once students gain experience with rubrics, they can help construct their own rubrics.

The evaluation techniques discussed earlier can also be used to assess a product or performance: anecdotal records, checklists, rating scales, and questionnaires. Now, try your hand at developing a rubric of your choice by completing Web Search: Rubrics.

This concludes our formal discussion of evaluative instruments. Table 10.4 gives a summary of these instruments. Review Table 10.4 and complete Task 10.2 which was designed to test your understanding of the material.

TABLE 10.4

Evaluation Instruments

Instrument	Description
Standardized Tests	A commercially developed test that samples behavior under uniform procedures.
Teacher-Made Tests	An evaluative instrument developed and scored by a teacher to meet particular classroom needs.
Rating Scales	A scale of values arranged in order of quality describing someone or something being evaluated.
Checklists	A list of criteria, or things to look for, on the basis of which a performance or an end product is to be judged.
Questionnaires	A list of written statements regarding attitudes, feelings, and opinions that are to be read and responded to.
Performance Assessment	Assessment in which students create an answer or a product that demonstrates their acquisition of knowledge or skill.

```
T   A   S   K       1 0 . 2
```

Evaluation Instruments

Respond to the following items. Check your responses with those given at the end of the chapter.

1. List six evaluative devices that can be used in the classroom.

   a. _____

   b. _____

   c. _____

   d. _____

   e. _____

   f. _____

2. All standardized tests are achievement tests.   (True/False)

3. The best evaluative device to use when comparing groups is a standardized test. (True/False)

4. The best evaluative device to use for the measurement of classroom goals and objectives is the teacher-made test.   (True/False)

5. The two basic types of test items used by classroom teachers are _____ and _____ .

6. A major problem associated with alternate-choice test items is guessing sensitivity. (True/False)

7. A rating scale is used to indicate presence or absence of a specified attribute. (True/False)

8. Define performance assessment and describe how portfolios can be used effectively in performance assessment.

   _____

   _____

   _____

   _____

9. A series of situations that require evaluation follows. Please indicate the best evaluation instrument to use in each situation: achievement test (A), teacher-made test (T), rating scale (R), checklist (C), questionnaire (Q), or portfolio (P).

   _____ a. A third grade teacher wants to know whether students' cursive writing has improved.

   _____ b. An eighth grade teacher wants to know how students feel about the poetry unit.

   _____ c. A school district superintendent wants to know how students in the district are doing compared to students in the state.

   _____ d. A driver's education teacher wants to know whether students are following the correct procedure for starting a car.

   _____ e. A mathematics teacher just finished teaching a unit on polygons and wants to know whether the material was mastered.

Continued on next page

_____ f. An English teacher wants to determine the growth over the year in ability to write a term paper.

_____ g. An art teacher wants to determine how well students can draw a series of figures.

_____ h. A fifth grade teacher wants to know how his students compare with other students in reading.

_____ i. A shop teacher wants to know the woodworking tools preferred by students.

Analysis and Reflections

Grades can be assigned on the basis of academic achievement, ability, level of effort, and attitude. What criteria and evaluation strategies would you use to determine grades? Share your criteria and strategies with the class.

Summary

- Evaluation is the process of making a judgment regarding student performance; measurement provides the data for making that judgment.
- Evaluation is an essential tool for teachers because it gives them feedback concerning what their students have learned and indicates what should be done next in the learning process.
- Evaluation helps you to better understand students and their abilities, interests, attitudes, and needs in order to better teach and motivate them.

Evaluation Types

- There are three types of evaluations: diagnostic, formative, and summative.
- Diagnostic evaluation is usually carried out prior to instruction for placement purposes.
- Formative evaluation is most often used during instruction to promote learning, while summative evaluation follows instruction and is most often used to judge the end product of learning.

Measurement Accuracy

- Every measurement device should be reliable and valid.
- Reliability refers to the consistency with which a measurement device measures some target behavior or trait.
- Validity is the degree to which an evaluative device measures what it is supposed to measure. The simplest is content validity.

Information Sources

- Teachers must develop skill in using the best information-gathering sources and the best data-recording instruments.
- Teachers must develop an understanding of the information obtainable from cumulative records, personal contacts, analysis, open-ended themes and diaries, conferences, and testing.

Evaluative Instruments

- Once a data-gathering technique has been chosen, an appropriate instrument for recording valid and reliable data must be selected. This selection will usually be related to the specific domain under study.
- Desired data may require measurement in the cognitive domain (achievement), the psychomotor domain (process or performance), or the affective domain (attitudes, feelings, or opinions).
- Measurement in the cognitive domain usually requires a test (achievement or teacher-made) or some type of written work, whereas measurement of processes and performances is usually best carried out through rating scales and checklists.
- The measurement of achievement is usually carried out through the use of teacher-made tests. These tests can be either objective or essay, depending on the outcome to be measured.
- Objective tests can consist of multiple-choice, alternate-choice, matching, or completion items, while essay tests can be made up of brief or extended items.
- The measurements of attitudes, feelings, and opinions are the most difficult to obtain and are usually best measured through observations or questionnaires.

Authentic and Performance Assessment

- Recently, attention has been directed toward authentic and performance assessment as well as toward the use of portfolios in the evaluation process.
- Authentic assessment measures students' abilities in "real-life" tasks and situations.
- Performance assessment requires that students create an answer or product to demonstrate the acquisition of knowledge or skill.

Activities

1. *Evaluation information*   Information to be utilized in evaluation can be collected through cumulative records, personal contact, analysis, open-ended themes and diaries, conferences, and testing. Make a list of at least five kinds of information that can be collected through the use of each of the six data-gathering techniques. Submit the list to your instructor.
2. *Class evaluation*   For a hypothetical class, list information-gathering sources and evaluative devices that you could use to evaluate cognitive growth, attitudes, and psychomotor skills. For your evaluation of cognitive growth, suggest the best type or types of test items to use for your purpose.
3. *Rating scale development*   Develop a rating scale that could be used to assist you in judging the social behaviors you desire in a classroom. If possible, use the scale in an actual classroom setting.
4. *Checklist development*   Develop a checklist that could be used to evaluate a student's performance in carrying out a task of your choice. If possible, use the checklist in a classroom setting.

5. *Self-assessment* Discuss the importance of student self-assessment. Outline three procedures or techniques that could be used for self-assessment by students.
6. *Performance assessment* Check with local districts on their use of performance assessment and portfolios. If used, in what subject areas are they being used? What are teachers' feelings regarding the use of performance assessment and portfolios? If performance assessment is not being used, is the district making plans for changing to some form of performance assessment?

Answer Keys

Task 10.1 Collecting Information
1. a. 2 b. 3 c. 1
2. *True* Summative evaluation is most often used to judge the final level of learning.
3. reliable; valid
4. Validity is the degree to which an evaluative device measures what it is supposed to measure.
5. a. Information from cumulative records
   b. Personal contact with students in the learning environment
   c. Analysis of student work
   d. Examination of student writing
   e. Visiting with parents and other school personnel
   f. Formal tests that cover the information taught
6. *True* Students often reveal internal feelings and attitudes when they write.
7. *True* Guidance counselors often work closely with parents and other individuals in students' lives.
8. *True* Tests provide the most objective and reliable information, whereas personal contact provides the least objective information.
9. a. *P* Observe the group to see what is delaying them.
   b. *A* Analyze the students' work.
   c. *P or O* Simply ask them or have them write about their feelings.
   d. *T* A test will tell you what they know.
   e. *CR* Check Mary's cumulative record for grades and achievement scores.
   f. *A* Give them an assignment and analyze the results.
   g. *P* Observe students in social situations.
   h. *T* Give the students a spelling test.
   i. *P* Listen to students.
   j. *O* Ask them to write their ideas.
   k. *CF* Hold a conference with Joe's parents.
   l. *P* Ask the class to discuss their views.

Task 10.2 Evaluation Instruments
1. a. Standardized tests
   b. Teacher-made tests

    c. Rating scales
    d. Checklists
    e. Questionnaires
    f. Performance assessment and portfolios
2. *False*   Standardized tests can be aptitude tests, general ability tests, or intelligence tests.
3. *True*   Standardized tests are normed and, therefore, can be used to compare groups.
4. *True*   Teacher-made tests should be written to measure the classroom goals and objectives.
5. objective; essay.
6. *True*   Students have a 50 percent chance of correctly answering an alternate-choice item by guessing.
7. *False*   A checklist is used to indicate the presence or absence of a specified attribute.
8. Performance assessment is assessment in which students create answers or products that demonstrate their acquisition of knowledge or skill. Portfolios are used to compile samples of students' work for evaluation of abilities, skills, and growth.
9. a. *R* Rate students on their cursive writing skill.
   b. *Q* Design a questionnaire on poetry, and have students respond.
   c. *A* Compare achievement test scores.
   d. *C* List the procedure to be followed, and check for each student.
   e. *T* Design a test on the material covered.
   f. *P* Set up portfolios for students and compile samples of their work over the year.
   g. *R* Design a scale for each figure, and rate students on each.
   h. *A* Compare reading achievement test scores.
   i. *C* List tools and check those used by students.

Theory and Research

Darling-Hammond, L. (1995). *Authentic assessment in action.* New York, NY: Teachers College Press.

Fiderer, A. (1998). *35 rubrics and checklists to assess reading and writing.* Ontario, Canada: Scholastic.

Gredler, M. E. (1999). *Classroom and assessment learning.* White Plains, NY: Longman Publishing.

Popham, J. W. (1998). *Classroom assessment.* Boston, MA: Allyn and Bacon.

Price, A. (1999). *Handbook for classroom assessment.* Reading, MA: Addison-Wesley.

Wyatt, R. L., & Looper, S. (1999). *So you have to have a portfolio.* Thousand Oaks, CA: Corwin Press.

References

Ahmann, J. S., & Glock, M. D. (1981). *Evaluating student progress.* Boston: Allyn and Bacon.

Airasian, P. W. (1993). *Classroom assessment* (2nd ed.). New York: McGraw-Hill.

Baron, M. A., & Boschee, F. (1995). *Authentic assessment: The key to unlocking student success.* Lancaster, PA: Technomic Publishing.

Brown, F. G. (1971). *Measurement and evaluation.* Ilasca, IL: F. E. Peacock.

Clark, S. N., & Clark, D. C. (1998). Authentic assessment—Key issues, concerns, guidelines. *Schools in the Middle, 7*(3), 50–51.

Ebel, R. L., & Frisbie, D. A. (1991). *Essentials of educational measurement* (5th ed.). Englewood Cliffs, NJ: Prentice Hall.

Farr, R., & Tone, B. (1998). *Portfolio and performance assessment: Helping students evaluate their progress as readers and writers* (2nd ed.). Orlando, FL: Harcourt Brace.

Goodrich, H. (1997). Understanding rubrics. *Educational Leadership, 54*(4), 14–17.

Herman, J. L. (1998). The state of performance assessments. *School Administrator, 11*(55), 17–18.

Hills, J. R. (1981). *Measurement and evaluation in the classroom* (2nd ed.). Columbus, OH: Merrill.

Mehrens, W., & Lehmann, I. (1975). *Standardized tests in evaluation.* New York: Holt, Rinehart, and Winston.

Meyer, C. A. (1992). What's the difference between authentic and performance assessment? *Educational Leadership, 49*(8), 39.

Mills, E. (1997). Portfolios: A challenge for technology. *International Journal of Instructional Media, 24*(1), 23–29.

Paulson, F. L., Paulson, P. R., & Meyer, C. A. (1991). What makes a portfolio? *Educational Leadership, 48*(5), 60–63.

Schurr, S. (1999). *Authentic assessment.* Columbus, OH: National Middle School Association.

TenBrink, T. D. (1982). Evaluation. In J. M. Cooper et al. (Eds.), *Classroom teaching skills* (2nd ed.). Lexington, MA: D. C. Heath.

Tombari, M., & Borich, G. (1998). *Authentic testing in the classroom.* New York, NY: Macmillan.

Making Systematic Observations

OBJECTIVES

After completing your study of Chapter 11, you should be able to:

1. Compare and contrast nonsystematic and systematic observation.

2. Differentiate among the three common types of data.

3. State two reasons why it is important to be able to differentiate among different types of data.

4. Differentiate between objective data and subjective data.

5. Contrast frequency measure, duration measure, and time-sample measure.

6. Explain the purpose of systematic observation.

7. Identify procedures an observer should follow in making systematic observations.

8. Apply systematic observation techniques to an observational experience.

9. Write accurate, objective reports of observational experiences.

10. Describe and use various classroom interaction observational techniques.

Your professional responsibilities as a classroom teacher include being both an active participant and an observer in a dynamic learning environment. As an active participant, you are a member of an ongoing social process, you plan and implement various educational programs, and you develop and implement a variety of instructional activities. As an observer, you are required to continuously collect information for both planning and management.

Accurate observations should help you answer questions such as: Am I asking enough questions? Should I plan more activities to teach this concept? Are the students ready to go on to the next unit? Is my seating arrangement appropriate? Are students staying on-task?

✄ Benefits of Observation

The information you collect as an observer can be used to analyze student learning, the learning environment, and student attitudes toward learning and schooling. Using these analyses, you will make certain conclusions about your teaching effectiveness and the progress your students are making academically and socially. These conclusions will then form the basis for the next phase of instructional planning. Reteaching may be necessary.

You can also collect information about student behavior and learning during the instructional process itself. This information will provide the ongoing feedback needed for classroom management and on-the-spot instructional adjustments, such as whether or not to terminate an activity, to use more examples, to provide more hands-on experiences, or to stop instruction and determine who is causing the disruption at the back of the room. The accuracy and effectiveness of these decisions will be directly related to the validity of your observations. Thus, when your observational skills are highly developed, you will know almost automatically what to do.

Finally, teachers who observe their own behavior can analyze the effectiveness of their teaching behaviors. For example, a teacher might ask: "Am I asking enough questions?" "Is my use of reinforcement effective?" "Do I dominate my class discussions?" "How do I react to different students?" With an understanding of information collection techniques and a conceptual and theoretical framework for analyzing teacher and student classroom behaviors, these questions can be answered. Thus, teachers who occasionally (about once a month) tape and analyze their lessons can often improve their teaching effectiveness.

✄ Types of Classroom Observation

There are basically two types of classroom observation: nonsystematic and systematic. With nonsystematic observation the observer or teacher simply watches and takes note of the behaviors, characteristics, and personal interactions that seem significant. Nonsystematic classroom observation tends to be anecdotal and subjective.

With systematic classroom observation, the observer typically measures the frequency, duration, magnitude, or latency of specific behaviors or events.

However, since classroom interaction is complex and fast-paced, it is difficult to record every instance of a targeted occurrence. For example, detecting which student disrupted a group activity or recited incorrectly during a group recitation would be difficult to observe.

One of the greatest obstacles to becoming an effective observer is the danger of misinterpreting what you see. Everyone has past experiences and biases that can easily distort what he or she sees. The concepts and systematic observation techniques presented in this chapter will help you overcome these problems.

✄ Types of Data

Systematically collected data are valuable only when they are used to improve the instructional process. Thus, the specific kinds of data needed will depend on what aspects of teacher or student behavior you are studying. A brief introduction to the major types of data and their instructional uses follows.

Valued data are "data that involve the judgment of an observer" (Hansen, 1977, p. 351). That is, the observer makes a value judgment regarding the observed behavior or event. For example, having observed the number of questions asked by the teacher, the teacher's use of movement or reinforcement, or the student's time on-task, the observer then makes a subjective statement regarding what was observed. Thus, following the observation, the observer might record "The number of questions asked by the teacher was appropriate," or "The teacher used movement effectively," or "The teacher didn't use enough reinforcement," or "The teacher was ineffective at keeping students on-task." Valued data, then, are nothing more than subjective value judgments on the part of the observer and are useful only when the observer's value judgments can be trusted to be consistent with tested techniques for effective teaching. For teachers seeking to improve their day-to-day instruction, this may mean taking notes on their own teaching skills or on student behaviors and making judgments regarding how appropriate they are. However, when the behaviors being observed are complex or when judgments external to the learning environment are to be made, descriptive or reproduced data must be collected.

Descriptive data are "data that have been organized, categorized, or quantified by an observer, but do not involve a value judgment" (Hansen, 1977, p. 352). This type of data demands that the observer decide to which behavioral category (if any) an observed behavior belongs. It also means counting the number of times a specific behavior is observed. For example, the observer might classify teacher questions as divergent or convergent, or classify teacher reinforcement statements as positive or negative, or label student movement as being necessary or unnecessary, or decide which teacher statements represent encouragement and record all such cases. Once they are recorded, a judgment must be made regarding the appropriateness of the observed behaviors. This judgment can be made by the observer, the teacher, or other interested individuals. The value of descriptive data is related to the observer's expertise in recognizing and categorizing specific behaviors and then evaluating their appropriateness, that is, in turning descriptive data into valued data.

Reproduced data have been recorded in video, audio, or total transcript (verbatim) form and can be reproduced when desirable (Hansen, 1977, p. 354). The data include a total reproduction of the targeted environment or behaviors. With this type of data collection, the observer might decide to record behaviors in the form of a list. Thus, the observer's record might consist of a list (verbatim) of teacher statements or student questions, or a list or diagram of the teacher's movement during a lesson. The data are valued only when the observer can be trusted to operate the equipment properly or to record the observed behaviors accurately. When data from verbatim reproductions are eventually extracted and used, they inevitably fall into one of the other two categories. Therefore, reproduced data will not be addressed further; you need only refine your skill in recording descriptive and valued data.

There are two important reasons for learning to differentiate between the two types of data. First, it seems likely that future teachers will increasingly observe one another in action. As more states and school districts implement minimum teaching competencies and adopt master teacher and career ladder plans (Zumwalt, 1985), inexperienced and less proficient teachers will be allowed to observe master teachers. Likewise, master teachers will be given the opportunity to observe and provide constructive feedback to fellow teachers. With this in mind, it is important to be able to interpret the observational language used by supervisors and other teachers who observe in your classroom.

Both descriptive and valued data can help you examine, refine, and modify your teaching skills. You need only decide which type is most useful for the purposes of the observation. You may collect one type of information for planning purposes or to provide the feedback you need during instruction and still another type to provide feedback to colleagues.

We look, but do we really see? Observing, especially in an objective way, is difficult to learn since it requires detachment. Too often we tend to include our own feelings, attitudes, and biases in what we observe. Therefore, inasmuch as the ability to make objective observations is a relatively unrefined skill for most novice teachers and for many experienced ones, it is a skill that must be developed and practiced. We shall now take a closer look at the process of making systematic observations.

⚔ Systematic Observation

Observations can, if made correctly, provide highly accurate, detailed, verifiable information not only about students and your own teaching but also about the context in which the observations are made. However, you must always keep in mind that behavior is complex and is the product of many interrelated causes. Those who observe human behavior can easily draw false conclusions. Specific skills and techniques that will help you study and analyze the teaching-learning environment in a systematic and objective fashion become essential for effective teaching (Brophy & Good, 1999). These skills will help you become more aware of and better prepared to control both your own and student behaviors and will ultimately lead to increased learning. Those parts of the learning environment that can be observed, classified, and controlled are the ones that can be used to facilitate learning.

Scientific observers not only acquire more accurate information than do casual observers, but they also apply what they learn more effectively because they follow certain procedures. Although observers who have developed their observation skills make special efforts to be unbiased and objective, even those who are highly trained tend to be selective in what they see. That is, everyone chooses which behaviors or actions to pay attention to and which to ignore. For example, teachers often ignore the negative behaviors of their better students while responding to the same behaviors on the part of poorer students.

Given any situation, a wide range of observations is possible. No observer can monitor everything that takes place in a classroom, because classroom environments are just too complex (Clark & Starr, 1986). For instance, if you are recording the interactions in a reading group, it would be difficult to record accurately all the behaviors occurring in the rest of the classroom. One way to overcome this difficulty is to observe only a small group (such as the reading group) or the behavior of only a few students. The target group can be studied intensively, and their behavior will often mirror what takes place in the total classroom.

Another focusing strategy is to limit the number of behaviors you look for at one time (five or fewer in the beginning). This is an especially useful technique for beginning observers or for teachers participating in self-evaluation. One simply cannot record data during the act of teaching. Audio or video recorders can be extremely useful in such situations since they permit repeated observation. Beginners should probably concentrate on the same behaviors for several days at a time.

Developing an observational plan is necessary if you are to make accurate recordings within an observational setting. Systematic observation represents such a plan in that it provides a useful means of identifying, studying, classifying, and measuring specific interacting variables within the learning environment. Systematic observation requires that you develop specific observational skills, such as the ability to:

1. Differentiate between objective and subjective data.
2. Determine the setting in which the behavior will be observed.
3. Determine the method for observing and recording the targeted behaviors or events.
4. Determine the interval of time the environment will be observed.

Individual plans may differ with respect to these elements, resulting in totally different observations. However they may differ, some type of systematic observation plan is needed in order to generate the kind of reliable data needed for instructional improvement.

Objectivity in Observation

Behavior can be defined as "that which is observable and overt; it has to be seen and it should be countable" (Tillman, Bersoff, & Dolly, 1976, p. 262). It is impossible to be completely objective in the collection of behavioral data. The very decision of what to record, what not to record, or how to categorize the information involves subjective judgments. Thus, being objective does not mean discounting your feelings, attitudes, and thoughts; it simply means using them to produce data that are objective. You should always strive to record what is actually happening rather than what you think is happening and your interpretation of it.

The context surrounding behavior should also be observed, for very often it will be useful when drawing inferences and conclusions and arriving at decisions. You should think broadly about all behaviors in the observational setting and include in your collection of data such items as time, place, the people involved, and objects in the environment.

Good observation then involves selective interpretations of behavior as well as explicit descriptions of specific, observable acts. To avoid erroneous interpretations, the distinction between observable acts (behaviors) and **inferences** (interpretation of behaviors) must be kept in mind. Consider the following statements:

1. Terri likes to read.
2. Joe is a nasty child.
3. Robert is a good student.
4. Mary is very creative.

None of these statements describes overt, observable behavior. Terms such as *likes, nasty, good,* and *creative* are open to interpretation; they are really interpretive conclusions or inferences rather than objective happenings. Objectivity requires specifying the behaviors that lead to such subjective interpretations. For example, Terri may have asked to read aloud in class, which then led you to conclude that she likes to read. Also, terms such as *hot, cold,* and *humid* are concepts that exist in the perceptions of the beholder. What is hot or cold to one person may not be to another.

Observations must be objective if they are to be of value. Compare the following statements with those just cited:

1. Terri read five books this month.
2. Joe kicked and hit three other children today at recess.
3. Robert made no errors on his math and English examinations.
4. Mary wrote two stories for the school paper this year.

Note that these observations are overt, observable behaviors which can be counted. They could lead to the inferences and conclusions stated earlier.

Task 11.1 will help you to develop your skill at differentiating between the two types of data and between overt, observable behaviors and inferences and conclusions. Remember that observable behaviors should be countable, whereas inferences are interpretations of behaviors.

Even though you cannot always see a process or a characteristic directly, you can often make a reasonable judgment about whether or not it exists based on the behaviors of an individual. What you do is make an inference about the presence or absence of certain characteristics and processes based on behavioral evidence. This supporting evidence must be observable so that others can review it and decide whether or not they agree with your inference.

T   A   S   K   1 1 . 1

Classifying Data

Respond to the following items. Check your responses with those given at the end of the chapter.

1. Classify the following recorded data statements as being valued data (V) or descriptive data (D). Check your responses with those given at the end of the chapter.

    _____ a. The teacher used a student idea four times in the 50-minute period.

    _____ b. The lesson was appropriate for the class.

    _____ c. The teacher did not provide sufficient examples for the development of the concept.

    _____ d. The teacher used too much verbal reinforcement and not enough nonverbal reinforcement.

    _____ e. The same student, Cindi, answered five teacher questions.

    _____ f. The set induction activity for the lesson was appropriate.

    _____ g. The teacher used the lecture method for 20 minutes and the discussion method for 30 minutes in this lesson.

    _____ h. The teacher is effective at using wait time.

2. The following list contains observational statements. Some of the statements are observable behaviors and others are inferences. Check the appropriate category next to each entry.

	Behavior	Inference
a. Harry is lazy.	_____	_____
b. Johnny threw his book.	_____	_____
c. Mike closed the door.	_____	_____
d. May had tears in her eyes.	_____	_____
e. Darrell is very shy around adults.	_____	_____
f. Pam is easily influenced by other children.	_____	_____
g. David dropped his pencil.	_____	_____
h. Al is hyperactive.	_____	_____
i. James likes to play baseball and football.	_____	_____
j. Paul acts strange in physical education.	_____	_____
k. Nickie sat down.	_____	_____
l. Joyce handed in her homework assignment.	_____	_____
m. Frank likes any kind of music.	_____	_____
n. Helen acts in an intelligent manner.	_____	_____
o. Alan appears neurotic most of the time.	_____	_____

Analysis and Reflections

Objectivity is essential to effective teaching. Why is this so important? Write a paragraph or two about the importance of making accurate observations. Share your ideas with your class and instructor.

You must always be careful in drawing inferences and conclusions because you can never be absolutely sure they are accurate. For example, you cannot be sure of inferences you might make when you hear Tommy say, "I really like school!" Is Tommy saying this because he thinks you want to hear it? You can never be completely sure. Therefore, a major concern should be to maintain constant vigilance regarding the question: What behaviors constitute "reasonable" support for the inferences or conclusions being made?

Even though you can never be absolutely sure of the inferences you make, their justification increases in proportion to the observable behaviors supporting them. Observers who habitually make inferences based on little behavioral data are not carrying out the role and responsibilities of a trained professional. These same observers too often make unsupported instructional decisions.

The Setting

In most instances, the setting for your observations will be limited to the classroom or the school grounds. However, as a visiting observer you may be interested in only a limited part of the classroom. For example, you may only want information pertaining to a specific classroom group or class activity. However, even when you are limiting the focus of your observation, you should include environmental data that might influence the targeted behavior. Such things as holidays, temperature, and weather will often affect observed behavior.

Recording Data

Observational data should be coded in a manner that is easy to record and use (Cardno & Piggot-Irvine, 1997). There is no observational system that is suitable for all situations. Symbols can often be used to represent specific behaviors, and they can be recorded on seating charts or other convenient forms such as the one shown in Figure 11.1. The particular system used to record data should be simple and tailor-made to the specific observation. For example, if only one behavior is being observed, you might use a simple X on your seating chart to record it. Simplicity in the recording of data is especially important when you must make observations as you teach. However, as mentioned earlier, when many behaviors are to be recorded or when the behaviors are complex, it is best to use an audio, video, or outsider observer to collect data. Table 11.1 lists examples of symbols that should prove useful in recording data.

Behaviorial data can also be recorded using different types of measures, such as frequency, duration, or time sample. **Frequency measurement** is employed when you want to determine the number of times certain behaviors are exhibited in a specified length of time. You simply keep a tally of the number of times the behaviors are exhibited.

Duration and time-sample measurements involve data that may not be discrete. That is, it may involve behaviors that continue for a length of time or that take some time to occur.

Duration measurement involves either the length of time a specific behavior continues or the time needed for its occurrence following a given direction or

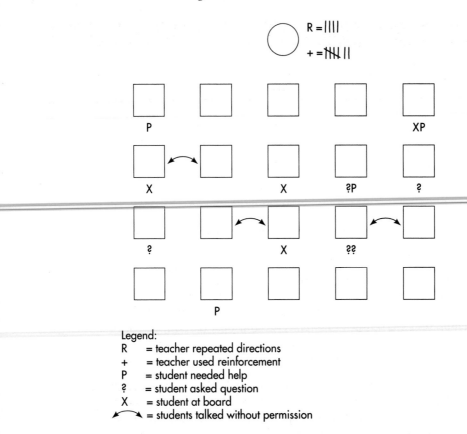

Legend:
R   = teacher repeated directions
+   = teacher used reinforcement
P   = student needed help
?   = student asked question
X   = student at board
⟶ = students talked without permission

FIGURE 11.1   *Recorded Data for Classroom Observation*
The circle represents the teacher and the squares represent the students.

signal. The time during which a student plays with a disallowed object, or the time it takes for students to turn to the correct page in a book would be examples of duration measurement.

Time-sample measurement is used to sample behavior at predetermined time intervals, such as five minutes or 15 minutes. The behavior can be continuous or discrete. You simply check for the behavior at the end of the specified time interval. For example, you might want to check whether students are on task at 5-minute intervals and make a record of those who are and those who are not.

Observation Time

The time when data is to be collected is usually determined by the teaching-learning situation and the type of data. If you are an observer in another teacher's classroom and are looking at teacher behavior during instruction, the data should not be collected during seatwork or independent study periods.

TABLE 11.1

Recording Symbols

Label	Symbol	Definition
Male	M	Individual is male.
Female	F	Individual is female.
Student Behaviors		
Correct response	+	Student answered correctly.
Wrong response	–	Student answered incorrectly.
No response	0	Student did not answer.
Inappropriate response	=	Student made inappropriate verbal response.
Student disruptive	D	Student caused problem in class.
Teacher Behaviors		
Reinforcement	+	Teacher used positive reinforcement.
Criticize	–	Teacher criticized student behavior.
Question	?	Teacher asked question.
No response	0	Teacher ignored student question or behavior.

Source: Adapted from T. L. Good and J. E. Brophy (1987), *Looking in Classrooms.* New York: Harper and Row, p. 76.

However, in making general observations, you will be interested in all aspects of behavior in the environment for a specified period. For most purposes, 45 minutes appears to be an adequate period for a representative sampling of behaviors in the learning environment.

You should also keep in mind that your presence in a classroom as a visitor may influence some behaviors within the observational setting. This influence, in general, usually tends to decrease over time. Therefore, it is wise to spend some time in the setting before recording your observations.

✖ Arrangements for Observation

Observations made without a definite purpose or preconceived plan can be both tiresome and unprofitable. Although such unplanned experiences might be interesting, or even entertaining, to the novice observer, over a length of time the whole experience can become an ordeal. Unplanned observation experiences are generally nothing more than "look-and-see" exercises with "catch-what-you-can" outcomes. However, if you are prepared for the observational experience, know what is to be accomplished, and are equipped with the correct techniques, you can obtain valuable firsthand information. To understand what is to be accomplished and to learn the necessary techniques, at least two basic conditions must be met.

First, you need to know exactly what behaviors to observe in order to achieve the intended purpose. Moreover, you need to know how to use the information once it is obtained. Second, in order to develop a plan of action for the observation, you need to be able to see behaviors as both separate, discrete phenomena and as interactive within the dynamics of the observational site. These two conditions are discussed in the following section.

To get to the heart of what is happening in an observational setting, you must give your full attention, something that is not easy. Making objective observations is so strenuous, in fact, that you can generally only do it for short periods. There will be times when you will want reasons and meanings behind what is happening and will therefore, if possible, record exact wording. At other times, voice quality, body posture, facial expressions, or gestures should be noted. Whatever data are needed, the use of systematic observation techniques will greatly enhance the recording of the data.

⚔ Writing Behavioral Descriptions

Writing a behavioral description of your observations is a difficult task, but it is a prerequisite to making accurate assessments of the learning environment. Tillman et al. (1976) offer the following guidelines:

1. Focus only on behaviors that relate to or affect the situation you are observing.
2. Record, whenever possible, everything that happens in the immediate environment. Attempt to report all conversation verbatim.
3. Report all behaviors sequentially.
4. State descriptions of behavior in a positive way. Avoid stating what did not take place.
5. Try not to report more than one behavioral observation in a sentence, except for discrete, short, sequential behaviors.
6. Keep a running account of the actual times of behavioral observations.
7. Do not make interpretations of behavior. Record all observations in standard English and do not theorize.

Attention to the suggested guidelines should improve the accuracy of your observations as a visiting observer or as a teacher in your own classroom. To improve your accuracy even further, an observation form, such as the Site Observation Record Form shown at the end of this chapter, can be used to record data. This form allows you to record recurring behavior with a minimum of record-keeping time. You simply record a behavior the first time it occurs, or prerecord the targeted behaviors, and then tally each occurrence in the Frequency column. However, it is essential that a precise description of the collected observations be written immediately following the session. Since descriptions hastily written during the observation are often imprecise, it is best to write them in a more formal manner afterward. This point is especially important if the observations are made as you teach. The guidelines described earlier should be used in writing a formal observation report on a form such as the Behavioral Description Form shown at the end of the chapter.

If the dynamics of classroom life are the object of analysis, a technique known as interaction analysis is quite useful. Before we conclude our discussion of observation with a brief look at this technique, complete Expansion Activity: Classroom Observation.

⚔ Classroom Interaction

Teaching is not, as some critics and teachers seem to think, just a matter of teachers talking and students listening. Effective teaching involves interactive communication patterns that are skillfully directed. Thus, observers and teachers should be interested in looking at and analyzing classroom interaction patterns. From such an analysis, one can learn whether a class is teacher-dominated or pupil-dominated, whether it is open or repressive, and whether the teaching style is direct (student freedom to respond is minimized) or indirect (student freedom to respond is maximized). A detailed description of such an analysis can be found in the Amidon, Casper, & Flanders (1985) training manual.

There are a number of methods for looking at classroom interaction. They vary from simple to complex, with many requiring the services of either an observer or a recorder (audio or video).

Even though the simpler schemes are not as useful as the more sophisticated methods, they can be helpful in detecting glaring faults in the use of various teaching skills. The simplest of these methods calls for the observer to tally each instance of teacher and student talk as, for example, T T P P T T T P T T T P P T T T T T P T. Although this record shows how often the teacher talks compared to the students, it does not reveal how long each talked. In a somewhat more sophisticated form of this method, the observer sits at the back of the room and records on a form such as that shown in Figure 11.2 the number of times each person speaks. Often the class seating chart can be used to record the data. The disadvantage of this technique is that an outside observer is needed.

The two techniques just described can be refined to yield more information by having the observer record who is talking at regular intervals, about every three or five seconds. This variation has the advantage of telling you which class members are interacting, how often they interact, and approximately how long each person speaks.

One of the more sophisticated and best-known interaction analysis techniques is the Flanders Interaction Analysis System (Amidon et al., 1985). This system is commonly taught to teachers, supervisors, and counselors who want to view typical patterns of verbal exchange in the classroom. The Flanders system is

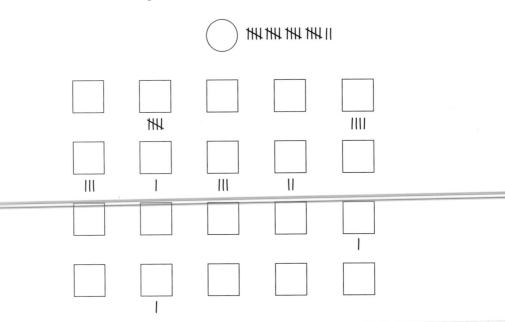

FIGURE 11.2 *A Simple Form of Interaction Analysis*
The circle represents the teacher and the squares
represent the students.

concerned only with verbal behavior. It is assumed that classroom verbal behaviors give an adequate sampling of the total classroom behaviors. In the Flanders system, classroom verbal interaction is divided into the 10 categories listed in Figure 11.3. By memorizing and practicing the code, the observer need only write down a single number to represent a type of verbal activity. To conduct an observation and analysis, the observer records the category of action in the classroom every three seconds or whenever a change in category occurs. At the conclusion of the observation, the observer arranges the records into a 10 by 10 matrix for further analysis. A detailed analysis of the matrix reveals the dynamic of the classroom and the general classroom atmosphere. By using this system, a teacher or observer can draw conclusions about the classroom climate and make inferences about the communication strategies fostered in the classroom.

The Flanders system is a complex technique. Therefore, some observers use a simplified version. In this version the observer records the interaction going on in the classroom on a form such as that shown in Figure 11.4, but does not arrange the tallies in a matrix. The simplified version does not give as clear a view of the classroom as does the complete system.

The Flanders Interaction Analysis System gives you an excellent overview of the verbal interaction in your classroom, which should give some important insights into your own teaching. If you tape-record your class, it is possible to apply the analysis without the use of an outside observer. There is insufficient space in this chapter to fully develop the Flanders procedure, but detailed information about it and matrix analysis can be found in the Amidon et al. train-

Teacher Talk	Indirect Influence	**1.** *Accepts feeling* Accepts and clarifies the feeling tone of the students in a nonthreatening manner. Feelings may be positive or negative. Predicting or recalling feelings is included. **2.** *Praises or encourages* Praises or encourages student action or behavior. Jokes that release tension, but not at the expense of another individual; nodding head, or saying "um hm?" or "go on" are included. **3.** *Accepts or uses ideas of students* Clarifying, building, or developing ideas suggested by a student. As teacher brings more of his own ideas into play, shift to Category 5. **4.** *Asks questions* Asking a question about content or procedure with the intent that a student answer.
	Direct Influence	**5.** *Lecturing* Giving facts or opinions about content or procedures; expressing his own ideas, asking rhetorical questions. **6.** *Giving directions* Directions, commands, or orders with which a student is expected to comply. **7.** *Criticizing or justifying authority* Statements intended to change student behavior from nonacceptable to acceptable pattern; bawling someone out; stating why the teacher is doing what he is doing; extreme self-reference.
Student Talk		**8.** *Student talk—response* Talk by students in response to teacher. Teacher initiates the contact or solicits student statements. **9.** *Student talk—initiation* Talk by students, which they initiate. If "calling on" student is only to indicate who may talk next, observer must decide whether student wanted to talk. If he did, use this category.
		10. *Silence or confusion* Pauses, short periods of silence, and periods of confusion in which communication cannot be understood by the observer.

FIGURE 11.3 *Summary of Categories for the Flanders Interaction Analysis System*

Source: E. J. Amidon, I. G. Casper, & N. A. Flanders (1985), *The role of the teacher in the classroom: A manual for understanding and improving teacher classroom behavior* (3rd ed.). St. Paul, MN: Paul S. Amidon, p. 8. Reprinted by permission.

CATEGORY	TALLIES

Teacher Talk	Indirect	1.	Accepts feelings.
		2.	Praises or encourages.
		3.	Accepts or uses ideas of students.
		4.	Asks questions.
	Direct	5.	Lectures.
		6.	Gives directions.
		7.	Criticizes or justifies authority.
Student Talk		8.	Student response.
		9.	Student initiation.
		10.	Silence or confusion.

FIGURE 11.4   *Simplified Version of the Flanders Form*

Expansion Activity: Monitoring Behavior

Most of us find it difficult to monitor student behavior and our own teaching behavior as we teach. Outline a plan for accomplishing this important task. Form small groups and share your plan with each other.

ing manual (1985). Now take a few moments to complete Expansion Activity: Monitoring Behavior.

⚔ Ethical Considerations

We must address one final issue before concluding this chapter: the confidentiality of observation information. Statements about observational information should never be made in front of unqualified personnel. Observation information should be discussed only on a need-to-know basis. It is equally important to refrain from talking about observations or other school business outside the school, no matter how great the temptation. Talking to colleagues about observations or behaviors in public places is also professionally unethical.

T   A   S   K   1 1 . 2

Making Observations

Respond to the following items dealing with the observational process. Check your responses with those given at the end of the chapter.

1. How can a teacher make his/her observations more objective? _____

   _____

   _____

   _____

2. One should always develop a plan of action related to what to observe and how it is to be recorded prior to making an observation.   (True/False)

3. One can never be absolutely sure that an inference is correct.   (True/False)

4. A recording of the time it takes for a student to be seated after being told to do so is an example of time-sample measurement.   (True/False)

5. An observer should write a precise description of an observation as soon as possible after making the observation.   (True/False)

6. Observers should never include their own interpretations in observational data. (True/False)

7. All classroom interaction schemes require the use of an outside observer to carry out the observation and analysis.   (True/False)

8. The Flanders Interaction Analysis System can be used in a classroom to reveal the general existing dyamics. What benefits can be gained from the use of this system?

   _____

   _____

   _____

9. Observation data should only be shared _____ .

Analysis and Reflections

Why is it important to keep observationional information confidential? Write a short paper on this important issue and submit it to your instructor.

This completes our brief study of making systematic observations. Complete Task 11.2 to check your understanding of the concepts presented in the last few sections.

Summary

- The teacher is both an active participant and an observer in the classroom environment.
- Accurate observations help teachers answer many questions.

Benefits of Observation

- Teachers are required to make continuous judgments and decisions about the learning process.
- Analyzed observation information forms the basis for what needs to be done in the instructional process. Judgments regarding what to teach next, how best to teach it, who needs extra help, what material to use, and so forth need to be made.
- Teachers must make decisions during instruction regarding changes in the planned lesson, pacing of the lesson, management of the lesson, and so forth.
- Observation information gives teachers insights into their own teaching behaviors.

Types of Classroom Observations

- There are basically two types of classroom observation: nonsystematic and systematic.
- Nonsystematic classroom observation tends to be anecdotal and subjective. Systematic observation typically measures the frequency, duration, magnitude, or latency of specific behaviors or events.

Types of Data

- There are three major types of data: valued data, descriptive data, and reproduced data.
- Teachers may collect one type of information for planning purposes or to provide feedback needed during instruction and another type to provide feedback to colleagues. Collecting the best type of data is a relatively unrefined skill not only for most novice teachers but for many experienced teachers as well.
- Skill at making accurate observations must be developed and practiced. The validity of these judgments and decisions depends to a large extent on the ability to make accurate observations.

Systematic Observation

- Skill at being an observer and making valid observations is essential for teachers. Systematic observation will improve a teacher's ability to make valid observations.
- Subskills associated with making systematic observation include: (1) the ability to collect the type of data best suited for the purpose of the observation; (2) the ability to differentiate between behaviors and inferences; and (3) the ability to plan for the observational experience with respect to the setting to be observed, the recording of data, and the observational time.

Arrangements for Observation

- Observation should be made with a purpose in mind. One should prepare for an observational experience.
- Collecting accurate observational information requires the observer's full attention.

Writing Behavioral Descriptions
- The writing of accurate behavioral reports will greatly assist a teacher in reaching accurate, final conclusions. This is often a difficult task.
- A precise description of collected observations should be written immediately following an observation session. This should be a more formal description of behaviors and/or events.

Classroom Interaction
- Learning comes best through interaction.
- Teachers should periodically look at their classroom interaction using one of the many observational schemes available.
- The best-known and most commonly used technique of interaction analysis is the Flanders Interaction Analysis System.

Ethical Considerations
- Collected observational information is confidential. It should be discussed only on a need-to-know basis.
- Talking with colleagues about observations or behaviors in public is professionally unethical.

Activities

1. *Observation of present setting*   Using the Observation of Present Setting Worksheet on page 312, record observations of your present setting. Record your observations in the order they are noted and limit the observation time to five minutes. When finished, compare your observations with others who have observed the same setting. Consider the following in your comparisons:
   a. The observations selected: Were they the same or selective?
   b. The sequence of the observations: Were they the same?
   c. The strategy used to make the observations: Was a strategy used by everyone or were the strategies different?
2. *Systematic observations*   Complete several observational activities in different teaching-learning environments. Use the Site Observation Record Form on page 313 to record your observations. As soon as possible after your visit, write a formal description of the observations using the Behavioral Description Form on page 314. Plan the following before you make your observation:
   a. The specific behaviors to be observed.
   b. The type of data to be recorded.
   c. The type of measure to be employed.
3. *Classroom interaction*   Complete several classroom interaction observational activities in different teaching-learning environments. Use various techniques for looking at the different classroom interaction patterns.

Answer Keys

Task 11.1 Classifying Data
1. a. *D* The observer simply recorded the number of times student ideas were used.
    b. *V* The subjective value judgment of "appropriateness" was made by the observer.
    c. *V* The value judgment of "insufficient" was made by the observer.
    d. *V* "Too much" and "not enough" are value judgments.
    e. *D* The observer recorded the number of questions answered by a student.
    f. *V* The subjective value judgment "appropriate" was made by the observer.
    g. *D* The observer simply recorded the methods used and the time.
    h. *V* "Effectiveness" is a value judgment.
2. a. *Inference* "Lazy" is open to interpretation.
    b. *Behavior* Observable action.
    c. *Behavior* Observable action.
    d. *Behavior* Observable action.
    e. *Inference* "Shy" is open to interpretation.
    f. *Inference* "Easily influenced" is a conclusion.
    g. *Behavior* Observable action.
    h. *Inference* "Hyperactive" is open to interpretation.
    i. *Inference* "Likes" is a conclusion.
    j. *Inference* "Strange" is open to interpretation.
    k. *Behavior* Observable action.
    l. *Behavior* Observable action.
    m. *Inference* "Likes" is a conclusion.
    n. *Inference* "Intelligent" is open to interpretation.
    o. *Inference* "Neurotic" is open to interpretation.

Task 11.2 Making Observations
1. Some possible techniques are to limit focus of observations, develop an easily used code, record observations on a seating chart or other form, develop and use checklists, or use audio or video equipment.
2. *True* You cannot possibly observe and record everything that happens in a classroom. Therefore, you must decide on what to look for and plan a simple way to record it. A plan will result in more accurate information.
3. *True* No matter how much positive data is collected, there is always a possibility that an inference could be false.
4. *False* This is an example of duration measurement.
5. *True* A precise description should be written as soon as possible so that important information will not be lost.
6. *False* Care should be taken in interpreting behaviors, but some interpretation often is helpful in achieving insight regarding the interactions of the classroom.

7. *False*   The teacher can utilize most of the schemes. However, training is often desirable for proper utilization of the more complex forms.
8. The system can be used to give insights into whether a teacher indirectly or directly influences student behavior. Proper data analysis can also give teachers other information about their teaching style.
9. on a need-to-know basis

Theory and Research

Boehm, A. E., & Weinberg, R. A. (1996). *The classroom observer: Developing observation skills in early childhood settings.* New York: Teachers College Press.

Borich, G. D., Martin, D. B., & Bayles, D. L. (1998). *Observation skills for effective teaching.* New York: Merrill Publishing.

McNeely, S. L. (1997). *Observing students and teachers through objective strategies.* Boston: Allyn & Bacon.

Power, B. M. (1996). *Taking note: Improving your observational notetaking.* York, ME: Stenhouse Publishing.

References

Amidon, E. J., Casper, I. G., & Flanders, N. A. (1985). *The role of the teacher in the classroom: A manual for understanding and improving teacher classroom behavior* (3rd ed.). St. Paul, MN: Paul S. Amidon.

Brophy, J. E., & Good, T. L. (1999). *Looking in classrooms.* New York: Addision-Wesley Publishing.

Cardno, C., & Piggot-Irvine, E. (1997). *Effective performance appraisal: Integrating accountability and development in staff appraisal.* Auckland: Longman.

Clark, L. H., & Starr, I. S. (1986). *Secondary and middle school teaching methods* (5th ed.). New York: Macmillan.

Good, T. L., & Brophy, J. E. (1987). *Looking in classrooms* (4th ed.). New York: Harper and Row.

Hansen, J. (1977). Observation skills. In J. M. Cooper (Ed.), *Classroom teaching skills: A handbook.* Lexington, MA: D. C. Heath.

Tillman, M., Bersoff, D., & Dolly, J. (1976). *Learning to teach.* Lexington, MA: D. C. Heath.

Zumwalt, K. (1985). The master teacher concept: Implications for teacher education. *Elementary School Journal, 86,* 45–54.

Observation of Present Setting Worksheet

Setting _____

Date _____   Time: from _____ to _____

Observer _____

Observations in Sequence

1. _____

2. _____

3. _____

4. _____

5. _____

6. _____

7. _____

8. _____

9. _____

10. _____

11. _____

12. _____

13. _____

14. _____

15. _____

16. _____

17. _____

18. _____

19. _____

20. _____

Site Observation Record Form

Observer _____ Date _____

Site _____

Grade/Subject _____ Time: from _____ to _____

Description of observed environment _____

_____

_____

_____

_____

_____

List all observed behaviors during the observation period. If the same behavior occurs more than once, indicate it by marking tallies in the frequency column.

Observed Behavior	Frequency

Behavioral Description Form

Name of Recorder _____ Date _____

Site of Observation _____

Grade/Subject _____ Time: from _____ to _____

Describe, in observable terms, the enviroment within which the observation took place.

_____

_____

_____

_____

_____

Describe, in behavioral terms, behaviors observed during observation session.

_____

_____

_____

_____

_____

_____

_____

_____

_____

_____

_____

_____

_____

_____

_____

Instructional Tools

Some key assets to success as a teacher are well-designed media, good technological support, and effective unit planning. Indeed, instructional media and technology and effective unit planning can often make or break the instructional process.

Chapter 12 explains the role and importance of media and technology in teaching. The focus is on how to use these tools to improve instruction. This chapter helps you choose and use appropriate media and technology for specific learn-ing intent. The strengths and limitations of specific media and technologies will be explored. The chapter also addresses the Internet and the impact computers are having on the educational process and their future role in schools and classrooms.

Chapter 13 explains the components of a well-designed unit and gives you a chance to design your own unit. The seven components of a unit plan are briefly analyzed.

Instructional Media and Technology

Objectives

After completing your study of Chapter 12, you should be able to:

1. Supply practical guidelines and prerequisites for selecting instructional media.

2. Describe the materials selection process.

3. Identify sources of printed materials available to classroom teachers.

4. Identify the advantages and limitations of textbooks and programmed texts as instructional tools.

5. Describe a model and a mock-up and their appropriate uses.

6. Describe the uses, advantages, and limitations of commonplace teaching devices.

7. Describe the characteristics, advantages, limitations, and uses of motion pictures, video technology, and computers as instructional tools.

8. Describe the instructional and curricular uses of technology in the classroom.

9. Describe the Internet and its classroom uses.

Real-life experiences are best to promote learning, but they are often difficult to provide in the classroom. Most experiences in the classroom will be through verbal symbolism—written and spoken works. High-achieving students are generally able to cope with a great deal of symbolism, while slow students and younger students have difficulty learning without firsthand experiences. To a limited degree various multisensory instructional aids—texts, pictures, simulations—can be used as substitute for needed firsthand experiences in the classroom.

Instructional media can range from the most common teaching tools, such as textbooks and chalkboards to newer forms, such as films and videos, to high-tech aids, such as computers, CD-ROMs, the Internet, and closed-circuit television. Technology is revolutionizing education at all levels of the teaching and learning process. The information superhighway is impacting education across the globe. Successful teachers must be aware of the new technology—what beneficial characteristics it offers and how it may best be incorporated into the teaching-learning process. If nothing else, this information and know-how will help reduce classroom boredom for both teacher and students.

When you are planning, using, and evaluating the success of various teaching aids, either singly or in combination, it is important to keep in mind certain basic criteria.

1. The motivational value of the media and technology should be assessed in light of the teaching-learning situation and the desired learner objectives.
2. Instructional media and technology must be planned as an integral part of the lesson. They will be of little value if there is insufficient time for their proper use or if other lesson components make them inappropriate.
3. The user should know how to use the technology and ascertain that everything is in working order before exposing students to it.

If instruction is to achieve maximum effectiveness, learning experiences should involve students as much as possible (for instance, through manipulation of objects, writing, and real-life situations). In effect, students should learn by doing. You should plan instruction so that students use as many of their senses as possible; learning is usually most effective and long-lasting when all the senses are engaged.

⚔ Role of Instructional Media

Instructional media can play several roles depending on whether instruction is "teacher-directed" or "student-directed" (Heinich, Molenda, Russell, & Smaldino, 1996). The most common use of teaching aids is to support a "live" teacher in the classroom. Indeed, the use of appropriate instructional media in the classroom can motivate, contribute to understanding, encourage participation, help maintain interest in a lesson, and enhance learning. The effectiveness of the media will depend on the teacher.

Teaching aids can also be used in situations where students are working alone or with other students. These forms of media usually come as an instructional package with objectives, guidance for achieving the objectives, materials, and self-evaluation provided. In some cases, an instructor is needed to serve as a consultant.

Distance learning is rapidly becoming a worldwide form of instruction. In distance learning the teacher and students are separated during the learning process and instruction is delivered by some form of instructional media: books, teacher-developed print material, paper-and-pencil tests, audiocassettes, videotapes, videodiscs, computers, or "live" through radio and broadcast television.

Instructional media play an important role in the education of exceptional students. These children often need highly structured learning situations because of their disabilities. Instructional media can be adapted and specially designed to make instruction more effective and enhance achievement.

✖ Selection of Instructional Materials

The selection of commercial materials, especially textbooks, is usually the responsibility of a professional committee operating at the district, school, department, or grade level. The selection of materials for individual classrooms—magazines, pictures, models, and so forth—is usually the responsibility of the teacher (Tipton, 1998). In both cases, you, the classroom teacher, still need to make professional judgments about the appropriateness and worth of the materials for your classroom. Committees and teachers should develop appropriate questions to meet their own goals. All instructional materials should be evaluated for their appropriateness against an established set of criteria. At a minimum, the following questions should be considered.

1. *Do the materials fit the goals and objectives?* Materials should fit the goals and objectives of your course as well as your unit plan and lesson plan.
2. *Are the materials well designed?* The materials should be durable, attractive, and appropriate in size; print should be readable and in a comfortable type size.
3. *Are the materials suited to the reading level of the students?* This will require that you read through the materials and make a judgment on readability.
4. *Does the difficulty level of the materials match the abilities of the students?* Highly motivated students can usually handle a lower success rate than low-achieving students.

Additional questions related more specifically to content are listed in Table 12.1.

✖ Printed Materials

Printed materials remain the most commonly used educational tools in school classrooms. Indeed, a tremendous amount of reading material suited for most school curriculums is available to classroom teachers. Textbooks remain the major source of printed information used in teaching, but other printed materials include workbooks, paperback books, newspapers, and magazines.

TABLE 12.1

Questions Related to Materials Selection

1. Is there a need for the material? Does it contribute meaningful content to the lesson?
2. Does the material further the goals and objectives of the lesson?
3. Is the material current and accurate?
4. Is the material appropriate for the maturity level and experience of the students?
5. Is the material suitable for the reading level of the students?
6. Are the ideas, concepts, and points of views well expressed?
7. Is the physical presentation of the material acceptable?
8. Is the material presented at a pace that allows for reflection and review?
9. Are the materials worth the time, effort, and expense?

Printed materials can be either published commercially or prepared by the teacher or school. Preparing your own materials takes time and money, so examine your needs and existing materials carefully and ask yourself the questions in Table 12.1 before you decide to create new materials.

Textbooks

Textbooks are the most common instructional aid available to teachers, and the most powerful (Lorber & Pierce, 1983). They are convenient and versatile and permit random access to information. Textbooks may be used alone, with other media, or as a source of course enrichment and supplemental material. Textbooks are generally easy to obtain and portable and provide access to concepts and information in both written and visual form (Brown, Lewis, & Harcleroad, 1983).

One major advantage of textbooks is that they help teachers plan their lessons by providing a unifying theme for classroom instruction and suggestions for organizing and structuring a course. In effect, textbooks offer a common selection of subject matter and readings—arranged in some logical order—and they can be used in focusing on content. Textbooks, especially teachers' editions, often offer a selection of teaching-learning tactics, strategies, activities, and questions. These textbook aids are designed to enhance understanding of the content and facilitate learning.

Aids that often appear at the beginning of a chapter include an overview, instructional objectives, focus questions, and key terms. Aids that occur throughout a chapter include headings, highlighted key terms, tables, marginal notes and discussions, and illustrative material such as graphs, charts, and pictures. Aids that come at the end of a chapter include summaries, discussion questions, problems, review exercises, sample test questions, suggested activities, suggested readings, and glossaries.

Instructional aids or teaching aids designed for teacher use are often provided as supplements to the textbook. They include (1) teacher's manuals, (2) skills books or exercise books, (3) test questions, (4) transparencies, (5) lesson plans, (6) reinforcement activities, (7) enrichment activities, (8) bulletin board ideas, (9) computer software, and (10) audio- and videocassettes. Moreover, textbooks also frequently provide sources and information relative to other teaching materials and tools.

Before they read the actual text, students can use the instructional aids and supplementary materials to acquaint themselves with the general approach and the information and concepts to be learned. While students are reading the chapter, the aids provide examples of concepts and supply supplementary information. Learning is reinforced after reading and critical thinking encouraged through chapter summaries, end of chapter activities and exercises, and problems.

Workbooks often accompany textbooks. At the lower grade levels, workbooks are often used separately to provide exercises for practice and drill in language arts, reading, science, social studies, and math. At the secondary grade levels, workbooks are often used in different content areas as a supplement to the textbook for practice. The value of workbooks depends on how they are used. Too often workbooks are used as a form of busywork to keep students occupied or, even worse, as a substitute for teaching. When using workbooks, always keep in mind that they tend to overemphasize factual and low-level information.

Textbooks also offer an economic advantage in that they generally last a long time and can be used repeatedly. Indeed, textbooks offer, in a single volume and in a variety of ways (written, pictorial, graphic), a variety of information in an economic package.

Finally, textbooks lend themselves to self-pacing. As such, they can be adapted to independent study, tutorial endeavors, and individualized instruction. Textbooks, then, can allow students without reading problems to acquire information quickly and efficiently and help learners grasp the relationship between cause and effect (Lorber & Pierce, 1983).

There are also disadvantages associated with the use of textbooks. However, most of these disadvantages stem from misuse. Indeed, Lorber and Pierce (1983, p. 109) point out that, "perhaps the greatest single misuse of texts is allowing them to dictate what will be taught." Teachers may let the textbook assume too great a role in classroom curriculum decisions. Textbooks can sometimes give rise to "textbook teaching"; characteristically, the teaching process becomes a regimental routine of assigned readings and recitations, accompanied by responses to questions at the end of the chapter. Finally, textbooks can lead students to put emphasis on "reading to remember" or "finding the right answer," which may tend to stifle critical thinking, problem solving, and student interaction and creativity. Thus, using textbooks inappropriately may relieve students of the need to do their own organizing and prevent them from thinking and drawing conclusions independently. However, keep in mind that high-quality textbooks help students learn when they are used appropriately. You should check to see that your textbooks are organized in a manner that enables curricular goals and objectives to be reached. You should check that the content—both written and visual—is appropriate, suitably sequenced, and at the desired reading level. Also, make sure that texts are physically attractive and that quality teachers' guides, teachers' editions, and other supplemental materials are included.

⋇ Common Instructional Media

The chalkboard and overhead projector are perhaps the most common teaching tools. These devices can be found in almost any classroom, but most of us fail to think of them as instructional media. The overhead projector is but one of several projection devices available to classroom teachers.

Chalkboards

Chalkboards are found in practically every classroom in the nation. Some educators view the chalkboard as the most useful and versatile of teaching tools. They are always there and ready for use. They can be used with a high degree of flexibility and give teachers the opportunity to present planned and unplanned information. Teachers can use chalkboards to reinforce oral explanations; to outline key elements of lessons; to show graphs, sketches, and diagrams; and to help clarify difficult concepts.

Chalkboards are sometimes misused. Indeed, learning can cease with the simple swipe of an eraser if the information is removed too soon. One cannot save information on the chalkboard without rendering the chalkboard useless for other purposes. Messy writing or writing in letters too small to read can also limit the usefulness of the chalkboard.

Transparencies and Overhead Projector

Overhead projectors and transparencies are unique in that "material may be shown graphically in segments and overlays, revealed progressively, annotated with student comments, and/or revised as the lesson progresses" (Kerr, 1990, p. 197). **Transparencies** are a popular, widely used instructional tool. When used creatively, transparencies can be an exciting instructional medium for presenting ideas to small or large groups. Indeed, transparencies are a very simple and effective means of communication and can be made quickly and easily by classroom teachers. Success with transparencies usually depends on the quality of the content and physical characteristics of the finished product and on how proficient a teacher is in operating the overhead projector.

Transparencies can be beneficial instructional tools in several ways. For one thing, they allow the teacher to remain at the front of the classroom facing the students. Thus, their use provides a high degree of classroom control; student attention goes to the content on the screen when the projector is turned on and returns to the teacher when the projector is turned off. Also, since transparencies do not require a darkened room, the teacher is able to retain a brightly projected colored image with the classroom lights on. Further, transparencies can be prepared in advance and may even serve as a viable substitute for chalkboards. Transparencies are commercially available in a variety of subjects and at varied levels of sophistication and understanding.

Limitations associated with transparencies stem from poor production techniques and teacher inexperience. Lack of skill in using thermal machines and thermal film may cause some teachers to make transparencies of poor quality. If the words on the master copy are too small or if too many words are crowded onto the transparencies, the result will be a cluttered, hard-to-read image.

Films, Slides, and Opaque Projectors

Audiovisual equipment in the classroom today is lighter, more energy-efficient, and easier to operate than it was in the past. Films, slides, and opaque projectors have largely been replaced by televisions, videocassettes, and videodiscs, which are relatively inexpensive and offer greater instructional flexibility.

Real-Life Objects and Models

Instructional materials do not have to be exotic or expensive to have educational value (Heinich, Molenda, Russell, & Smaldino, 1996). Objects drawn from real life, and models of real-life objects, are sometimes all that will be available in remote rural school districts with low budgets.

Real-life objects can be some of the most involving, accessible, and intriguing educational materials used in the classroom. For instance, coins, plants, animals, tools, and machines offer the potential to stimulate students' imagination and attainment of concepts. Real-life objects are especially appropriate for students with limited life experiences or who are encountering a subject about which they have had little or no direct experience.

A model is a three-dimensional representation of a real-life thing. The model may be smaller, larger, or the same size as the thing it represents. Models of almost anything—from cars to the human body—can be built or purchased for classroom use. Indeed, constructing or assembling models can be appealing classroom projects. Such activities can sharpen both cognitive and psychomotor skills. These models can provide learning experiences that real-life things cannot provide.

A model can also be used to represent an abstraction of a complex process. The model United Nations is a typical example wherein students assume the roles of ambassadors and address global issues and problems. Girls and Boys State is another example of a model where students assume the roles of city officials, run for election, and are elected to state offices.

Many educators recommend real-life objects and models when realism is essential for learning. They provide the direct involvement often needed to internalize the concept being taught.

Mock-Ups, Simulations, and Games

Mock-ups are representations of complex devices or processes: for example, a mock-up of a nuclear reactor or an internal combustion engine. Mock-ups illustrate the basic operations of a real-life device without the associated risks and costs and can be used to clarify complex concepts. The most sophisticated type of mock-up, the simulator, is a device that gives students the ability to experience an important aspect of real life.

Simulations are abstractions of the real world, involving objects, processes, or situations. Simulated games involve situations with goals, rules, and rewards. Simulations were first used successfully in military, business, medical, and public administrative arenas and have now become popular in education, particularly in conjunction with computers and VCRs. Indeed, many simulations are now produced commercially for teachers. However, more often teacher-made simulations are used in the classroom, since they can be geared to specific classroom goals, students, subjects, or grade levels.

Educational games are activities with goals, rules, and rewards. Educational games have been an important instructional tool in elementary schools since the early nineteenth century. Educational games are not designed solely to amuse; they make social and cognitive contributions to learning. For example, checkers and chess can challenge the mind; they involve logic and sequencing of moves. Monopoly can be used with young children to enhance counting and dealing with the value of money.

Pictures, Drawings, and Charts

Pictures, drawing, and charts are relatively inexpensive instructional materials. Many can be obtained at little or no cost. They can be used appropriately at all levels of instruction and in all disciplines. For instance, they can be used to stimulate creative expression, such as writing stories or poetry; to help sharpen interpretation skills, such as economic predictions from charts; to show motion, such as a drawing showing how to perform a motor skill; or to develop decoding skills, as in the interpretation of intent from a cartoon.

Pictures, drawing, and charts are readily available in books, magazines, newspapers, and catalogs; they can also be produced by teachers or students. They should be appropriate for the intended instruction and of sufficient size for use with a class or group of students.

This completes our brief overview of common instructional media. Complete Task 12.1 to check your understanding of the information presented on commonly used instructional materials and aids.

New Technologies

Textbooks may be used less frequently, as new media and technology, such as videos, videodiscs, videocassette recorders, and computers, enter the classroom. The new forms of technology enable teachers to expand the classroom in which learning takes place and greatly enrich student learning experiences (Newman, 1992; Tipton, 1998). Teachers can bring the outside world into the classroom and provide instruction that goes far beyond what can be delivered in the classroom alone. The new media and technology provide a more direct

T A S K   1 2 . 1

Common Classroom Instructional Materials

Check yourself on the following concepts. Check your responses with those given at the end of the chapter.

1. Three prerequisites regarding the proper selection of media and technology include:

   a. _____

   b. _____

   c. _____

2. The selection of classroom materials is generally the responsibility of either _____ or _____ .

3. Printed materials in most classrooms are usually limited to a textbook.   (True/False)

4. Chalkboards are losing their usefulness as classroom teaching aids.   (True/False)

5. The major limitations associated with transparencies stem from _____ and _____ .

6. Real-life objects are especially appropriate for use with students who have had limited life experiences.   (True/False)

7. Describe a model. _____

   _____

8. Games have little educational value.   (True/False)

Analysis and Reflections

Most teachers use transparencies. Create a transparency using a variety of appropriate pencils and in a variety of sizes. Project the transparency to determine the best size, color, and type of markers for good visibility. Share your conclusions with the class.

approach to instruction. Video and computers have rapidly become key instructional technologies used in both formal and informal education. Video can combine motion, color, and sound in ways that can dramatize ideas better than any other medium. Students can experience the past, present, or future. They can be transported inside the human body, around the world, or out beyond the solar system. Likewise, teachers can use computers as an aid in a multitude of ways, ranging from tutor to student tool. Let's now take a closer look at these versatile forms of technology.

Motion Pictures, Videos, and Television

Motion pictures and video allow teachers to communicate by using the two most direct channels for learning: sight and sound. Both depict motion, promote the building of a common base for experiencing and understanding the world in general, and impact the emotions. Both are flexible media in that they enable step-by-step demonstrations and observations to be shown and repeated in critical sequences. Moreover, both allow observation of items and events that are too dangerous or too difficult to view because of time, distance, and size limitations. Both may be used to present problem-solving situations, promote critical thinking, and depict historical events, and both may serve as springboards for further study, research, and learning. Finally, they can provide teachers with an avenue for enriching and supplementing instruction.

Motion pictures offer several specific advantages over video. Certain special techniques are better suited for motion picture technology than for video—techniques such as animation, long-range photography, microphotography, and time-lapse photography, as well as slow-motion photography and slow-motion projection. Additionally, films are available from a wider range of sources and in a greater number of subjects and titles than videos. However, due to the increasing popularity of video instruction brought about by the availability of more efficient, inexpensive video equipment and the rising costs of motion pictures and associated equipment, this imbalance is changing. Some observers suggest that video will replace motion pictures—except for large-screen projection purposes (Bullough, 1988).

Motion pictures are limited in certain respects. For instance, they do not adapt well to flexible pacing of the material presented. Some may present material too slowly for some students and too fast for others. Motion pictures may also present incorrect information, promote misconceptions, and distort reality, leading to possible misinterpretations of intended messages. In some cases they may also contain unacceptable material.

A major advantage associated with video is that it can be produced economically and easily on a local-school basis. Only a limited amount of equipment is necessary, and it is generally user-friendly and becoming more portable. Videotapes come in cassette format and are fairly inexpensive. Further, they are reusable and easily duplicated.

Video is immediate. It allows the quick recording of information and, if desired, immediate feedback. As such, recorded information can be easily and quickly transmitted live to special audiences or delayed and used later. Stop-action and slow-motion capabilities make video particularly valuable when teaching such topics as the circulatory or digestive system, the passage of a bill through Congress, or the trajectory of a missile. In cases where programs are taped from other sources, however, remember to be careful not to violate copyright laws.

Easy production and flexibility can benefit students as well by inviting them to get involved in their learning. For example, students may be permitted to prepare programs dealing with careers and community problems, record guest speakers, make class movies, or record field trips.

Video programs also have certain limitations. In fact, all the limitations cited earlier for motion pictures may also apply to video programs. Video may present other specific problems. For one thing, students come to school as users of television, with its rapid-paced, canned, general-entertainment format.

Teachers may not be able to hold students' attentions very long. Even when video programs are produced by professionals, their level of sophistication and interest may not match that of the programming to which students are accustomed.

Since video is generally viewed in small-screen format, many students may not be able to see what is presented very well. Even when large video projection capabilities exist, they are expensive, and too often the video images tend to become poorer in quality when enlarged or viewed at an angle. Some educators also maintain that the capabilities for providing feedback to students are lacking with video, especially with respect to instructional television programming.

Television programming is an immediate, widely available, and frequently used instructional tool. It is sometimes considered the most pervasive medium in our society. Today, television has become a common medium for instruction. Programs may be locally produced, purchased, or rented or they may be received via broadcast or closed circuit from a commercial or public television station.

Broadcast programs are sent through the air and received by antennae or microwave systems, while closed-circuit programs are sent and received via fiber-optic cable. Interactive video technology networking to provide instruction at distance location is an example of a broadcasting system (Musial & Kampmueller, 1996). A videotape playback unit (VCR) is a simple example of a closed-circuit system.

A distinction is usually made between educational and instructional television. *Educational television* is designed to inform or educate in general, whereas *instructional television* is designed for specific classroom instruction and objectives. Instructional television is selected by the teacher to meet course or program objectives. Broadcast and closed-circuit programming may serve either purpose.

Finally, you need to consider the role that motion pictures, videos, and television will play in your classroom. They should be used with specific lesson objectives in mind. You should make certain that the content of media presentations is appropriate for your intent. To this end, you should preview all programs before they are viewed by students. As noted earlier, before viewing, students should be alerted to what they should look for, a technique that enhances the likelihood that they will be attentive to media presentations in a meaningful way.

Videodisc and Interactive Video Technology

A **videodisc** is a compact disc (CD) on which a tremendous quantity of visual information is stored. For example, one videodisc can store up to 54,000 separate frames of still images, up to 50 hours of digitized stereo music, or 330 minutes of motion images with sound (Heinich, Molenda, & Russell, 1989). Put another way, one disc has the storage capacity of more than 600 carousel slide trays. There are still other advantages of videodisc technology: Videodisc technology permits random access and retrieval of any one piece of information. Material can be stored in full-color, full-motion format or as still visuals with sound. Videodiscs can be used for distributing almost any set of instructional materials. And their small size permits easy storage and minimizes mailing costs.

Computer system components and video system components may be linked to form an interactive video system, thus tapping the benefits of both systems and creating an excellent instructional tool with tremendous potential. The user can individually access, sequence, and pace both sound and images. Such a multimedia learning environment can be a powerful practical method for individualizing and personalizing instruction. In effect, interactive video systems allow learners to become more involved in their learning.

A simple video playback unit consisting of a monitor and a VCR (for running videotapes) offers the most primitive level of interactive video. Students "interact" with the unit by manipulating, as desired, such controls as PLAY, FREEZE/PAUSE, FORWARD, or REVERSE. A computer equipped with a CD-ROM drive offers a more sophisticated interactive unit with greater storage capacity. Students use the computer to control access to the verbal and visual information on the disc. Figure 12.1 shows the standard configuration of an interactive video system. The videodisc provides the video portion of interaction video. The images can be presented in slow motion, fast motion, or frame by frame (as in a filmstrip or slide display).

Videodisc technology does have limitations. Videodisc players are expensive and most do not permit local school recording; copies of programs must be made at remote sites, and they tend to be rather expensive. Such limitations may discourage widespread use of videodisc technology in most public

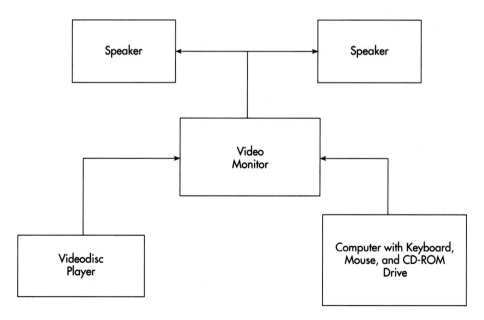

FIGURE 12.1 *Basic Components of an Interactive Video System*

schools. Concentrated efforts are needed to lower the cost of the technology and make it more widely available.

Computers

Computers can be a powerful tool in a teacher's repertoire (Siegel, Good, & Moore, 1996). With the advent of microcomputers, computers have become commonplace in modern society. Their popularity and educational value has had an irreversible impact on schools. Indeed, with their word processing and record-keeping capabilities, quick and easy spreadsheets, and high-quality graphics programs, computers have established their effectiveness as management and instructional tools.

Figure 12.2 diagrams the basic components of a personal computer. The physical components constitute the *hardware.* The central processing unit (CPU) is the computer's "brain." It performs the commands you specify, carries out calculations, makes logical decisions, and so forth. The programs that tell the CPU what to do are the *software.* Read-only memory (ROM) consists of the control instructions that have been "wired" permanently into the computer's memory; these are programs that the computer will need constantly to run and perform internal monitoring functions. Random-access memory (RAM) is the flexible part of the memory. The programs and data being manipulated by the user are temporarily stored in RAM, then erased to make way for the next program or stored on floppy disks, compact disks, or in the computer's hard drive for future access.

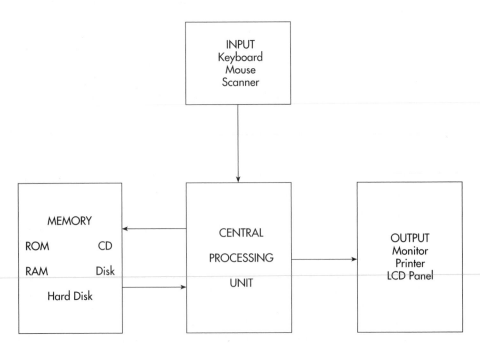

FIGURE 12.2   *The Basic Components of a Personal Computer*

Input devices transmit information to the CPU. The most common input device is a keyboard. Other input devices include the mouse, joysticks, track balls, scanners, and graphic tablets. *Output devices* allow the computer to send information to you. Common output devices include a video monitor, an LCD panel, and a printer.

A computer's memory size is usually described in terms of how many bytes it can store at one time. Essentially, a byte is a single character (such as "A" or "?"). You will often hear statements such as "My computer has 32 megabytes of RAM," or "My hard drive will hold 10 gigabytes." A gigabyte is approximately one billion bytes.

Software has gradually improved in quality and variety and is now available for all subject areas and grade levels. Indeed, current software presents whole units and courses of instruction. The newer software permits a variety of student responses, with branching to appropriate levels of instruction based on the correctness of students' responses. If students fail to master intended skills or concepts, the software breaks down the concept using analogies, examples, and suggestions rather than simply repeating presentation of the subject matter. Moreover, overall instruction is made more appealing and enhanced through the use of graphics and sound.

The selection, evaluation, and purchase of classroom software should be based on how well the program sustains student interest and, more important, how well it addresses intended goals and objectives. More specifically, you should focus on (1) how well the software appeals to students and acts as a motivator, (2) how well the software helps students master intended skills and concepts, and (3) how well the software encourages and develops higher-level thinking.

Computers can greatly expand the types of instruction received by students, improve on current teaching modes, and free teachers to increase their personal attention to students (Solomon, 1992). Indeed, positive experiences can come from meaningful interactions with computers as students learn concepts concurrently with the application of those concepts, for example, when computer training exercises are integrated into computer programs that actually call for students to use spreadsheets while using the training programs in business education classes.

Computers and computer labs have become less expensive and more versatile, and if schools know their potential and have the proper software, the capabilities are limitless. However, interest in adapting computers to serve as instructional tools needs to be nourished.

Computers characteristically offer many advantages as management and instructional tools. Their success has flourished with the increase in availability at less cost. Computers permit the use of flexible, practical, and effective self-contained units of instruction; allow vast amounts of data and information to be quickly stored and used for reference, manipulation, and problem solving; and provide several sources of output, including by screen, printout, and signals passing over wires to remote places. Also, as noted earlier, they may be used for controlling other instructional tools, such as slides, filmstrips, motion pictures, and video programs.

Generally, computers represent good motivational tools. They encourage students to become actively involved in the learning process. Further, they make fewer errors than teachers and do not get irritated, tired, angry, distracted, or impatient. Indeed, computers have become so sophisticated that they can mimic human instructors in response to students. Moreover, computers also benefit students by helping them develop a sense of accomplishment, and in so doing improve their self-confidence. Additionally, computers and computer software are available to serve the unique needs of students from diverse backgrounds, including the advanced, the below average, the learning disabled, those from low-income families, and those with limited English skills. Another major instructional advantage of computers is that, with the appropriate software, they can be used by both teachers and students for word processing, record keeping, and desktop publishing. As such they permit teachers and students to produce, save, retrieve, edit, and print both text and visuals for term papers, letters, pamphlets, newsletters, brochures, grade reports, or books.

Most school computers are desktop computers rather than mainframes. Utility programs are now available specifically for teachers and administrators that facilitate such functions as scheduling, record keeping, test writing and analysis, or puzzle generation. The instructional role computers have assumed in the classroom has taken two forms: computer-managed instruction (CMI) and computer-assisted instruction (CAI), which is sometimes referred to as computer-based instruction.

Computer-Managed Instruction   The primary purpose of **computer-managed instruction (CMI)** is to help both the instructor and the student in the management of records. Specifically, teachers use it for handling student records, diagnosing and prescribing materials, monitoring progress, and testing. The computer can be used to store information about students and about relevant instructional materials. Students can take tests on the computer or input information into a personal portfolio. Moreover, computers can diagnose the learning needs of students and prescribe optimal sequences of instruction for them. Essentially, computer-managed instruction does not provide instruction, but it may contain instructional programs or activities; that is, the programs can provide activities that focus on identified student needs.

Some computer-managed instruction packages will include instructional objectives, instructional activities, corresponding test items, and instructional support. In such systems, computers often are used for testing students' competency mastery; for recording each student's mastery progress; for diagnosing weaknesses, recommending remedial work if necessary, and indicating when the student is ready to move on to the next step; and for providing needed additional practice.

Teachers who have become proficient with the appropriate computer-managed instructional software can manage instruction with these computers and maintain sophisticated records on students. Indeed, as teachers develop lessons and test items for the units they teach, they can be programmed into the computer for random selection when the time comes for use. Moreover, teachers will find word processing programs useful in producing course outlines, handouts, and tests. Furthermore, teachers will find the use of database information systems in collecting and recording information and spreadsheet information extremely useful in recording grades and calculating end-of-term grades.

Computer-Assisted Instruction **Computer-assisted instruction (CAI)** usually serves one individual student at a time, as part of the instructional activity. The major strength of computer-assisted instruction is that it is interactive: Information, questions, and other stimuli flow from computers to students, but then the students can provide input that shapes the next computer output.

With computer-assisted instruction, acquisition of information and development of skills is accomplished through the use of a computer system and a computer software program. The computer system usually consists of a CPU, a data-storage system such as a disk drive or hard drive, a monitor or display unit called a *cathode ray tube*, and a keyboard. Programs may be designed to fit individual needs at any desired ability level, pace, or degree of complexity. The four main types of programs for computer-assisted instruction are drill and practice, tutorial activities, simulation, and games.

Drill and practice programs are the lowest level of computer use. They lead students through a series of examples to increase dexterity and fluency in a skill. That is, they contain exercises that repeatedly put the student into contact with quantities of information, facts, problems, and relationships for the purpose of learning and mastering concepts and skills or committing material to memory. Drill and practice is used predominantly for math drills, foreign language drill, vocabulary building, and the like.

Tutorial programs are designed to emulate a human tutor: The computer acts as the teacher. The computer initially presents new information; depending on student responses, it may present additional or supplemental information. The initial presentation and follow-up responses to the student may take the form of written explanation and descriptions, questions and problems, or graphics and visual illustrations. Tutorials are generally more sophisticated than drill and practice programs.

Simulation programs call on the students to role-play and model reality. Essentially, students confront real-life situations. That is, they make decisions while emulating or interacting with "real-life" or "close-to-life" situations and processes in order to learn from their responses. Simulations are especially helpful and thought provoking when they ask students to make decisions concerning situations or processes involving risks or dangers. Students can now conduct experiments; experience past events, current happenings, or future possibilities; and consider what-if problems through simulations.

Gaming programs engage students in activities where they must follow specific rules that differ from those of real life in order to reach a specific goal. Attaining the goal usually entails competition—group against group, as in volleyball; individual against individual or machine, as in chess; or individual against a standard, as in bowling. To be challenging, goals should have a roughly 50 percent probability of success.

Whatever form of computer-assisted instruction is used, it is usually appealing to students. Programs involve students and give them some control over the rate of their learning. Moreover, they can often improve instructional effectiveness and efficiency.

Although there are definite advantages associated with computers as instructional tools, some educators criticize them because of what they consider characteristic limitations. For one thing, computers are still expensive; critics suggest that dollars spent on hardware, software, and maintenance would be better spent for more teachers, higher salaries, or other instructional materials. Some fear that computers may replace teachers. Others fear that they stifle creativity, limit social interaction, emphasize narrow facts at the expense of broad generalizations, limit the imagination, and dehumanize instruction.

The use of computers is also criticized because of perceived instructional limitations and problems, such as the limited range of objectives being taught by computers. Most computer-based instruction cannot effectively teach affective, motor, or interpersonal skills. Even in the cognitive domain, current programs tend to teach at the lower levels of knowledge and understanding. Copyright problems, the poor quality of some software programs, and incompatibility among software programs also can limit their effectiveness. Further, some teachers fear using computers because they are too complex to understand.

Additionally, logistical environmental concerns may limit the use of computers. For example, having to deal with issues like placement of the computers, supervision of users, maintenance, and acquisition of supplies may cause some teachers not to bother using computers as instructional tools.

The Internet

Most school districts in the United States are either getting wired or are making plans to get wired for the Internet (Levinson & Surratt, 1999). But, what is the Internet and how can it be used in the classroom? The **Internet** was established to let computers all over the world talk to each other. The Internet was originally developed to be a military communication system that would survive a nuclear war. It was later funded by the National Science Foundation as a research support system. If an individual or school district has a computer, a modem, and a phone line, they can obtain access to and use "the Net." Today, the Internet is becoming an indispensable teaching/learning tool. It can provide several basic services: the capability to logon to other computers on the Net; electronic mail, or e-mail; newsgroups; access to files from remote computers; online database searching; and access to the information system of the twenty-first century, the World Wide Web.

The future of the Internet is uncertain, but one thing is for sure: It will be a critical component in our educational system. In fact, Bissell and Newhoff (1997) view the Internet "as the most promising resource for strengthening the nation's K–12 education system." It is presently creating educational opportunities for teachers and students to gain access to distance education and unlimited resources. The Internet allows teachers and students to tap into world information sources right from their homes and classrooms (Federman & Edwards, 1997).

Expansion Activity: Internet Use

The Internet can be an effective tool for teachers in any subject and at any grade level. How can teachers make use of the Internet in various subjects and at various grade levels? Form groups of four and five and generate ideas for elementary, middle school, and high school teachers. Share your group's ideas with the class.

Teachers and students in remote rural schools can now access the Library of Congress, visit countries around the world, tour museums, communicate with other teachers and students, and dialog with educational experts.

School districts and classroom teachers can improve instruction through the effective use of the Internet. Teachers and students can learn the latest information and developments in thousands of fields, search the card catalogs of some of the greatest libraries in the world, get instant information on almost any conceivable topic, and discuss world issues and news of the day. Hundreds of Internet websites and hyperlinks have been created that can be valuable resources for school districts and classroom teachers. For example, more than 1,000 lesson plans, organized by subject and grade level, can be reviewed in the AskERIC Virtual Library. They can be accessed by selecting AskERIC Lesson Plans on the menu of the AskERIC Virtual Library at web address **http://ericir.syr.edu.**

The Internet provides a place where teachers and students can explore and grow. The Internet is a powerful tool that teachers can use to give students an even greater opportunity to explore the world around them. However, the Internet also contains much unacceptable materials for students. Clearly, the Internet can be a valuable asset to teachers. Complete Expansion Activity: Internet Use to explore your future plans for using the Internet.

Technology in the Classroom

The use of technology in the classroom is a quiet revolution. Although most teachers still teach through traditional methods, others are realizing the potential of multimedia, the World Wide Web and Internet, and other information-based forms of instruction. Technology in the classroom can have many benefits because it (1) emphasizes active learning, (2) responds to different learning styles, (3) enhances collaborative learning, (4) increases individualized learning and self-paced study, and (5) encourages greater student independence.

No one could have predicted technology's impact on the lives of students, parents, communities, and teachers, but the changes brought about have been meaningful. As a rule, technology has fostered the development of a renewed emphasis on writing, literacy learning, and hands-on mathematics and science. Technology affords teachers the opportunity to plan a number of activities at the same time.

It has been found that multimedia can speed learning and increase student retention levels. Some of the multimedia programs that can be used in the classroom are Claris Works, WordPerfect, HyperStudio, PowerPoint, electronic gradebooks, and Digital Chisel. Educational activities can involve e-mail, building web pages and links, performing research for class and individual projects, and creating multimedia projects. Some specific uses of multimedia programs follow.

1. Programs such as Claris Works, WordPerfect, and Microsoft Word offer integration of word processing, outlining, test construction, newsletters, flyers, certificates, presentations, drawing, painting, spreadsheet computation and charting, database management, and communications. By integrating several of these features, with or without an Internet connection, one can make slide presentations, link frames, add Quick-Time movies and compose documents for research report writing.

2. HyperStudio is a multimedia program that has the ability to bring together text, sound, graphics, and video. It uses a hypertext type format to create various pages and links. It can be used to create programs and presentations. HyperStudio can be used with or without an Internet connection, but with an Internet connection it can be used in conjunction with either MediaLinker to access remote Internet sites or by using the web browser, MacWeb.

3. PowerPoint is the premier presentation software. Originally designed for business it has great applications for the classroom. The most distinctive feature of PowerPoint is its extensive use of visuals. As such, PowerPoint presentations are generally motivational to students. Presentations can be used to introduce new material or to supplement an adopted textbook.

4. Electronic gradebooks are designed to assist teachers with the tedious job of recording grades and preparing grade reports. Most of these programs are very flexible and easy to use. Indeed, most give users a vast number of grading choices. Most allow teachers to print a variety of individual reports to be sent home to parents. Some programs can be linked to the Internet so parents can check their children's grades with just a few clicks.

5. The Digital Chisel is a multimedia authoring tool specifically designed for teachers and students to allow them to create storybooks, reports, interactive presentations, question sessions, school projects and so on. It contains hypertext and hyperlinking. Projects may also contain questions that create records which can be stored for grading.

The use of multimedia enables the teacher to work with students to construct projects that incorporate text, images, sound, and movies. The students' work can be viewed by many audiences and can be used as an authentic assessment of what was studied in the classroom. The presentation of multimedia projects can be offered in many ways. The students' work can be taken home on videos or cassettes and can even be uploaded to the Internet for the parents to download at home.

Administrators and teachers also value e-mail because it saves time and money. For example, e-mail can be used by administrators to communicate with teachers and to distribute the weekly bulletin. Teachers can communicate with each other and with other school personnel. Moreover, since many homes now have access to e-mail, administrators and teachers can communicate with parents regarding how well their children are doing. One of the most exciting aspects of the new technologies is that they break down the four walls of the classroom and open up the learning environment. The technology can unite students with their own communities as well as with peers in other nations, and it gives them access to international libraries, databases, and museums. The opportunities are virtually unlimited.

Over the past few years visual presenters have been surfacing in many classrooms. What are visual presenters? The visual presenter (also known as video presenter, visualizer, Elmo, video imager, and several other names) is a video camera mounted on a stand, which is very close in appearance to a photographic copy stand. Operating on a similar principle as the opaque projector, the visual presenter displays two dimensional objects such as photographs, documents, and graphs. Unlike the old opaque projectors, the presenter can also image parts of three-dimensional objects that could include a page from a book or a machine component. Thus, a visual presenter can be used in place of an opaque or overhead projector to project written pages or pictures onto a screen.

There is also a downside to technology in the classroom. Some education specialists contend there is no evidence that using computers or the Internet will improve student achievement. Nevertheless, districts are pouring billions of dollars annually into the latest hardware. Is such a strong commitment a truly sensible course? Indeed, it is projected that American schools will invest $5.2 billion in technology this year, outpacing last year's $4.3 billion. However, only 15 percent of teachers have appropriate computer training. Critics warn that the billions being spent on classroom technology are billions not going to other essential functions. Term papers and other homework are often taken from computers, while students' favorite Internet sites reportedly have to do with sports, cars, and movies. Meanwhile, American students lag behind other nations in math, science, history, geography, and reading.

The introduction and use of technology in schools and classrooms will not automatically increase student learning. To accomplish this end, educators must rethink how schools are organized and rethink curriculum and instruction. Teachers and administrators must know how to use the hardware and software. More importantly, they must know how to use these tools to create appropriate learning experiences for students. As teachers gain easier access and receive

Web Search: Using Technology

Access Internet URL website **http://aaps.k12.mi.us/~northsid/classtech-topten.html#students** which lists some ideas for using technology in the classroom. Using the top ten lists on the Internet site as a guide, generate a list of ideas for using technology in the subject or at the grade level you plan to teach. Share your list with the class.

training in the use of the latest technology and as technology resources expand through electronic networking, instruction will be enhanced and we should see students becoming more active, confident, motivated, and achieve at higher levels. Let us now look at some of your ideas for using technology in the classroom by having you complete Web Search: Using Technology.

T A S K   1 2 . 2

New Technologies

Check your understanding of the following newer technology concepts. Check your responses with those given at the end of the chapter.

1. A major classroom benefit derived from videos is the realistic you-are-there feeling it communicates to students.   (True/False)

2. A major problem associated with the videodisc is the lack of space to store data. (True/False)

3. Explain what is meant by an *interactive video system:* _____
_____

4. The basic component of a personal computer that carries out the calculations, processes, and control commands is referred to as the _____ .

5. Describe the four main types of programs used in computer-assisted instruction (CAI):
   a. _____
   b. _____
   c. _____
   d. _____

6. Describe the Internet and how it can be used effectively in the classroom._____
_____
_____
_____
_____

7. Give a rationale for the increased use of technology in the classroom._____
_____
_____
_____
_____

Analysis and Reflections

The quality of instruction can be improved through the use of technology. How would you use technology in developing: inquiry-based and discovery activities, problem-solving activities, performance-based assessment, real-world applications, and social learning skills? Write a short paper relative to your ideas and submit it to your instructor.

This concludes our discussion of various newer technologies. Complete Task 12.2, which will check your understanding of this section.

Summary

- Planning for the use of media and technology should be an integral component in preparing for teaching.
- Instructional media often can enhance teaching effectiveness. Indeed, to a limited degree, various multisensory instructional aids can be used as substitutes for first-hand, real-life experiences.
- Plan your instruction so that students use as many senses as possible.
- The use of media is especially important to slow and younger students who often have difficulty learning through only verbal symbolism—written and spoken words.

Role of Instructional Media

- The role of media depends on the mode of instruction—teacher-directed or student-directed. The most common use is to support a "live" teacher.
- Media is essential when instruction is delivered through some form of distance learning.
- Media plays an important role when working with exceptional students.

Selection of Instructional Materials

- Many forms of instructional media are available to teachers, including the textbook, other common learning tools, and newer technologies. Commonly used instructional media include printed materials, the chalkboard, overhead projector, real-life objects, mock-ups, simulations, games, pictures, drawings, and charts.
- Newer technologies available to teachers include video, motion pictures, computers, and the Internet. Each of these media forms has advantages and limitations.
- The best media to use in any given situation will depend on (1) the teaching-learning situation, (2) the learner objective and value of the media to the lesson, and (3) the ability of the user to use the media correctly.

Printed Materials

- Printed materials remain the most common aid to instruction in the classroom.
- The textbook continues to be convenient and versatile and permits random access to information.

Common Instructional Media

- Chalkboards and overhead projectors are found in practically every classroom. Some educators view them as being the most useful and versatile teaching tools available to classroom teachers.
- Real-life objects, models, mock-ups, simulations, games, pictures, drawings, and charts can be inexpensive educational aids. They can be valuable resources for districts with low budgets. Real-life objects are especially appropriate for students with limited life experiences.

- Models, mock-ups, simulations, and games can be used to provide learning experience.
- Pictures, drawings, and charts are easily obtained at low cost and can greatly enhance the learning of complex concepts.

New Technologies

- Videos, videodiscs, videocassette recorders, and computers are relatively new media forms. This newer technology provides more direct involvement in instruction.
- Interactive video and computers are the only media tools that are two-way communicators. The ability to respond to the user's input makes interactive video and computers among the most powerful media available to teachers.
- Computers have assumed two roles in the classroom–computer-managed instruction (CMI) and computer-assisted instruction (CAI). The purpose of computer-managed instruction (CMI) is to assist both the teacher and student in the management of records. Computer-assisted instruction (CAI) comes in four different program formats: drill and practice, tutorials, simulations, and games.
- Most school districts are making use of the Internet to improve the effectiveness of teaching and learning. The Net is fast becoming an indispensable teaching/learning tool.
- The use of technology can speed learning and increase student retention. Some of the multimedia and programs that can be used in the classroom are Claris Works, WordPerfect, HyperStudio, PowerPoint, electronic gradebooks, Digital Chisel, e-mail, and visual presenters.
- No one form of instructional media is going to be the means to accomplish all ends in the teaching-learning process. The various commonly used media and the newer technology give teachers a number of ways to deal with the wide range of student temperaments, backgrounds, and learning styles encountered on a daily basis.

Activities

1. *Classroom visitations*   Visit several classroom teachers and discuss with them how classroom materials are selected in their schools. Discuss how they use the more common instructional media and the newer technologies. Compare your findings with what you have learned about media in this chapter.
2. *Multimedia*   Develop a 30-minute multimedia lesson that incorporates the chalkboard, transparencies, and motion picture or filmstrip and then microteach it.
3. *Technology stores*   Visit a local computer store and, if possible, view a demonstration of hardware systems and word processing units. Visit a video store and view how a videodisc player and interactive video system operate.

Answer Keys

Task 12.1 Common Classroom Instructional Materials

1. a. Nature of teaching-learning situation assessed and learner objectives determined.
   b. Media and technology planned as integral part of lesson.
   c. User knows how to correctly use media and technology and associated hardware.
2. individual teachers; committees
3. *True*   The textbook is the only instructional aid used in many classrooms.
4. *False*   Chalkboards are still the most widely used tool.
5. poor production techniques; the teacher's inability to use them correctly
6. *True*   Real-life objects give students new experiences.
7. A model is a three-dimensional representation of something.
8. *False*   Games have been an important instructional tool since the early nineteenth century.

Task 12.2 New Technologies

1. *True*   Because motion pictures are multisensory, they sometimes can make one feel like they are a part of the action.
2. *False*   Videodiscs can store vast amounts of information and material.
3. A video system linked to a computer system that empowers an individual to control images and sounds.
4. central processing unit (CPU)
5. a. Drill and practice exercises related to information, facts, etc.
   b. Tutorial programs that present new information
   c. Simulation programs that present "real-life" situations
   d. Gaming programs used to develop skills
6. The Internet is a communication system that lets computers all over the world talk to each other. The Internet allows teachers and students in the classroom to tap into world information sources, to visit museums, and to communicate with other people. The Internet also gives teachers access to the latest information and planning materials.
7. Technology can help teachers put more emphasis on active learning, help them respond to different learning styles, help enhance collaborative learning, increase individualized learning and self-paced study, and encourage greater student independence. Technology can also assist teachers in communicating with parents, other teachers, and administrators.

Theory and Research

Bitter, G., & Pierson, M. (1999). *Using technology in the classroom* (4th ed.). Boston, MA: Allyn and Bacon.

Heinich, M. (1999). *Instructional media and technologies for learning*. Paramus, NJ: Prentice Hall.

Knapp, L. R., & Glenn, A. D. (1996). *Restructuring schools with technology.* Boston, MA: Allyn and Bacon.

Maurer, M. M., & Davidson, G. (1999). Technology, children, and the power of the heart. *Phi Delta Kappan, 80*(6), 458–460.

Snyder, T. (1989–1998). *Great teaching in the one-computer classroom* (5th ed.). Watertown, MA: Tom Synder Productions

References

Bissell, J., & Newhoff, S. (1997). *Guide to the Internet in educational psychology* (2nd ed.). New York: McGraw-Hill.

Brown, J. W., Lewis, R. B., & Harcleroad, F. (1983). *AV instruction technology, media, and methods* (6th ed.). New York: McGraw-Hill.

Bullough, R. V., Sr. (1988). *Creating instructional materials* (3rd ed.). Columbus, OH: Charles E. Merrill.

Federman, A. N., & Edwards, S. (1997). Interactive, collaborative science via the net: Live from the Hubble Space Telescope. *The Internet in Education: A Supplement to T.H.E. Journal,* 20–22.

Heinich, R., Molenda, M., & Russell, J. D. (1989). *Instructional media and new technologies of instruction* (3rd ed.). New York: Macmillan.

Heinich, R., Molenda, M., Russell, J. D., & Smaldino, S. E. (1996). *Instructional media and new technologies for learning* (5th ed.). Englewood Cliffs, NJ: Prentice Hall.

Kerr, S. T. (1990). Alternative technologies as textbooks and the social imperatives of educational change. In D. L. Elliott & A. Woodwards (Eds.), *Textbooks and schooling in the United States.* Chicago: University of Chicago Press.

Levinson, E., & Surratt, J. (1999). Is the Internet the most important educational event since McGuffey's reader? Who knows? *Converge, 2*(4), 60–62.

Lorber, M. A., & Pierce, W. D. (1983). *Objectives, methods, and evaluation for secondary teaching* (2nd ed.). Englewood Cliffs, NJ: Prentice Hall.

Musial, G. G., & Kampmueller, W. (1996). Two-way video distance education: Ten misconceptions about teaching and learning via interactive television. *Action in Teacher Education, 17*(4), 28–36.

Newman, D. (1992). Technology as support for school structure and school restructuring. *Phi Delta Kappan, 74*(4), 308–315.

Siegel, J., Good, K., & Moore, J. (1996). Integrating technology into educating preservice special education teachers. *Action in Teacher Education, 17*(4), 53–63.

Solomon, G. (1992). The computer as electronic doorway: Technology and the promise of empowerment. *Phi Delta Kappan, 74*(4), 327–329.

Tipton, M. (1998). *Techniques for planning and producing* (4th ed.). Dubuque, IA: Kendall/Hunt Publishing.

A Well-Planned Unit

Objectives

After completing your study of Chapter 13, you should be able to:

1. Identify and describe the various components of a unit plan.

2. Develop a unit plan for a specifc subject and grade level.

3. Evaluate a unit plan relative to established criteria.

4. Reflect on issues that can impact planning.

Planning is an essential undertaking for teaching to be successful. Generally, planning requirements will vary at different localities around the nation. However, there is no single best format for a unit plan. Particular formats may sometimes be best for specific disciplines and/or topics. Theoretically, there is also no set time duration for a unit plan. Some units may extend for only several days while others will extend for a few weeks. The duration often depends on the subject, interest, and students. Whatever the format and duration, planning remains a critical component in the quest for excellence in teaching.

In reality, teachers and school districts will use a variety of unit planning formats. The format presented in this textbook is commonly used by many teachers. The unit components include:

1. A topic
2. Goals and objectives
3. Content outline
4. Learning activities
5. Resources and materials
6. Evaluation

This chapter will examine the components of a well-designed unit plan in some detail. To be a successful teacher, you need to know how to create a good unit plan. Therefore, we will ask you to write a unit for a topic of your choice. A well-written unit plan will be presented. We will then analyze each component of the plan and ask you to write the component for your own plan. Commonly asked preservice teacher questions related to the unit plan will be addressed. An examination of each component of a unit plan will provide a better understanding of its role in teaching.

✴ Teaching Preparation

This text has reviewed the many components of teaching, and while doing so, undoubtedly, you have reflected on your own knowledge and abilities as a teacher. Now it is time to prepare a unit plan for a subject and grade level that you intend to teach.

The logical first step in your preparation to teach is to write the course topic outline (Forsyth, Jolliffe, & Stevens, 1995). For many beginning teachers the course topic outlines for their courses will be presented to them by a peer and/or administrative curriculum committee and the beginning teacher must adhere to the description as published in the course of study and state guidelines. However, there are usually three general sources that will help you discover what to teach: state department of education curricular publications, school and/or district courses of study, and school-adopted textbooks.

✴ The Unit Plan

A sample unit is presented in Figure 13.1. The unit plan links together the goals, objectives, content, activities, and evaluation for the desired period of time. It determines the overall flow for a series of lessons over several weeks and reflects

TOPIC	**Subject/Grade**	**Duration**
The Power of Communication	Language Arts/7th Grade	3–4 weeks

GENERAL GOALS FOR THE UNIT

The goals of this unit are to help students:

1. Communicate more effectively in writing.
2. Develop social skills needed when communicating in a group or at work.
3. Experience the difficulties of communicating without a common or standard language.

SPECIFIC OBJECTIVES

As a result of this unit of study the student will be able to:

1. Practice speaking and writing skills.
2. Expand their vocabulary and become aware of the impact of word choice.
3. Identify various purposes for written communication.
4. Analyze personal habits of writing.
5. Identify the function of writing in daily life.
6. Employ those higher level cognitive skills that require the student to analyze, synthesize, evaluate, and create.
7. Evaluate written work.

CONTENT OUTLINE

I.   Writing Purposes

   a. Entertain
   b. Explain or Inform
   c. Describe
   d. Narrate

II.   The Writing Process

   a. Planning
   b. Organizing
   c. Writing
   d. Editing
   e. Revising

III.   Communication Skills

   a. Your Message
   b. Your Audience
   c. Your Purpose
   d. Nonverbal

IV.   Communication Cycle

   a. Sender
   b. Decoder
   c. Interference

FIGURE 13.1   *A Well-Planned Unit*

Continued on next page

LEARNING ACTIVITIES

1. Students must arrange themselves in alphabetical order by middle names without using their voices or any kind of writing utensil. Introduction to the unit.

2. Group discussion about the difficulties of communicating without a common or standard language base.

3. Group students and have them create a cluster of people in the community that will be invited to speak to our class about ways they use writing to communicate. (Encourage students to seek a variety of career types, including housewives and Mr. Moms.)

4. Write letters of invitation to selected people in the community. Use writing process to plan, organize, write, edit, and revise letters.

5. Study textbook chapters about the communication cycle, listening skills, and speaking skills.

6. Role play to practice skills needed to introduce a speaker. Textbook pages 845–851.

7. Use telephone skills learned on page 844, to confirm speaker's acceptance to speak to our class. Confirm date and time, as well as topic to be presented.

8. Listen to the invited panelists to gain information about their use of writing skills. Make a list of ways speakers use writing. Note any body language, or interference that affects the message being presented.

9. Watch a PowerPoint presentation that outlines the four basic purposes for writing.

10. Prepare a chart titled "Why People Write." Group the information from panelists into the four basic purposes for writing.

11. Summary discussion of the communication process.

12. Unit exam.

RESOURCES AND MATERIALS

Posterboards and markers or (large sheets of white paper)
Textbook
Telephone access
PowerPoint presentation
Projection machine

EVALUATION

Textbook chapter concept questions
Role play activities will be pass or fail
Participation
Unit test
Why people write charts

Source: Developed by Susan Moore, Konawa Public Schools, Konawa, OK. Used with permission.

FIGURE 13.1   *A Well-Planned Unit* (Continued)

Topic	**Subject/Grade**	**Approximate Duration**

General Goals

1.
2.
3.

Specific Objectives

1.
2.
3.
4.

Content Outline

Learning Activities

Resources and Materials

Evaluation

FIGURE 13.2   *Unit Template*

an understanding of both the content and processes of instruction. We will now analyze the different components of this unit plan. Using the template shown in Figure 13.2, you will assemble the essential parts of your own unit plan.

The Topic

How does a teacher determine the topics to be taught? This task will vary from district to district. However, units are generally outlined around a general theme or idea (the unit topic). The unit tends to be the single unifying structure around which lessons are prepared. Note the unifying structure of the sample unit titled "The Power of Communication" shown in Figure 13.1. A sequential course topic outline might be prepared or selected by a single teacher or a team of teachers, or it might be prepared collaboratively with the students (Smith & Johnson, 1993). Be aware that beginning teachers sometimes have unrealistic expectations about the amount of content a heterogeneous group of students can study, comprehend, and learn over a period of time. Other examples of unit topics could include sentences, the Civil War, thermodynamics, the heart, or the short stories of Hemingway.

Your Turn

It is time to begin building your own unit plan. Select two or three related chapters from a textbook that you might use when you begin to teach. Give the selected content a unifying unit title. Project an approximate duration for your unit. Record the information on your unit template.

Unit Goals

Why do teachers write goals? Aren't objectives enough? The unit goals establish what the unit is about and what the students are to learn. They are the broad outcomes that students should achieve upon completing the total unit. Goals give focus and direction to the unit. As pointed out in Chapter 4, goals are broad statements of the purpose or learning intent of the unit. Note the broad intent of the goals in the sample unit in Figure 13.1.

Your Turn

Write one or more goals for your unit. Make sure your goals represent the broad purpose of the unit instruction.

Specific Objectives

Do you really need objectives for classroom learning? How many objectives should a teacher write for a unit? The specific objectives are the subordinate skills that students must learn in order to achieve the goals. They help students identify the important points in a unit—what they should know and be able to do when the unit has been completed. Each of the daily lesson plans associated with the unit should include one or more of the specific objectives. On the average, the daily lesson plan should contain no more than two or three specific objectives. Lessons prepared for younger children should be even shorter and should focus on attaining perhaps a single objective.

The inclusion of explicit objectives in a unit or daily plan should never inhibit you from capitalizing on unexpected, serendipitous learning opportunities during the implementation of a lesson. You should continuously monitor students so needed adjustments can be made relative to your instructional intent.

Your objectives should also be a guide for your assessment. The type of assessment item used should not only measure accomplishment of the objective but should also be compatible with the objective being assessed, covert or overt or a combination of both.

Your Turn

Write specific objectives for your unit. The objectives can be either informational or instructional. However, make sure the intent is clear and that they are subordinate to your goals.

Content Outline

What is the purpose of the content outline? How much information should be included in the content outline? Where do you get the content? The curriculum in most elementary and secondary schools is organized around the academic disciplines (history, chemistry, language arts, mathematics, and so forth). Even though this organizational structure is often criticized, it is likely to remain for some time.

Normally, a unit plan outlines what content is to be taught. It is the substance of the plan, the information to be presented, obtained, and learned. It is the information selected to meet the specific objectives and goals of the course. To make sure your unit actually covers what it should, you should write down exactly what content you intend to cover. The amount of detail will vary. Generally, you will want to outline the content of your instruction. However, you don't want to have pages of notes to sift through. Nor should you read your lesson to students. You should be familiar enough with the content so that an outline (in detail, if necessary) will be sufficient for instruction. At a minimum, it should include a "key word" checklist of the material to be presented, arranged in the order that you intend to teach it. The content outline shown in Figure 13.1 is typical for an experienced teacher. Think of the unit plan as similar to the text of a speech to be delivered. Speakers giving a speech for the first time often need to follow a set of detailed notes or perhaps even a word-for-word text. As they gain experience, they find less and less need for notes and can proceed more extemporaneously.

The content for a unit might come from a chapter or chapters in an adopted textbook or from major sections of a curriculum guide. A note of caution, most curriculum guides have been developed by experienced teachers and cannot be expected to fit the preferences of all teachers. They do, however, provide a helpful overall design to follow.

Your Turn

Develop the content outline component of your unit. Outline the content to be covered during the entire unit. Include as much detail in this section as you feel will be needed to do an effective job of teaching the unit.

Learning Activities

How many activities should be included in a unit? Should they all be the same type? What criteria should be used in selecting activities? Should you put time limits on your activities? The learning activities are generally established as a series of tasks that will contribute to attainment of the intended objectives. You should make sure the activities are feasible; that you can afford the time, effort, or expense; that you have the necessary materials and equipment; and that the activities are suitable to the intellectual and maturity levels of your students.

The initial activity should be planned to introduce the unit. It should arouse student interest, inform students of what the unit is about, and provide a transition that bridges the unit topic with what students have already learned. The activities that follow should be developmental activities. Developmental activities should form the bulk of the plan. They include activities that present information, demonstrate skills, and provide reinforcement of previously learned materials. The final activity or activities should be culminating and bring the unit to a close.

Activities should be chosen that will enable students to learn the content. Generally, you do not want to put time limits on your activities. An activity should be continued as long as it is beneficial to students. However, be reasonable regarding the appropriate amount of time for your activities. Also, do not feel obligated to design or select one activity for each objective, some of the best activities will serve multiple purposes and allow students to attain several objectives. Only major or special activities, such as speakers, group work, field trips, research reports, buzz sessions, projects, experiments, summaries, and summative examinations, need be listed. The recurring or common activities can be included in the daily lesson plan.

Note that the sample unit plan in Figure 13.1 includes a carefully planned introductory activity. This activity is followed by a series of developmental activities. The unit is closed with a group activity and discussion activity to tie the concepts together.

Your Turn

Design and/or select activities for your unit that will result in the acquisition of your stated objectives. Be sure to include an introductory activity, developmental activities, and at least one culminating activity.

Resources and Materials

What classroom resources and materials should be included in a unit plan? This section of your unit plan should provide a checklist of essential materials you expect to use to teach the unit. This list should include reading materials, community resources, technology, handouts, and lab facilities—in short, anything that the student does not have that you must supply. Suffice it to say that you need to identify resources and materials that will enhance the learning experience. It should guide you in assembling the resources and materials needed to carry out instruction.

> ## Your Turn
>
> Now that the activities have been planned, list the resources and materials that you will need to obtain to teach the unit. List only materials students will not normally have available on a daily basis.

Evaluation

Why evaluate? How often should you evaluate? What kind of evaluation is best? Who should do the evaluation? Assessment of student progress in achievement of the objectives (formative evaluation) should permeate the entire unit. Plan to gather information in several ways, including informal observation, portfolio assessment, observation of group work, project assessment, and paper-and-pencil assessment. You must make decisions about assignments, diagnostic tools (such as tests), and the procedure by which grades will be determined.

The unit assessment must be consistent with the specific objectives. Evaluation can be conducted by students or the teacher or both. In addition to objective appraisal, the evaluation should provide information for improving the unit plan. Note the different types of evaluation used in the sample unit in Figure 13.1. The evaluation includes both performance assessment and pencil-and-paper assessment.

> ## Your Turn
>
> Plan your unit evaluation. Include at least one pencil-and-paper assessment and one performance assessment. Make sure your assessment evaluates the attainment of your objectives.

You should now have a complete unit plan. Complete Expansion Activity: Unit Evaluation which will help you evaluate your unit.

✖ Approaches to Unit Planning

The unit plan presented in this chapter was chosen for its brevity and simplicity. This does not make it a superior plan, but such brief units are often used by teachers. Indeed, the sample unit has been taught several times over the years. Do you think the unit is too skimpy? What do you think of the format? Is the content outline adequate?

Expansion Activity: Unit Evaluation

Use the ten evaluation questions listed below to evaluate your unit plan. Evaluate it yourself first, modify it, and then have your modified version evaluated by at least three peers. Based on feedback from your peers make final modifications and submit the final version to your instructor.

Unit Evaluation

Questions	Yes	No	Comments
1. Are goals clearly stated?	___	___	1.
2. Are specific objectives clear and practical?	___		2.
3. Is the planned content appropriate for the grade level?	___	___	3.
4. Will the plan's content contribute to achievement of the objectives?	___	___	4.
5. Is the plan workable, given the time frame, needed materials, and other logistical considerations impacting the class?	___	___	5.
6. Does the introduction engage students, motivating them to want to learn?	___	___	6.
7. Are the activities clear and manageable and related to the lesson objectives?	___	___	7.
8. Is a well-designed closure provided to reinforce learning, convey a sense of completeness, and synthesize the content of the lesson?	___	___	8.
9. Are materials appropriate for the grade level, adequate to meet the needs of all students, and valuable to the lesson?	___	___	9.
10. Do evaluative criteria provide the necessary data to determine how much students have learned from the lesson?	___	___	10.

Additional Comments:

New teachers should check with their supervisors before planning and writing units for their courses. Some school districts have a preferred approach for developing units. Some districts require teachers to submit units for final approval, while others give teachers more professional autonomy.

Summary

- Planning is essential to effective teaching. However, requirements will vary from district to district.
- There is no one best planning format. There is also no set time duration for a unit plan.

Teacher Preparation

- The first step in planning is to develop a course topic outline.
- There are three sources that will help teachers plan what to teach: state department of education curricular publications, school and/or district courses of study, and school-adopted textbooks.

The Unit Plan

- A unit plan links goals, objectives, content, activities, and evaluation for a period of time.
- A unit topic tends to be a single unifying structure around which instruction is planned.
- Unit goals establish what the unit is about and what students will learn. They give the unit focus and direction.
- Specific objectives are the subordinate skills that students must learn in order to achieve the goals. They also guide your assessment.
- The content of a unit is the substance of the plan, the information to be presented, obtained, and learned. It is the information selected to meet the objectives.
- Essential materials and resources should be listed in your unit plan.
- Assessment of student progress should permeate the entire unit.

Approaches to Unit Planning

- Experienced teachers usually write rather brief simple plans.
- New teachers need to check on district requirements for planning. Some districts require that unit plans be approved, while others give teachers professional autonomy.

Activities

1. *Planning style*   Do you notice any patterns in the way you plan? Are there ways you can facilitate your way of planning? For example, do you need to set aside time for peace and quiet to plan or can you plan anytime and anywhere? Write a couple of reflective paragraphs on your planning?
2. *Planning for diversity*   Make a list of the ways teaching in a diverse society impacts your planning. Will planning for diversity impact your planning? Will the community impact your planning?

Theory and Research

Bell, D., & Ritchie, R. (1999). *Towards effective subject leadership in the primary school.* Philadelphia, PA: Taylor & Francis.

Crombie, W. (1997). *Curriculum innovation.* Philadelphia, PA: Taylor & Francis.

Jacobs, H. H. (1997). *Mapping the big picture.* Alexandria, VA: Association for Supervision and Curriculum Development.

Passe, J. (1998). *Elementary school curriculum.* New York: McGraw-Hill.

References

Forsyth, I., Jolliffe, A., & Stevens, D. (1995). *Planning a course.* Philadelphia, PA: Taylor & Francis.

Smith, L., & Johnson, H. A. (1993). Control in the classroom: Listening to adolescent voices. *Language Arts, 70*(1), 18–30.

Appendix
State Teacher Certification Addresses and Telephone Numbers

Alabama:

Teacher Certification Office
State Department of Education
Gordon Persons Building
Montgomery, Alabama 36130-3901
Telephone: (205) 242-9560
http://www.alsde.edu/default.asp?

Alaska:

Teacher Certification
Educational Finance and Support
Services
P.O. Box F
Juneau, Alaska 99811-0500
Telephone: (907) 465-2831
http://www.educ.state.ak.us/Teacher
Certification/

Arizona:

Teacher Certification Unit
Department of Education
1535 West Jefferson
Phoenix, Arizona 85007
Telephone: (602) 542-4367
http://www.ade.state.az.us/certification/

Arkansas:

Teacher Education and Certification
Department of Education
State Capitol Mall, Room 107B
Little Rock, Arkansas 72201-1021
Telephone: (501) 682-4333
http://arkedu.state.ar.us/teacher.htm

California:

Commission on Teaching Credentialing
1812 9th St.
P.O. Box 944270
Sacramento, California 94244-2700
Telephone: (916) 445-0184
http://www.ctc.ca.gov/credential-
info/credinfo.html/

Colorado:

Colorado Department of Education
Teacher Education and Certification
201 East Colfax Avenue
Denver, Colorado 80203
Telephone: (303) 866-6628
http://www.cde.state.co.us/index_
home.htm

Connecticut:

State Department of Education
Bureau of Certification and
Accreditation
P.O. Box 2219
Hartford, Connecticut 06145
Telephone: (860) 566-5201
http://www.state.ct.us/sde/cert/
index.htm

Delaware:

Department of Public Instruction
Certification and Personnel Division
The Townsend Building
P.O. Box 1402
Dover, Delaware 19903
Telephone: (888) 759-9133
http://www.doe.state.de.us/certifi-
cation/dpi_home.htm

District of Columbia:

Department of Certification and
Accreditation
Presidential Building, Suite 1013
415 12th Street N.W.
Washington, D.C. 20004
Telephone: (800) 433-3277
http://www.k12.dc.us/dcps/home.
html

Florida:

Florida Department of Education
Teacher Certification Section
Collins Building
Tallahassee, Florida 32399
Telephone: (850) 488-5724
http://www.firn.edu/doe/menu/t2.
htm

Georgia:

Department of Education
Teacher Certification
1452 Twin Towers East
Atlanta, Georgia 30334-5070
Telephone: (404) 657-9000
http://www.gapsc.com/TeacherCer-
tification.asp

Hawaii:

Department of Education
Office of Personnel Services
Teacher Certification, Room 302
P.O. Box 2360
Honolulu, Hawaii 96804
Telephone: (808) 586-3269
http://www2.k12.hi.us/Home
Page.nsf?OpenDataBase#teach

Idaho:

State Department of Education
Teacher Education and Certification
Jordan Office Building
Boise, Idaho 83720
Telephone: (208) 332-6884
http://www.sde.state.id.us/certifica-
tion/default.htm

Illinois:

State Teacher Certification Board
100 North First Street
Springfield, Illinois 62777
Telephone: (800) 845-8749
http://web-dev.isbe.state.il.us/teach-
ers/Default.html

Indiana:

Indiana Department of Education
Teacher Education and Certification
State House, Room 229
Indianapolis, Indiana 46204-2798
Telephone: (317) 232-9010
http://www.ai.org/psb/

Iowa:

Board of Educational Examination
Grimes State Office Building
Des Moines, Iowa 50319-0147
Telephone: (515) 281-3245
http://www.state.ia.us/educate/
programs/boee/index.html

Kansas:

Department of Education and
Certification
Teacher Education and Accreditation
120 East 10th Street
Topeka, Kansas 66612
Telephone: (913) 296-2288
http://www.ksbe.state.ks.us/cert/
cert.html

Kentucky:

Department of Education
Division of Teacher Education and
Certification
1823 Capitol Plaza Tower
Frankfort, Kentucky 40601
Telephone: (502) 564-4606
http://www.kde.state.ky.us/de-
fault.asp?m=45

Louisiana:

Teacher Certification
Department of Education
P.O. Box 94064
Baton Rouge, Louisiana 70804-9064
Telephone: (504) 342-3490
http://www.doe.state.la.us/doe/
asap/home.asp?I-CERTIFICATION

Maine:

Division of Teacher Certification
State Street Station No. 23
Augusta, Maine 04333
Telephone: (207) 287-5315
http://janus.state.me.us/educa-
tion/cert/cert.htm

Maryland:

Maryland Department of Education
200 West Baltimore Street
Baltimore, Maryland 21201
Telephone: (410) 767-0412
http://www.msde.state.md.us/certi-
fication/index.htm

Massachusetts:

Bureau of Teacher Certification
Department of Education
1385 Hancock Street
Quincy, Massachusetts 02169
Telephone: (617) 388-3300
http://www.doe.mass.edu/cert/

Michigan:

Michigan Department of Education
Teacher/Administrator Preparation
and Certification Services
Box 30008
Lansing, Michigan 48909
Telephone: (517) 373-3310
http://www.state.mi.us/mde/
off/ppc/office.htm

Minnesota:

Department of Education
Teacher Licensing and Placement
616 Capitol Square Building
550 Cedar Street
St. Paul, Minnesota 55101
Telephone: (651) 582-8866
http://www.educ.state.mn.us/licen/
license.htm

Mississippi:

Division of Instruction
Office of Teacher Education and
Certification
P.O. Box 771
Jackson, Mississippi 39205
Telephone: (601) 359-3483
http://mde.k12.state.ms.us/license

Missouri:

Department of Elementary and
Secondary Education
P.O. Box 480
Jefferson City, Missouri 65102
Telephone: (573) 751-0051
http://services.dese.state.mo.us/

Montana:

Office of Public Instruction
Certification Services
State Capitol
Helena, Montana 59620
Telephone: (406) 444-3150
http://www.metnet.state.mt.us/

Nebraska:

Department of Education
Teacher Certification
301 Centennial Mall South
Box 94987
Lincoln, Nebraska 68509
Telephone: (402) 471-0739
http://nde4.nde.state.ne.us/TCERT/
TCERT.html

Nevada:

Teacher Certification
Department of Education
State Mail Room
215 East Bonanza
Las Vegas, Nevada 89158
Telephone: (702) 687-9141
http://www.ccsd.net/HRD/NVDOE/

New Hampshire:

Office of Teacher Education
State Department of Education
101 Pleasant Street
Concord, New Hampshire 03301
Telephone: (603) 271-2407
http://216.64.49.52/certification/
teacher.htm

New Jersey:

Department of Education
Office of Teacher Certification
3535 Quakerbridge Road
CN 503
Trenton, New Jersey 08625-8276
Telephone: (609) 292-2045
http://www.state.nj.us/njded/edu-
cators/license/1111htm

New Mexico:

Education Preparation and Licensure
N.M. Department of Education
Santa Fe, New Mexico 87503
Telephone: (505) 827-6581
http://sde.state.nm.us/index.html

New York:

Division of Teacher Certification
State Education Department
Room 5A11, Cultural Education
Center
Albany, New York 12230
Telephone: (518) 474-3901
http://www.highered.nysed.gov/
tcert/

North Carolina:

Public Instruction
Division of Certification
Salisbury and Edenton Streets
Raleigh, North Carolina 27611
Telephone: (919) 733-4125
http://www.dpi.state.nc.us/
licensure/lifaq.htm

North Dakota:

Department of Public Instruction
Office of Certification
Capitol Building
Bismark, North Dakota 58505
Telephone: (701) 328-2264
http://www.state.nd.us/espb/

Ohio:

Ohio Department of Education
Division of Teacher Education and
Certification
65 South Front Street, Room 1012
Columbus, Ohio 43266-0325
Telephone: (614) 466-3593
http://www.ode.ohio.gov:80/www/
tc/teacher.html

Oklahoma:

Teacher Certification
2500 North Lincoln Boulevard
Oklahoma City, Oklahoma 73105
Telephone: (405) 521-3337
http://sde.state.ok.us/pro/tcert/
profstd.html

Oregon:

Teacher Standards and Practices
Commission
580 State Street, Room 203
Salem, Oregon 97301-3782
Telephone: (503) 378-3586
http://www.ode.state.or.us/tspc/

Pennsylvania:

Department of Education
Bureau of Teacher Preparation and
Certification
333 Market Street, 3rd Floor
Harrisburg, Pennsylvania 17126-0333
Telephone: (717) 772-4737
http://www.pde.psu.edu/certification/teachcert.html

Rhode Island:

Department of Education
Office of Teacher Certification
22 Hayes Street
Providence, Rhode Island 02908
Telephone: (401) 277-2675
http://instruct.ride.ri.net/

South Carolina:

Department of Education
Teacher Certification Section
1015 Rutledge Building
Columbia, South Carolina 29201
Telephone: (803) 734-8317
http://www.state.sc.us/sde/commques/certcont.htm

South Dakota:

Office of School Standards
Division of Elementary and
Secondary Education
700 Governors Drive
Pierre, South Dakota 57501-5086
Telephone: (605) 773-3553
http://www.state.sd.us/state/executive/deca/account/certif.htm

Tennessee:

Tennessee Department of Education
Office of Teacher Licensing
6th Floor North, Cordell Hull Building
Nashville, Tennessee 37243-0377
Telephone: (615) 532-4880
http://www.state.tn.us/education/lic_home.htm

Texas:

State of Texas
Division of Teacher Certification
1701 North Congress Street
Austin, Texas 78701
Telephone: (512) 469-3000
http://www.sbec.state.tx.us/

Utah:

Utah Office of Education
Teacher Certification
250 East 500 South
Salt Lake City, Utah 84111
Telephone: (801) 538-7741
http://www.usoe.k12.ut.us/cert/

Vermont:

Department of Education
Education Resources Unit
Certification Office
State Offices Building
120 State Street
Montpelier, Vermont 05620
Telephone: (802) 828-2444
http://www.state.vt.us/educ/

Virginia:

Department of Education
Unit for Teacher Education and
Certification
P.O. Box 6Q
Richmond, Virginia 23216-2060
Telephone: (804) 371-2522
http://www.pen.k12.va.us/go/VDOE/Compliance/home.html

Washington:

Department of Education
Professional Certification
Old Capitol Building
7th and Franklin
Olympia, Washington 98504
Telephone: (360) 753-6773
http://www.k12.wa.us/cert/

West Virginia:

Department of Education
Office of Educational Personnel
Development
1900 Kanawha Boulevard East
Building 6, Room B-337—Capitol
Complex
Charleston, West Virginia 25305
Telephone: (800) 982-2378
http://wvde.state.wv.us/certification

Wyoming:

Department of Education
Certification/Licensing Unit
Hathaway Building
Cheyenne, Wyoming 82002
Telephone: (307) 777-6248
http://www.k12.wy.us/ptsb/index.
html

Wisconsin:

Bureau for Teacher Education
Certification and Placement—Box 7841
125 South Webster Street
Madison, Wisconsin 53707-7841
Telephone: (800) 266-1027
http://www.dpi.state.wi.us/dpi/
dlsis/tel/licguide.html

Glossary

A

Academic learning time   The engaged time, or time on-task, that results in performance or achievement of 80 percent or more.

Achievement motivation   The need to achieve at a task for its own sake rather than for an extrinsic reward.

Achievement test   A standardized test designed to measure knowledge of a particular subject or battery of subjects.

Advance organizer   An introductory statement to students that provides a structure for new information that is to be presented.

Affiliation motive   The intrinsic desire to be with others.

Allocated time   The time set aside for each of the planned school activities (teaching, lunch, recess, etc.).

Analysis   Cognitive learning that entails breaking down material into its constituent parts so that it can be understood.

Anxiety   A feeling of uneasiness and tension associated with the fear of failure.

Application   Cognitive learning that entails the use of rules or processes in new and concrete situations.

Assertive discipline   A classroom management approach developed by Canter and Canter that stresses the need for teachers to communicate classroom needs and requirements in clear, firm, unhostile terms.

Authentic assessment   A subset of performance assessment that requires realistic expectations set in real-life contexts.

B

Behavior   Actions that are observable and overt; they must be seen and should be countable.

Behavior modification   The manipulation of observable behavior by altering the consequences, outcomes, or rewards that follow the behavior.

Between-class grouping   A system in which students are assigned to classes on the basis of established criteria.

C

Charter schools   Schools run independently of the traditional public school system but receiving public funding; run by groups such as teachers, parents, or foundations. Charter schools are free of many district regulations and are often tailored to community needs.

Checklist   A list of criteria, or things to look for, on the basis of which a performance or an end product is to be judged.

Classical conditioning   Repeatedly pairing a neutral stimulus with a stimulus that elicits a response until the previously neutral stimulus alone elicits the response.

Closure   See **Lesson closure.**

Cognitive approach   Emphasis on the viewpoint that factors within the individual account for behaviors.

Cognitive set   See **Set induction.**

Cognitive style   The means by which individuals process and think about what they learn.

Commitment   Affective learning that involves building an internally consistent value system and freely living by it.

Comprehension   Cognitive learning that entails changing the form of previously learned material or making simple interpretations.

Computer   Electronic device that can store and manipulate information, as well as interact with user. Commonplace in many classrooms and in everyday life.

Computer-assisted instruction (CAI)   The use of computers for presenting instructional information, asking questions, and interacting with students. Individualized instruction administered by a computer.

Computer-managed instruction (CMI)   The use of computers for managing student records, diagnosing and prescribing instructional materials, monitoring student progress, and testing.

Concept   A category into which a set of objects, conditions, events, or processes can be grouped based on some similarities that they have in common.

Connectionism   An approach to learning in which learning results from the associations or connections forming between stimuli and responses.

Content validity   The degree to which the content covered by a measurement device matches the instruction that preceded it.

Continuous reinforcement schedule   A pattern in which every occurrence of a desired action is reinforced.

Convergent question   A question that has only one correct response.

Cooperative learning   The formation of mixed-ability (low, middle, and high) groups that work together cooperatively on assigned tasks and are rewarded on the basis of group success.

Creation   Cognitive learning that entails combining elements and parts in order to form a new whole or to produce an evaluation based on specified criteria.

Creative thinking   Putting together information to come up with a new understanding, concept, or idea.

Critical thinking   Complex thinking based on standards of objectivity and consistency; not the same as intelligence.

Curriculum   The planned and unplanned learning experiences that students undergo while in a school setting.

D

Decision making   The making of well thought out choices from among several alternatives.

Deficiency needs   Maslow's term for the four lower-level needs in his hierarchy: survival, safety, belonging, and self-esteem.

Delayed reinforcement   Reinforcement of a desired action that took place at an earlier time.

Demonstration method   Instructional method in which the teacher or another designated individual stands before a class, shows something, and tells what is happening or what has happened or asks students to discuss what has happened.

Descriptive data   Data that have been organized, categorized, or quantified by an observer but do not involve a value judgment.

Diagnostic evaluation   Evaluation administered before instruction to determine students' areas of strength or to identify specific learning problems.

Disabled   Having an inability to do something.

Discovery learning   Instructional method that focuses on intentional learning through supervised problem solving according to the scientific method. Students are encouraged to learn concepts and principles through their own exploration.

Discussion   Term often used by teachers to describe teaching methods that rely on verbal exchange of ideas.

Divergent questions   Questions for which there are many correct responses.

Duration measurement   The length of time during which an observable behavior continues, or the time interval between the communication of a direction or signal and the occurrence of the required observable behavior.

E

Empirical questions   Questions that require integration or analysis of remembered or given information in order to supply a predictable answer.

Engaged time   The actual time individual students spend as active participants in the learning process.

Evaluation   The process of obtaining available information about students and using it to ascertain the degree of change in students' performance.

Evaluative questions   Questions that require that a judgment be made or a value be put on something.

Exposition teaching   Teaching method in which an authority—teacher, textbook, film, or microcomputer—presents information without overt interaction taking place between the authority and the students.

Exposition with interaction teaching Authority-presented instruction followed by questioning that ascertains whether information has been comprehended.

Extinction   The gradual disappearance of a behavior through the removal or the withholding of reinforcement.

Extrinsic motivation   Motivation created by events or rewards outside the individual.

F

Factual questions   Questions that require the recall of information through the mental processes of recognition and rote memory.

Fixed reinforcement schedule   A pattern in which reinforcement is dispensed after a desired observable behavior has occurred a constant number of times or after a constant length of time.

Focusing question   A question used to focus students' attention on a lesson or on the content of a lesson.

Formative evaluation   Evaluation that takes place both before and during the learning process and is used to promote learning.

Frequency measurement   A measure of the number of times specified observable behaviors are exhibited in a constant time interval.

G

Goals   Extremely broad statements of school or instructional purposes.

Growth needs   Maslow's term for the three higher-level needs in his hierarchy: intellectual achievement, aesthetic appreciation, and self-actualization.

H

Halting time   A teacher's pause in talking, used to give students time to think about presented materials or directions.

Handicapped   Possessing an impairment that limits one's activities.

I

I-messages   Clear teacher messages that tell students how the teacher feels about problem situations and implicitly ask for corrected behaviors.

Imitation   Carrying out the basic rudiments of a skill when given directions and supervision.

Inclusion   The practice of providing for learners' special needs within a regular classroom environment.

Independent study   Instructional method in which students are involved in activities carried out with little or no guidance.

Individualized instruction   Instruction that has been designed to meet each student's needs, interests, and abilities.

Inference   The process of interpreting direct observations to form interpretive conclusions.

Informational objectives   Statements of learning intent that are abbreviations of instructional objectives in that only the student performance and the product are specified.

Inquiry learning   Instructional method that focuses on the flexible yet systematic process of problem solving.

Instructional objectives   A clear and unambiguous description of instructional intent with student performance, product, conditions, and criterion specified.

Instructional strategy   The precise global plan for teaching a lesson, unit, or course. Its two components are the methodology and the procedure.

Instructional time   Blocks of class time translated into productive learning activities.

Interdisciplinary team teaching   A group of teachers who work collaboratively to teach an integrated curriculum and integrative units.

Intermittent reinforcement schedule   A pattern in which correct responses are reinforced often but not following each occurrence of the desirable behavior.

Internet   System established to let computers communicate with each other.

Interval reinforcement schedule   A pattern in which reinforcement is dispensed after desired observable behavior has occurred for a specified length of time.

Intrinsic motivation   An internal source of motivation associated with activities that are rewarding in themselves.

K

Knowledge learning   Cognitive learning that entails the simple recall of learned materials.

L

Learned helplessness   The learned perception, based on experience, that one is doomed to failure.

Learning   A relatively permanent change in an individual's capacity for performance as a result of experience.

Learning style   The set of cognitive, affective, and physiological behaviors through which an individual learns most effectively; determined by a combination of hereditary and environmental influences.

Lecture recitation   Teacher presents information with no overt interaction with students.

Lesson closure   Teacher actions and statements designed to make a lesson content understandable and meaningful and to bring the presentation to an appropriate conclusion.

Likert scale   A five-point attitude scale with linked options: strongly agree, agree, undecided, disagree, and strongly disagree.

M

Magnet school   A school that focuses on special themes (i.e., art, music, drama, etc.) or curriculum areas (i.e., science, mathematics, language arts, etc.).

Mainstreaming   Moving handicapped students into classrooms with nonhandicapped students.

Mandated time   The set amount of time, established by the state, during which school is in session.

Manipulation   Independent performance of a skill.

Mastery learning model   A five-step pattern of instruction that emphasizes the mastery of stated objectives by all students by allowing learning time to be flexible.

Measurement   The assignment of numerical values to objects, events, performances, or products to indicate the degree to which they possess the characteristic being measured.

Methodology   The patterned behaviors that form the definite steps by which the teacher influences learning.

Modeling   Presentation of the values or behaviors of an admired person as an inducement to students to acquire those values or behaviors.

Motion pictures   Series of still pictures taken in rapid succession that give illusion of motion when projected.

Motivation   The influences of needs, desires, and drives on the intensity and direction of behaviors.

N

Negative reinforcement   Strengthening the likelihood of a behavior or event by the removal of an unpleasant stimulus.

No-lose tactic   A problem resolution tactic whereby teacher and one or more students negotiate a solution such that neither comes out the loser.

Nonverbal reinforcement   Using some form of physical action as a positive consequence to strengthen a behavior or event.

Norming group   A large sample of people who are similar to those for whom a particular standardized test is designed and who take the test to establish the group standards. The norming group serves as a comparison group for scoring the test.

O

Objective   A clear and unambiguous description of instructional intent.

Operant conditioning   A type of learning in which the probability or likelihood of a behavior occurring is changed as a result of procedures that follow that behavior.

Outcome-based education (OBE)   An education theory that guides curriculum by setting goals for students to accomplish. Outcome-based education focuses more on these goals, or outcomes, than on "inputs," or subject units.

P

Performance assessment   Assessment in which students create an answer or a product that demonstrates their acquisition of knowledge or skill.

Planning   A sequential decision-making process in which it is decided what should be taught, how best to teach the desired content or skills, and how best to determine whether the content or skills have been mastered.

Portfolio   A systematic, organized collection of evidence designed to illustrate a person's accomplishments and represent progress made toward reaching specified goals and objectives.

Positive reinforcement   Strengthening the likelihood of occurrence of a behavior or event by presenting a desired stimulus.

Precision   Psychomotor ability to perform an act accurately, efficiently, and harmoniously.

Premack principle   The use of a preferred activity as reinforcement for a less preferred activity.

Primary motives   Forces and drives, such as hunger, thirst, and the need for security, that are basic and inborn.

Probing questions   Questions that follow a student response and require the student to think and respond more thoroughly than in the initial response.

Procedure   A sequence of steps and activities that have been designed to lead to the acquisition of learning objectives.

Productive questions   Broad, open-ended questions with many correct responses that require students to use their imagination, to think creatively, and to produce something unique.

Prompting questions   Questions that involve the use of hints and clues to aid students in answering questions or in correcting an initial response.

Q

Qualified reinforcement   Reinforcement of only the acceptable parts of an individual's response or action or of the attempt itself.

Questionnaire   A list of written statements regarding attitudes, feelings, and opinions that are to be read and responded to.

R

Rating scale   A scale of values arranged in order of quality describing someone or something being evaluated.

Ratio reinforcement schedule   A pattern in which reinforcement is dispensed after a desired observable behavior has occurred a certain number of times.

Reality therapy   Therapy in which individuals are helped to become responsible and able to satisfy their needs in the real world.

Receiving   Affective learning that involves being aware of and willing to freely attend to a stimulus.

Redirecting   The technique of asking several individuals to respond to a question in light of or to add new insight to the previous responses.

Reflective listening   The act of listening with feeling as well as with cognition.

Reflective teacher   Teachers who think deeply about the theory and practice of teaching.

Reflective teaching   The continued self-monitoring of satisfaction with teaching effectiveness.

Reinforcement   Using consequences to strengthen the likelihood of a behavior or event.

Reliability   The consistency of test scores obtained in repeated administrations to the same individuals on different occasions or with different sets of equivalent items.

Reproduced data   Data that have been recorded in video, audio, or verbatim transcript form and can be reproduced when desired.

Responding   Affective learning that involves freely attending to a stimulus as well as voluntarily reacting to it in some way.

Ripple effect   The spreading of behaviors from one individual to others through imitation.

Rubric   A scoring guide that helps establish uniformity in evaluation of a student.

S

School-based management (SBM)   The shift of decision-making authority from school districts to individual schools. Such proposals vary, but they usually give control of a school's operation to a school council composed of parents, teachers, and local administrators.

Secondary motives   Forces and drives, such as the desire for money or grades, that are learned through association with primary motives.

Self-fulfilling prophecy   Actions or behaviors that occur because of a belief or prediction that they will occur.

Semantic differential   A seven-point scale that links an adjective to its opposite; designed so that attitudes, feelings, and opinions can be measured by degree, from very favorable to highly unfavorable.

Set induction   Teacher actions and statements at the outset of a lesson to get student attention, to trigger interest, and to establish a conceptual framework.

Silent time   The time the teacher waits following a student response before replying or continuing with the presentation.

Simulation   Instructional techniques in which students are involved in models of artificial situations or events designed to provide no risk experiences for students. Also sometimes referred to as games.

Socratic method   The method used by Socrates, which involved asking a series of questions of one student while classmates observed; each question changed the student's course until the student eventually totally disagreed with his or her own earlier answers.

Standardized test   A commercially developed test that samples behavior under uniform procedures.

Stimulation approach   Emphasis on the viewpoint that factors outside the individual account for behaviors.

Stimulus-response psychology   The study and practice of learning how to vary individuals' behavior by varying their stimuli.

Summative evaluation   Evaluation used to determine the extent of student learning upon completion of instruction.

T

Teacher-made test   An evaluative instrument developed and scored by a teacher to meet particular classroom needs.

Teaching   The actions of someone who is trying to assist others to reach their fullest potential in all aspects of development.

Team planning   Coordination of teachers' instructional approaches among disciplines.

Team teaching   A plan by which several teachers, organized into a team with a leader, provide the instruction for a larger group of students than would usually be found in a self-contained classroom.

Television programming   Broadcast video signals, such as commercial television programs, that are received and shown on a display unit.

Thinking   The act of withholding judgment in order to use past knowledge and experience to find new information, concepts, or conclusions.

Thinking skills   Ability to use the mind or intellect in exercising judgments, forming ideas, and engaging in rational thought and reason.

Time on-task   See **Engaged time.**

Time-sample measurement   A sampling of the environment for specific observable behaviors at predetermined time intervals.

Token reinforcement system   A system in which students perform actions or behaviors desired by the teacher in order to earn neutral tokens that can be exchanged periodically for rewards.

Transparencies   Still, projected material including images and words placed on clear acetate or plastic film.

U

Usability   In regard to a test, practical considerations such as cost, time to administer, difficulty, and scoring procedure.

V

Validity   The ability of a test to measure what it purports to measure.

Valued data   Data that involve a value judgment on the part of an observer.

Valuing   Affective learning that involves voluntarily giving worth to an object, a phenomenon, or a stimulus.

Variable reinforcement schedule   A pattern for the dispensing of reinforcements, in which the number of desired responses, or the length of time during which desired responses have occurred, varies.

Verbal component   The actual words and meaning of a spoken message.

Verbal reinforcement   Using positive comments as consequences to strengthen a behavior or event.

Vicarious reinforcement   An individual's strengthening of a behavior or an event in order to receive the consequences obtained by others who exhibit the same behavior.

Videodisc   A platter resembling a phonograph record used for storing visual materials for presentation on a display screen.

Vocal component   The meaning attached to a spoken message, resulting from such variables as voice firmness, modulation, tone, tempo, pitch, and loudness.

W

Wait time 1   The initial time a teacher waits following a question before calling for the response.

Wait time 2   The total time a teacher waits for all students to respond to the same question or for students to respond to each others' responses to a question.

Within-class grouping   A system for accommodating differences between students by dividing a class into groups for instructional purposes (i.e., reading groups, mathematics groups, science groups).

Y

You-messages   Teacher messages that attack students.

Index